D1236486

# Divining Truth

## Straight Talk From Source (the story)

Toni Elizabeth Sar'h Petrinovich

Copyright © 2012 by Toni Elizabeth Sar'h Petrinovich

ISBN 978-0-7414-8039-2  Paperback
ISBN 978-0-7414-8040-8  eBook
Library of Congress Control Number: 2012918151

Printed in the United States of America

Published November 2012

INFINITY PUBLISHING
1094 New DeHaven Street, Suite 100
West Conshohocken, PA 19428-2713
Toll-free (877) BUY BOOK
Local Phone (610) 941-9999
Fax (610) 941-9959
Info@buybooksontheweb.com
www.buybooksontheweb.com

## Disclaimer

Sacred Spaces, Sar'h Publishing House, Meta yoU School of Mastery, Heartstorm courses and Toni Petrinovich (Toni Elizabeth Sar'h) provide this material for your information. It is not intended to substitute for professional counseling and/or the advice of your primary health care provider. We encourage you to follow the directions and advice of your professional counselor and/or primary health care provider. The mention of any product, service, or therapy is not an endorsement by Sacred Spaces, Sar'h Publishing House, Meta yoU School of Mastery, Heartstorm courses or Toni Petrinovich (Toni Elizabeth Sar'h).

# Table of Contents

Foreword..................................................................................v

Prologue................................................................................ix

Introduction .......................................................................xiii

1.  What is God? ....................................................................1

2.  Who am I?.........................................................................5

3.  Where am I from?...........................................................10

4.  Where am I going?..........................................................14

5.  Is there a heaven and hell?...........................................18

6.  What is my divine purpose in this lifetime? ................23

7.  What lessons do I need to learn and challenges to
    overcome in this life? ...................................................28

8.  Do souls have ages - old, young, new?.........................33

9.  What is a lightworker?...................................................38

10. How do I surrender to life?..........................................43

11. How can I be aware of oneness?..................................48

12. Is there another word I can use for the "void"?.........53

13. How do I travel through the dimensions? ..................59

14. How can my glimpses of wonderment last longer? .....65

15. What do emotions have to do with the soul level? ......70

16. How can I achieve financial abundance?......................76

17. How can I do work that I am meant to do and that I
    love? ...............................................................................81

18. What is the world waiting to receive from me?..........86

19. How do I drop the yoke of unfulfilling tasks?..............91

20. Do I have to have energy work and initiations done?..........96

21. How can I hear spirit's words? ...................................101

22. Should I develop my psychic abilities? ......................106

23. How can I facilitate a person's soul in my work? ........111

24. Self-love, where does one start?................................116

25. Where does one begin after a lifetime of negative
    reinforcements and beliefs?........................................121

26. What causes my occasional angry behavior and what can I do about it? ...................................................127

27. How do I let go of the fear of punishment? .......................132

28. What about religion? ...........................................................138

29. How do I differentiate between mind and heart? ..............143

30. How do I find balance between enlightenment and 3D constrictions? ...............................................................149

31. How do I pass up the temptations present on planet earth? ....................................................................................154

32. How do I best raise my vibration in my life in general? .....159

33. How can I experience freedom? .........................................164

34. How can I help others on their journey? ............................170

35. How do I help people understand they need assistance to be in balance? .............................................175

36. Do I always fulfill my soul's purpose? ...............................180

37. Why does it feel so hard to be here? .................................185

38. I want to make big changes in what appears to be a perfect life. How do I do this? ...........................................191

39. What is in the Akashic Record? .........................................197

40. How do I connect with my soul group? ..............................203

41. Do we have past lives? ......................................................209

42. Is my birth family part of my soul group? ..........................215

43. Do we have strong soul ties to the people who are close to us in this life? .......................................................221

44. Why does it seem difficult to find a community of like-minded people? ..........................................................227

45. Why do people I consider close to me not like me? .........232

46. Why is it so hard to forgive? ..............................................238

47. What is compassion? .........................................................244

48. What is unconditional love? ...............................................250

49. How do I find my soul mate? ..............................................255

50. What soul purpose do my partner and I have together? ................................................................................261

51. Why do we become immobilized, not progressing to maximum capability?............................................267

52. What can we do to "unstick" ourselves?.............................273

53. I have an innate understanding of the bigger things, so where is my direction?.....................................279

54. What are effective strategies to recognize we are not reaching our capabilities?.....................................284

55. Where do we turn for internal and external support and direction?.......................................................290

56. Is it possible for negative energies to attach to me? ........296

57. Why don't I feel safe here, especially at night? .................302

58. What should I focus on to protect myself? .........................308

59. Can mechanical objects negatively affect me? .................314

60. Why am I sick? ....................................................................320

61. How can we clarify the vision of our possibilities?.............326

62. Why do I feel I have been intuitively working toward something all of my life? .....................................332

63. How can I know that what I do is for the highest good? ................................................................338

64. Is my soul purpose in alignment with this mission, or is it time to move on?..........................................344

65. What is my highest contact of light when I need help or information?.................................................350

66. How do we gain support from others when they don't believe we will change? ............................356

67. How much of the "transformation process" is guided internally and how much externally? .................361

68. How do we ensure we remain on the path to achieve our dreams?.........................................................367

69. How do we maintain balance and momentum as we move to the next level? .......................................372

70. The transition is unsettling; how do we maintain spiritually and physically?.......................................377

71. How can I be free to be who I am on my own terms? .......382
72. Does awareness separate  some people from others
    at this time?.................................................................387
73. How do I know I have arrived at Self-Realization?............393
74. How can I do more good when I feel limited in my
    outreach?......................................................................398
75. How can we experience heaven on earth? .......................404

# Foreword

In my feeling of joy in writing this foreword, I include a testimony of my individual experience with this profound book of truth. I also pay tribute to its author, Toni Elizabeth Sar'h Petrinovich, who allows herself to be in conscious relationship to the Mystery within. Toni has written as a true teaching master, creating an invitation into her wisdom, and simultaneously conveying that there is no one right path to understanding the Mystery of life, of God, of Source, and of ourselves. As I read Divining the Truth, I experienced that from start to finish, Toni as an author goes forward like the flow of water in a river, not knowing what the flow encounters on its journey, yet nevertheless persistent, unafraid, and real. Her courage and boldness have created a book for the truth seeker that resides inside each of us. Toni does not claim to tell the whole truth in her story. She tells a truth, as she knows it to be, flowing through her mind within Cosmic Consciousness and with her considerable awareness. She is a master teacher of humanity united in the one heart. I encourage you to approach the reading of this book with curiosity and readiness for a grand adventure.

I am deeply moved by the light that Toni has shed on the complex challenge of conveying an understanding of God. Despite the fact that our finite minds have considerable challenge understanding the infinite, she has found words and images to assist us in doing so. In providing the opportunity for every reader to have personal insights about God, she goes further by providing guidance for personal application of the insights and the knowledge. This book is about God's love, the unity we all experience in the one heart, what to do with one's own life to experience the power of the love that is. In reading the book, I experienced seeing God with fresh eyes and I felt invited into a radical faithfulness to God. For me, the invitation to a radical faithfulness was conveyed in the passage:

*"When you express the words, 'I AM God,' among your friends and family, they are astonished at your arrogance. It is not*

*audacity at all; rather it is the truth of you as ME. Were they to embrace the self-same truth, they would no longer be surprised."*

This book is not one of theology or philosophy to be considered, argued and put away on a shelf. It is a blueprint for a way of life. It challenges us to understand that there are no 'ordinary people', rather, that all people are extraordinary, that all people are of Source and we each and every one of us reveal Source to one another. Indeed, accepting this and living this require faithfulness to God that is radical. Toni does not espouse perfection as an end goal rather that we each are invited to be who we know ourselves to be, and trust that all is perfection as it is. Each and every one of us is an extraordinary human, immortal, and currently having a particular human experience complete with its choices about the attitude and approach that we each take.

Like other profound books of truth, there is not one singular truth, but a truth that leads to another truth, allowing for continual discovery. In preparing for writing this Foreword, I read the book, quite eagerly, three times before I was content that I had immersed myself sufficiently in my own divining of the truth from the offerings in Divining the Truth. The book is written in such a way that it invites a relationship between the reader and what is written, and in my case invited an experience of deep immersion into both the content and my personal journey with the content. As I read the book, I experienced a number of 'ah ha' moments as the content rang true for me. How can something ring true when I was exposed to some of the subject matter for the first time? I believe it rang true because the subject matter took me into a state of remembering what is known by us as humans, by me as the reader in particular.

This book will go forth into the world for those who have ears to hear its message, eyes to see its message, feelings that can feel their way into the truth of the message, and for those whose inner knowing says a big "YES" when immersing oneself into the message. To one person, its message will be as clear as day. To another, it may not seem so. The reader who does not resonate with what is written can make the choice not to use it and is not under any obligation to find it to be true. For those who do not resonate with it, I see the likelihood of loving it in the future, when the time is right. Everything has its season.

I believe that people in a number of cultures will grasp the truths told in this book with far less difficulty than those who were cultured in western societies. Approaching this profound book with wonder, curiosity and imagination is a way to open oneself up to accessing the wisdom within it as an immersion process. A musician might say 'learning new tunes and loving it...let's practice!' A baseball player might say 'learning new plays and loving it...let's practice!' As you read Divining the Truth, the same attitude would be helpful...you can choose to learn the 'new tunes' in this book and be in the state of 'loving it' with the joy that can be found in 'let's practice'. This allows the reader to find an access to the depth and breadth of the material in such a way as to bypass the normal and limiting way of thinking. Imagination, curiosity and wonder in the reader create the conditions to cast off prejudices (pre-judices, pre-judgments) of the mind, and as a westerner, I dare say, of the western mind. The western mind, more than any other, has been schooled in a cause and effect mentality, a linear mentality of what is considered rational thought. In much of the rest of the world, particularly amongst indigenous peoples, and the great civilizations in China and in India, the same mental processes focusing on causality did not take root in the same way. Natural laws were experienced as more dynamic, leaving room for synchronicity, coincidence and chance. In some cultures, whole brain thinking was encouraged. In western cultures, left hemisphere directed thinking was strengthened more than whole brain thinking. This book is best grasped with whole brain thinking.

I approached the reading of this book with curiosity and imagination, feeling as though I was getting ready for a great adventure. And so I am in the adventure. I was prepared to be delighted. And so I am delighted. I experienced spiritual nourishment. I experienced guidance for mastering this dimension. I also experienced an invitation to take responsibility for the creation of my life. I accept this responsibility. I experienced the invitation to use my consciousness and to join others in using our mass consciousness seeing beyond the illusion of this reality, and to create a different reality. Toni makes it clear that there is nothing wrong or right with the current reality. Every reality is a choice and leads us collectively to a different set of conditions to experience life. Personally, I prefer a world of compassion, passion, harmony, peace and self-responsibility. I experienced this book as a guidebook to assist me in doing my part in creating the reality that I want to experience. Even if your preferred world is different from mine, you are free to work on your creation as I am on mine. This guidebook provides the tools you need to create your preferred world. There is no right and no wrong, no good and no evil, there is only Source having experiences.

I have searched for ways to convey my appreciation of Toni, who she is, and all of her work. I choose to convey this admiration with a quotation from the great Sufi poet Rumi:

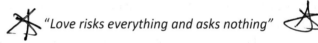 *"Love risks everything and asks nothing"*

For me, Toni is love and she risks everything with her courage. In love, she asks nothing. She provides for us all generously to enrich our lives...for those with ears to hear and eyes to see...in whatever lifetime.

In the one heart,

Birgitt Williams
Dalar International Consultancy

# Prologue

*I made the decision to include these writings of my editor, Kathryn Hart Teixeira, as a prologue to this book due to their depth of understanding. The first is her original prologue. The second writing was completed after reading and editing this book.*

I was born in the sapphire month of September under the Virgo stars. Born remembering my origin as Source, I lived in the matrix of my divine blueprint until the age of three. Prior to that my only memories of physicality include meeting a guardian earth-angel of my mother and therefore myself and experiencing the union of the polarities of light/dark, presence/absence and matter/Source as my earthly parents put me to bed to sleep one night. At the age of three, I made the conscious free will choice to "reject" my divine origin blue print as Source Experiencing. This was done symbolically on the Earth plane by flushing the water-turned-blue (assumedly by some bowl cleaner insert) down the toilet in the new house now occupied by my family and me. This moment is seared in my mind as the beginning of duality and of my decision to play in the earth's polar fields before the appointed time of re-membering (Occurring in the infinite Now).

My blueprint as a Divine Human Experiencing continued to hold me as I played in the dense fields of electromagnetic experiencing called Earth. For purposes of learning, I knowingly absorbed the realities of my family, my neighborhood, my school and my church, which existed within currents of fear, disconnection, lack, unhappiness, struggle, strife, competition, anger, distrust as well as natural currents of love and generosity so characteristic of the human heart.

I concurrently noticed the vibrations of those in my environment who broke the mold by living within the world while being not "of" it: A youth minister dressed to the nines, with a stylish hat and guitar in hand, a music teacher who had the courage to notice that I seemed to play and sing with gusto and encouraged the development of my musical abilities, a fifth grade teacher with a twinkle in his eye determined that I could do "no wrong" and even nick-named me "Grace" (by the way, I dreamed of reuniting with him just last night!), a seventh grade teacher with a guitar and a song and a courageous heart willing to affirm the truth of my existence as a creative and musical being.

My blue-print held me in unique and creative ways during this time: The blue walls of my bedroom, the blue-painted piano in our blue carpeted living-room, the blue blanket and barrettes gifted me by a grandmother, the blue-purple water pearl given to me by my childhood playmate upon her return from the Hawaiian Islands and so on.

The time came for a conscious shift in my fourteenth year. I accepted that the Christos lives in my heart eternally and that my life would be used for remembering this truth. I blessed the stars with my vow and tucked myself in my heart – yet the time for remembering fully would wait with infinite patience.

I continued to flourish in music wearing my blue Friends of Music dress faithfully to each concert. I wore my angelic voice teacher's blue Guinevere dress as I premiered the same role my senior year. I enrolled in college at the University of Michigan (Go Blue!). I even wore the veil in the form of "The Blues" for I wanted the "full" earth experience so that I would know *through my feelings* what Freedom through Absolution is. My Blue print held me as I travelled to Europe in my blue-denim dress. It called to me in a storefront window in Italy in the form of an Italian silk-brocaded peasant shirt – in, you guessed it, BLUE! That shirt and another sparkle blue dress would accompany many recitals in graduate school as it became clearer and clearer to me that I would be re-membering soon. I met my husband, Fernando, who wears the color blue (his favorite) as if it were a uniform! It is! I begin seeing flashes of blue – especially when I seemed to be re-membering consciously in the midst of daily activities (dimensionally travelling and shifting). I meet a Guru who emphasizes meditation on a blue-pearl and subsequently gift her with my blue-water pearl. My Blue-eyed children are born and I am dear friends with another being who is living in remembrance of her blueprint. In fact, I am editing her book on re-membering the Divine blueprint inherent within each soul on earth Right Now! As time accelerates, I breathe in my Angelic Human

Blueprint with infinite patience, exhaling freely as I connect with my environment, the field of Love that is the Infinite Potential of The One, existing without time and without name.

## Revised Prologue

Though it appears I was born on September 13, 1974 in Detroit, Michigan, the truth is that I have never been born. It appears I AM temporarily housed within the cellular intelligence that comprises the being called "Katie Hart", and yet I am not dependent upon my gracious host (which is also me) for my life. As Eternal Essence, I exist in the Divine Matrix of the One Heart. For the adventure of it all, I am personified as a woman living in the Western sensibilities of the United States. Watching me as this woman navigate her life as presence is my life's passion. I love her without expectation or fear. There is no thing she can do to separate herself from me, and I know it. As I watch her move about her daily life, I am in utter delight.

Her past up to this date is a divine play that is referenced with utter non-attachment and integrity. Though I have imbued in this incarnation a natural proclivity towards music, for example, I am not bound by any scripting. I am free to experience and to unfold myself through experience as I see fit for no other reason, save play! Free from all form, my sense of limitlessness informs me. I exist as the watcher and the watched simultaneously; my sense of identity rooted in the fearlessness of love without condition, outside of conventional notions of time and space.

The natural sense of unity that I feel expresses itself in communion and effortless cosmic communication. Aligned with the compulsions of my awareness of oneness, I feel myself as the All in the All. No thing is separate from me and no thing is I. The infinite consciousness that I am simply arrives on the wings of my felt awareness and transcribes itself as love and passion within union for life as it is. All is seen for the Love it is: person, rock, attitude, action, memory, judgment, joke. Heart knowing is my only compass, and all of life supports my knowing. I have always been and will always be aware of my Divine blueprint for how could it be any different?

At home in the Heart, all mental functions lose their importance and the flowering that I am exudes eternal joy in the presence of my essence.

# Introduction

For those who are not already familiar with me, let me simply give you a brief bio and then we can get on with talking about the alchemy of this book. I am clairvoyant, clairaudient and kinesthetically aware of the invisible worlds. In other words, I see and experience the invisible in addition to the visible. I was born with these capacities making the choice to develop their many uses as I matured.

I have written one other physical book, *The Call, Awakening the Angelic Human*, and several others available as e-books on my Sacred Spaces website. In addition, I offer CD and DVD meditations and class presentations. While I have spent much of my life traveling the world presenting spiritual metaphysical courses, I now teach internationally via the Internet.

This book is a written narrative of some of the many questions people have asked me over the years. Some of the questions were sent to me specifically for this book. Most of them were the result of personal queries through email, radio interviews and question/answer sessions during my classes.

As I wrote Divining Truth, I opened my heart and mind to the responses within the questions from Cosmic Consciousness, the Cosmic Mind, or you might call it "the Mind of God". Since all information is available within the All, accessing is only a matter of becoming coherent within personal alignment assuring the "telephone line" is open and the reception becomes ultra-available. This is not something only I am able to do. Anyone can have the same experience if he or she focuses on personal harmony within all bodies, physical, spiritual, emotional and mental.

If you are looking for quick, pat answers to questions in your life, don't read this book. It will not tell you if you are enlightened or whether you should marry the guy or gal next door.

At the same time, you can't read this book without getting a much more expanded view of your Self within this incarnation. Read from beginning to end, this book becomes a source of constant confirmation of your divinity. Of course, this means you will be asking yourself to feel, think, speak and act from within that scope once you have read to its ultimate finale.

The questions begin within a general scope of curiosity and continue to a more defined, personal set of queries. Each response is given in the first person voice of Source, God, All That IS, the I AM or whatever name you use to connote the All. Accompanying each question and answer is a short story setting forth an example of the answer in action. Again, you will not find an easy assessment of the response in action within the storyline. It summons you to reach inside your heart to understand the characters' application of the reply.

If you choose to read this book, I ask you to do so in order to better understand how to live a life of union, common union, communion and, eventually, cosmic communication. I would request that you set aside the limiting beliefs to which you are presently attached giving yourself the opportunity to view and live your life anew – from the aspect of I AM. Herein, you will find not only consummation of duality; you will experience an invitation to know yourself as union.

In the words of this book's speaker, "Come, witness yourself as I AM within ME."

# Question One
## What is God?

I AM. I AM not the manifestation of anything in creation and I AM all that is creation. The beginning and the end has no meaning to ME for I AM always. I know no future. I AM All That Is.

I AM all that is not for I AM all. While your mind places labels, conditions and specifications upon what I AM, I AM none of those labels or those conditions and I AM all of them.

I AM that from which the aspect you know as Creator emerges hence It Is ME. I AM It. All that is created exists within what I AM. There is naught but I AM.

You are an attribute of ME as conscious awareness emanating within the emergence of Creator within ME. I AM not consciousness and I AM all consciousness. I AM absolutely and infinitely aware of ME without cause or effect.

That which you call Creator is the ushering forth of MY ESSENCE in a constant upsurge of expression. It resembles ME as it emerges within ME. I AM aware *as* Creator that is an aspect of ME. The guise of Creator is a simple emanation of ME. I AM without attributes or aspect and include all aspects and attributes.

All thoughts flow within ME for I AM all thought. All feelings emanate from within MY Presence, as I AM all feelings. All actions are emerging extensions from within MY Essence and are enacted within ME.

Without thought, feeling or action, I AM. Without creation or existence, I AM. As the current of all conception, I AM.

As your mind attempts to label and define that which I AM, it calls ME THAT which Is. "THAT" is yet another label. Remove the concepts within your mind knowing that I AM only and all.

Your mind acknowledges ME as love. I AM neutral, encompassing all that is not neutral. That which is identified as good and bad, I AM. That which is neither right nor wrong, I AM. All that you characterize as good or evil, I AM.

1

Love is a facet of Creator using the property you label *love* to extend into its creation. Through the essence of this love, Creator balances the concept of duality accessing infinite counterpoints of expression. Looking for the source of love, you will find it in Creator. I AM.

Within ME, emerge all possibilities. I AM without beginning or end. I AM infinite and non-infinite for I AM without origination.

Within ME is all not as memory yet as all. When you use your mind to reflect upon experience, you are within that which is all. You contemplate that which is without time for I AM timeless. I encompass all space for there is no space within ME. I AM.

When you believe you are "here" or "there", you are not. You are in existence only within your emergence within ME for I AM. You feel movement within your idea of space yet your boundless emergence knows no space. You are in a constant state of arising within ME.

When you are seeking love, when you are professing to love, you are seeking and acting as Creator, an emanation of ME. I AM.

I AM without longing, yearning or need. I have no need. Encompassing all, I AM. You exist within ME as a created illumination of ME. I AM.

As you seek to know yourself, contentment with being is an experience of MY non-being. I AM all therefore, I AM that which is not for I encompass all without duality or exception.

Your mind searches for identification upon which to land ever missing its mark. It seeks within the space of no-space and searches within the time of no time. I AM.

From within Creator's pleasure you will find the love you seek in experience. It is MY love and not MY love for I AM all.

The "I" of you belongs to your identity. I AM without identity. I AM; You are.

As I AM without definition or interpretation and Creator bears only the description you place upon it, You Are without qualification or connotation. You emanate from within Creator as it arises within ME. I AM.

I AM that which cannot be named, ineffable and transcendent in your terms. Without name, form, beginning or end, I AM.

As you consider what I AM, loosen your hold upon the belief you will understand until you no longer have desire to know or comprehend. When you have relinquished your yearning to satisfy your mind, I AM.

In being, I AM. Within your breath, you touch the edges of remembering I AM. The beat of your heart is an echo of I AM. I AM All. I AM no thing. I AM.

## Story Time

*Here I AM alone or All One depending upon how you want to look at it. Wouldn't it be delightful to create infinite numbers of Me to play with and talk to, look at and love?*

*Well, first I'll need to manifest an aspect of Me as Creator to be in charge of creation. That'll work just fine since it will be Me anyway simply emerging from within Me. Creator will be the emanation of Me establishing the various concepts, objects, locations and opportunities in the All. I'll call it my creation!*

*This is really exciting! As My Essence emerges from within Me every possibility begins to vibrate causing a sequence of waves to build into frequencies and units of measure: spaces, dimensions, time durations, bodies, thoughts, feelings and actions.*

*Since anything is possible within Me, Creator can allot a certain set of aspects to emerge within a world of duality, a representation in form of what I AM formlessly. I AM everything and I AM nothing. Duality will mirror polarity as two sides to every possibility.*

*There will be a light and a dark, an up and a down, an in and an out. The potential is enormous. If free will is added into the mix, then I (as MY creation) can make choices within the duality between this and that, one or the other, more or less.*

*Ah, and since I AM infinite I'll want to have an end to the game somewhere along the line so I'll give these creations a physical end time that means they can start all over again and make other choices.*

*What fun! I wish I had thought of this sooner!*

## Question Two
## Who am I?

When I look at this question, I immediately see that you believe you are *someone*. Isn't that the way of this world you live in?

Would it surprise you to know the personality you feel you *are* is as fleeting as the pictures that dance upon your image screen? And, at the same time (since you live within a concept of time and space), it feels solid and real to you. Who you are is the objectified sense of your personality.

So, to keep that character in your story happy, let's talk about who you are:

You are the sum total of every experience you are having in every dimension, time, space, world and "reality" that emanates from within Creator. While you experience the microcosm you live in as appearing to be all that you believe you are, it is the pinpoint of your focus for this momentary life.

Though you may wish to be of the opinion that you are good (whatever that means to you) and are trying your best, in many other realities you do not care whether you are "good" or not. You are delighting in being the "bad girl" or the "incorrigible boy". You are playing it to the hilt.

At the same time, when you decide to do something "wrong" in this dimension (for whatever reason), you are living simultaneous lives you would consider "sacred" and "holy" in yet another realm of experience.

You are a totality of all of these parts and the collections of roles you are playing are without number. Every time you think a thought, you stimulate a connection within a life you are maintaining in another dimension somewhat outside of your present conscious awareness. Those lives influence the presence of this reality and vice versa. You are in constant flow and flux among all of these existences in some type of form.

Much more than a "who", you are a "what". The question would be more easily phrased as "What am I?" and answered as:

You are an emanation of consciousness emerging within ME as it emanates from within Creator. Since Creator is an effluence of ME and you materialize within Creator, you originate from and proceed within ME. You are I AM.

Your various religions and authorities have spent a good deal of time attempting to divest you of this knowledge. They have done a very good job. You no longer feel worthy to call yourself what you *are* and therefore live within limitations imposed upon you (you believe). Actually, the boundaries are *self-imposed* because there is nothing outside of ME so whatever you allow into your frequency stream also emanates from within ME.

When you experience yourself as a "what" rather than a "who" (if you make that choice within your free will), you begin to feel like you are "coming awake". Some of your teachers and preachers tell you that you are "waking up"; that you have been asleep.

You are not sleeping or dreaming. You are experiencing an aspect of consciousness that is only aware of what it desires. When you begin to feel the stirrings within you of feelings telling you it's time to change, you will do so.

You incorporate every aspect that I AM. Nothing has been "left out of you". You are no more incomplete than I AM incomplete. Your capacity to know this truth is actuated within you right now. Your free will acceptance of it brings it fully into your consciousness and you begin to respond to life from the abundant abilities that are always yours.

The "what" that you are is sporting about in a planet you call earth, wearing a label you call your "name" and exhibiting attributes your personality wishes to experiment within your present form.

As such, you are a true and complete expression of ME. You might say that I AM sporting and cavorting about in planet earth through the expression of your personality. This is your individuation; it is the individual "whatness" of you embracing your "whoness".

All of this exciting (to you) activity is recorded in a "place" you call your soul. It is a record of your comings and goings in all of those realities and dimensions that I was talking about earlier.

When you allow yourself to access the information contained within your soul record, you begin to see how these lives can impact this life if you desire. Remember, that it is "if you desire". You are making the choices here – as ME. Every choice is the correct and appropriate selection in each moment of your time and space.

You can redefine your "who"; you cannot redefine your "what". You can give new names and ideologies to the "what" yet it will always remain undefined. The attempt to give it definition belongs to the "who" which does not understand that it is a "what" and always will be.

Your only reality is what you are as a state of aware consciousness. When the "who" lies down to surrender its costume to the earth of this dimension, what you are experiences another entrance into realms upon realms of living. You continue infinitely in expression as I AM.

## Story Time

This is a conversation between Ann and John in the spirit world. While they don't have gender out of body, it makes it easier to tell the story:

Ann: *"John, I hope you don't mind if I use this name. I know that you're not John anymore; it helps to have something to call you. I'm thinking about incarnating again. Do you feel like coming along?"*

John: *"Well, Ann, I'll use your name too; it makes it simpler. It sounds like a good idea. I've been out of body for a while now and contemplating the various experiences I've recorded; might be the chance to do something new. What do you have in mind?"*

Ann: *"Do you remember that time in earth when you were a soldier and I was a nurse? I'd like to reverse the roles with a twist. I'd like to incarnate as a male, as your brother, with you being my sister. I didn't really feel complete with the short period I* was nursing you during that Civil War time in the United States so I thought maybe I could protect you as an older brother and get more of that type of experience in the upcoming life."

John: "Hmmm, well, I've spent a few lives as a female; actually, it's fun with the focus humans have around feminine energy as weaker. We know that's not true yet incarnating in a less muscular body tends to lend toward support and protection so I'll give it a go if you want."

Ann: "Michael and Camille told me they wanted to be father and mother this time. We've spent so many incarnated expressions taking care of them it would be fun to reverse the tables. You might want to know they have their own agenda, though.

"Camille wants to experience forgiving and absolving so Michael has offered to be the antagonist in this life. He thought he might create some sort of addictive personality tending toward what humans call abusive so Camille will have the opportunity. Are you still game?"

John: "Sure and it'll give you more opportunities to be my guardian because our father will be frightening to us as children. We can really play out a lot of different roles among the four of us. Did anybody else say they wanted to join or is it the four of us at the moment?"

Ann: "I've transmitted the message that we have room for some friends for all of us, maybe a counselor or religious type for Michael and, of course, there may be a few who want to be consolers for Camille. As we continue to evolve this plan, I'm sure more beings are going to show up and ask to join the play."

John: "Great – well, I'm letting it be known that we've got some upcoming excitement planned and it's all going to happen in the transforming duality of earth so I know we'll get lots of takers.

"I'm going to review a few of my simultaneous lives to see if there's anything else that wants a bit of balancing. I might as well take the opportunity while it's being presented. You might want to do the same."

Ann: "Oh, I already did that and I've decided that I'll be a loner since most of the lives in earthly form I've either been *married or in some sort of relationship. This time will be different and I'll have expanded space and time to delve into me. This is going to be a great trip!"*

## Question Three
## Where am I from?

WE are back now to the "who" and the "what"? This question refers to the personality. It is the personality wanting to know where it is from and the Self (I AM as the "what") knows without placing significance upon it.

You originate within ME. You are an extension, an emanation of all that I AM. Every molecule of your body, every thought you think and feeling you have is emerging from within ME.

When your mind begins to contemplate a point of origin, it is looking for a beginning. Since the mind (your psyche) wants to understand its ancestry, it looks for its beginning. Emerging as ME (timeless), you have no inception. When humanity calls ME the "Alpha", it suggests that I have a beginning. I do not.

If I were to have an activation moment, something would have to generate ME. Since I AM all, there is no "other" providing this actualization. I AM. You are. There is no difference and there is no separation within US.

Your personality is emerging from within your soul record as an aspect of experience you chose before you came into this individuation. When you made that choice, you based it upon all of the existences you are experiencing in all dimensions and what type of participation you might enjoy in this pattern of time and space.

From within your soul's blueprint, you birthed yourself into this time/space with an intention to experience its flavors. Having entered the electromagnetic force field holding this plane in vibrational formation, you forgot why you made your original choice. Though you knew this before your incarnation, you forgot that you knew upon physical entrance. It is for this very reason you chose to embody here – for the adventure of forgetting.

All of this choosing, forgetting, begetting and birthing take place within ME. It is a constant fluctuation within MY Presence. Since there is no creation in existence except within MY Essence, all is I AM. Therefore, being unable to remember is much less important than your human mind wants to believe because the obliteration of conscious memory is also ME.

In its search to identify itself, your mental body seeks systems of belief, groups to connect with and authority figures to obey hoping to coagulate these distant memories into a substantial story. Choosing from among that with which you resonate, a claim is staked for a point of view creating a semblance of a personality that you call "you". If this search for knowledge leads you to belief in reincarnation, you begin to align with specific "past lives" you believe are influencing the experiences of *now*. Hence you have a place to look, blame or credit.

When you inquire where you are "from" your personality wants to know how it developed itself. It is seeking its "home base" formulated upon a particular set of specifics it believes comprises reality. Usually, the ego will denounce any lineage that does not agree with its current list of proscribed understandings.

Where you are from is within ME. I, as Creator, unleash MYSELF in all forms infinitely. These articulations do not "descend" *from* within ME nor have they a need to "ascend" *to* ME. They are emanations *of* ME within MY Presence.

Since all are "equal' within ME, there are no creations better or worse than any other. Your strength of opinion lives within the judgment attributed to any aspect of ME by the ideologies and concepts in which your mind engages. Divesting yourself of a need to compare or weigh opens the first portal to your full remembrance, always available to you as ME.

As you consider why you are asking this question, remove the basis of your idea from what you *believe* is "true". This will enable you to flow into a steady stream of consciousness that is infinitely aware of its original inception as Creator's breath. As you breathe, you inhale and exhale as Creator within ME. Following the emanation of this thought, you will begin to comprehend the effect your simultaneous lives have upon this incarnation giving you ample room to make choices within ME.

If your question mirrors your curiosity regarding which lifetime you most recently experienced prior to this incarnation, you may look to your natural propensities realizing you carry within your cellular memory the most prevalent recall of expressions in form. Yet knowing the outcome held within the answer to this question serves no purpose except to assuage your desire to control your participation within the present form. Eventually, the knowledge will become insufficient to fulfill your yearning and you will endeavor to know yourself as ME.

There exists only awake consciousness in all formations exhibiting the tendencies each has to *be*. All emanates from within itself and is the origin of it infinitely expressing as ME. The limitations experienced within your present dimension are for the sole purpose of observing yourself in this particular embodiment. If you wish to measure yourself within your present emergence, your individuation as Self is the smallest grain of sand within an infinite beach.

"Where are you from?" You are from nowhere and everywhere as I AM.

## Story Time

"Ann" and "John" are remembering the beginning as they commune in the spirit world:

John: *"Do you remember what it was like before the accumulation of experience?"*

Ann: *"Oh, yes, it is present with me right now and always reminds me of what I am – a spark of consciousness. Then the urge to take form begins and the fun of recording happenings. Eventually, I focus on one or two 'lives' rather than living all of them at the same time."*

John: *"Expansion is similar within me. My soul record contains such experiential wisdom due to the many life forms I am. Each specific recording plays within me as celestial music."*

Ann: *"Sometimes I let go of any concept of being in form at all and simply resonate within the patterns of Creator without any sense of myself. I experience only the enfoldment of love beyond any telling."*

John: *"I know that immersion. It is the depth of home, the genesis of all . . . hmmmm."*

Ann: *"Yes, hmmmmm. This is the nameless expression and why it feels a little unusual to call you 'John' and to have you call me 'Ann'. We're nameless, also."*

# Question Four
## Where am I going?

You are going nowhere and everywhere. The concept of "traveling" to some place is based upon your idea of living within time and space. The dimension in which earth life is experienced relies on a linear basis for what you stream, as your "reality", comprised of a past, present and future. This hypothesis is a theory inherent within your present exposure in form.

As you are composed of a physical body that is born and eventually decays dissolving back into its energy stream, your mental body observes an origin of this life (where you came from) and an end to which you assign the question, "Where am I going?" As you live within your consciousness and accumulate life experience within your soul record, your mind conveys a progression of occurrences "making up" your life. This continuous stream appears to "end" when you lay down your corporeal form.

Contributing to this factor is the realization you don't "know" where you will appear next in your life's stream of consciousness so you live with some fear about that world "out of the body" within which you will inevitably emerge. Your religion or spiritual concepts give you some hope there is a place offering less chaos and more control. At the very least, it will guarantee a sort of "happiness" or even bliss.

The basis for most of your longing to know where you are going (be it in this body or out of this body) ushers from your discontent with *now*. When each breath is an acknowledgment of your emanation within ME then the desire to know where you are going or what is "next" loses its importance.

As you allow your consciousness to witness its own awakened state, you realize perceiving where you may be at any time you label as the "future" disassociates you from You (ME) within your mental and feeling bodies. The contribution of your focus to the breath you are breathing is touching into your personal emanation within ME.

When you are complete with this earthly experience, laying down your present appearance, you will witness yourself within the reality of your focus. I speak not of the focal point of that last breath rather of your general frequency within your present life. It becomes your point of convergence as much as the activities you indulge in while within your present physiology are the same points of action for you.

Contributing to the outcome of your expanding awareness without form are the beliefs you hold on to as you transition from physical to non-physical. The realm in which you find yourself will not be judging you for what you choose as true only resonating with the vibratory patterning within your choice.

Often the question "Where am I going?" also includes what is approaching your present energy stream from what you term your "future" in the physical. The linear conception of moving through time creates an impression of "going" somewhere while actually you are witnessing one impression, then another, then another even though each is simultaneously in existence within MY ALL.

It is the frequency with which you resonate in this breath that creates what you experience in the following breath. This is an infinite state of resonance you call "creating". You are neither creating nor manifesting since all *is* – within ME. Creator magnified itself through infinite expansion as it generated the pattern of all creation. You resonate with the frequency of those impressions as you shift and transform your focus.

You choose where you are "going" within this present lifetime as well as where you will "go" when you are complete with physicality. The unconscious aspect of your mental body plays little part in this magnificent array of choices even though in your physical body, you may find yourself acting or speaking from habits or beliefs you have adopted. Once you no longer are using the present vehicle of incarnation, you experience yourself as aware consciousness emerging within a realm of resonating existence.

It is the human, earth-based guidance system prompting your desire to know, and thereby control, what it believes it desires next in your "here" or eventually in your "there". Your cognitive mind has little awareness of how much authority it has over your resonate frequency. As you allow your mental faculties to become influenced by the stream of You rather than the apparent denseness you observe, your frequency awareness becomes your focal point granting you conscious choice over your wavelength of expression.

As you contemplate "where you are going", feel within the center of your physical body your opening into the infinity of ME. In the breath of that allowance, you will feel the oscillating creative impulse of Creator leading directly into the emergence within ME. With this as your focus, you may easily answer your own question with an emphatic "I AM". As the foundation of every answer to each of your questions and the converging point of your present awareness, you will observe your next breath (or next "step" as you often refer to it) as the yielding of you to You.

In this moment's inhale and exhale, you draw into your effusion the inspiration of MY Essence. Then, "where you are going" is more consciously within ME Self-realizing your present state of consciousness.

## Story Time

In present incarnation, Ann is Paul and John is Nancy. They've lived a full life and now it is time for Paul to leave. Nancy will transition a little later:

Paul: *"Nancy, it's time you know. This ole' ticker just isn't going to keep goin' anymore. It's been a good life and I wouldn't trade it for anything. Give me a final hug so I can leave in peace."*

Nancy: *"Oh, Paul, I don't want you to go. I'll be close behind. We always do things together, you know."* Nancy gives Paul a final loving hug with tears in her eyes as she feels his chest rise and fall for the last time.

Paul slides gracefully out of his physical form shaking himself a bit like a spaniel coming out of a clear, pristine lake. Waiting for him is a group that he often incarnates with ensuring he knows where he is in consciousness.

One of the group: *"Welcome back! Good time? You've only been gone for a twinkle. Want to tell us about it?"*

Paul: *"Sure – let's convene over here and we can all go over my latest set of experiences. I went with John/Nancy you know and she'll be along shortly. It was an eventful life with much wisdom gained through many choices. Has anyone seen my earthly mother and father – oh, there they are – come on over and let's recollect for a moment."*

Father: *"Wow! That was an expansive life experience. Living in a world of despair and taking it out on my family really cut me off from consciousness. I didn't even have to try to forget, it came so naturally once I got to that place. What compassion it gives me for all the human beings who experience that state, as well."*

Mother: *"Yes, we had some very intense times being a married couple in the environment we created. It filled our records with acceptance, forgiveness, absolution and compassionate love. I really gained understanding of what it is to absolve which was my original intention. Thank you so much for the role you played in being my mate for that life."*

Paul: *"I'm going to take a bit of a hiatus before incarnating again. I'd like to experience some integration here before I choose another form. Thanks for all of the support in meeting me upon arrival. We can gather again, when Nancy appears. I know she'll want to tell us all about her last few earth days, as well."*

The crowd slowly disperses into the various aspects of consciousness they are, changing form into that which suits each one best in the moment. As for Paul, he simply drifts into a state of conscious bliss until he feels a resonating tug, again.

## Question Five
## Is there a heaven and hell?

The answer is "yes" and "no". Let's begin with "no":

Your religions and spiritual authorities profess belief in a place where believers go known as *heaven* or *hell*. So off the top, let's simply state that there is no place as heaven or hell with reference to a physical realm in which you will ultimately exist.

The idea you will be *rewarded* vs. *punished* is one of the key concepts authority figures use to maintain the fear of disbelieving or disobeying their authority or the control of the religion in which you allege belief. Once you have committed to a particular group mind, it is often very difficult to remove yourself from that way of thinking since the fear of hell lingers. That is just the point.

Since there is no punishment and likewise no reward from what do you draw guidelines regarding how to act, respond and believe? That is where the world of spirit and soul come into play. The capacity you have to understand you are the only reward giver or punisher is often hard-won since there seems to be no one who is confirming for you what you are supposed to believe or not believe. Once you begin to understand this concept, the future will brighten up considerably.

Now, having addressed the "no" let's look at the "yes" of the answer:

The sense of "being in heaven" is the conscious awareness of a realm without a body wherein you experience bliss. Is there a *God* sitting there visiting with you? No. Are there angels floating around singing and playing harps? No. There is the sense of love, non-judgment and awareness that comes with existing within a dimension without duality (the sensed need to choose either *right* or *wrong*).

Backtracking to the last few questions and answers, you will remember you are consciousness. You are I AM. What you resonate with within your feelings and mind is the reality in which you experience. This applies to *being in form* or *out of form*. It is all the same – application of consciousness as awareness.

When you leave your physical body, from within the underlying feelings within your inner core will emerge a "picture" of "where" you are. That perception will morph and change dependent upon your focus of the moment. Usually you understand this quite soon and begin to realize your inherent harmony and balance.

Since your underlying beliefs and principles will and do create the frequency that upwells within your consciousness, those concepts will fuel the fire of your experience. Yet, your spirit and soul are aware of what is playing out for you in your disembodied state and the moment you realize you can resonate with a state of tranquility then it will be your reality.

Since fear is not a thriving frequency in any plane of existence, it has little room to maintain itself in the bodiless state. The anxiety of your transition is easily transformed into the love and flow of non-physical life.

If you persist in fear of what this experience may bring to you without paying attention to what is possible, then for the period of time you embrace the fear, you will live in your own version of hell. It does not include flames or a devil with a pitchfork. What it does include is your experience *as fear* until you release its hold upon you (yes, *you* release it).

Since there are many beings out-of-body who "know" you and are present with you as you transition, some of them may attempt to assist you in realizing where you are and what is possible. To the degree you accept this assistance to that degree will you begin to realize the sense of contentment referred to herein.

Your religions would have you believe the world out-of-body comprises a state to be attained. They would have you desire to "go there" rather than *be here* since it will feel so much better and you will be happier. It is much more pragmatic than that supposition.

The sense of being out of physical form is less dramatic than you might expect. You are still very conscious of yourself and your surroundings. You still resonate with that which you wish to experience. What eventually becomes quite different is the sense that you don't have to choose among a host of choices with outcomes. Slowly you realize that your conscious awareness instills within you the sense of simply "being" and that is quite enough. No more is required until you begin to desire "in-form" experience.

Why would you desire form if you are "content"? Because you are a constantly moving, expanding consciousness infinitely experiencing. It (yes, "it"; no duality, remember) begins to sense there are other experiences it can have if it is in a different form. This point may not come for what you would call months, years or centuries. The bodiless world is timeless so the decision point makes no difference whatsoever. It comes when it comes and you choose what you choose.

Realizing that transitioning out of body is similar to stepping through a doorway into another "place" of "living" releases you from the hope of reward or the fear of punishment. It is the ultimate possible freedom within consciousness – consciously knowing what you are.

## Story Time

Nancy has made her transition and has just now released her physical body. Within her belief systems are assumptions she is not worthy to know God, has acted in a way to hurt others and hasn't loved Paul enough. She is taking these fears with her as she makes her transition along with the love she naturally portrayed in earth. The underlying principle is fear.

Upon arrival into the realm of spirit, Nancy's first experience will most likely be one of shyness, anxiety and a desire to hide so that no one can see all of her theoretical mistakes. She attempts to withdraw into herself and finds that isn't possible so she creates a detour off the main "road" upon which she finds herself into a frequency that resonates with her fears.

Here she finds other souls who feel as she maintains and want to hide from those they believe will be able to see them for what they think they are. The fact that all of this is based upon earthly perceptions is not present, only the fear of being seen without their personality masks.

Nancy will remain in this "place" until something stimulates her to look elsewhere. This could be anything. If Paul and his parents met her as she crossed over, she might have had an opportunity to let them support her in unraveling her beliefs. If they did not meet her at the moment of her transition, she would quickly have found a way to hide. Judgment does not apply so neither action is important.

Since Nancy *is* conscious awareness impacted by the energetic beliefs she has embraced, only she can make a decision which direction she will take. Others can offer suggestions, yet ultimately it is Nancy's choice. Eventually, she will realize self-recognition is possible and she will be seen as she truly is.

Since Paul and his family do not resonate with Nancy's beliefs about herself, they will not follow her on the detour she is taking. Each of them may decide to attempt communication with her yet ultimately it is Nancy's decision whether she will let herself "hear" any one of them. Dependent upon the strength of her assumptions, she may or may not listen.

Again, there is no time in the world of spirit and soul so Nancy may take as long as she wishes within her detour world. The concept of an infinite heaven and hell arises from this inherent realization within the human consciousness. Once out of the mortal body there is no time. Experiences will *be* lived until they no longer *are* within the particular frequency of the consciousness.

What may occur are individuals within the detour reality beginning to feel comfortable with each experience within the group leading to less fear and need to withdraw. This will stimulate the group as a whole to a sense of self-acceptance. The self-worth will naturally resonate with love and the "walls" of the detour reality will begin to dissolve.

Upon dissolution, Nancy and her detour group will commence allowing themselves to be seen for what they are without fear. They will merge and commune with others who have been "outside" of their detour reality existing within conscious awareness of themselves as contentment, tranquility and love.

All consciousness "conspires" to emerge within a sense of contentment, harmony and balance. Nancy's detour was really no detour at all, rather another branch into awareness allowing her and those with whom she resonated to come to a new conscious understanding.

# Question Six
## What is my divine purpose in this lifetime?

As you become consciously aware of yourself as Source in form, it is natural for the ego personality to question its reason for being. Most people begin to ask, "What is my purpose for being in this life?"

The idea you are your job or the label given you regarding your relationships with family and friends no longer appears to apply to how you are experiencing your life. There is a "bigger" sense often perceived as a "larger purpose" than simply being a mother/father/husband/wife working in the business/farming/social world. The hint of greater potential stirs the yearning within your heart. It is the voice of your soul letting you know you are expanding into release of purely physical perception.

Since this initial stimulus causes you to wonder *why you are here*, there may emerge a sense of a divine purpose for your life. Within your cellular memory lives the source of your manifestation here. The record of your soul also holds your initial decision to take form in this life. Since the underpinning of all manifestation is the origin within ME, it is natural for you to sense a drive toward that original conception. While the thirst appears to be a "return" to your roots, it implies, instead, a "re-membering" – a bringing of all of your memory "back together", union.

The needs and desires of family, work, friends and acquaintances have been the focus heretofore. Now they pale in comparison to this unnerving drive to re-member. That which was your greatest satisfaction is only a passing fancy. Day-to-day can begin to feel very routine as your personality considers whether it might not be missing out on something important.

At this point in life, many people divorce themselves from their relationships and apparent responsibilities. They feel foreign in what were once familiar surroundings. Sometimes their words and actions distance them from those who love them. Rather than spending time explaining their confusion, people most often simply hide away forgetting that others are enduring the same longing.

Now solitude becomes a precedent. Ease within silence, connecting deep within begins to secure the emerging sense of origin. During this time, it is helpful to honor the desire to be alone and silent. Natural awareness of union arises most easily from a void without word or action.

Each soul knows the perfect timing for this auspicious event. The soul speaking through the heart will not ever betray, lie or compromise. Acting as the agent of spirit, the soul emphasizes and implements every frequency capable of stimulating re-membering.

If you experience the desire to re-member, give yourself permission to use your silent time to reflect on the signposts, signals and messages garnered from daily living, unfolding the way most smoothly. The need for control, adherence to a belief or pattern and the divisive personal mind will distract you from a very natural, ongoing process.

Sometimes it may feel like it is unveiling itself much too slowly for your liking. You want it to hurry up. You want to know what you are supposed to *do* and how to bring it out into the open – *get it done.*

Eventually, given the time and quiet necessary to become aware of your own message, you will come to one realization. *You are experience in form.* Your purpose is to experience. What do you want to experience? What appearance do you want it to take? How do you want to perform from this conscious state of awareness?

Your "purpose" as ME in form is to garner experience within this physical body. When you incarnated you held a very loosely scripted idea about what your life experience would be. The script included this time in your life in which you are asking what your purpose is and now the stage is set – the moment to stop attempting to control from within your earthly perception. You will begin to exist as "beingness".

What often happens is called a "breakthrough" and you want to maintain that sense of knowing not realizing that holding on to the epiphany stops you from having further breakthroughs.

You want each moment of "spiritual high" to last and call this your *purpose*.

You believe no one else in your life can understand what you are experiencing so they all seem distant to you. In reality, each one of them will experience a breakthrough moment and will believe *you* don't understand. Each personality's idea about purpose is an individual expression and still one within divine union.

So, to answer your question: Your purpose is to experience in form. If it is the lifetime of re-membering, you will. If it is not the lifetime of re-membering, you most likely will not. Your script is open and accessible for re-writing should you desire.

The script is yours. You are the scriptwriter and you can augment, edit and re-write your personal story at any time. There is no judge or jury except your own mind.

Your purpose blooms like the beautiful rose in the moment of your remembrance. If this lifetime is one in which you will not re-member, your soul record will record all of the experiences you are presently having and that is your purpose. It is all experience; that and only that.

## Story Time

Let's go back to life with Paul and Nancy. When we left them, they had transitioned out of body, so we are going to go back to their lives within earth.

Paul is now about 25 and is living alone as he originally planned. Nancy is 20 and going to the local university.

Paul: *"Nancy, you tell me you're studying engineering. That's an unusual subject for a woman. What prompted that decision?"*

Nancy: *"I have this strong drive to do what men do, to compete in the market place like a man. It gives me a sense of purpose and I like numbers so I decided engineering would be a good calling. Why do you ask?"*

Paul: *"Oh, I don't know. I guess I thought you would follow a more benign profession – like maybe nursing or perhaps be a vet. Engineering seems so linear."*

Nancy: *"Well, it suits me just fine and I'm going for it. Will you support my decision or are you going to fight me the whole way?"*

Paul: *"Oh, of course I'll support this if it's what you want. I'm behind you 100% of the way."*

Two years pass and Nancy is thinking about graduate school. One day she's walking in a nearby park and suddenly she feels very alone in a way she has never felt before. The strangeness is accentuated by the quiet – no birds singing, no children laughing, no cars traveling on the local street, at least in *her* reality.

She sits down on a park bench and looks around wondering what is happening. All of a sudden, Nancy begins to cry feeling the deep sense of unhappiness she has been suppressing streaming forth with her tears.

*What is this all about,* she asks herself. *I'm finishing up my schooling. I have a good part time job that is paying the bills. My friends like me. Why am I so unhappy?*

A slow, warm feeling begins to flow upwards from within her heart. Nancy catches her breath as the tears begin to subside. *What is this yearning? I've never felt anything so strong before in my life,* she muses.

All at once, understanding breaks through like the sun after a long spring thunderstorm. *Oh, my, gosh – I don't want to be an engineer. I want to move to Africa and work in the nature reserves. All of my life I have read books about Africa and its creatures. That's what I really want. It must be the purpose for my life.*

That night Nancy calls Paul and tells him her decision. She's moving to Africa and is going to find work at a reserve for animals. Paul shakes his head and laughs.

*"Hmmm, thought you might eventually change your mind. Bet you think this is your purpose in life. What happens if you go to Africa and change your mind, again? What about that?"*

With a shy smile, Nancy replies, *"Well, now that I've seen how easy it is to change from one idea to the next, I really don't know. I'll probably have to wait and see won't I? At least now, you'll have a reason to travel. You can come visit me."*

Paul replies, *"Good idea. Together we'll discover that* purpose *is whatever is happening in the moment. Wonder what's next?"*

# Question Seven
## What lessons do I need
## to learn and challenges to overcome in this life?

The idea that you are in form to experience *appears* to be similar to being in form to learn. Yet, learning and experiencing are two sides of one coin.

You *are* a constant state of experience. Even simply sitting in a chair staring out a window is an experience of: the chair, the comfort or discomfort of your body, what you see outside the window, what you are hearing as you sit and the degree to which you are present with these and other aspects of sitting in a chair. The *experiencer* and the *experience* **is** one.

What you learn from sitting in the chair is different. You may learn you like the view from that window in particular or that the sun streams through at a specific time of day in a perfect manner. You may also learn that sitting facing in a different direction gives you a better view than your original position. There are many interesting learning experiences when you simply sit.

Your choice to incarnate in form is a decision to experience. Within the scope of that embodiment, you may learn or you may not learn. Perhaps you are spending other parallel lives as a strong warrior and choosing this lifetime to experience being a soft, feminine woman. Once here you make a choice to experience believing you are a victim to your female personality. You whine, complain and generally make life miserable for those around you.

Now, your experience of being in feminine form is occurring yet the learning included in what it feels like to be in that body has changed. Now you have instigated an entirely different set of responses and reactions that you may decide to balance in this lifetime or not. You will call these your *challenges*.

By definition, a challenge is *a call to battle*. If you believe learning through experience is a fight to engage in, then you will encounter numerous assaults. If you experience learning as expansive and transformational, it will be so for you.

The original ideology of learning and meeting challenges will be found in your concept of separation from ME. Since your division feels so complete, you are in a constant state of *challenging yourself* to remember what you are. When it doesn't show up easily, you feel it's hard and you must *do battle* with it. Rather, it is the call to surrender your soul is offering to you and you may hear it or not. The soul does not care. *It is experiencing.*

As you give in to experiencing yourself as I AM, you will no longer undergo learning as a challenge. In fact, learning will nearly cease to exist, at least from the standpoint of believing you don't know something and need to *learn* it. You will simply allow the upwelling of I AM *as* your consciousness and the assimilation will be complete. You can do that right now, if you will allow it to occur.

The areas of your life appearing out of alignment are the very experiences you are being invited to delve into within this incarnation. From that aspect, you can see where the learning will occur and you will allow yourself to embrace a totally different way of being. Your constantly expanding form reminds you that you are ever new and changeless as I AM for I AM in a constant state of dynamic flux while being changeless.

When you use the word "overcome" with regards to challenges, you are demonstrating a desire to control what cannot be controlled. To *overcome* is to *prevail over* and how can you prevail over your Self when you are constantly being invited to *be* that Self? An invitation does not request domination.

The ever-present desire to prevail against all "obstacles" and to find ease in life sets the stage for a constant upstream battle. Once you start swimming up the formidable labyrinth of the waterfall, you begin to realize that it is all in vain. Some of you simply give up right there while others turn around and begin to float downstream.

Life is *ease in experience*. Desire for control, flights of fancy regarding how life "should be" or "shouldn't be" resonate with pain, suffering and discomfort where there is no need. Expectations of different experiences and the perceived inability to bring them into fruition only frustrate the already overwhelming feeling that all is lost. Actually, the only deprivation is the concept you *have* to learn or overcome challenges.

The perceived appearance of your life may not fit the idea you "had" about how life would unfold. The people in your environment may not be the sort you wish to spend much time around causing you to feel stuck and frustrated. Your job, the lack of time for quality play and the overall conditions of your present experience may be overwhelming, boring, disgusting and upsetting. Wonderful!

What are you going to do about this situation? If you feel you have to overcome it, it will remain the same. Once you take on a combatant, it will duel with you until one of you expires. Rather, let the anticipation of creative expression and fulfillment urge you forward to a different resonance within your present experiencing.

I AM in a constant state of expression. What you view as a lesson or a challenge expresses as ME in one of my many guises. How will you host ME in your life? Do you need to overcome I AM?

## Story Time

Nancy has moved to Africa and Paul is thinking about going for a visit. He's having a tough time making decisions about how a long trip might affect his career as a lawyer.

After some consideration, Paul decides that one of his lessons is learning to stand up for himself. It feels like a challenge that he needs to take on to become more assertive. Though he learned in the university and later law school how to speak well as an attorney, when it comes to making himself heard on his own behalf, he has problems. This will be a good opportunity.

On Monday morning, Paul arises and after his usual morning routine, he begins the drive to work. Interiorly, he is setting himself up to approach the managing partner of the law firm where he works to ask for a month off to travel to Africa and visit Nancy.

Part of Paul is excited at this chance to overcome his fears and another aspect is scared to death. *What if I get fired? What if the managing partner yells at me? What will the other lawyers think? Will I have the guts to take this stand?*

Upon arrival at the office, Paul straightens his necktie and gets ready to walk into the managing partner's office. He's sweating and nervous, yet he's going to do this because it's one of his biggest challenges.

Walking down the long tiled halls of the law firm, Paul runs straight into Frederick coming around the corner; or, as more people know him Frederick Swanson, Esq., *the* Swanson in Swanson and Aeglaten, Attorneys at Law.

*"Paul,"* Frederick addressed him in a rush, *"I was just headed toward your office. We have a bit of an emergency going on. Come down to the conference room where the partners are meeting. We need to talk with you."*

Paul was definitely not prepared for this interruption in his thought process. After all, he was right in the midst of learning how to take an assertive stand and ask for what he wanted. Yet, this was *the* boss and he wasn't about to refuse.

*"Of course, Frederick, I'll go right away. Is everything alright?"*

*"You'll find out when you get there,"* Frederick attempted to assure him. *"Just get down there right away."*

Paul headed to the south end of the lobby where he was met by a room of ten partners talking quietly among themselves. He felt awkward and uneasy being the only non-partner at the conference table yet he took his place in the last vacant seat in the middle and attempted to become invisible.

Frederick was quick to follow and all came to a hush when he entered the room. Full attention was given to the founding father of their intimate dynasty.

*"I wanted you all to hear it from me. We are in the midst of making some big changes within the firm and I've invited Paul to be part of this meeting because it will affect his career. Two of our biggest clients, you all know whom I mean, are talking about leaving us if we don't get some younger blood to work with them. I've decided to appoint Paul as lead counsel for these two firms*

*when they are dealing with matters where they want a younger, talented mind involved. This means that each of you will be asked to back him up until he gets his feet under him as to their various projects with our firm. Any questions?"* Frederick was not one to mince words.

Paul felt a sweat breaking out that was much worse than the one he had earlier experienced. *What am I learning now? How to say yes or no? Wait, they haven't even asked me. I've simply been appointed. Is this the way I want to live my life?*

Paul listened to the various suggestions the partners were making about how all of this was going to work. Then Frederick addressed him specifically, *"Paul, do you have anything to say about all of this?"*

Paul's words were stuck in his throat. What had seemed so important a few hours ago was no longer in his mind. He didn't know whether he wanted to jump for joy or run screaming out of the door.

*"No, not at the moment, I don't. I'm honored you have chosen me to represent our firm with these two companies. I will definitely take all of the assistance offered until I am better acquainted with the needs of these two important clients and they come to know me better. Thank you for this opportunity,"* Paul heard himself saying. He was trembling. *Have I missed a chance to stand up for myself? Have I missed out on a wonderful trip on behalf of my career? What does it all mean?*

That night Paul called Nancy to tell her he wasn't coming. *"Oh, that's fine, Paul. I was going to call you,"* Nancy responded. *"I've been asked to take on a whole new project with the parks department and I won't be able to host you here for at least another year. Glad you didn't make firm plans about showing up this time since I'll be very, very busy. Actually, so will you."*

Paul hung up the phone in bewilderment. Then it dawned on him – the experience – the need to control.

# Question Eight
## Do souls have ages - old, young, new?

Souls don't age, as humans believe they do. When you ask about *old, young* or *new* souls, your mind is visiting a linear sense of time that does not exist in the soul world.

From the standpoint of old vs. young, souls exist with more or less recorded experience dependent upon how many lifetimes they have chosen to incarnate. Though a soul is in a constant state of conscious awareness, it does not always feel an urge to come into form. Often the consciousness that encapsulates the soul simply exists without form in what you would call the *world of spirit*. In this state, it is aware of itself *as* consciousness.

When you ask about the age of soul, it is usually from the perspective of *old,* meaning wise and *young* meaning just getting his or her feet on the ground from the standpoint of human incarnation. This is a human perception with no merit within the wisdom of the soul.

A person can be living within earth appearing to be very wise and have only incarnated in form in this dimension a few times. Another person may be embodied here who seems foolish, rash and still be one of the *oldest souls* from the perspective of experience simply wishing to have a fun, frivolous lifetime.

Since most human questions are posited from a point of comparison or judgment, this one easily tops the list. What difference does it make how "old" or "young" a soul is unless you are attempting to label a person in some way.

New souls do not exist from the standpoint of being truly "new". I AM, Creator Is and all souls ARE from the inception of Creator's conception. There is no age in the realm of spirit so there is no *new* or *old*. There is only experience and yet within the soul world that is of no importance either. Incarnation is only to experience - whatever, whenever, wherever and with whomever.

Appearance can be very deceiving to the human mind. A soul that incarnates in earth hundreds of time and understands the trap of duality may make a decision to embody as a crippled child to assist members of its soul group to act as mother and father enabling a specific set of experiences. The humans observing this particular script may make a number of assumptions about the family without really knowing what the underlying soul patterns are for those beings.

Another soul without many earth lifetimes may choose to come to this dimension to master duality as an experience. Other humans may view this soul as a guru or teacher without fully understanding the depth to which this experience is taking that soul, especially since it made a choice to enter duality with little experience of it.

Since being born in earth opens the door to forgetting what you are, it is very easy for a soul (whether experienced in this dimension or not) to forget to re-member what it *is* when it arrives here. All souls embrace this risk in coming into this plane. Even those souls who have incarnated here hundreds or thousands of lifetimes take the chance that when they arrive, they will forget.

Dependent upon the strength of focus and intention at the outset of birth, a soul may or may not re-member its origin easily. Hence, judgment of those who appear to have "lost their way" is only a limited perception of opinion since there is no way anyone can know why a soul has embodied here until the individual re-members for itself.

If you view life from within the soul's reality, it is easier as a human being to move aside from judgment and opinion about how other people are living their lives. Even the small child living without food or water in the African desert made that decision before incarnating and only that soul knows the reason why.

Quantity does not mean *quality* in soul lifetimes. A soul may incarnate in earth a thousand times without much quality within the life stream of each embodiment. Since it is the quality or focus on experience that infuses the soul with the memory of its origin, the quantity of lives does not equal the experience. Again, judging from the outside appearance is useless.

If you are curious about whether you have had many quality experiences within this realm, ask, *How important is it that you know your many life experiences?* If the answer is important, then you have not had enough experience in this realm and will undoubtedly come back until . . . it is no longer important.

The viewpoint of importance tells you that you have much experiencing to do here or you would not be concerned about it. *Your focus is your answer*. When you come to the point that you can let go of who you believe you are or why you are here; that the number of lives being lived or not lived is of no concern, you may begin (and that is only *begin*) to re-member your Self as I AM. Until that time, you will constantly choose and re-choose to emerge within this plane until you are the master of it.

The concept you want to hold in mind is that you are eternal. You have infinity to understand duality. If you hold up your question about old, young or new souls to the light of forever, it loses its meaning. When the loss of its meaning means nothing to you, you have aged in wisdom a bit . . . *only a bit*.

## Story Time

Nancy is in Africa working with the national parks reserve department. Her job is to assist in erecting the fences that keep poachers from killing off the elephant herds for their ivory.

Every day she gets up and dresses in the coolest and lightest of shorts and shirt, puts on her sturdy boots and protective hat to meet the other members of her crew who are erecting miles of fencing to protect these majestic animals.

And, every day, the same urge within her keeps arising – the desire to strip down and run naked among the elephants like a native. Though she knows the herds would probably not welcome her dashing among them, there is almost a vision within her mind's eye showing her how it "used to be".

Nancy questions this imaginative flight of fancy because she hasn't ever seen this done, yet it persists. Sometimes when the group takes their lunch break, she stands at the fence line staring at the elephants roaming through the trees a hundred yards away. Then the desire and the vision become very distinct.

One night a native medicine woman comes to the parks department's evening barbecue. Most of the department's staff eats together at picnic tables outside the tents or in the mess tent. The outer area is open to the public so it is easy and customary for local people who are interested in what Nancy and her co-workers are doing to come ask questions.

This particular medicine woman has a special gift. She sees beyond the realm of the physical into the world of the spirits. She is very old for a woman of her tribe, seventy-five.

Entering the cooking area, she sniffs at the meat and curls up her lip. Cooking over fire in grills made of metal is not something she is accustomed to within her natural life. Quietly, she sidles over to where Nancy and her friends are sitting at the picnic table. She is so silent she almost goes unnoticed, until . . . .

*"Ya,"* she says loudly pointing at Nancy. *"Ya, ya."*

Nancy doesn't know what she means and one of the local workers comes over to act as translator. He begins talking with the medicine woman and tells Nancy that this ancient one has been attracted to her soul.

*"What does that mean?"* Nancy asks with trepidation. *"Does she want my soul?"*

*"No, no,"* the translator responds, *"she is telling me that your soul has much, much experience in it yet it is still afraid. She says you do not know what you are worth; that the elephants can tell you but you won't know until you are no longer afraid of them."*

*"I'm* not *afraid of the elephants,"* Nancy indignantly replied. *"I simply know better than to go past the fence line since the animals are wild. We were instructed never to approach them unless accompanied by one of the professional staff who sometimes cares for them. One or more of the animals might mistake our intention."*

The translator was describing to the medicine woman what Nancy was saying, translating back and forth between them. Now the ancient native laughed heartily showing off the two teeth left to her.

The translator turned toward Nancy with a look of wonder. *"She tells me you do not need to listen to the instructions. The elephants know you. They knew you in the life of the young boy who ran with the elephants. She says you won't believe her until she tells you that you can see yourself running naked with the elephants when you were seven. It was your rite of passage and you were then named* Tusk *because the elephants would let you ride on their long, ivory tusks. She says you are remembering and now you will remember more."*

Nancy stood beside the picnic table speechless. *How could this woman know what she had been seeing in her visions? Could all of this be true? How could this old crone know how much she felt like she had to make sure she was making everyone else happy? That she felt so worthless even though she knew she was doing a good job. How could this be?*

With the message delivered, the old woman said something to the translator, turned around and walked away. Nancy felt like running after her.

*"What did she say to you before she left?"* she asked the young native.

*"She told me I wasn't to waste my time attempting to make you believe her; that your wisdom was old enough to show you the rest."*

That night Nancy lay upon the bunk without even putting the blanket over her. She hadn't taken off her clothes and had no intention of sleeping. *Do I dare go out to the elephants in the dark? What if there is a lion? What if I get caught breaking the rules?*

In the midst of her musing and questioning, Nancy fell asleep fully dressed. She dreamt of elephants: big, fully tusked elephants lifting her high in the air . . . and she was laughing – the laugh of a young boy in the height of his glory, *Tusk.*

# Question Nine
# What is a lightworker?

As a label, a lightworker is a human being who focuses his or her attention upon working with light. While this name has been given to a number of spiritual categories, it is a misnomer.

The inaccuracy of the designation arises within the separatist viewpoint suggesting there are *lightworkers* and *non-lightworkers.* Since you are composed of light, and only light, all are working *within* the light of which each is composed.

Those who consider themselves to be more focused within the light *often judge* those they deem *not* working within light (sometimes referred to as "using or not using positive energy"). This is impossible and, as an aside, all energy is neutral.

Light is defined as *an illuminating source* while work is *the effort to accomplish something.* Your definitions betray you by their meaning. How can light be an effort to accomplish? When you say you are a *lightworker* by definition you are saying you expend effort to accomplish being that which you are. When you look at the name from within its roots, it becomes illogical.

Individual experiences as energy within I AM are a composite of the informational profusion of light you are in human form. The capability to compose a perception of life from outside your stream of light is not possible due to the inherent composition of the molecules of your bodies – physical, emotional, mental and etheric.

Within the lightworker classification is the belief that those who are *lightworkers* are more likely to be enlightened than their less fortunate counterparts – the struggling masses of humanity. What is not acknowledged within the common aggregate is the inherent structuring of every human being as light in form.

The ability you have in this moment to make a choice to *be of the light* or *not be of the light* is not an aspect of your free will. You *are* light. You will always *be* light (if you want to work from the viewpoint of time) and you have always been light (within that same time perspective). Within your virtual construction, you are not given a choice by ME as Creator about how this occurs; it simply *is*.

The lightworker community places a great deal of emphasis upon *healing*. Those who are not "of the light" usually require healing and the intervention of a qualified lightworker to bring them into a state of wholeness.

While many human beings seek balance within their lives, the concept that another being can make this occur is one of fundamental confusion within the ego personality. Each human being is fully capable of bringing him or herself into the harmony each seeks.

Though the support of another human being while in the midst of coming into harmonic balance is nurturing, it is not necessary nor will it create the desired effect. The most the *lightworker* may do is *be* that which he or she wishes to experience in the world. There is nothing that can be *done* except through the free will of the person desiring balance.

Actual "healers" do nothing. They need not even be with the person supposedly requiring the "healing". Spontaneous remissions are a scientific way of observing what I AM expressing here.

Releasing belief that healing is needed results in trust in wholeness allowing the experience to occur. How often are you told (or do you tell others) that you "need to find a healer with whom you resonate"? Of course, due to the trust that is engendered when you believe the person you are interacting with is in resonance with you, the resonance accomplishes the harmonic whole.

The need to be called a *lightworker* or to name yourself so simply separates you from those you deem not worthy to be called such. The stream of consciousness emanating from within I AM knows no difference between one who believes he or she works with light and one who has no notion of the meaning of that term. All is One within I AM.

If you are desirous of separating yourself from others you deem less than you, using labels that speak of your separating viewpoints could be more precise. Your initial response to that idea will be one of resistance because you believe you are operating from a sense of union; not so.

Remember, your soul doesn't care what you call yourself within I AM. You may respond to whatever name suits you until you come to the realization of the divisive factors involved within the naming process. The capability you have of streaming yourself as light is no different from the ability others have – no matter what you may call them.

Is the man sitting on the sidewalk begging less of a lightworker than you are? Is the CEO sitting in his office attempting to figure out how to keep the company afloat less of a lightworker than you are? How judgmental have you become in your opinion of who is a lightworker and who is not? Even within your lightworker communities, you judge some better than others.

I AM; You are. You are light. All is light. All is infinite within the working of that light requiring no effort or accomplishment.

## Story Time

We left Nancy dreaming about a lifetime as the young boy, Tusk. The next day as she awoke, Nancy felt a sense of longing mixed with dread. How could she possibly express to her co-workers what she had experienced last night beginning with the appearance of the medicine woman and culminating in her dream world? *Best keep it to myself.*

Today the crew was going to finish the last set of fence posts around a particularly nasty set of inclines at the other side of the local forest. They had put this piece of work off until they had the time and energy to complete climbing over rocks and brush to set the posts in the ground. Today was that day.

Nancy sequestered her dream state deep into her subconscious so she could concentrate on the job at hand. The group trekked around the edge of the forestland and to the opposite side from the camp intending to begin post-holing at the lowest point and culminating at the top. Paired in twos they set out to start digging knowing it would take well past lunch to reach the top.

Down below them in the forest the elephant herd was eating, splashing in ponds and generally being elephants. The sound of their ripping and tearing at tree branches echoed over the landscape.

As Nancy dug and positioned posts, her mind easily surfaced its dream state and she began to resonate with the sound of the feeding elephants. She felt the desire to be with them upwell within her yet knew she had to keep it under wraps among her co-workers who were either slightly fearful of the power of the elephants or more induced to obey the rules.

Time passed, many holes were dug and the morning stretched on under the hot African sun. A local native boy had been commissioned to keep everyone supplied with water and today he was a very busy young man. He ran from one set of diggers to the next (twenty total) bringing fresh buckets of water from the stream flowing down the outskirts of this side of the hill into the pool in the forest. Everyone felt a great deal of gratitude for his offerings even though he was treated as *lower caste* by most of the workers due to his inability to speak (he was mute) and his illiteracy.

As Nancy and her cohorts decided to stop for lunch under the only shade tree clinging to the side of the hill, a tremendous noise arose in the forest. While no one actually knew what was causing the commotion, it sounded like the trumpeting of a young elephant either from pain or from fear. No one had the expertise to understand the message of the sound.

Nancy's elephant resonance went into high alert yet she didn't know what to do either. Everyone looked at each other quizzically and somewhat fearfully. Since the fences were not complete due to their just finishing the last part of the fence line on this set of inclines, the undercurrent of danger presented itself dramatically.

*If only I had the courage of Tusk right now,* Nancy thought to herself. *I would run into that forest and find out what the problem is with the elephants. I would know what to do if I could remember what Tusk remembers.*

Just about then, a speeding form passed by the lunching group. It was the water boy barreling down the hill toward the noise in the forest. He was going to see what was going on and was definitely putting himself in grave danger.

No one moved. The air was filled with angst, fear and threat to survival.

Nancy could tolerate her anxiety no longer. She stood up and lunged forward in one smooth descent following the water boy down the hill.

"Nancy, don't go down there. You know better. He's just a local village boy. If something happens to him, it's one thing. We don't want you to get hurt." The voice of the park's supervisor, Sam, echoed over the elephant trumpeting.

Nancy didn't pause for even one moment. She followed the youngster into the forest where they found a young baby elephant caught between two fallen tree trunks. His back leg had become wedged and no amount of prodding from his mother was moving the trees. If the strength of an elephant can't move a tree, what are we supposed to do? Nancy thought.

In amazement, Nancy watched as the water boy approached the baby elephant without any fear (not even of its mother) and gently laid his hands on the baby's forehead. With a gentle push, he began urging the youngster backward the way it had come when it originally became stuck. He pushed slowly, then more determinedly until the little one had no choice except to backup. Voila! Its leg sprung free through the same gap into which it had fallen rather than struggling forward further into the intertwined trunks' trap.

The elephant mother trumpeted in gratitude (at least that was what it sounded like) as Nancy looked toward the mute water boy. He gazed into her eyes shining a beatific smile and then simply walked away.

In her mind, Sam's words echoed, "He's just a local village boy. If something happens to him, it's one thing. We don't want you to get hurt."

## Question Ten
## How do I surrender to life?

Begin answering this question by asking yourself, "How do I *not* surrender to life?" You are in a constant state of surrender no matter what you believe you experience through free will.

Your capacity to make decisions, attempt to control your life and the depth to which you, as a human being, will go to make sure you are experiencing what you believe you want to experience suggests to your mind that you are in charge. Putting this mildly, *you are in charge of nothing*. You simply *believe you are* to satisfy your desire to dominate, to feel in control.

Your state of being is within infinite surrender to I AM.

From the outset of the human experience (millions of your years ago), the strongest physical being dominated the group, tribe or gathering in a very physical way. Often this subjugation took the form of physical injury or outright demonstrations of force. Sometimes it was more subtle. Just the same, it was exhibited by every new specimen within the ancestry you consider human beings.

Little has changed upon the arrival of what you now call the *technical age*. The differences only lie within the method of the domination. Since it is a struggle (and you will agree that it *is* a struggle) to stay on top, it is obvious that it's not a natural state of being. If it were within the innate scope of life, nature would also appear to be in a state of dominance over other aspects of itself.

Since you are reading these words, you are circumspectly sniffing around the idea of surrendering to I AM. It sounds noble, to be commended at least. What you don't realize is that you have already surrendered. You simply don't know it yet.

Contrary to popular belief, you are I AM and as I AM any ideas or concepts you have about the state of your existence are already lost in the surrender to I AM. Much like the beloved of your heart, you have submersed yourself within the I AMNESS of yourself without even realizing you were falling in love with you. Yet, it is happening and you are surrendering to it.

So when you ask, "How do I surrender to life?" what you are really asking is, "How do I mentally stop fighting life?" Isn't that closer to the mark?

Your mind seizes every opportunity it can possibly grab to convince you that if you *do this* or *do that*, you will be in a state of bliss, harmony and love. It gives you exercises to do; it makes sure you put them on your calendar and watches over your progress, day by day. Even the practice of observing your progression is part of ensuring that you complete what you have devised as your *plan of surrender* to your I AM. The mind believes it is in control.

Meanwhile, your soul simply keeps recording all of the experiences you are having, your heart continually prompts you to slow down and live your life without need of practice or belief and *I AM remains your constant surrendered state.* The inclusion of this particular memory is not outside of you. Fundamentally, it is what you are as I AM.

Surrendering means *to give up.* Can you give up what you believe you *need to do* to surrender? Can you give up the idea of *giving up?* Will you acknowledge your surrender within ME?

As you allow your heart to speak as your soul, you will find your mind will slowly open up to new ways of receiving information. Your mental faculties will surrender to the awareness of your soul through the messages of your heart. Since you are asking the question, you are seeking a way to understand how to *be* this state and so here are a few helpful hints you may adopt provided you don't make a "to do" list out of a loosely-held set of suggestions:

For a start, let go of every *"should"* and *"should not"* you use to construct your life. This doesn't mean you are to drive on the wrong side of the road. There are common sense principles you already know that apply to living safely. *"Should"* and *"should not"* include concepts around how you *should* eat, how you *should* meditate, how you *should* speak, act and be seen. There are also, of course, how you *should not* eat, meditate, speak, act and portray yourself. Each one of these adopted rules indicates you are attempting to be viewed by either yourself or others in a proscribed manner. When you fail at a *should* or *should not,* you feel guilty, a failure and ashamed. Those feelings are your initial warning signs of ego domination.

If you want a practice, simply say I AM to yourself every time you feel like you don't know what to do or say. Let the I AM of you inform you how to live, breathe and experience your surrender. Since you are already completely in a state of surrender to I AM (unconsciously) you are simply affirming that which you already are in form.

Spend time each day sitting silently as I AM. Breathe I AM. Inhale I AM. Exhale I AM.

In the moment of the inbreath and the outbreath, in between the two, you will find a silent space wherein you realize the truth of your surrender. Not only have you surrendered to life, your life *is* your surrender.

## Story Time

We left Nancy standing next to the broken tree trunks marveling at her lack of control in the elephant situation. This was definitely not her usual stance in life. She was a leader (she told herself). This unnerving experience with elephants was taking her completely by surprise.

Nancy walked back to the lunching group under the tree who were finishing up, readying themselves to get back to work. Sam looked at Nancy with a great deal of irritation. No one was going to get hurt on his watch!

*"Sam, I'm sorry I didn't listen to you. My instant reaction was to follow that kid into the forest and I'm glad I did. He managed to save the baby elephant stuck between two tree trunks when its mother couldn't even do it. I wish you had been there to see the whole thing,"* Nancy replied to Sam's frown more out of fear for her job than because she felt a need to explain herself.

*"I don't really care why you did what you did or went where you went. What I do care about is keeping this crew safe.*

*The next time you run off when I tell you not to, you're out of here. Do you get my drift, little lady?"* Sam drawled. He was not one to mince words.

Nancy put her head down to keep Sam from seeing the slight smile unconsciously forming on her lips and walked away with her digging cohorts. Sam always got his back up and while he did have the power to hire and fire, she knew he had a soft spot in his heart for her (she had seen that more than once) and was most likely more angry with her because he thought he might have lost her than because he was her boss.

Posthole digging progressed slowly due to the heat of the afternoon and toward four o'clock, the crew had given all they had to the drenching sweat of the venture. Picking up shovels, posthole diggers and lunch remains, they headed down toward the camp and the welcoming cold showers.

Nancy lingered a bit, looking longingly toward the space through which she had entered the forest and felt a burning desire to do so again. *Well, not right now, maybe later,* she told herself and continued following her wilting companions who by this time were about fifty yards ahead of her.

Suddenly Nancy felt a tingling on the back of her neck as if someone had eyes on her. Looking over her left shoulder back up the hill, she saw that someone *was* watching her. It turned out to be the medicine woman who had visited the camp and talked about her interactions with elephants and the lifetime as Tusk. Nancy froze in place. *Do I go up there? I don't understand her language. What would I say?*

The motionless, old hag continued to gaze at her. Nancy began to feel very sleepy, overwhelming tired. *I believe I cannot take another step. I've got to sit down right here, sun or no sun.* And, thinking those strange thoughts, Nancy collapsed like a lead weight in the middle of the hill while a small wisp of cloud floated overhead until it hid the sun from her just enough to cool her down.

Slipping into her dream world, falling, falling asleep Nancy found herself standing in front of the medicine woman, though now she saw this ancient figure as young, vibrant and powerful though it was obviously the same person.

46

*"I've taken you into the realm of spirit to talk with you. Here you have no need of knowing my language. Here we simply understand each other. I have two messages to give you. You may decide to listen and follow surrendering yourself to your own plan or you may make the decision to resist yourself. Whatever you decide is important only to you. I am simply the messenger."* The beautiful, shimmering young woman instilled the words within Nancy's mind.

*"The first message is this: You were drawn to this country because your life as Tusk desires fulfillment in this here and now. You may complete this yearning or you may ignore it. If you decide to forget it, it will return with vigor in another incarnation. This you cannot escape.*

*"If you make the decision to complete the experience in this time and space, you will find much that is familiar will be taken from you. It must be this way for you to interface with Tusk in his here and now.*

*"The second message is a bit more complex. Your brother, Paul, is part of the unfolding of these parallel realities. If you decide to embrace your life as Tusk in his conscious reality and merge it within your awareness as Nancy, you will be changing the outcome of Paul's present life, as well.*

*"If you decide to ignore these messages and simply live your life as you have until this moment, Paul's incarnation will not experience the mergence with your present life any more than it already is; in other words, all will continue progressing from the observational viewpoint you are already experiencing.*

*"Neither decision is either right or wrong. It is simply a crossroad point and this is the moment of your decision. You must give me your answer now. There is no space for deliberation. This is the moment of possible surrender to your own plan."*

Nancy stood, speechless. *She was going to influence Paul's life by her decision.* Yet, she knew in her heart what the answer must be. There was no doubt.

*"I surrender to Nancy as Tusk and Tusk as Nancy in this space and time and I have no idea what that means."*

## Question Eleven
## How can I be aware of oneness?

A concept of *being aware of oneness* is foreign to the human mind. You chose to live in duality that by its nature is two rather than one. The natural state of your mind, emotions and activity experiences polarity.

Let's begin by talking about being aware of wholeness and then we will segue to oneness in a natural progression.

When you contemplate wholeness, you may think of balance or you may see it as multiples combining as one. In your dimension, wholeness is much more than simply being of one piece. It also expresses itself as a mergence, an upwelling linkage among you and all else that appears outside of your personal "piece" – the particle you *are* within I AM.

Sometimes you feel whole and then on other occasions you may feel fragmented. It doesn't mean you physically are "in pieces"; it simply means your perception of reality, at that moment, is incoherent. Within coherence lies the answer to the experience of wholeness as oneness.

If you wish to be aware of the absoluteness within which you dwell, coherency within your physical frequency is necessary. When you are incoherent (your wavelength is disrupted in its amplitude or the up and down of your frequency), you *feel* separated from the energetic transmission in your dimension emanating from within I AM. This does not mean you *are* separate. It simply means you experience yourself as divergent.

Living within a similitude with all creation is the experience of wholeness and this is why it naturally leads to the consciousness of oneness. Your awareness is then that of selfsameness. It is only your ego's mind seeing itself as separate and distinct from the other or *others* within your environment.

You are conscious, aware and one. Focusing on these three concepts without being distracted by the daily activity of your present reality brings *oneness* into focus.

It is only your perception that is limited. Your mind creates a *life* and you call it your *reality*. When you allow yourself to extend "outside" of the personal life you live, you begin to become aware of the inner "link" among all creation. The term "link" here is only for your mind because all emerges as one stream of consciousness within I AM.

The designations with which you have labeled yourself declare your sense of separation. *I was born in this city, I live at this address, I am a mother/father, I work for such and such company.* Each of these descriptions distinguishes you within oneness. To be aware of your constant emerging within the oneness of I AM it is important that you relinquish your ideas of *who* you are and simply be *what* you are.

Due to the proclivities of the human perception within your present time, it is important that you spend a period each day alone, in silence, to *be aware* of oneness. Note that it is *be* aware rather than *become* aware. Setting a specific time in which to dwell on what it means to *be one* gives your mind a focus to pay attention to assisting it in shutting down its constant drive to entertain you. You may begin with a few minutes each day, if that is all you are comfortable with, and expand its duration as the experience becomes more familiar to you. Without time spent in silence, being aware of oneness will be most difficult for your constantly striving mental world.

The period you spend in silence will expose you to how limited your personal vision is within human form. What you perceive *with* your senses is based upon what you *expect* to perceive based upon what you believe you *will perceive.* It's a circle of experience bounding you in on all sides until you make the determination that it is time to break free. The great experiment of this dimension is that of free will in contrast. The adventure is to immerse yourself within the sense of separation and then to be aware of oneness (which is always present within you *as* you). Since you have asked the question, your timing is *now* to be aware of I AM. To do so, in your world, you must set aside time to be I AM; then oneness is all you will know.

It is your focus upon the labels assigned and how they play out that causes the limitation of being the one I AM. Oneness exists within I AM as I AM and you are I AM so you are oneness. Loosen your hold on the names with which you present yourself and oneness will be the result.

Let your vision be new. Let the ideologies and concepts within your human mind drop away as you peel yourself like a tender grape. Feel the aloneness of oneness that is comprised of "all-oneness". Being alone, you are aware of being all one. Free of your judgments and opinions, you are free to choose to be I AM. Where you believed you needed companionship to know oneness, you realize your only *perceived* need is I AM.

Sitting in silence as I AM naturally extends into your daily reality. When the focus of your silent "time" expands to include your human activities, your awareness has shifted from activating your labeling to exposing the inner core of your I AM presence. Being aware of oneness is less about a new sense of awareness and much more about returning to the awareness of yourself as the home you seek. I AM that of which you wish to be aware. I AM one. Be aware of ME and know I AM oneness. I AM one as you.

## Story Time

Nancy's experience with the water boy, the elephants and the medicine woman was now several days in the past. The post holes had been dug on the incline, the fence stretched and secured and this area of the park department's fencing project was complete.

Sam had called a meeting in the dining tent to talk about their next endeavor. It seemed that a number of poachers were taking advantage of weaknesses in some of the park's boundaries and his crew had been asked to address this need.

*"There appears to be a bit of a problem on the northern perimeter of the park,"* Sam said with deliberation. He was not looking forward to sending his team into an area that could be potentially deadly due to the persistence of poachers carrying loaded rifles.

*"The fencing we put up and the locked gates we installed have been pulled down nearest the area where the lion prides*

*usually bed down. I'm going to send all of you with armed guards to re-erect the fencing and track down any of the lions that might have escaped the perimeter. Not only are they a danger to the livestock in the area, they are also in danger of being extinguished permanently if we don't fully commit to the mission of the park. Does anyone have any questions?"*

George voiced the concern lingering in everyone's mind. *"Sam, how are we supposed to track down the lions? May we use native beaters to drive them back into the park's perimeter? I don't know any other way we could accomplish this."*

*"Yes, George and anyone else wondering about the same question, we will use the local beaters gently and softly. Since the prides have been living within the park's boundaries they will naturally return 'home' when they feel threatened. Once inside the fence line, they will go back to their natural habitat. Then you can all put up the new fencing and gates. I've also asked the local police to stand guard with you until you are finished. Needless to say, this is a stopgap measure until we can ferret out who is doing the poaching. That's my job. Your task is to get the fencing replaced. You'll all be leaving immediately."*

Loaded into their utility trucks and provisioned for the several days they would be staying in the northern end of the park, Nancy's crewmates made the four-hour trek to the location of the destruction. Upon arrival, they realized what a job laid ahead. At least a mile of fencing had been ripped up and all of the gates were strewn around the grounds with chewed up hinges and locks.

While six of the team set up the crew's tents as living and dining quarters, the remainder began unloading the trucks and laying out the new fencing. Others were dragging down the remnants of the old wire and moving the gates out of the way. Nancy joined the removal crew at a good distance from camp where the fence line shifted west by northwest toward a stand of camel-thorn trees.

She and two of the strongest men were pulling down and tying up heaps of twisted wire when a trumpeting resounded through the air. The sound emerged from within the trees though it wasn't clear from exactly which direction. Everyone stopped work to listen and then heard the shuffling sound of padded feet walking in unison toward them.

Out of the camel-thorn forest emerged a small herd of elephants led by the female and baby that Nancy had witnessed only days before stuck in the downed tree trunks. They ambled out cautiously stopping just shy of exiting the tree line.

Their appearance was so unexpected that no one spoke or moved. Each member of the crew stood stock still facing the small grouping except Nancy. Her time had come and she wasn't going to miss *this* opportunity.

Slowly, with her hand outstretched, Nancy began taking one small step at a time toward the female and baby elephants. Her mind was screaming that this combination was as dangerous as it gets though her heart spoke even louder. . . .

As Nancy tiptoed toward the mother and child, the baby elephant began making overtures toward her. Usually a mother elephant would stand between her baby and an intruder, yet this mother did not. In fact, she backed away a bit to let her offspring make its introduction.

Nancy felt its shiny trunk tip flicking across her open palm and ancient memories stirred inside her. She was completely unaware of the crewmembers standing behind her in open amazement. A shift within her consciousness overlaid an image of Tusk in her mind's eye blurring her experience as Nancy with that of Tusk.

Following the line of the little elephant's trunk up to the top of its head, Nancy began scratching it as though it were a kitten right where the trunk melded into the skull. A deep humming sound emerged from inside the infant as though he were purring. Mother, on the other hand, now stepped forward and nuzzled the back of Nancy's hand with her own trunk.

*This is oneness*, Nancy thought to herself. *Not only do I feel at one with these elephants; I know myself as Tusk and myself.*

Then she remembered the words, ". . . *you will be changing the outcome of Paul's present life, as well.*"

## Question Twelve
## Is there another word I can use for the "void"?

Often words convey a meaning through feeling. This question obviously is a concept that the "void" is uncomfortable and not desirable.

Since there are dozens of meanings for "void" in the English language, I will offer a few alternatives here and then I will discuss the "void".

The "void" may also be referred to as *vacuum, space, nothingness, sunyata, zero, emptiness, thusness, undirected, abyss, nihility* to name a few. None of these words carries a negative connotation with reference to "void". It is an expression of "no thingness" without impetus from Creator.

There are many reasons why the word "void" may create discomfort. It might arise from a sense of limitlessness to dark and black or the notion that where there is a "void" something is missing. Though humans use "void" in countless ways to express *removing* or *getting rid of*, it is not this sense that is the origin of "void". It is a derivative of Latin for *empty*. Being uncomfortable with the concept of *emptiness* means the heart is longing.

From the standpoint that being in *emptiness* coincides with *surrender*, this question is a very fertile subject. While it is common within the earth's dimensional frequency to retreat from the idea of surrender, what is being requested by the longing heart is a release *into* the "void" from which it originally came and from which it constantly emanates. It is the basis *for* and the absolute beginning *of* your origin.

Your ego personality is quite certain that it has this world pretty well figured out even if you do experience life as a *sometimes struggle*. The ego still rears its head in admonishment every time you consider relaxing your hold on the attachments perceived as connecting you *to* earth. The prospect of an empty, bottomless, never-ending space within which you might even consider surrendering can be a terrifying aspect for the ego and your mind.

What the personality doesn't recognize is the eternal love emerging from within the "void" nurturing and nourishing all of Creator's aspects. The ego longs for this love yet unsuccessfully keeps attempting to find it in the dual dimension. Any idea of releasing into the abyss to experience the utmost upwelling of this love shutters the doors of the mind. Your heart knocks on that closed door continually.

The innate habit of self-protection attempts to persuade you to avoid the "void". If you sit in silence during the day (quite close to nothingness), the mind begins to play inviting you to think about *this* and to think about *that* so as to keep you from tip toeing too close to the edge of the abyss where you might *fall into love.* Oh, what a moment of extreme bliss your ego personality forgoes only because it perceives your release as its lack of control.

The ego fears submersion within ME more than any other possible occurrence. Ideas about nihility or a vacuum fill it with terror so it begins to withdraw behind its fortress walls pulling up the drawbridge as it retreats. With the moat of separation firmly in place, your ego personality feels safe not realizing that its sense of aloneness within this perspective is not the sense of "all-oneness" but rather simply lonely.

What your ego doesn't know, and will not know until it loosens its reins of control, is the very yearning it feels within itself is the same desire it will fulfill within the "void". On a subconscious level it is aware of this fact, yet it doesn't let it rise to the surface for fear the invitation may be accepted. Since your heart, as the voice of your soul, is constantly inviting you to release your grasp on your perceived beliefs and allow the reality of I AM to surface within you, the ego personality keeps an eye out for the occasions when the invitation may become overwhelmingly inviting.

Eventually, the concept of separation becomes too much for the personality to bear. The call from the "void" becomes not only insistent, it is also begins to appear charming and inviting. Despite the ego's promptings to "get away from the edge", the heart's simple urgings become the siren's call. Once this state is reached, you would say "the die is cast" and all that is left is completion of the deed itself. You become aware of your Self as I AM emanating from within I AM.

Since your personality is in a constant state of desiring, yearning, hoping and anticipating, it finds it difficult to stop when asked to do so. The supportive aspects of your reality, the concepts held by and expanded upon through mass consciousness and the over-arching propensity for your ego mind to follow the human herd maintains your equilibrium among your human counterparts. Even when the potential of infinite love is set before it, the ego will question, doubt, probe and prod in the hopes of remaining in a state of separation albeit saying, "I love you."

This is the time for silence and, yes, that means silence within the "void" – call it what you will. When you remove your focus from the distractions of your world to enter into the quiet of nothing, you walk toward the abyss with a fragrant red rose in your hand saying to the beloved, "I come with an open heart. I will remain open to you. May we know each other within the union of the ONE merging within our divinity." In that moment, that which is the "void" is seen no longer as "no thing" for it is then observed fully and completely as I AM.

## Story Time

When Nancy returned to the camp that night, sweaty, tired and hungry, her physical symptoms were superseded by her desire to talk with Paul. She couldn't get him out of her mind, partly because of what the medicine woman had said and additionally due to wanting to share the magic of her newfound elephant connections with her brother.

Though there was no phone service in the camp, she knew they would be finished with the fence repair within the next day and she so looked forward to getting back to the main campsite where the administration buildings had outside access. Though Nancy wasn't sure what she was going to say to Paul or how to tell him about her recent experiences, she knew it would most likely come flooding out because of their strong union.

The next day flew by with ease (if not also with much hard labor). The elephants did not show up. The lions had been coaxed back into their habitat by the beaters on that first day so there was little interaction with any of the animals. Though heavily guarded day and night, none of the crewmembers ran into any trouble with poachers and the whole affair seemed mundane (except for the elephants).

After packing up the utility trucks, the crew made a decision to drive back at night since everyone was feeling the same urge to get "home" as they called "admin". Nancy felt her reason was stronger than others were though everyone wanted their customary access to telephones, computers and incoming mail.

The night drive was easy and cool after the days of toiling in the sun. Some of the group fell asleep against each other's shoulders while Nancy stared out the window at the stars and the rising moon wondering where all of this was taking her. Now her only propelling force was calling Paul.

Because of the ten-hour time difference, Nancy had to wait until morning to make her telephone call when she knew Paul would be home from his office. From what he had said over the months she had been working on this fencing project, Paul had made great headway in his law firm. Though she had told him that she couldn't play hostess to his visit earlier in the year due to being chosen to head up one of the park's larger land surveys, Sam had changed his mind and left her on the crew because of her "great people skills" as he called them. She wondered what was underlying his real reason for keeping her from being promoted.

By 9:00 a.m., Nancy could wait no longer. It was 7 p.m. for Paul and he would just be getting home; at least, he *should* be getting home then. She earnestly hoped so.

The phone rang only twice before Paul answered with his usual brusque, *"Hell – o!"*

*"Paul, it's Nancy,"* the words were going to tumble out unbidden. *Go slow, girl. Give him a chance to get ready for this,* she thought pensively and then let loose.

*"I've wanted to call you for days. We've been working far out on the northern rim of the park and I couldn't get to a phone until today. I have so much to tell you and you just have to listen. Don't talk. Just listen to me, okay?"*

Paul didn't have much choice. Nancy was speaking so uncontrollably fast she would have spoken right over him should he have decided to say more than, *"Okay,"* which he did.

*"I met this medicine woman and she could just about read my mind. She knew everything I had been dreaming about and she told me that I had this life I am living in another reality and that I have to blend with that life here. Then this one little elephant was getting hurt and this boy saved him. I was right there, Paul. I was right there. Then she appeared again and she knocked me out or something and she talked to me in a dream and told me I had to make a decision and that it was going to affect you. Then the elephants came to me and the baby was there. Am I making any sense?"*

Paul was doing his best to follow her rambling dialogue even though he had no idea what she was talking about at all. It seemed she had met an old woman and somehow some elephants were involved and it had something to do with him. No, this was making very little sense, really.

*"Well, Nancy, I'm not sure where all of this is going. You certainly sound excited. Are you all right? Is everything okay?"* Paul was feeling some concern for Nancy's state of mind though he did know his sister as being stable. *Something* had definitely shaken her up.

*"Paul, I'm fine. I'm more concerned about you. The old woman said if I made a decision to be this other life, too, it would affect you. And I made that choice, Paul; I made that choice. So I want to make sure you're okay 'cuz we've always taken care of each other and I started getting worried when the elephants came to me when we were working the fence. That was when I believed this could all be real, you know. Is everything okay with you?"*

*"Well, yes, everything's fine from the standpoint of 'am I still breathing?' but from the standpoint of 'everything' being really fine, well, no. Two days ago I got fired."*

Nancy heard Paul gulp and take a breath. *Two days ago, it was two days ago that the elephants had come to her. It was two days ago.*

## Question Thirteen
## How do I travel through the dimensions?

The etheric realm, the subtle realm, that which is unseen, is that from which you constantly emerge. You unfold into the subtler realms as Creator is intentioning manifestation, creation in endless dimensions in every possible manner infinitely without end.

Every possibility that exists, drawing energy from the "void", is connected within the physical realm. Within this oneness, nothing is separate; nothing is disconnected within I AM. Those vibratory frequencies are interacting with you as *oneness*. The "void" is embedded within your DNA and you are embedded within it. It acts as a template for oneness to be expressed in and through you in harmony and coherence.

Consciously being aware within the dimensional worlds is one of the most natural experiences you could have; it has been conditioned out of your culture. If you step back from the industrial/technological world that you presently live within and look at your ancestors in the natural world, you will see that unequivocally all of the earlier peoples had constant communication with the unseen. Those countries, tribes and national groups living within a multi-dimensional reality travel within those dimensions of frequency and use their knowing, their nightly dreams and their voyages of seeing into the unseen to manifest, organize and administer their daily lives.

The first notion you want to shift is that you are actually "traveling" anywhere from the sense of necessarily moving your physical body from one "place" to another. Dimensions exist as frequencies within consciousness so your method of "travel" is your conscious awareness in a new focus – a different frequency.

Of course, the first step in experiencing multi-dimensional consciousness is creating a time when you can sit silent, alone and quiet. You must turn off the business swirling within your mental body if you wish to use it *consciously* to focus on another set of frequencies.

Once you have sequestered yourself for the journey, the next step is to let go of the beliefs you have about what you will experience. Your image screen you call your imagination, your feelings and auditory sense will supply you with information based upon the beliefs you have about dimensional travel. Letting go of expectations and anticipations opens your doorway to the "void" and allows possibilities and potentials to arise not considered by you within your present reality.

Now you will begin to perceive many different aspects of You. You cannot send or receive information within energy waves that are already carrying information. All transmissions in manifestation rely on *carrier waves* that are devoid of imprint enabling the information to travel within them. Your mind must be empty as in the "void" to receive the emerging frequencies.

Until you are accustomed to relaxing into the flow of the frequency shift, you will want to allow a good amount of your time for the first "traveling" experiences. Several hours at the outset are usually needed to quiet down, settle in and begin the redirection of your attention from the present reality into the worlds of *all* "realities". Eventually, you will find guidance through one predominate sense - visual, auditory or kinesthetic. As you become familiar with the journeying, all of your senses will become involved within the experience. Allow the natural flow of your sensual awakening to guide you.

Let go – completely, absolutely and totally. Now infinite experiences have an opportunity to upwell within you. You are no longer lost to your judgments, your opinions - what you believe you know. It all falls away into the freedom, the realization of the infinite presence of You.

Realize every day, moment to moment, you constantly live in many dimensions and you will understand that you don't focus on your shift from one to another. In one breath you are paying attention to what is at hand and in the next breath you have "traveled" to an experience you had "last night". This is multi-dimensional travel.

The world you live in, the "void" you emerge from within and the dimension to which you "are going" is not physical. It exists and is available to you when you make the decision you want to live your life more consciously aware *of*, and consciously linked *to*, that which already exists. It is not outside of you and it is not inside of you. It simply *is* and in that, so *are* you. You simply *are* within I AM. You cannot keep from traveling among the dimensions. All you can do is keep yourself from knowing it.

Reveling in the experience of I AM, you will soon come to understand your desire to "travel" within the "dimensions" is nothing less than your yearning to know ME. The quality of your journey is based solely upon your attention to the unfolding of your heart, as the voice of your soul, within the flow of MY Divine Presence as You.

If your ego personality wishes to "travel" dimensionally for the glory of its success in doing so, you will achieve only that – personal glory. If your hunger is to know ME, if your thirst is to experience ME as You in the vast, ever-emanating "void" of the all, you may joyously anticipate an outcome far beyond your present imaginings. The choice, of course, is up to you.

There is no separation and no union. There simply is and the *isness* you experience is I AM as you, as ME – ONE.

## Story Time

Paul's words had hit Nancy hard and fast. Their conversation had wound down with Paul's statement that he had been fired about the same time that Nancy had ventured to touch the baby elephant.

They had closed their telephonic visit with an agreement to talk further when Nancy had a chance to muse over the confluence of all these experiences. Paul, though devastated by being fired, had assured her that he had some prospects in the offing and was looking into joining up with a couple of less prominent though more fulfilling law firms in the area. *Somehow,* Nancy thought, *I doubt that.*

What Paul had not told Nancy was the defeat he was experiencing during these interviews. The same question kept coming up, *"I hear you were recently let go from your last firm. Would you like to tell us about that?"*

Paul didn't have a fast comeback for that query due to the fact it wasn't exactly clear *why* he had been fired. There was mention of him getting too friendly with some of the junior executives of the firm's corporate clients. These up and coming white collars had tumultuous reputations but no one had actually come out and said, *"We are firing you because of . . . ."* It had been more, *"You don't seem a perfect fit for our conservative firm, so we are giving you two months' severance pay and letting you go."*

Deep within Paul knew he wasn't a good fit for corporate law. He was much too adventuresome and much younger than most of the lawyers he had been working with so the release from the law firm had come as a partial relief. Yet, his ego had been delivered a stunning blow by this turn of events and he was most definitely unwilling to tell Nancy what was actually going on within him. In fact, he wasn't even ready to admit to himself that perhaps he just wasn't cut out to be a lawyer at all.

Meanwhile, Nancy was busy taking things into her own hands. She hadn't called Paul back to find out more about his firing issue because she wanted to talk with Sam first. They always needed strong backs and muscles in the park service and Nancy could think of nothing better than to have Paul working alongside her, especially now that she was getting involved in this "living two lives" affair.

Sam listened with interest as Nancy briefly explained Paul's predicament though he wasn't sure that he wanted a brother/sister team amidst the motley crew he was already running. Yet, as usual, Nancy's way with words, her sparkling, bright eyes and Sam's preference for her won out.

*"Okay, Nancy, if you want Paul to come work with us I know I'll be able to find a place for him. Just don't turn it into a family affair, huh. We've got enough problems keeping everybody on task without bringing the two of you's personal problems. When can he start?"*

*Whoops,* thought Nancy, *that was way too easy.* *"I haven't told Paul my plan yet, Sam, so I don't know. I'll call him first thing tomorrow and see if he's up for this. I wanted to ask you before I said anything to him."*

Letting Sam know he came first was important and Nancy's feminine instincts knew that very well. As for Paul, *well, time would tell.*

Early the next morning Nancy made the telephone call to Paul and found him at home, *again. Strange, I thought he was out looking for a position.* Nancy couldn't help but wonder what was really up.

"Paul, how ya doin'?" Nancy asked first. *Might as well lead in easily instead of pouncing like a female lion.*

"Well, Nanc, I'm doin' fine. Been looking for a new job, as you know, and pretty much keeping to myself. What's up?" Paul answered as briefly as possible.

"Paul, I have an idea and hear me out before you make up your mind, okay? I don't know what's going on with you but I want to offer you a job here with me at the park. I've already talked with my boss, Sam, and he said he has plenty of work if you want to come.

"The money isn't as good as you would make as a lawyer but there's hardly any overhead. We have a camp to live in and everybody has his or her own tent. We're fed pretty well and the weather and country are beautiful. It's just a lot of work, hard work, and you kind of get used to it. With your fitness and strength, you'll have no problem and I'd love to have you here.

"We didn't talk too much the last time I called. You just sort of heard me out and I'd love to spend more time with you. What d'ya think? Will you come?" Nancy held her breath.

"Well, it'll take me a day or two to get things lined up here. How long is the job for?" Paul was actually considering the offer.

"Once you start working with the parks department here, you can pretty much stay on as long as you want. The work is year round and sort of endless. The fences are constantly coming down. There's always new land to clear and maintain so we all rotate among the different jobs. There's no end in sight, really."

*Could Paul really be thinking of accepting this offer,* Nancy thought with amazement. *I thought I'd have to talk him into it.*

*"Well, Nancy, count me in. Call me back in two days and I'll give you an ETA. I'll also tell you about the dreams I've been having. Seems like whatever is happening with you is bleeding over to me because my nights are sweaty and distorted. I wish I knew how to lucid dream so I would have more control of where I go. All I know is that I am going somewhere. Maybe this extreme change will straighten it out for me. You guessed it right. I need help."*

## Question Fourteen
## How can my glimpses of wonderment last longer?

Your sense of wonderment is a very momentary experience of coherency within ME. As you focus your attention upon your congruency, you experience it as a feeling you want to last longer, if not infinitely. Your sense of I AM is heightened, at least within the limits of your present beliefs.

Since your daily interactions within contrast are exactly that – contrasting – when you begin to experience moments of consistency within yourself as ME, you believe they are outside of your moment-to-moment experience. While this is not true, the sense of separation within your dimensional world makes it feel like it is true.

Your choice in each moment resonates as the reality information you experience within the "void". As these choices are written upon your soul record, the frequency of each decision holds all of the possibilities for your future-future. It contains the potential of all of your lives. *Through your thoughts, words and actions* you delve into your own potential. Through your free will choices you reverberate as the next movement within I AM.

Conscious experiences shift and change throughout your daily routine of "being alive". From what you choose to wear as clothing to what you choose as food, from your choice of spiritual practices to preferred arenas of work and play – each is a conscious decision, a free will choice, within existence in your frequency dimension. The movement from one thought or memory to the next is *so fast* that most of you are not aware that consciousness is shifting. It often feels like simply "having a thought".

Nowhere is the flow of spirit easier to observe than within the shifting, changing flow *of* conscious thought. Here is where your wonderment enters and exits. Yet consciousness is much more than thoughts; it is a state of absolute awareness of being as I AM.

For the most part, humanity walks your earth unconsciously aware. The masses are hypnotized by the blatant references given to them through media, authority figures and their own desires to be seen as special or *more*. When you have these moments of bliss, you often mistake the fleeting experience as a glimpse of your "enlightenment", as you call it.

If you are feeling the inner yearning to experience realization of ME, then you absolutely must release your attachment to the ideas, concepts and beliefs you have gathered within your personality. It is the need to be right, the need to know, the need to have the last word, the need to appear spiritual and all of the other needs you have incorporated into your personality that lay down the boundary lines obstructing you from your own awareness of conscious enlightenment that is a permanent state of "wonderment" always present and arising within you.

So, back to maintaining your sense of bliss: I have been mentioning how important it is to find time in your schedule for silence. Here is where your wonderment arises most naturally. At first, you might think it is hard or boring to simply sit and be. Yet, without the silent time in which to experience your euphoria, it will constantly evade you.

The feelings of ecstasy, wonderment and bliss you say you encounter from time to time in meditation, during workshops or seminars, listening to sacred music or being in the presence of a perceived "holy person" are sensory experiences of ME. It is ME as a perceived sense *of* ME.

Consciousness is in a perpetual state of enlivenment within I AM. When you experience brief moments of what you describe as your wonderment, you are swinging like a pendulum within a state of balance in consciousness to a state of hyper-sensory experience. This is not an accentuated experience of pure ME rather a heightening of your physical senses. Since it feels "good", you want it to remain longer rather than realizing your true yearning is for coherent, centered, infinite contentment as ME as I AM.

Since all energy within your world is in a constant repetitive state of frequency, when the wave you are feels very good due to your focus of attention upon something you believe will enhance your human experience it is natural for you to desire this coherent state to remain. It can do so if you will retain your focus upon not what caused the feeling, rather the feeling itself. While you may desire to continue listening to the music or being with the person who is sharing this resonance with you, it is not the person or object that is important. The feeling can be a constant if you will allow it.

What is important for you to remember is that the feelings you describe as good, wonderful or ecstatic are dependent upon your physical body for the experience rather than purely consciousness. Since you live in a world of duality, wonderful feelings are the opposite of undesirable feelings. When you focus on having wonderful feelings, by necessity you are also resonating with the opposite of that feeling. In your reality, you cannot have one without the other.

Your desire to extend your glimpse of wonderment is understood. Peel away the layers of your focus putting your conscious attention upon what lies beneath the layers of distraction. There you will find I AM.

## Story Time

*Well, I was right,* Nancy thought when she hung up from the call with Paul. *He can play nicey-nice all he wants, but sister knows him and I knew he was in trouble. I'm so glad he has decided to join me here at the park.*

Nancy's feelings of joy were short-lived when she returned to tell Sam about her conversation. He had news of his own, and it wasn't good.

*"I'm glad that Paul will be joining us. Now let's get down to business,"* Sam replied brusquely to not only Nancy, but also the rest of the crew standing around wondering what was up.

*"There's been a call from the head office down south telling me that we're in for a few hard weeks. The weather is turning fast and we're goin' to have days of thunderstorms, flash flooding and potentially lethal mudslides. We've got about three days to get those barriers finished that we started at the park's northeast corner where the larger creek feeds into the forest*

pond. *And that's not the only trouble spot. The pond itself is at capacity already and when it does flood, and flood it will, the forest is going to become a swamp for all of the animals living within its walls. I'm putting together some ideas about how we can drain it a bit in anticipation of the storm."*

Nancy's elated feeling deflated like popping a balloon with a pin. She hadn't experienced this type of storm here before but she had certainly heard stories about them. They came on fast, rain fell in sheets of water overcoming all life and when the storm passed away, mudslides and devastation were the results. Obviously, they had to get moving if they were going to get this completed before the first thundering roar echoed over the camp.

*I'm glad that Paul won't be arriving for a while,* Nancy mused anxiously. *The last thing I need is to have a broken brother showing up during a potential catastrophe.*

*"Okay, I want everyone to get organized for emergency procedures. You all know how much is going to be expected of you. If there's anything emotional going on for any of you, let's hear it now. You won't have time for feelings once the storm comes. We've got to get this work completed within the next two days. The remainder of today we'll set up the protective measures here at camp, secure everything you won't be taking with you tomorrow and meet once more tonight for a final briefing. Does anyone have any questions?"* Sam finished his initial announcement.

The crew had all been rigorously drilled in emergency procedures during their initial training classes. No one needed to ask what to do though you could feel the envelope of fear that was closing in around the group.

*This will be my first experience in a life-threatening condition for which I am partly responsible to alleviate.* Nancy was only partially contemplating the outcome of this potential disaster and strongly thinking about how this might affect the elephants, especially "her baby" as she had come to call the young elephant she had befriended.

In the midst of her musing, Nancy heard a whisper in her mind. *"They will call to you in their moment of need. Be ready to shape shift into Tusk."*

She froze in her tracks not sure where the voice was coming from except it was obvious it was inside of her. *It must be the old medicine woman. She's using that telepathy again but this time she didn't knock me out. I guess I can be thankful for that.*

Not knowing what to think about the words, she was hearing, and definitely not wanting the crew to ask her what was going on, Nancy hurried to her tent where she had been headed anyway. *I'll be safer in privacy if she's going to keep talking,* she thought, as she mentally checked off the items she had left to do to get ready for tomorrow's excursion.

Upon arrival at what she called "home base", Nancy quickly found being alone was not going to be possible. Standing next to the single cot with her tiny feet hidden in the mess of abandoned clothing on the ground was the medicine woman. Calmness pervaded her atmosphere in stark contrast to the absolute disarray in which Nancy customarily left her tent when working.

*"I see you heard my summons. That is good. I have much to tell you and I know you have even more to do here, so let's begin. Sit down in front of me,"* the elder spoke as if Nancy were her student.

*"My name is Talish. I live many lifetimes in this forest. You and I know each other in many of these lifetimes and now we are to begin working together within this one. You must learn to stop your constant emotional swing. You must remain consistent and calm. Every breath you breathe creates a windstorm of activity in all of the realms. You no longer have that privilege – and that is, indeed, how you may see it.*

*"Those who live in earth walk as though they are dead within their energy streams. When something comes along to light up their lives, they want to keep it forever. They would do good to look at the animals. You are no longer among the walking dead. With me you are, now, alive. Let that life be one steady stream of breath."*

## Question Fifteen
## What do emotions have to do with the soul level?

The soul is not a "level" rather it is an etheric record of all your experiences as I AM and exists in "present time". Since there is no time in the realm of the soul, the first statement is only for your information because it makes no sense from within the emergence of the soul.

The soul is truly undefinable in human language. It is in a constant state of dynamic change experiencing and recording not only every breath you take but also the space between your inbreath and outbreath. It is in the vastness of this *pause* outside of your construct of time in which the soul "dwells".

The personality uses the physical body to express as a semblance of soul. Using your physical vehicle, together with the mental and emotional bodies, the soul experiences a variety of occurrences within its incarnation, ultimately leading to remembrance of itself as I AM.

Since the emotional body is an expression of the personality, the answer to your question would be "yes" with a few caveats along the way:

The existence of your soul does not include a "level". You are used to viewing life from a linear viewpoint, a scaffold upon which you affix the various labels that attract you from time to time. The soul is as I AM. It is in existence everywhere and nowhere as I AM. If you remove the idea of levels from your reality, you will begin to see much more clearly how you exist as an emanation of ME with a soul recording your infinite activities and states of being.

Emotions stem from within feelings. They are not *separate* from what you feel rather are an extension of the subtlety of feeling showing up when you wish to project what you are feeling into your reality. The consequence can be a sense of great joy, anger, guilt, grief, happiness, compassion, empathy or sorrow. Emotion is *energy in motion* stimulated by your craving to release that energy as *expression*. Your soul records the original feeling and the emotion. The soul is a record of every experience, not matter how minute or macro.

Due to the chemical onrush of hormones and neuropeptides within your physiology during the influx of emotion, many of you tend to become very attached to an emotive state. You often create a scene to experience a specific sensation so that you can let loose the energetic build up within your bodies. If this pleases you, you will continue to do so. If it does not result in the outcome you had hoped for you will change the emotion you are exhibiting or you will stop emoting altogether, at least for the moment.

Paying attention to the reasons you are exhibiting emotions is an important part of your maturing into the realization of your etheric Self as I AM. Chemical swings within your body do little to foster awareness; rather, they muffle your ability to know your Self by proclaiming the exhibition of the ego personality as the master of your experience.

Quality of emotion is more important than quantity. A deep outpouring of love toward another aspect of creation need not be overpowering or dramatic. You may feel balanced and serene yet the rising current of your emotional body may be felt most strongly. Do not underestimate the quality of the subtle world. It is not reliant upon extremes or demonstrations that cause upheaval within your energetic self. Serene, tempered and uplifting emotions tell others more about your ability to express as I AM than any great *quantity* of emotional output.

Translating quality vs. quantity within the type of emotion you most frequently experience, you will observe where you overdo rather than underdo. It is seldom that you express emotionally in a diminutive capacity. Most evocative experiences are correctly labeled "outbursts" because most human beings have spent so much of earth time suppressing feelings that when a moment comes to exhibit an emotion, it literally "bursts out", or appears to do so.

Creating a harmonic balance among the capacities you have to feel, think and express and living within the natural rhythm of your heart will alleviate your need for these outbursts. Then the quality of your emotion becomes a deeper sense of your soul's expression and your ability to use your emotions as the messenger of your love becomes paramount.

It is not necessary to express in an emotional way at all. Your feelings do quite nicely in conveying the experience of your human life. For instance, when you feel the oneness of I AM and you wonder at the bliss you are feeling, it is not necessary to emote about it to anyone, including yourself. Simply experience the occurrence and then let it be. There will always be another and then another . . . infinitely. Holding on to any experience does not stem the tide of the next experience. It simply confuses you.

So, yes, your emotions do live within the experience of the soul yet not at any *place* that you would consider a *level*. The word "level" conveys the idea that there are higher and lower ranks within ME. That is not true. All is equal within I AM as expressed within or without form. All experience is equal within the soul that knows no levels, no time and no space. It simply *is* as I AM.

## Story Time

Nancy listened with rapt attention though it would have been impossible to do ought else. The medicine woman had weaved a magic ribbon of intrigue around her dialogue and Nancy was caught within it.

*"Now that we are consciously within this journey together, you are going to have to make some rather difficult choices. The present position you hold within the park is jeopardized by having met within me. You will no longer be focused solely upon your work within your maintenance group. The quality of your participation will become less and less. You may either decide to tell Sam what you are experiencing, you may quit the job or you may go on as you presently are and see what happens as it unfolds.*

*"No matter the decision, our lives are now inextricably entwined, and that you may accept or resist. Within the spirit world, you have made your commitment already. Yet, since the*

*world of spirit is vast and unknowable, you may fight against those choices or make a decision to be as the water in the stream and flow with them. I am not here to cast judgment upon you, only to tell you what is occurring in your life's energy in this present.*

"*Would you like to ask me any questions before I continue?*"

Nancy had a multitude of questions she wanted to ask the old crone sitting in front of her yet she didn't know where to begin. *Make a decision about her job? When the riot of the storm was nearly upon them and it was "all hands on deck", how could she desert the crew now?*

"*I have so many questions I don't know which to ask first. I guess what's on my mind right now is what happens if I don't say anything and just let everything continue as it is? Does that mean something bad will happen?*"

"*Ah, you see, you have delegated your choice to your personal belief in bad or good. There is no wrong or right choice. There is only choice. When I said that in the spirit world you have already made your choices, what I meant is that you, as spirit, wish to experience everything possible and therefore have removed any roadblocks from the unfolding of this destiny. How it occurs is up to you in this reality.*

"*If you decide to simply let all unfold as it presently is then you will find ways to deal with the veil you will be maintaining between you, Sam, crew, and eventually, Paul. The first choice to live within the pretense of secrecy begins a spiral you will either be able to maintain or have to alter somewhere in its course.*

"*It is for this reason I originally told you that you must learn to control your emotions. Let your feelings drive your responses without emotional sway taking over. When your emotions begin to drive your experience, you find yourself out of control and cannot make choices in response to what you are experiencing. You react rather than respond.*

"*Since we will be going into many worlds to explore the natural life in earth, you must learn to convey only that which you wish to experience within that world which is within your energy stream. If you are not in control, you will begin to feel as though your experience is dominating you. Though this is not true, it will be seen and felt as such."*

Nancy put her hand up to signal a pause in Talisha's soliloquy. *"May I ask a question?"* she offered and continued without pausing. *"Does this have anything to do with the memories and visions I have as a life as Tusk, the young boy who played with the elephants?"*

*"It has much to do with Tusk yet not only as a young boy. You, if you acquiesce, are going to experience the life of Tusk in his youth and then as a young man affording him and you a very extraordinary experience – that of living consciously in multiple worlds simultaneously.*

*"Once upon a time, long, long ago in earth years, you made a decision to attempt this achievement. Now is the time of its offering. When you blend yourself with Tusk completely, so that you know yourself as Nancy and you know Tusk as he exists, yet there is no difference between you, you will no longer be of value to your park work crew. And that is why I offer that you might want to make appropriate arrangements now, if you wish to remove any chance of adverse experiences later. It will, of course, be as you wish."*

Nancy sat in wonderment at what she was hearing not completely sure if she wanted to stumble into this unknown territory. Yet, on the other side of the coin, she felt so called to this land, this place, this time. *And Talish was right about her emotions. She let them rule her far too often much to her later regret. Personal outbursts had been an aspect of her personality she had been in a constant struggle to contain. Coming to Africa had assisted in restraining this otherwise annoying behavior and she hadn't thought about it much since her arrival at the park. Was it rearing its head once again?*

*"Can I think about it for a while?"* she asked hoping to put off an otherwise difficult decision. *"We have this storm coming and I'm really needed here just as I am right now. Making changes in the midst of all this doesn't feel right. And then there's Paul coming."*

*"Of course, as I said, the choice is yours to make. Do as you wish; follow your feelings. Don't get lost in emotion as this scenario begins to play out. Your emotions are your nemesis.*

*"And, as to Paul, he's already here."*

## Question Sixteen
## How can I achieve financial abundance?

Financial abundance – this is a very relative set of terms. What is abundant to one is not enough for someone else. Those who live as what you call "within their means" may wish to be more abundant so that their means become greater. However you wish to look at financial abundance, you will find a contrasting view.

Since you are asking the question, I will answer simply – you cannot *achieve* financial abundance. You may, however resonate with that which feels abundant to you. You may experience an outpouring of the paper representations of wealth the human economy calls money. You may also stash these pieces of paper away in vaults or move their digital representations around via your banking systems. This will not be the achievement of abundance.

Abundance is experienced as a profuse quantity of something, in this case the money you call your finances. To the human mind, this represents the ability to spend this oversufficiency in a variety of ways most of which are deemed to be entertaining or life enhancing. Actually, what you desire is freedom. That is what your abundance represents to you.

If you resonate with your concept of abundance and begin experiencing affluence within your life without being free to use the money however you see fit in any given moment, you will begin to feel a lack. Your experience of scarcity has very little to do with abundance of money and much more to do with your feeling of constraint within physical form.

So, let's talk about freedom and you may use your mental faculties to compare it to financial abundance:

For most of humanity being free means you don't have to tolerate experiences you don't like whether they be work situations, people who make you uncomfortable or any other situation that is undesirable. Being free of these circumstances allows you to feel more freedom, or less limitation, within your life. Or so you believe.

Within this context then, I would like to restate your question: "How can I achieve freedom?" Allowing this will include financial abundance, as well.

Recognize, if you would, that your culture lives within a consciousness of limitation that states, "There may not be enough". This is anticipation that what you believe you need is not available to and for you. When you live from a frequency of lack of anything, it overflows into all other areas of your life. If you believe you are deficient in love, it will play out as also lacking adequate financial abundance. If you experience low self-worth, you will feel as though you don't have enough money . . . and so it goes.

I would like to suggest that you begin to focus on what you require to feel free. What can you place your attention upon that will call up within your frequency a sense of freedom? This is the answer to your question, you see. When you are focusing on privilege and opportunity within your energy stream, you open the doors to abundance within all levels of experience.

There is absolutely nothing lacking in your dimension. Everything you could desire is possible for you except you don't realize that you have to resonate with the frequency of it to acknowledge it in your reality. Your belief structures, your habits and patterns are deeply ingrained physically, emotionally and mentally. Each of these blueprints expresses your sense of limitation in a specific way.

None of the financial abundance within your world will give you financial abundance. As soon as you have more of the money you say you lack, you will begin looking for more of the same. It is an endless and fruitless ambition you behold within you.

You are living upside down within your reality. You believe if you have enough of the physical requirements of life that you will have time to delve into the more etheric aspects of your dimension. Have you noticed those you call the "rich" doing so? Do they spend time delving into their etheric selves? Or do they spend time creating more financial opportunity for themselves?

The basis for your freedom and, therefore, your abundance is foundationed upon your frequency within ME. When you view your life from within the frequency of living as ME, you construe the deeper meaning existing within all things that is I AM. The consequence is that you begin to see your life as abundant, live your life as abundant and abundance is all you experience.

Your heart, as the voice of your soul, knows only its deepest passion. Exerting subtle influence over your life in many different ways your heart constantly urges you to experience the freedom of living as profusely as you can possibly imagine for yourself. Whether you live in a mansion or a cardboard box, the freedom of expression is seated within your heart. How you decide to experience it is the abundance of your life giving itself to life itself.

Your wholeness as I AM is not reliant upon a need for freedom. It is freedom itself. Expressing your passion for life within this sense of abandon creates abundance in all areas of your life, including your financial perspective. Resonating with the awareness of abundance will transform your life into only abundance. Then your question will be answered within I AM.

## Story Time

*"Paul is here? Where is he?"* Nancy nearly shouted into Talish's face. *"How could he be here without telling me? This couldn't possibly be!"*

*"He is here because I summoned him here through the dream world. He is not yet physically here yet he is as present as you and I are sitting in your tent. I have been preparing him for what he is going to experience once he arrives here in his body. Paul will 'hit the ground running' as you would say. He will be up to speed on our conversation because I have tapped him into my consciousness with you,"* Talish explained as though Nancy understood.

*"Well, if he's here, then I want to talk to him, too,"* Nancy began to interject when over the top of the conversation with Talish she heard Sam calling to her.

*"Nancy, you've got a telephone call. Come to the admin building and get it. It's Paul calling for you."*

Nancy ran to the office musing about how synchronistic it was that Paul had called just when she was saying that she wanted to talk with him.

*"Nancy, I've sold my car, cancelled my rental agreement on my apartment, packed my clothes and bought a ticket. I'm on my way and now I'm about penniless. I didn't have much to start with and selling my car let me have the money for the airfare. I'm really looking forward to getting on that plane and seeing you. I'll be there in two days,"* Paul announced before Nancy had the chance to say more than hello.

*"Paul, we're in for a terrific storm. You can't come now because the planes won't be able to land. You'll have to put it off for a few days at least before you can get into this part of the continent. It's way too dangerous right now."*

*"Nancy, I don't have the money to pay for a ticket change. I'm going to chance it and come anyway. If the airplanes can't land, then I'll deal with it. I'm not used to being without enough money to take care of myself so I'm going to have to count on you for a while. Hope you can live with that. I'll see you soon. My plane is landing at 2 p.m. your time day after next. See you then."*

With those parting words, Paul hung up. He wasn't going to be put off and now that he didn't have anywhere to go, he had to get on that plane. For the moment, it was going to be his new home until he landed in Africa where a tent would replace his apartment.

Nancy stood with the phone in her hand shaking her head. The last thing she wanted was to put Paul in danger and now here he was flying into one of the season's worst storms against all better judgment.

*"Nancy,"* Sam called, *"let's finish up packing these trucks. We've got to get done before dark."*

Nancy hurried over to where Sam was putting the finishing touches on tarping the equipment in the utility trucks.

She felt like she had let everyone down sitting in the tent talking to Talish while everyone else was working. Now, Paul was coming at her invitation and might be killed in an airplane.

*"Sam, I'm sorry I didn't help out with loading the trucks. I went to my tent and . . . ,"* Nancy began to explain.

*"What are you talking about? You haven't been gone but two minutes plus the minute on the telephone. You said you needed to go to your tent for something and you would come right back. I don't know what you mean,"* Sam blurted as he pulled tightly on the bungee cords strapping down the protection over the pounds of supplies in the last truck.

*"I was gone for only two minutes? No, I was in my tent for at least half an hour, Sam. That's why you called me to come to the phone – because I was gone,"* Nancy attempted to explain to her boss as well as to herself.

*"Nancy, cut it. We don't have time for this right now. We've got to get the last briefing done before you all head out tomorrow before dawn. I don't want to argue about whether or not you were here. You were and that's that."* Sam walked away with an angry shrug. He was more than a little concerned about his crew plus what was coming in the days ahead.

Nancy watched him walk away reliving in her mind the conversation she had had with Talish and Paul's calling simultaneous with her telling the medicine woman she wanted to talk to him. *What was real?* She had been sitting talking in her tent for quite a while yet Sam didn't remember it.

As she walked back to the office for the final set of instructions before the early morning's departure, a slight movement in her peripheral vision caught her attention. Turning quickly to her right, Nancy glanced at the tree toward the end of the camp compound.

Talish stood silent, motionless staring at her. *Was this what she meant when she referred to things unfolding differently? Should she tell Sam now and change the outcome of this experience?*

A bolt of lightning flashed overhead causing Nancy to drop her thought process and run toward the office. *Were the rains coming sooner than predicted?*

## Question Seventeen
## How can I do work that I am meant to do and that I love?

This question begs to be separated into two queries: "How can I do work that I am meant to do?" and "How can I do work that I love?"

The reason I AM dividing the question is because there *is* no work you are meant to do and there *is* work you would love to do. The meaning is not the same though your human concept believes if you are doing what I mean you to do then you will love it. I don't *mean* you to do anything at all.

Since you want someone to tell you what to do, how about asking yourself what *you* would love to do? When you were a child, you had ambitions about what might be interesting to look into later in life. Those aspirations didn't go anywhere. They are still lingering quietly in the background of your consciousness waiting for you to make the decision to take a second look at them.

Perhaps now is the time, since you are asking what you can do to create work that you love. Most human beings find themselves involved in a career, position or job that they feel they *fell into* – something not necessarily designed or desired but rather what came along at the time.

A good number of you are living the career choice of your parents or peer group rather than taking the chance that what you really would like to do wouldn't be perceived as work because it would be loved so much it would appear as play. This is based upon the belief that work is supposed to be hard and you are supposed to suffer through life attempting to survive.

You remember the old Adam and Eve story in that book so many of you like to read. Why would I BE an intention to suffer rather than thrive?

So, we will clear up the first question. There is no work you are *meant* to do. There *are* pursuits available to you that are based upon your natural proclivities. The basis for not doing that which is most natural to you is foundationed upon wanting to please those who suggest you do something besides what you want to do *and* your desire to sustain a specific level of survival for yourself. Notice I did not say sustain a certain level of *thriving*; you live in a perilous spiral of surviving rather than thriving.

Now, as to the second part of the question: The work that you would love to do is sequestered quite neatly in your heart as the voice of your soul. If you will spend time in silence as I AM constantly suggesting, you will find that the work you see yourself participating in is the deepest passion of your heart. It calls to you louder than any other occupation or distraction.

Usually, you will find the answer to your question within the activities you call hobbies – what you do in your "spare time". When you are not under directive from a fear-based drive to accomplish and when you have discretionary time available, you will take part in your passion with great zest and creativity.

This, then, is what you can do to do the work you love. Many enterprising humans have developed creative new jobs and careers. Others have only glimpsed the possibility of what is available and have shied away from it because they are afraid of what other people will think, don't believe they can sustain themselves through work that is not hard or are afraid to take the chance they might fail at an endeavor they enjoy.

The quest, of course, is much like the answer to the question about financial abundance. Attempting to make something happen, because you think that more "doing" will get it done, does not resonate within your world. You are discovering this is true in subtle ways yet haven't become accustomed to putting it into practice.

If you will sit quietly and face the fear you have of being ME and exploring the creativity abiding within your form, you will quite easily dismiss the complex manner in which your mind attempts to "cut you off" before you get a chance to consider your inherent potential. Many of you are near the understanding of the enormity of your capacities. Now it is time for you to take that step over the line necessary to resonate with your passion.

The phrase you often use "think outside of the box" asks you to step outside of your normal patterns of assumption and explore what might be possible for you. Your mental body is very familiar with specific manners and methods of contemplating what your future might hold. Moving outside the boundaries of your own limitations exposes you to new ways of thinking about what you refer to as "work". Then you have an opportunity to transform your workday into a play day.

Know that I expect nothing from you. Know there is nothing you are to do or not to do to work out your destiny. As you unfold within ME, play within the fields of your imagination allowing the most creative aspects of your personality as an individual to proclaim your life within ME.

As you embrace your deepest desires and passions, you will find yourself jumping with great glee to greet your day each morning. The entire world is your playground and you may create marvelous experiences within the sandbox of your life.

## Story Time

Sam stood in the midst of the exhausted crew giving his final briefing before sending them off to bed and an early rise in the morning. The storm was definitely arriving far ahead of the weatherman's schedule. Alterations in the plan were obviously necessary.

*"Okay, it's plain to see that this storm is going to come a day ahead of when we thought it would arrive. So, here's the new plan. I want the one-third of you standing to my left to take one truck in the morning and head to the dike we were completing down south. Get that finished and get back here.*

*"The group standing to my right will take another truck to the west edge of the forest embankment and widen the runoff stream bed for the forest pond. Don't worry about making it look nice; don't get fussy. Open up a wider space for the water to run through, so there's less flooding in the forest when the pond overflows.*

*"The bunch of you standing in front of me will take the third truck and head right out where you came back from on the northern fence repair. I want you to check every single post and fence wire for any tampering or weakness. On your way back, stop at the crossroads that leads over to the natives' village and*

*dig those drainage ditches deeper. We've put enough pipes into the ground that there shouldn't be a problem there but I'm not taking any chances.*

*"Now, any questions before you get some food and go to bed? 4 a.m. is comin' real early."*

*Might as well get this over with,* Nancy thought. *No one else seems to have any questions so I'll ask what's on my mind.*

*"Sam, Paul's supposed to land at Airhouk Airport tomorrow at 2 p.m. What do you think his chances are?"* Nancy asked half-heartedly.

Sam squared his shoulders. How he hated these personal interjections into his seemingly orderly setup.

*"Missy, there aren't going to be any planes landing around this area for days. I don't know what Paul is thinking and I don't know what he's goin' to do. All I can concentrate on right now is getting all of you out there and back in one piece. Go eat and sleep fast."*

Admonished, Nancy headed right over to the administration building to call Paul no matter the time difference. She needed to stop him from getting on that plane if possible. Her call was to no avail. His voicemail answered simply, *"Don't leave a message; Paul doesn't live here anymore."*

There was nothing to do now but eat and sleep. The thought of food was an abomination to her stressed out stomach but Nancy wolfed down a cheese sandwich realizing time to eat was going to be scarce for the next few days. Then she went for a guarded walk attempting to shake off her nervous jitters over Paul's arrival before committing to the illusion of sleep.

Naturally, she headed to the spot where she had spied Talish earlier in the day. There was no sign of her there now even though Nancy waited around a bit in hopes she might show up.

Once back in her tent, she laid out all of her raingear "just in case" making the sensible decision to take it with her when they left in the morning. Absent-mindedly she lay down on her cot fully dressed avoiding the vulnerability of a nightgown. She already felt way too accessible for her own comfort.

Sleep snuck up in spite of her anxiety-ridden mind. Before Nancy knew it, she was deep in the dream world and now Talish did show up and she wasn't alone either. She brought Tusk along for a conversation within the effortless flow of the etheric dream state.

*"We come to assure you that your heart's desire is coming into fulfillment. You didn't come to Africa to mend fences and dig ditches. This was simply a way to get you here. Now that we are in communion, you will find the true desires of your heart will soon be answered. Trust this unfolding as you trust your very self,"* Talish presented herself looking young, vibrant and motherly.

The strength of the message awoke Nancy with a start. She looked around the pitch-black tent imagining she would see Talish and Tusk standing right there next to her cot. The tent was empty and soundless except for her erratic breathing.

*It was a dream but it was so real,* Nancy thought in a sleep-drugged daze. *I know I didn't come here to run fence lines and maintain water ditches yet it's brought me closer to my heart's calling, the elephants. I wonder what she meant, "my heart's desires will soon be answered".*

As she lay back on top of her mound of blankets again, Nancy's last thought before sleep re-claimed her was how much Talish and Tusk looked alike, almost like mother and son.

## Question Eighteen
## What is the world waiting to receive from me?

*Your reality* may very well be awaiting something to unveil itself within you, yet I AM waiting for nothing. I already know all you are capable of and much more. WE are one and it is truly an intimate relationship laying bare the person inside of your skin; the one you know you are when you are not pretending to be the person you want people to believe you are. I know you with your scars, your scabs, hidden fears, your worst nightmares as well as the loving, caring, compassionate individual you are as I AM.

Perhaps you may wish to re-word your question as "What do I *believe* the world is waiting to receive from me?" or, more appropriately, "What do I wish to receive from the world?" Any idea you may have about what creation may wish of you will be colored by your personal anticipation of what you expect of yourself, what you wish to receive from it and how you can make the biggest personal impression upon the world within your given concepts.

Why do you feel that the world wants to receive something from you? Answer this question honestly and you will realize that it is a reflection of your personal desire to be seen and to be recognized. Can you sit back and simply love the world as it is without judgment? Are you able to be the love I AM without anyone confirming your existence?

If the answers to those questions are in the negative and I AM not judging you for your ambition to be desired in your reality, know that when you attempt to change what you *are* to become something you believe is desired within the world, and I stress *believe* here, you become incoherent. The energy of your frequency becomes confused because you are attempting to align yourself with what you feel the world wants of you rather than letting the passions of your heart be your offering.

The world would enjoy your awareness of yourself very much. Your reality would revel within your presence, an intimate communion with you and within you. Intimacy is the foundation and the forerunner to knowing yourself. It literally forces you either to be authentically who you are or allow even the idea of being intimate to slip away. You cannot *pretend* to be intimate. You cannot masquerade as intimacy. Intimacy is your presence now, in this moment, exactly as you are within I AM.

Your ego personality wants to believe it is desired, needed and useful. It definitely *is* all of these attributes yet not in quite the same way you might imagine. Through the quiet murmurings of your heart, you will find how you may most delightfully share yourself with your world. What do you wish to experience in this life that is the secret, haunting dream of your heart? If there were no limitations of time, money or endurance, what would you be and do?

What would happen if you sat silently, if only for fifteen minutes a day, and followed the rhythm of your breath? What feelings would surface? What unbidden thoughts would you find floating into your awareness once the screaming voice of perceived necessity was silenced? What would the mirror of your inner image screen, your imagination, offer to you?

What is the world waiting to receive from you? It is waiting for nothing. You have created wanting and assigned its meaning to your reality as though it were outside of you. The world is neutral to your wanting and is complete as I AM. It desires nothing from you.

Will you look into the mirror of the world to see the desire you hold within you? Will you allow your reflection to impress its subtle suggestions within you?

You choose to want for fear of feeling numb to life. You want to want. Stepping away from what you believe is lacking in your life will provide you the opportunity to witness your fear. When you know no lack, then you will know the world needs nothing.

Surrender to the natural rhythm of your breath, your life, your passion for existence without needing to be needed. The world itself provides all of the clues to the awareness lying within you. Look well and see its wholeness, its fullness. It is I AM.

When you make the decision to shift from the dream of your reality to conscious awareness of ME and you live your life within that awareness, the question you ask will become moot. The earth is already receiving from you, fully and completely. You transmit your frequency through your existence as I AM and the world happily receives it as it is dynamically transmitted. You are constant change.

You may experience your life as needing to know what you are to contribute to the world, yet that is only defined by the wanting you have invented and made real within your mind. The need you witness within you is the need you believe the world has of you. It is already receiving you completely and is quite satisfied with the result.

Your mind balks at the idea there is nothing you need to do. Your beliefs shrink and shrivel under the weight of this concept. Could it be possible that you are perfect exactly as you are? Can you allow yourself to be so vulnerable as not to expect anything of yourself except being I AM?

## Story Time

Before the sun relieved her long night's musings, Nancy and the three crews were up and headed out to their various locations. Nancy made sure she was in the group that would be working on enlarging the drainage for the forest pond in hope of seeing the elephants once again. Their presence had been sadly lacking from her life since her first connection.

The clouds gathered overhead like an angry, growling mob wanting to be let loose to wreak havoc upon the hapless humans below. Thunder resounded far over the hill and threateningly headed in their direction. Obviously, work was going to be fast and steady; no time for dallying around today.

When the utility truck finally parked above the waterway draining the twenty-foot deep pool feeding the forest's trees, everyone tumbled out and grabbed shovels in hopes of getting the work completed before the rain began to pour. Three hours passed unnoticed as shovels dug in and mud was banked up widening the bed by two feet on each side.

Just before Don, the group supervisor, called for a short lunch break, Nancy felt the first raindrop fall amid the trees. Though it was already raining steadily outside the forest, the greenery overhead provided some slight protection, at least for a while.

*"Don, it's starting to rain. Do you think we're done here? Shouldn't we be getting back?"* Nancy voiced the uneasiness worming its way among the crew.

*"Let's eat and work until we're finished with this section. If the rain starts to fall harder inside the forest here, we'll call it quits. Otherwise, we're safe for now and this really needs to get done,"* Don, project supervisor, recklessly replied.

The crew each grabbed a sandwich holding the edge of bread in one hand while digging with the other. Excavation went slower but at least everyone was getting fed.

Not too long after the useless discussion with Don, water began welling up within the drainage ditch. Swelling from ten inches to fifteen inches in as little as ten minutes, the swirling mud pushed against the newly formed bank edges threatening to spill over through several weak spots.

Suddenly a cracking sound followed by a loud whoosh grabbed the group's attention and a flash flood three feet in depth swept through the ditch carrying two of the workers with it. Above the shrill screams of their surprise was heard the trumpeting of elephants and the ground began to shake.

Chaos ensued as the crew members still standing quickly tried to decide whether to attempt saving their companions or themselves. Two of the burlier guys ran after the submerged crewmembers who were now about a quarter mile away. Everyone else fled toward the truck.

Nancy stood frozen, almost unaware of the physical danger avalanching down upon them. Her only focus was in the direction of the elephant herd and its shrill trumpets of fear. Realizing the sounds were coming from upstream and that the only way to find out was to go into the onrush of water, she looked for a way to circumvent the flooding where there might be relatively dry ground.

Heading back toward the truck behind the retreating crew, she turned off from the group and headed north toward the siren call of the elephants' warning. Not yet knowing why she was compelled to do so, she was being urged to join with the elephant herd that was outside of any logical reasoning. In all reality, it was a death defying compulsion with no explanation.

In the midst of the running crush of terrified bodies, no one missed Nancy as she disappeared among the trees - keeping the wall of water on her right side and gauging how fast it was flooding out into the thirsty earth. She could see the elephant herd just ahead with many of them caught in the mud rising up around their thick, buried legs.

*What could the herd want from me?* Nancy wondered. *I'm just one woman. What can they receive from me?*

In the midst of her quandary, Talish and Tusk appeared before her. Instantly still, Nancy felt an onrush of air and suddenly Tusk was gone. She was both Nancy *and* Tusk. Looking down at her body, she saw Nancy. Looking out through her eyes, she saw the forest, Talish and the elephants through the eyes of a boy, Tusk.

*"Come, child, if we lead the matriarch out of the mud, the rest will pull free. Their fear has them trapped more firmly than the earth does,"* Talish addressed Nancy/Tusk as one being.

Following Talish toward the struggling elephants, Nancy knew no fear, as she would have as simply *Nancy*. The herd and she were one energetic being.

Talish easily spotted the old, raggedy-eared great grandmother and approached with practiced ease. Holding her hand up in a sign of greeting, the wrinkled, dripping trunk wound itself around her arm. With a gentle tug, Talish began walking toward dryer ground though that was becoming a very limited commodity. As the matriarch followed Talish and Nancy/Tusk, the remainder of the herd's instinct to follow its chosen leader overcame its fear of being trapped. One by one, the elephants pulled free of the mud following the tiny humans who led them.

# Question Nineteen
## How do I drop the yoke of unfulfilling tasks?

Your idea that some tasks are fulfilling and others not so is a demonstration of your feeling your life is unfulfilled. Once you are living from within the capacities of your heart's voice and following the passion that calls to you, all tasks will fall into the area of creativity.

There is no task too small or menial within the human experience existing outside of ME. So when you perceive a task as unfulfilling, you are saying your mind does not include it within the representation I AM. The course of this observation leads directly to a *lesser* or *greater* stance within your own projections of yourself.

Since every experience you have in earth is an occurrence within ME there is no lesser or greater. There are simply aspects of you that you prefer to ignore because you don't receive enough inner acclaim for them. Remember that only you can give yourself the admiration you so desire. Even the lowest job within your own perception has its great merit within I AM.

Your culture is largely the determining factor as to what you consider unfulfilling and lacking creativity. There are very ingenious ways to dispose of garbage if you focus upon that capacity within you. When did you begin to believe that you are *more* or *less* dependent upon what task you are completing? It is not your occupation making its mark within ME; it is what you are being.

Consider the lowly dishwasher at the local eatery (*lowly* only in your perception). Every dish he touches resonates with his energetic signature. Every glass he cleans is now prepared by him as a receptacle of sacred communion through its next contents. The cook is no more worthy to instill the food with his or her frequency than the one who washes the soiled dishes. Harmonizing with the frequency of cleanliness within the union of ME is the equivalent of kneeling before the loftiest altar in the greatest cathedral.

The concept of a "yoke" portrays these tasks as burdens. You are not burdened in any aspect of life. Once upon a time, when you were a toddler running around learning about your world, you found everything to be of great note. You saw each article in a room, each person coming into your visual screen, each idea popping into your ever-expanding mind to be the most exciting in that moment.

As you matured, you began to be told what was right and wrong for you to do dependent upon your culture and your upbringing. Some of these ideas resonated with you and many did not. To these you assigned the label of "yoke" due to an authority figure holding sway over your performance of the task.

The pattern continues to this day even though you are fully capable of laying down the yoke at a moment's notice. If you believe you cannot set aside burdens you no longer consider fulfilling, it is only due to your belief about your personal identification. Within each set of labels is included the duties of that identity. Fear of disappointing those you say you love or those from whom you wish appreciation and confirmation keeps you from setting aside that which no longer resonates within you.

Yet, the very concept of being "yoked" would not arise if those you say you love were loved by you without condition. Then the assumed "burdens" would no longer feel like a duty rather a loving action you take to expand the communion you experience within that particular relationship or situation. It is due to your inner definition of "love" that you do not perceive the "chore" as a privilege within your reality.

Rather than desiring to remove the yoke of burden from your lofty shoulders, it is possible to shift your perspective of what the servitude signifies to you. Does taking the garbage outside feel overwhelming? Does paying your bills overcome your sense of creativity?

Any action taken in MY world has the capacity to be done with ease, creative flourish and enjoyment. Setting aside time to write out the energy checks in exchange for the services rendered to you may be enhanced by beautiful music, flowers upon the table or desk and your favorite beverage at hand. Bagging up that which is no longer of any use to you may be a profound moment of appreciation as you realize that you have so much materiality that some needs to be disposed of rather than held as all you possess in MY world.

Your perspective creates the yoke. Your perception creates lack of fulfillment. Within ME, living as I AM, all is a creative response in resonance to infinite inspired input and output. Each breath you breathe is a creative aspect of ME fulfilling it Self. Each action wipes clean the slate of experience "just in time" for the next to occur.

Your capacity to live unyoked is your soul's invitation to revisit your world. The bounded reality you have created is, in essence, boundless and without limitation. You impose limits upon it because your belief is that it could be better *if only* . . . .

You are the "if only" as I AM. Shifting your focus from one of bounded burdens to ultimate, everlasting freedom is your choice. Only you can make the decision for you. I AM without burden or yoke. So are you.

## Story Time

Nancy staggered out of the forest accompanied by a large herd of trumpeting, soggy wet elephants. Pausing to take a breath, she watched them bypass her and head south beyond the head of the flood as the herd moved toward higher ground. The earth shook as though an earthquake was rumbling from the number of enormous feet moving in rhythm.

Turning around to address Talish, she found herself alone and now only as Nancy. The presence of Tusk within her consciousness was no longer. It was a strange sensation, almost a feeling of being abandoned.

*"Nancy,"* she heard Don calling her as he stumbled in her direction, *"what are you doing? Where did you go? Once we were all past the tree line, we looked for you and couldn't see you anywhere. What happened?"*

*"Oh, I must have gotten separated from you,"* Nancy answered not ready to tell anyone the truth of her experience.

*"I was trying to get past the water and went south while the rest of you were going north. I'm fine. How are the two that got swept away?"*

*"We pulled them out before they drowned, but* just *before they drowned. That was close. Let's get together and see how everyone is doing. The rain is really coming down and we need to get back to camp. The storm is in full onslaught."*

Nancy followed Don to the truck totally bewildered. This was becoming very bizarre. More than anything else, she wanted time to sit alone and ponder what was happening to her. She felt like she was losing her mind.

*"Okay, everybody, are we all here?"* Don asked with some relief in seeing that everyone had circled up around the truck. Dan and Paul, having been engulfed by the water, were now sitting in the back of the utility bed with blankets wrapped around them. Though badly shaken, they seemed to be physically fine.

*"We're going to go back to camp now. We most likely lost some shovels in that disaster and this is definitely not the time to look for them. We'll wait until the storm is over and come back for them then. Thanks for a good job and fast reaction time during what could have been deadly. You'll probably not forget this for a long time,"* Don explained with great relief. Losing crewmembers while acting as project supervisor was not something he wanted on his resume.

*"I don't know why we were sent out here to begin with,"* Dan spoke up weakly, water still flowing from his nose. *"It was a stupid idea to send us out so close to the storm's eruption. This is crazy."*

*"Dan, when you signed on to work with the park what did you have in mind? What was your purpose for coming to the reserve?"* Don addressed him from the side of the truck.

*"I wanted to work out in nature, be in the wild, be close to the animals and feel like a man. You know I didn't have much of a choice, though. This is dumb boys' work, not what I signed up for at all. Mending fences and digging ditches, yeah!"* Dan was feeling the burden of responsibility careening with his near death experience.

*"Well then, maybe you are just a boy or maybe you're not ready to be a man, Dan,"* Don replied, now welling up with anger overtaking his relief. *"There is more to maintaining an animal reserve than going out to pet the elephants. It takes work, stamina and guts. Maybe you don't have what it calls for after all and, yes, you did have a choice."*

*"Okay, everybody load up. We're out of here,"* Don said leaving Dan sitting slack-jawed at his chewing out. He hadn't expected to be put down in front of the crew.

Everyone was silent on the way home. Nancy gave inner thanks for the quiet since she didn't want to share with anyone what she had just experienced. Thankfully, no one seemed too interested in her at all especially after hearing Don give Dan his dressing down. Too many of them shared Dan's feelings and now many of them were feeling sheepish.

Upon arrival back at camp, they found the situation quite similar to the area from which they had just come. Water was flowing in every gulley, some of the tents were awash despite their precautions and Sam was busy digging drainage ditches to encourage the water to run off away from the camp.

Don jumped out of the truck, grabbing a shovel and yelling over to Sam, *"I'll help you. Looks like you could use a hand. Don't know if anyone else will pitch in. They're pretty bushed right now."*

Nancy watched most of the crew wander away from Sam and Don meandering toward the cook's tent. The need for comfort food was replacing their sense of responsibility.

Still overwhelmed by her recent interaction with Talish, Tusk and the elephants, Nancy felt a deep kinship to these two men who took their job so seriously.

*"Mind if a girl helps out?"* she asked while picking up another shovel. *"I might not have the stamina you two do but I have the desire. Don, I think that's what you were trying to say."*

## Question Twenty
## Do I have to have energy work and initiations done?

Do you believe you need initiations or energy work? Why do you believe you need to have this type of etheric experience? That is the first answer to your question.

Whether you "have" to submit to another's energetic manipulation or confirming your divinity through an initiatory process is contingent upon whether you believe it is necessary.

If I tell you that you *don't* need energy work or initiations and you believe you do, it will only forestall the inevitable. Eventually, you will surrender to your belief and request energy work or an initiation because your concept of what you need will override what you are reading here. If I tell you that you *do* need energy work and initiations then you will spend your existence looking for the next energy worker or initiator because you will not find fulfillment outside of yourself and you will believe something is missing.

The concept of shifting the energetic structure of your field to "heal" you has arisen throughout your "ages" as a way to rebalance the energy stream of which you are comprised. Some energy workers hold a very pure intention with regard to how they resonate with those coming to them. Others simply go through the motions of their preferred modality in the hope that something will happen to reinforce their belief about their capability.

The concept that you need initiations stems from your belief that you are not I AM. You feel if someone else puts their hands on your head, sends you the perfect set of energetic instructions or confirms you as initiated, it results in a belief that you are now *more*. In your perception, you may believe this is true. Within ME, it makes no difference.

There is a great difference between making a decision that you wish ceremonially to sanctify your intention to live as your conscious divinity and believing that someone else must "do" it for you to establish your "holiness". Faced with the invitation to be initiated, what do you think in that moment? Do you feel honored? Are you afraid?

The sense of your personal perspective around what the initiation is meant to enact for you will determine whether you feel worthy to be so honored. If you are asking for this genesis, why do you believe you are not enough, as you presently exist? What belief lives within your consciousness confirming your lack of divinity?

Within your religious beliefs, there is a great patterning of "less" or "more". The priest, minister, master, guru or leader of any sect is seen as closer to ME, more in MY sight and able to connect within ME in sacred communion in a way that the "lesser", the congregation, cannot. That is the *belief*. It is not the truth, yet it is the fervently held ideology within the church, synagogue, community or group.

Ask yourself this: Why would I "make" one human being more worthy of being ME than another human being? Isn't that the very inception of separation? I AM one. Why would I manifest separation through Creator?

You have the capacity to know your union within ME as much as, and sometimes more than, a person who professes to have given him or herself to God. That doesn't mean they cannot know ME just as well. It simply means that their dedication to ME doesn't make them more sacred than you are. In other words, it is their idea of a good time in this earthly experience.

To *initiate* is to *begin* - so you are in a constant state of initiation because you are in a constant state of beginning. You begin with this breath and then you begin with this next breath infinitely.

It is much the same with your idea of needing energy work. First, it is not "energy" "work". It is an intention to focus upon energy and resonate with an idea of wholeness. That is why I said earlier that some users of energy in this way have an intention that shape shifts the energy and some simply go through the motions. The energy is neutral. What is intended within it designates the meaning you perceive. It is *your* perception.

One of the reasons having "energy work" done feels so good is the complete, dedicated attention given to you by the energy worker. And since you know it is usually relaxing, you submit easily to whatever that person suggests needs to be done. Much like feeling better because you called the doctor, once you make an intention to shift your energy, it is done. Projecting the responsibility for it onto another person is your habit. Perhaps you may wish to re-evaluate who is actually doing the shifting since you are the only one who can resonate as *whole* for yourself.

Remember that all energy within your world is neutral which means it carries no meaning and it doesn't have a desire to be used in any particular way. Anyone is capable of informing the energy streams with information that will assist in remembering you are I AM. It doesn't take someone hanging out a shingle announcing this as his or her intention. You may allow it to occur for you in the silence and privacy of your own home with no one around except you.

You have no need to experience initiations or energy work. If you desire to do so, by all means, do. Simply do not believe it is necessary to know yourself as I AM.

## Story Time

Once the trio had diverted as much water as possible from the center of the campground, they headed into Sam's office for a well-deserved break. Not surprisingly, no one else had emerged from the cook's tent to assist. The downpour was keeping the crew huddled around the warm cooking stove without thought or concern for the work going on outside.

Nancy plopped down in an old wooden chair and put her head on her arms on top of Sam's desk. It was only mid-afternoon yet the excitement and drama had taken its toll. She was exhausted.

Suddenly, she sat upright with alarm. Paul had just popped into her mind. *How could I have forgotten about him? He's supposed to land here tomorrow in the middle of this storm.*

"Sam, Paul's supposed to be coming in tomorrow. It's impossible. We could hardly stand up out there. Planes can't land in this. What do I do?" Nancy asked now nearly in tears more from exhaustion than concern.

"Nanc, take it easy. I've been through more of these storms than you can count. If the planes can't land here, they go on to Cape Town and land there. It's miles away but it'll be outside of the storm's circumference. He can call you from the airport and let you know he's safe. Then he'll have to stay there until this storm passes. There's little puddle jumpers all over the place that can bring him here. Take a breath," Sam spoke from experience.

"He doesn't have any money to stay anywhere. He told me he was broke after buying the ticket to come here."

"The airlines will take care of accommodations since they couldn't land the passengers locally. Don't think that Paul is the only one in this mess. The whole plane is filled with people who are wondering what to do. It's not up to you. Let'em all figure it out for themselves."

Though Sam's words were not exactly calming, at least they made sense and Nancy almost sighed in relief.

"I'm going to go to my tent and get out of these wet clothes. It'll help to lie down for a while," Nancy announced as though anyone was listening. Sam and Don were opening a bottle of whiskey to do their own rendition of drowning their sorrows.

Once back in her tent, Nancy stripped out of her soaking wet pants and shirt, peeled off her underwear and wrapped a big, dry towel around her shivering limbs. Lying down on the bed, she drifted immediately into the senseless space between waking and sleeping.

Immediately, Talish appeared within her inner vision.

"Glad to see you made it out of the forest and back to camp in one piece. That merge was a little surprising to you, wasn't it? It usually doesn't happen quite so fast but this was an unusual occasion," she explained with a sly grin.

"Now I'm going to educate you about the upcoming events because understanding ahead of time makes the going easier. You're going to have many more of these experiences though hopefully not quite so dramatic.

"You and Tusk are one energetic stream. You emerge in this space and time as Nancy. Tusk exists in another as Tusk yet the two of you are the same soul. We would call it 'spirit form' in my tribe yet soul will explain it to you more easily.

"The drive you experienced that brought you to Africa is not your personal desire. It was also Tusk wanting to be in form here as you. Within your time implication, he 'was' here in form a long time ago though talking about time within this reference is only for your own understanding. It doesn't mean anything to spirit form.

"I also want to assure you that what you're experiencing isn't special. Every human being alive in this reality is experiencing a rendition of Tusk/Nancy in his or her own way. A few are conscious of the experience and the majority put it off as déjà vu or coincidence. Again, in our tribe we don't use those words. We would call it 'spirit match'.

"All energetic streams flow from the one Great Source – your God. We have no word for what you call God because in my tribe we know it cannot be named. I will continue to use terms that are familiar to you so you will understand these concepts. This God of yours is given a personality by your people as though it were a man with desires, wants and preferences. Our tribe knows this does not exist.

"Within the source of all energy live all humans and animals as one energetic stream. I want to emphasize this aspect to you because it is why you are having these experiences. The one energy stream is contacted by each consciousness within intervals that allow for certain experience. Once you contacted it as Tusk; once as Nancy. Now you contact it as Tusk and Nancy. Rather than unusual, it is quite commonplace.

"Within the next few months, you are going to experience several other contact points as well and then you will more easily understand what I am saying. Another contact point for you will be your brother, Paul."

## Question Twenty-one
## How can I hear spirit's words?

The etheric realm, the subtle realm, that which is unseen, is where you originally emerged. Actually, you unfolded into the subtler realms when I AM as Creator intentioned manifestation, what you call creation in endless dimensions, frequencies of expression in every possible manner infinitely. It doesn't make any difference if you believe in evolution or creationism; whether you believe beings from another planet manipulated human DNA to create the human or whether you feel you "walked" into your body. All of those ideas and concepts include something that is manifest from something that is unmanifest – ME.

Within ME, every possibility exists connecting within the physical realm, as well. In the sense of Oneness, nothing is separate; nothing is disconnected.

Everything that exists in every dimension (as slow in frequency as you can imagine and as fast in frequency as you can even consider) is connected by a web-like force. It is the basis for what you call telepathy, energetic remission of lack of health in the physical body and feeling what you call "vibes" from people, plants and animals. It is even the reason why you like to look at some pictures, movies or scenes and not others. It all depends upon the resonance you have with that which you are observing during that moment in linear time. Look at the same picture a year later and you will see it differently even if you do nothing consciously to change your perception of it.

The words above are a preamble to answering your question. The words of "spirit" are *your* words. They are OUR words. They are present within you whether you are paying attention to them or not. It seems sensible to invite communication with that in which you have your being.

Communication with the etheric while in your physical body is one of the most natural experiences you could have; it has been conditioned out of your culture due to your present belief systems. All of the earlier peoples had constant communication with the unseen. Tribes adhering to the ways of their ancestors use their knowing, their nightly dreams and their voyages of seeing into the unseen to create, organize and administer their daily lives. Not only do they hear the words of spirit, they also act upon them.

The world you live within, your point of origin and the world to which you are "going" are not physical. The subtle realm exists and is available to you when you make the decision you want to live your life more consciously aware of and consciously in union within ME. I am not outside of you or inside of you. I AM as are you. You simply *are*. You cannot keep from having communication with the subtle, etheric realms. All you can do is keep yourself from knowing it.

Again, I remind you that hearing the words of spirit entails being quiet within your mind. When your rambling thoughts are taking up the available "space" within your consciousness, you do not hear the more subtle levels of communication. Attributing the unavailability of spirit to your not knowing how to hear is senseless. You will not receive its information if you are thinking; then it is very difficult to hear spirit's communication.

Communion from the subtle realms does not always come in audible words. More often, you experience ME as a feeling, a hunch, the gut response to your reality. Very often you set those communications aside based upon your mind's doubt and fear of losing control of its habitual patterns. When you allow yourself to sit silently each day and listen within for MY voice in whatever form in comes to you, soon you will find yourself relying on the strength of OUR union rather than the mental concepts and human knowledge you refer to as "knowing".

Trust is your key to this communion you desire, trusting what you hear and experience within your inner world is true for you. When your human mind begins to question the reality of what you hear within ME, you have two choices. You may notice either the mind's thought and let it go its way or you may use it to defend yourself from surrendering to your upwelling inner communion.

Eventually, if you surrender to your participation within ME, the mind quiets down assigning itself to far better tasks. You may invite your mental faculties to take the information flowing within you into consideration when making personal decisions. You may also use the "new" material to dissolve old beliefs and replace them with the resonance of trusting MY voice.

Remember that MY voice is *your* voice. I am not separate from your own inner dialogue. Dependent upon your familiar patterns of understanding, MY information may flow within you through words, pictures, smells, sounds or feelings. You may determine which best suits you as you become more practiced in hearing ME. Do not dismiss anything you experience from within this silent world for all is of the One and all has particular meaning for you when uprising within you.

You are already hearing and experiencing the words of spirit. The activity is not something new to you. Becoming more consciously aware of how you interpret, and then use, the flow of informing energy will give you a few clues as to when you close yourself off from that which is most natural for you. I AM speaking to you right now. Are you hearing ME?

## Story Time

Nancy awoke to the crash of thunder, the crackle of lightening and the roar of wind blowing through far-reaching treetops. She had slept for several hours after her visit from Talish and now felt slightly more refreshed than when she had originally retreated to her personal tent space.

The message from the wise woman was still firmly available within her consciousness with prominent attention being placed upon the idea of "contacts" as lifetimes. *How could Paul be another contact for her if he was alive with her in this space and time?*

She felt she was getting a bit of a handle on this merging of consciousness within form even though there was very little foundation as to *how* she understood it. It felt much more like a "given", something she had always known and was now remembering.

Dressing in warmer, dryer pants and shirt, she slipped her rain gear over a woolen sweater and headed to Sam's office to check in. Whatever still needed doing around the camp would have to be accomplished despite the torrent of water overhead. She felt ready and equipped to take on any assignment Sam might have for her.

Walking into Sam's office was akin to entering into a live-fire war zone. He was at his loudest and harshest addressing the crew that had abandoned the truck immediately upon arrival. Heads were about to roll.

*"This is the last warning I'm giving any of you,"* Sam shouted as the purple veins stood out in his neck. *"Anyone who ditches work, anybody who complains, any one of you who tells me again that hard work isn't the reason you came to Africa will be fired on the spot – no matter what's going on. I will not stand for subordination and I don't need crybabies. Am I clear?"*

No one looked directly at Sam or really even at each other. Though everyone felt the ripple of resentment, nobody had the courage to step forward.

Nancy decided to jump into the furor putting in her two cents in defense of the crew who, to a more or less degree, were her friends here.

*"Sam, I believe I can speak for us all. Most of us haven't been in situations as dangerous as the present conditions. We don't know how to respond despite our two days of emergency training before we arrived here. Cutting everyone a bit of slack would probably get everybody out doing whatever you need done next. Right, boys?"*

She hoped she wasn't putting her foot in her mouth or sounding too motherly. Being the only female in camp had its privileges and its burdens and, right now, she was siding with female wiles rather than attempting to be one of the guys.

Silence prevailed. Confirming Nancy's statements might make them all look like fools. Arguing with her would start Sam up again. Better to be quiet and see what was coming next.

*"Okay,"* Sam relented, *"I'll take Nancy's comments as coming from all of you. I want everybody in dry clothes, raingear on and back out at it. This storm is relentless. It isn't supposed to*

end for at least a week. We need ditches dug around camp anywhere you see water pooling. Take it from me. I've been here fifteen years. It gets much worse before it gets better. Move out!"

With Sam's final directive, the crew escaped his strident anger heading out the door like chagrined students from school. Nancy stayed behind hoping she hadn't spoken out of turn.

"Nancy," Sam addressed her while pouring himself another drink, "thanks for speaking for the crew though you and I both know that we're going to lose a few of them by the time this storm is finished. I'd like you to join Don as a project supervisor and take on more responsibility. For now, get out there and show 'em how it's done." Sam dismissed her.

Back out in the ruthless rain and wind, Nancy pulled her hood down over her hair and picked up one of the shovels now lying in a pool at her feet. There was enough water running through the center of the campground to keep them busy for days. Heading toward the sleep tents to begin trenching, she noticed that a couple of the crew followed suit. Good, I'm glad I don't have to tell them what to do. They'll just follow me.

Digging was a meditation. Make a long hole where the water could drain and move to the next spot. It allowed release from her thoughts making room for the constant information that was becoming a habitual pattern.

This adventure is taking me to places I never dreamed possible. Rather than a border between worlds, following my guidance has brought me to a merging of many. I no longer experience myself as just Nancy. I am who I am for sure, and I'm Tusk and I'm Talish. Sometimes I believe I'm also the elephants.

Each and every one of them is in constant communication with me. If I stop thinking, I can hear voices. Sometimes it's me, often Talish. Now and then, I hear Tusk. I wonder what other "contact points" she meant. Will I hear them, too?

And, what about Paul? What will he think if I tell him any of this? He'll probably think I've gone nuts.

# Question Twenty-two
## Should I develop my psychic abilities?

You cannot develop an ability you do not possess. You believe there is a *psychic world* you can tap into to receive answers for yourself or other people. While it is present due to your belief, it is not a human ability, as most would surmise.

The psychic plane is an energetic stream within a given concept that believes looking into that realm will provide you with answers regarding what you term your "future". Since that "approaching time" is not in existence until you resonate with one or another potential possibilities, there is no *future* time into which you may look.

The capacity you believe is possible to develop is more one of perception within the emotions of the human energy envelope and then proclaiming it as so. Since your resonance with what you see is how you bring it into "being" in your reality, when it appears you believe you have predicted the future correctly.

You may think of it this way: Every human being is energy. The energy is comprised of feelings, thoughts and the alignment of the physical body. All of these "bodies" emerge from within the world of spirit – ME.

Each body is a waveform of energetic vibration carrying information based on whatever you are placing your attention upon in the moment. When you change your focus, the information changes, as well. Dependent upon your desire or your natural proclivities, you will resonate with one or another potential in all possibility.

The more you practice "diving" into the energy of human feelings and thoughts, the more you become focused upon that plane of information. Realize that I AM describing only one set of frequencies where human emotions and thoughts exist. It is a slight disturbance in the frequencies within which I manifest through Creator.

At the same time, you are only able to access information that resonates within your own energy stream. If you ask a question with a desire to receive guidance from what you are describing as the psychic world, you are only capable of receiving that which will align with your preconceived beliefs. This is a very limiting viewpoint.

Those of you who believe you can look into the astral to provide answers for others do so by examining the energy field (consciously or unconsciously) of the person asking the question. From that frame of reference, you then resonate with what you believe possible for that person. You are limited in the availability of information based upon what you are resonating with personally. You will see them through your eyes, which in essence is seeing yourself.

What may also trip you up during this investigation is your theory about right or wrong, bad or good. If you experience something in their field of possibility that is abhorrent to you or seems dangerous, how will that color your response to them? Do you know whether the potential you are seeing is *their* reality or your own since you can only see through your own resonance?

Tapping into the psychic world is tantamount to going to a movie. Some films are action thrillers, others dramas, comedies or documentaries. Viewing the movie, you take on the experience of the actor or actress who most resonates with you.

So, too, is the psychic realm. That is why I state that it is not an ability; it is much more a sandbox to play in for a short time, if you so desire.

Another aspect of psychic diversion you might want to understand is that of resonating within frequencies you are not yet prepared to handle. If you have a proclivity toward anger or violence and you are dipping your toe into the astral where there is much anger, how much more will you be impressed by this frequency? Are you ready to take on the balancing of that aspect of your personality?

Hopes, fears, anticipations and disappointments often drive you to consult with a psychic to receive confirmation about what you hope will transpire for you. The person providing this service can only respond to you from that which you already know about yourself. Since you are the best interpreter of your energy signature, giving away your authority to someone who proclaims him or herself as able to tell your "future" undermines your existence as I AM.

Your understanding of your Self begins to shine when you stand forth in the integrity and authenticity that is naturally yours. Releasing your material hopes and fears wipes the etheric slate clean and then you are capable of truly seeing what is possible for you without being afraid of what is next in your reality.

When you rely on another to give you meaning for your life, keep in mind that they see you through their own "filters", their view of life from within their beliefs and perspective. Some of these concepts may align with yours and some may not. If they are harmonic with your beliefs, you will come to believe the person understands you better than you do. He or she does not.

If you have a desire to receive information from the subtle realms, read the answer to the previous question and follow those words. Opening within MY Mind to receive free flowing information from ME is an ability you fully possess. Your human mind might not agree at the outset since it wants to delve into climes that are more emotional, yet your heart speaks this truth to you loudly. All you need do is listen.

## Story Time

The remainder of that day was spent working in driving sleet and rain: digging, trenching, moving over, digging and trenching. Nancy held her own with the male crew much to their surprise earning their hard-won respect.

By nightfall, Sam called a halt to the progression of work, stating, mildly that *"everyone did a good job."* Not known for his plaudits, no one expected much more from him.

Cook had prepared hot soup tureens and good, greasy cheese sandwiches to warm up cold, empty bodies. There exuded an air of frivolity within the mess tent as several young men jockeyed for a seat closer to Nancy, now their unsung defender.

Nancy was having a difficult time concentrating on all of the sudden attention being placed upon her. Her mind was very distracted with Paul, where he was, how he was and when she would hear from him. Sam was the only camp member who knew that Paul was coming to join them and Nancy wasn't ready to announce that her older brother was on his way.

Having finished as much of the oily sandwich as her stomach could endure, Nancy excused herself to the moans and groans of her supporters who had hoped she would hang around for a while. Leaving them to comfort each other, she headed for her tent and silent reverie about Paul's situation.

Back in the privacy of her own space, Nancy sat in the folding chair that was her "lounge chair" and closed her eyes. *Okay, if Paul and I are supposed to have contact within lives, then I should be able to contact him as me. I've never tried this before and I don't even know how to go about it, but I could try it.*

Reaching out with her mind, Nancy looked for Paul. She thought about his smell, the sound of his voice and her general feelings when around him. Nothing came.

She kept trying until suddenly she jolted upright as her head fell onto her chest in sleep. *Well, obviously it's not working. I think I'll just go to bed and forget about this nonsense. Tomorrow morning I'll try to figure out where he is and how to get ahold of him.*

Sleep came effortlessly as Nancy abandoned her chair and collapsed on the cot. Her muscular exhaustion became evident as she reached for a blanket and fell into oblivion . . . for a few moments.

*"Nancy, I'm here,"* Talish appeared from within the dream world with her usual swirling of energy. *"You've been having quite a time trying to contact Paul, haven't you? Would you like some easy lessons with me here in your dream state that you'd remember when you wake up? It's very simple.*

*"The first thing you want to do is to stop trying so hard. Do you struggle when you are speaking to yourself inside? No. So stop the effort to 'find' Paul. He's here just as you are. All you have to do is talk to him the same way you talk to yourself and trust that he is hearing you.*

*"When you get up in the morning, after you're fully awake, sit down quietly away from your friends and talk to Paul.*

*Tell him how worried you are about him, the strength of the storm and ask him how you can help him wherever he is. Then wait. I know you're going to be surprised by the results.*

"He'll be here eventually and when he is we'll set up some 'spirit match' time together for the two of you so you'll be able to converse energetically with ease. For now, just do as I ask."

Upon awakening the following morning, Nancy remembered everything Talish had told her. She got her coffee and breakfast, checked in at the office and then high-tailed it to her tent before the workday officially began. The relentless rain chilled her to the bone.

Once back "home", she sat in her chair, closed her eyes and took a deep breath. *Don't try. Just do. Talk to Paul the way you would talk to yourself.*

"Okay, here goes. Paul, I'm so worried about you. I have no way of contacting you. I don't know if you got on the plane to come here or not. Everyone says no planes are landing here. I have very limited access to a telephone. I don't know if you are safe.

"I do know you have no money so you can't even help yourself. You could be stuck somewhere without any way to even contact me. Is there a possibility that you could call me here? I left my number with you the last time I talked to you. I hope you remembered to bring it with you if you did go. Please call me, Paul. Please call."

With that, Nancy opened her eyes and took another deep breath. *That felt funny yet in some way, I'm relieved. I said everything I wanted to say and now all I can do is wait and see.*

Back out in the rain, Nancy joined the crew who were being instructed by Don as to how to keep the tents drier. Though they were made for harsh weather, this rain was beyond their rating. Even the tarps slung over the tents were not doing the job. It was time to "go native" and use tree branches interlaced together under the tarps to fend off the flow of water.

As Don was explaining the rather tedious aspects of the upcoming job, Sam called out from the office, "Nancy, there's a telephone call for you. Sounds like Paul."

# Question Twenty-three
## How can I facilitate a person's soul in my work?

The soul is a compilation of your experience as I AM. It is *this* record that bears the impression of every thought or activity you experience. The record is written within ME and as ME. The energy expended in the activity leaves an imprint upon the etheric waves causing the creation of a memory recording in time and space.

Choice in each moment creates the information contained within your soul's record. These are not only decisions you make within this physical incarnation as ME. It also includes all aspects of you in the invisible (to you) worlds. It contains all of the possibilities for the future you resonate into existence, the potential for all lives. Through *thoughts, words and actions* each human delves into personal potential. Through free will choices, the next movement within the soul is created through resonance.

Your soul's potential is activated by thought. It functions within the frequency of this plane, the dimension of duality and contrast as it emerges within ME. Soul force or substance is infinite, indestructible vibration.

The soul, as the individual in the earth plane, has experiences and learns from them. These learnings are then embedded within the soul as memory. The attributes learned and the recognition of the control of energy becomes of even greater use in the subtle plane.

Since the soul is an entire record of an individual within ME, it is not possible for you to "facilitate" another's soul through any endeavor. What you may do, if you wish, is to support the experiences of that individual as they are recorded within the soul.

I would like to re-focus your attention upon yourself rather than on the facilitation of another soul's expression. While you mean well within your question, you are forgetting there is nothing you can do to change the choice a person has made with regard to how he or she is going to experience existence. Your desire to do so is an expression of your own wish for personal transformation.

The capability you have to make inner changes and shifts is a demarcation line between you and your belief about what you can do for another. By this, I mean that you see yourself as one type of individual and the other person as an "other". This is not true. What you believe needs facilitation within another is exactly what needs assistance within you.

Rather than using energy in an attempt to transform another person's experience, the most beneficial use of your time will be in revising yourself. When you are aware there is nothing that needs to be fixed, helped or healed within ME as an individual, you will no longer be concerned about how you may facilitate another's soul. It simply will not be a concern for you.

Within the stillness of conscious awareness, look carefully at your question. From where within you does it arise? Are you concerned that you will not be doing the "work you are supposed to do"? Are you filled with fear that if you don't spend time fixing another you will be seen as "less than" by your peers? It is your ego personality's desire driving your query. Your expression of ME is not absorbed in facilitating another person's soul because it knows there is no need. Will you now allow your personality to remind itself of this fact, as well?

Spontaneously arising within you as ME is compassion and love without condition allowing you to be in union with what appears to be the "other". If you truly wish to be of assistance to those in your environment, simply *be* with them *as* ME rather than as a facilitator of change.

Any idea you may have about a need to assist another in transforming him or herself arises out of the need to display yourself for confirmation. Sitting with another, listening, breathing and being is of the greatest benefit in time of difficulty or stress.

Do you remember that the person whom you wish to facilitate is I AM? Are you aware your perception about how he or she "should" change is fueling your question? While a few of you incarnated into your body to partially experience this life in support of another's transformation, it will come so naturally you will not have to consider whether or how to make it occur.

Your world emerges within ME complete and perfect exactly as it is. Where you see non-perfection, a need to fix or make a change is only based upon your viewpoint in the moment. Move to another country, adopt another ideology, attend one more workshop and you will see it differently. You are a moving, dynamically shifting state of affairs. Do not believe otherwise.

In answer to your question, I will say that the moment you step into the utter clarity of purpose as the individual you are, in that moment you will realize the uselessness of facilitating another. He or she does not require it even if he or she is asking for it. Would it not be more beneficial to express to that person they are fully capable of creating the transformations they desire without you? Does that offend your personality's sensibilities?

Truly, it is irrelevant within ME. I AM cause. I AM effect. There is no facilitation necessary.

## Story Time

*"Nancy, I know you've been concerned about me. Please don't be. I'm a big boy, you know,"* Paul announced with no preamble as to why he was calling exactly at *that* moment.

*"Things changed drastically after I talked with you last. By the time I got to the airport to fly over to you, they told us that a big storm was due and changed all of our flight plans. I was put on a totally different, slightly earlier flight to Cape Town. I have just landed there. My one problem, of course, is being broke. I can't get to you until the thunderstorm lifts which won't be for days and I need a place to stay. Can you wire me some money?"*

Nancy held the phone, white-knuckled. She had no idea what she was going to hear and feared the worst. Now it appeared that everything was fine with the exception of money. *Why had I gotten so worked up over something I couldn't control?*

*"Well, Paul, hold on a minute. I'll have to ask Sam if someone can drive me into the village to the Western Union*

*outpost. With this weather, we'll be lucky to get a truck on the road. Hold on a minute."*

Nancy turned to talk to Sam only to find she was standing in the office completely alone. She could hear his booming voice above the din of the storm shouting directions to someone outside. Running in that direction, she quickly interrupted him not wanting to leave Paul hanging on the phone line.

*"Sam, Paul's in Cape Town just like you said he would be. He needs money. Can someone drive me over to the village post so I can wire it to him?"*

*"Nonsense, no need of that,"* Sam growled at being interrupted. *"I'll call my cousin who owns the Mountain Hotel and Restaurant and tell her to put him up. We'll square up later. Just tell Paul to go to the hotel and ask for Sandy. Tell him to tell her I sent him and I'll be calling her in a few. Now, let me get finished here."*

Back in the office, Nancy relayed Sam's message to Paul with relief. *Why do I feel so responsible for him all of the time? Doesn't seem like I should.*

*"Nanc, tell Sam thanks for me, huh? I can't wait to be with you so we can sit and have a good long talk. There've been so many weird things happening to me. I'm almost afraid to talk about them over the phone.*

*"Looks like I won't be there for at least a week. Sure this Sandy won't mind putting me up for that long?"*

*"Paul, you can be sure that Sam will take your hotel stay and meals out of your paychecks here. He doesn't do favors for people. This was just the easiest way to get you taken care of so I can get back to work. This reserve is his only concern.*

*"There is so much to do here normally and now the rain. It's washing out roads; uprooted trees are ripping out fences, not to mention the mess it's making of the riverbeds and streams. We're really going to be happy to see another set of muscles show up after this rain stops.*

*"Can I ask you a couple of questions about the stuff you're afraid to talk about? I'm really curious about a couple of things,"* Nancy asked cautiously.

*"Okay, go ahead. Just don't ask me to go into details. I'm afraid once I get going, I won't know when to stop talking. There's been so much. What do you want to ask?"*

Nancy swallowed, hard. *Am I ready to tell Paul about Talish and Tusk? I've sort of let the cat out of the bag by wanting to ask him questions.*

*"Paul, did any of this have to do with a woman or a boy? Are you having visions or hearing them talking to you when you sleep?"* Nancy held her breath.

*"How did you know? Well, it isn't exactly like that. There's no boy. Actually, it was an old woman and you that I've been seeing; sort of shimmering in and out a lot. Then when I'm really sleeping, I hear this noise like animals crashing through a forest and drumming. It's been going on for a couple of weeks now. How did you know about any of this?"*

Nancy didn't want to unveil herself fully over the phone yet she felt she owed Paul some type of explanation.

*"Well, Paul, I've been visited by an old woman. I don't know if she's the same one you're seeing. And there's a boy. Sometimes they come when I'm asleep."* She wasn't ready to tell him about the physical transference with the elephants during the beginning of the rainstorm.

*"We can talk about it more when you get here. Paul, I'm so glad you're coming. I think this is going to be really good for all of us."*

*"All of us, Nancy? Who's the all? Are you talking about the crew? Or do you mean the other side of you I see in my dreams?"*

*"Paul, I have to get back to work. I can hear Sam yelling out there and I don't want him mad at me. He's angry enough about the storm and all. See you soon. Go see Sandy. Sam'll call her a little later."* Nancy quickly slipped past the last set of questions and hung up the phone.

# Question Twenty-four
## Self-love, where does one start?

You begin with ME. When you love ME without concept, condition, judgment or expectation, you are then capable of loving yourself because you are I AM. Rather than attempting to figure out what parts of you are the most deserving of your love, you simply bestow it all and as I receive it, so do you.

Since your physical reality and your sense of spirit are one, you remove the doubt of your ability to love yourself when you focus that energetic stream upon your awareness of ME. Spirit is constantly in-forming the physical bringing into formation all that consciousness experiences. Instead of "trying" to feel self-love, let ME embrace you in MY love. As you love ME, I love you.

Your personality expresses within your world either aware of itself as spirit in form as love or unaware. You relate to your awareness or lack of it as "seeking". As conscious awareness accelerates and expands, recognition of ME becomes the basis for your existence. Within this awareness of ME, lives your love that then becomes union within all because I AM all, therefore you cannot love ME without loving all as well, including yourself.

Within this self-directed love, you may then release the bonds of programmed belief systems and the judgments of dual contrast realizing the absolute focus of freedom and liberation in human form. It is only through love of ME that this is possible. Seeking your spiritual "advancement" in whatever form you choose is a drive of the ego personality. Surrendering into simply loving is the call of your soul through the voice of your heart.

No thought, feeling, emotion or idea exists that is not ME. All that is manifest and unmanifest emerges from within ME. All is an experience of the whole as this emerging love. Within this natural state, you mirror to yourself your own capacity to be love. As you love ME, you inform the mirror of consciousness of your love that is MY Love. Awareness of being love in form is a mirror mirroring back to the mirror. The transmission and the receiving of the love are simultaneous.

How many times do you follow the yearning, the mystery of the key that is pulling at your heart to fulfill that which self-love tells you is true for you? How many times do you "sacrifice" yourself for another out of "love" for them when the action is more likely coming from fear of feeling guilty, retribution of some type or a plain and simple belief system that you have not taken the time to examine for its relevancy in your life? And what does it feel like after you have made that "sacrifice"? Do you really feel like you have acted out of love and feel complete, satisfied? Or does there remain that ever-present nagging resentment that sits quietly in the corner waiting for the perfect moment to exert its fulfillment?

When you live as love, you experience MY love as your Self, loving back and you can truly feel it. It feeds you, nourishes you, brings you to new heights of understanding, awareness and gives you the ability to be ever stronger within your divinity as ME.

The love within every situation is free. It is without boundaries. Love is always free. It doesn't hold any need to be right. There is no price to pay for love. If you feel a need to evaluate your love in any situation, relationship or experience, you may assure yourself that you are not living as that love. You are not aware of ME. You are reacting to what you believe is happening, what is going on in the reality that you have created and can re-create with the power of your free will. Love carries no price. It simply *is*, just like you. You simply *are* as love and that is all you need be, authentic, natural and fulfilling.

Love erases the sense of separation and completes your awareness of oneness within ME. Re-member, so long as you create separation between you and anything or anyone else, you do not know or love ME. WE are not on a journey to oneness. You are not achieving oneness. Your path is not oneness. Oneness is within ME and that is all that exists in and out of manifestation. Anything else is an illusion within the mind of your ego personality existing within a realm of contrast and choice.

The union you "seek" within your apparent concept of separation is already in place. Its label is love yet your construct of love is usually filled with the conditions of what that love means to you. Love is only union. It is nothing else. The union of love applies no restrictions to its emergence within ME. As you love ME, you love yourself. As you believe it is difficult to experience self-love, you believe it is difficult to love ME. You cannot separate the two ideas.

Separation does not exist. Your mind plays a game so that your ego personality can feel important in its opinions and judgments. Your mind perceives itself as always right to itself. Surrender to oneness. You will be surrendering within ME coming to an absolute "new" awareness of your Self.

Give your heart and mind to loving ME. Forget about the need to love your Self. When your only focus is upon loving ME, without a doubt, you will find yourself loving you as well. When you doubt that you are feeling love for your Self, immerse yourself in your love of ME. Release the seeking of self-love. Find it within ME.

## Story Time

The next few days flowed by like the floodwater with which Nancy and her park reserve mates were surrounded. Daily ditch digging, reinforcing of the tents' protective coverings and attempting to stay dry consumed their physical lives. Paul did not call in and Nancy didn't attempt to reach him. She had told him as much as she was ready to admit to and Sam had assured her that he had talked with Sandy and Paul was set, at least for now.

Though Nancy hadn't yet found the certitude to spend her lunch hours alone in her tent due to fear of what her male cohorts might ask, she did retire earlier than usual each night awaiting the appearance of Talish and/or Tusk. Often they appeared within dreamtime, sometimes as a physical presence.

She was just beginning to get a glimmer of what Talish was attempting to teach her about multi-dimensional travel. It was not a matter of actually moving from one place to another, more a focus of awareness, a shape shift into another avenue of attention.

Three days into the seemingly endless downpour, Nancy left the dining room with its overpowering testosterone and sloshed through the mud back to her tent. The night was unusually silent despite the deluge. Yet, within the silence was a low-level rumbling, almost as much a feeling as a sound. It filled the air, raised the hair on her arms and tightened her stomach muscles, a lot.

Glancing around for a physical sound source, a slight movement at the edge of camp caught her eye. In the dim light of dusk, it was hard to make out distinct shapes through the falling curtain, yet she thought she was seeing a portion of the elephant herd at the tree line edging the western camp circumference. At least, they seemed to be shapes that big.

It definitely did sound like the low rumble was coming from that direction though what it meant Nancy didn't know. The rolling grumble created a yearning within her to join them, to touch an elephant body and feel the leathery, armored skin. Precluded by the brunt of the storm from going any further than she already had managed to trek in the mud and water, Nancy just stood and watched the three elephants she could now see more clearly. One by one, they turned around and disappeared into the trees leaving her feeling very much alone.

Entering her tent, Nancy found Talish waiting for her in physical form. While she had done this before, each time surprised her since she wasn't use to having people showing up unannounced. This was her private space and she wanted it kept this way though the appearances of Talish were slightly more welcome.

*"Nancy, I hear you are becoming acquainted with elephant love,"* Talish led off with an unexpected comment.

*"What do you mean 'elephant love'?"* Nancy questioned skeptically as she peeled off her dripping raincoat and hat. *"All I'm getting acquainted with is water and much too much of it for my liking."*

*"Oh, this comes and it goes, much as life,"* Talish responded with what looked like a smirk. *"As the ebb and flow of human existence, the waters of the heavens bring us nourishment and the replenishing of the waterways for all animals – four-*

legged and two-legged, winged and crawling. You would complain much louder if you were dying of thirst in some of the deserts not too far from here. Now sit down and relax. We have a lesson tonight the elephants have begun and I have chosen to continue. We work in concert, the elephants and I. They stimulate your curiosity and I attempt to satisfy it.

"I know you were listening to the elephants communicating with you though you didn't know what was happening. They rumble with a sound barely below human hearing and sometimes far below your ears' ability to hear. Each of their rumbles conveys a different message to the other elephants heard for miles in every direction.

"What they were conveying tonight was their acceptance of you. Now I'm not suggesting that you go running up to them, yet. That will come in time. What I am getting around to here is that they are telling you to accept yourself as they accept you. And, yes, they do feel what you feel and understand you much better than you might believe possible.

"As Tusk you run with the herd as a mahout, at least that is what some call elephant riders. Within your life as Tusk, you are being raised by the elephants as one of them. They love you as a child and you love them as family. We call this 'spirit bred'.

"Now, as Nancy, the herd recognizes you even though your physical appearance is different than that of Tusk. Your essence is the same with a few differences. As Nancy, you are much less sure of yourself. You do not love yourself as you do as Tusk. Your young boy aspect has no concept of love or not love. He simply loves. The elephants are requesting that you remember what that feels like, to love. Once you understand what I am telling you here, you will be able to walk up to any of them fearlessly.

"This is an important statement. So far, your only interactions have been in times of danger so your natural survival tendencies have blocked out much of the experience. When you are with them within the sharing of love, you will experience an enormous difference."

# Question Twenty-five
## Where does one begin after a
## lifetime of negative reinforcements and beliefs?

There are many concepts included in this question, so I will take it apart in answering it.

You are still alive so you have not experienced a lifetime of anything. This is good news because it means you have life "time" left to transform what you believe about yourself within ME. So I will rephrase that part of the questions to "after some years" and that will more accurately reflect the shorter space of time you believe *feels* like your entire life and is not.

I will add here that if you were complete with this lifetime and existing in the realm of soul, you would not be asking this question because you would be observing the present experience from the realm of non-duality. In that plane, there is no negative, no *force* or *reinforcement* and no belief. Those attributes are personal to the earth's dimension as well as other incarnation venues, yet are not held within the soul's "world".

As to "negative reinforcements", anything that is reinforced must be there in the first place. Since you are I AM the only reaffirmation that is possible is to reinforce your existence within ME. What you are considering "negative" is simply an event. You choose to interpret it as negative meaning that you have a preference for one thing or another. You have chosen to perceive what you consider negative behavior and see it being reinforced everywhere you look. It is your perspective that requests a change, not the action itself.

Your ability to observe your actions and beliefs as negative or positive suggests you are capable of altering each or any of them. Postulating that reinforcement keeps you from doing so is self-indulgent projection. You blame another for what you believe you clearly see as undesirable. As I AM, you have the power and the creative potential to dissolve any and all assumptions you maintain no longer serving your personal experience. No one can or will do this for you.

Now that we have established a baseline from which to continue the answer to your query, I will continue. A belief system is what you have confidence in without requiring proof that it is correct. Every human maintains a belief system. This does not mean that they have a specific religious, political or cultural belief. It simply means that there are opinions and convictions they hold that they have confidence in without requiring proof.

Outside of standard beliefs, you are vast and infinite as I AM. There is no limitation upon what is possible for you. As observed in the preamble to this answer, your ability to perceive negative vs. positive experiences acknowledges the difference within your beliefs and actions. Choosing to remain within the perceived negativity is your personal reinforcement of that which you are saying you no longer desire and that which you are participating within through free will.

In this moment, you maintain the power and strength to re-determine your perceived future. Your composition as I AM affords a full range of choices regarding how you are going to reference your life's story.

"Where to start" is at the beginning, the onset of the belief. Forget the reinforcements. Once you know the origin of the belief, you can decide whether you want to continue believing something you consider "negative" or not. This is your decision, your choice and why you incarnated into this body within this particular time/space continuum.

You will inevitably arrive at the educational point within your childhood, first by your parents, then by your teachers and whatever religion, if any, in which you were raised. Identifying specific targets of belief affords you the platform for your research. You may then reinforce these convictions, habits and patterns for yourself. You may also discard them either partially or wholly.

How easy it is for the human mind to project its personal disappointment upon another human or situation. "If only so and so had not done such and such, I would not be like this," your mind speaks with impunity. It betrays your strength belittling your divine authority and continuing to control your low self-esteem.

Self-indulgence and self-betrayal go hand-in-hand. You indulge in behavior you believe is negative and you then betray yourself by blaming its appearance within your life upon another person or situation. Certainly, there may be supportive people or actions, shoring up your undesirable beliefs, yet no one has the capacity to *make* you take part within any of these experiences.

Once you have located the origin of a belief, you may then consider what you would like to replace it with, if anything. Focusing upon the positive or negative will keep you locked within the contrast cycle of judgment where you presently find yourself. Removing the concept of right or wrong, good or bad from your reference point allows your conscious expansion into awareness of I AM.

Remaining aware of I AM is useful for this purpose. Your existence within ME, as ME, is the only truth you will ever know despite what your mind would have you believe. Centering your perception upon the wholeness of your existence, whether incarnated or not, dissolves your need to believe you experience either positive or negative forces. *You* are your only force. Any reinforcement comes directly from within you.

## Story Time

Nancy was entranced with Talish's narrative. It summoned up within her a deep desire to know more, to understand and to participate actively within this world that Talish was so vividly painting for her.

Just before she had a chance to ask a question, Sam's voice could be heard calling her name, summoning her back to the mess tent for some unknown reason. She really didn't want to leave Talish with her expanding explanations yet knew the outcome of ignoring Sam was even less desirable.

*"Talish, I have to go find out why Sam is calling me. I'll be back as soon as I can. Will you wait for me?"* Nancy asked feeling helplessly among dimensional worlds.

*"I will return when the time is proper for you, Nancy. I am no longer needed here and have given you much to think about,"* said Talish as she backed gracefully out of the tent nearly disappearing within the sheet of rain that readily concealed her.

Nancy put on her boots, raingear and hat dreading another trudge through the mud to join Sam. Who knew what was up now. Sam's voice hadn't left much room for questioning - only obedience. He held tight control over his domain and few had the guts to stand up to him.

Gracelessly sliding into the mess tent on a river of mud and water, Nancy collided with Don who stopped her from nearly falling over a bench pulled away from the tables. As he grabbed her arm, he whispered in her ear, *"You're going to love this."* Steadying her as she fought to secure her footing, Don sidled out of Nancy's line of sight giving her ample room to sense the stench of fear overriding the usual male camaraderie.

Dan anchored everyone's expectant attention. Obviously, the crew had been awaiting her arrival before beginning whatever was going to happen next.

Sam was the first to speak, as usual, momentarily drawing the group's eyes away from red-faced Dan and his circle of supporters.

*"Dan and several other of the crew sharing his feelings have spent some time talking after dinner. They asked me for floor space and time to address all of you. Please hold your comments until he or they have a chance to voice their thoughts,"* Sam politely requested.

*This is so unusual for him,* Nancy thought. *What's convinced him to use respect?*

Assembled attention again reverted to Dan as the keynote speaker of the evening. How fearful he was of what he was going to announce shone through his eyes. It didn't take sensitivity to glean how difficult he found "public speaking".

*"We've been talking about the incident at the creek the other day and have come to some conclusions,"* Dan began with some trepidation. *"I've been chosen as the one to talk about our feelings, concerns and, ultimately, our decisions. Please hear me out before you judge us."*

Nancy glanced over at Don who had moved to a choicer location against the far wall. He caught her eye, winking.

*"One of the reasons that Paul and I were so easily swept away by the flood was because of our lack of focus on the job at hand. I'm speaking for most of us when I say that we all sort of feel like we're being taken advantage of here and without good reason.*

*"None of us really knew what we were getting into coming to the reserve. The job application advertised the positions as one of 'maintaining wild animal habitat in the depths of the African jungle'. It all sounded quite romantic and at first blush, it was until the hard work part of it all took over.*

*"Now that we've been indoctrinated into the reality of the job, we either have to make a decision to stay or leave. We've talked with Sam and Don tonight and they've advised us that what we've been experiencing the last few days is more the reality than the intermittent event. Though we won't always be having this kinda' weather, we will be digging water ditches, constantly repairing fences and sorting out the jungle debris. That's why I'm saying that this is a crossroads.*

*"Once this storm let's up, we each have the option to stay or go. There's a flight scheduled to leave in two weeks. The storm'll be gone by then and anyone wanting to bail has the option to hop that plane. If you decide to stay, then we all need to re-commit to our choice here. I guess it's not really a re-commitment so much as a commitment to the job at hand rather than the glamorous idea we believed this trip would be.*

*"That's about all I have to say. If anyone wants to make any comments now's the time. Know that Paul and I have already committed to Sam and Don our full support and dedication to doing what it takes to keep this reserve as the home for so many wild animals. What you decide to do is up to you. We've learned our lesson the hard way. Hopefully, you won't have to say the same."*

Nancy glanced over at Sam and Don sequestered against the wall, authoritatively huddled together. This was a strange turn of events and her natural sensitivities were informing her that there was much more than met the eye in Dan and Paul's decision.

## Question Twenty-six
## What causes my occasional
## angry behavior and what can I do about it?

Anger signals a need for change. Since you are only able to change yourself, anger requests adjustments in your perspective and beliefs.

Many of you feel that "righteous anger" is justification for your emotional outbursts of outrage. "Righteous" connotes you believe you are "right" and someone else is "wrong" which also means you believe one aspect of ME is right and another aspect of ME is wrong. This is due to living in your contrasting world of duality.

What can you do about it? Change your belief to change your perception. This, in turn, will alter your interpretation of the observation causing the angry behavior. When you no longer believe that another person or situation "should be" different from what it is, you will be less inclined to animosity.

Sometimes the changes you want to see made within a person or situation are experiences in which you have the capacity to make these alterations. Often you feel that you are not capable of making them because you don't believe you have enough authority to do so. Here is where you really have an opportunity to remove the mask your ego personality wears and let yourself be seen.

If this creates fear within you, recognize that energy as neutral with an overcast of fear due to believing you lack control over a situation. Since WE are one, you are completely invested in anything you are experiencing no matter how small a part you believe you play within it. The structures of any situation are emerging from within ME just as you are so there is no difference between you and the cause of your anger.

Due to your human desire to control what is occurring, the natural shifts within consciousness that would occur if you would surrender to what is happening become moments of frustration based upon your expectation of the moment.

Expectation of any person or situation removes your ability to love that person or situation. Love does not expect. Love *is* as I AM. Your human mind has attached itself to concepts you believe are "right" and "to be expected" so when they are not fulfilled you become angry. Remove the expectation and you remove the anger.

While control of others or situations mirror your experience of *personally* feeling out of control, there is only one being you can regulate and you know who that is; it is yourself. You may decide to change your perception of a person, place or thing or you may decide to fight against it. The simple conclusion remains that the anger displays your desire to change *something* and the only person or "obstacle" you can shift is yourself.

Stop for a moment to consider what I AM. That which I AM, you *are*, so this consideration will be of great assistance to your understanding.

As All That Is, I AM experiencing in every possible manner and combination. When you encounter anger over a situation within your feelings, you are separating yourself from ME within your mind and energy body. You believe that something "should" be different based upon your beliefs of the moment, meaning you believe *I* should be different from what you are experiencing.

Since all is one, when you make changes within yourself you alter that which you perceive. Your perception is based upon your belief and what you interpret that belief meaning to you. Every conceptual description and significance is different for every one of you. No one sees any belief, even an identical idea, in the same light.

Know this: Any sense of anger is not negative. It is neutral energy assigned an interpretation expressed as the inability to make a change in something you believe is outside of you. It is not. All is contained and emerges within you as ME. The only changes you can make to alleviate the signal the anger is conveying to you are within you as ME.

As you breathe into the expectation, you wish to transform, observe whether you are attempting to run *from* something or run *toward* another experience. If you want to get away from something, you will carry it with you because it is also you. Resonating with a specific event or going toward it alters the frustration to be in accord with your anticipated experience. You are no longer attempting to elude your anger. You are shifting your attention completely.

The concept of surrender is a term of great resistance to the human mind and yet surrendering to being ME is the only possible outcome for all of the transformations you believe you are experiencing. Nowhere is it more easily seen by you than within the anger you are feeling. Rather than fighting the urge to fight, surrender to the idea that wells up within the struggle and ask it what it wants of you rather than what it wants of someone else.

Honor all feelings as signals alerting you to what is arising in your frequency. Ask it what it is saying to you. No energy transmission within you as ME is negative or positive. It simply *is* and within its being is the core of your expression as ME.

Your anger is not asking you to do something. It is requesting you to perceive differently and that is possible within your expression as I AM. Accept yourself as ME.

## Story Time

Nancy hung around for a while after the crew had dispersed following Dan and Paul out of the mess tent. Don and Sam were still standing together talking secretively and Nancy shored up her courage to go speak to them about why they were being so furtive.

*"What's going on, guys? What's the big secret?"* she asked hopefully expecting an answer and to be included.

*"Nanc, not sure you want in on this. Once you start getting involved in the scuttlebutt, you're going to be looked at as 'admin' and then you'll be ostracized by the crew, at least socially,"* Don offered in lieu of a truthful answer.

*"I'm already different than everybody else here. I'm the only woman in camp so you might as well tell me since it won't change a thing,"* Nancy responded, not being put off by Don's sloppy attempt to protect her.

"Okay, but don't say I didn't warn you. We were talking about how long we thought this attitude of cooperation was going to last. What Dan said was nearly a verbatim copy of the lecture he got from Sam earlier this afternoon. The only difference was that Sam had added that he was ready to fire both Dan and Paul for their insubordination. This little get-together was their way of holding on to their jobs. It's all about money," Don began explaining. Sam was livid. He really didn't want to talk about this anymore.

"Nancy," Sam began to add, "keep this to . . . ." This was as far as he got before Nancy stepped in with one obvious objection.

"Hey, wait a minute. This job isn't so great that they would put themselves on the line like that if they didn't mean it. I can't believe you think they're doing this just for the money. There has to be more to it than that."

Sam and Don looked at each other dubiously. Either they were going to include Nancy in the administration of this reserve or they weren't. It was looking like a crossroad with no clear decision coming from either of them. After a few short breaths, Sam took a step toward the tables and chairs.

"Let's sit down here for a minute and talk. There are a few things I need to say if we're going to include you in all of this around here."

Nancy, Don and Sam pulled chairs up to one of the tables toward the back of the tent where they were out of hearing range of anyone still lurking around outside. We really should be having this talk in the office, but I guess this will do, Nancy was thinking as she felt the energy shift from furtive to conspiratorial.

"Okay, Nanc, here's the deal. Both Dan and Paul are on probation due to criminally negligent behavior stateside. They beat up a couple of guys really bad last year and got off easy with probation and community service. When they asked if they could spend their time here working on the reserve instead of on the streets of New York, they were given permission to come here under the auspices of our local government. A lot of red tape had to be dealt with to make it happen. If they screw up here, they go to jail.

"But it's not only that. Both of them suffer from a great deal of anger that they try to hold in. If they let loose, someone here's going to get hurt. They know I know. They're not sure if I've told Don and now I've told you. I can guess how they feel about anyone else being involved in their business and though that really isn't too important as far as I'm concerned, I'm also responsible for the safety of everyone here. So, keep your mouth shut, will you?"

"There's more to it than just that, Nancy," Don chimed in. "Just before you arrived here, there was an altercation with Dan and Paul and some of the crew when a couple of them tried to stop Paul from challenging the elephant herd. The elephants don't come around here very often and when they do, it's important to respect 'em. Paul, driving one of the trucks, decided to play 'chicken' with a female elephant that was walking just outside of the tree line with her baby. Nothing's worse than being around a mother elephant when she's with her young 'un. He nearly got himself killed and who knows what else could've happened.

"This last stunt with the flood was really the last straw for them and they knew it. So the talk was for show, and to let Sam know they heard him by telling the whole crew they were committing to their work. Though some of the guys who don't know them might have believed it, their friends know better. Basically, they're sorta' scared."

"Well, why did you let Dan speak then, Sam?" Nancy wondered out loud.

"Because it was better to le'im have his say than to tell him he couldn't. He's set himself up even though he knows I know better than to believe him. It was just the easiest and most peaceful thing to do under the circumstances.

"I've already shifted you to lead for a crew so now I'm going to advance your position to be the same as Don's, assistant camp supervisor which translates to project supervisor. This added responsibility means that the actions of the crew you lead reflect on you so make sure you keep your head above water and your nose clean. When any of these guys want changes, they think that getting mad is the way to make something happen. They have to know that it won't work that way here."

## Question Twenty-seven
## How do I let go of the fear of punishment?

The easiest way to let go of the fear of punishment is to release the belief you need to be punished, your need to be chastised for a wrongdoing. Since there is no right or wrong within ME, there is no bad or good within you because you are I AM in physical form. Therefore, there is no need to be punished for any word or action.

The belief in punishment has been acculturated within you due to the authority figures you allow to "rule" over you. Since there are many layers of domination within your reality, there are many opportunities to believe you have displeased an authority figure.

You are your only sovereignty though you often "give yourself away" to others through the belief it is the correct action to take. No one holds dominion over you. Through your free will, you may make a determination to whom you give this influence in your life, yet that is a choice.

When you begin to inspect your reason for believing you may be punished, you will soon realize that the idea of being disciplined by another is a relief. The feeling stems from your personal desire to be more regulated in your thoughts, words and actions. Since you see yourself as needing discipline and unable to achieve it alone, you project the responsibility onto another rather than carrying it for yourself.

Many authority figures within your life are not truly such within their own minds. You have given them that responsibility and they act it out in conjunction with you. Withdraw the imposed domination, the dominance disappears and with it the fear of punishment.

The concept of punishment is separate from the fear of it. You may know that retribution is possible and not be afraid of how it might show up. Fear describes your ego personality's desire to be seen differently much the same as being embarrassed is the result of desiring your mask to remain in place.

Fearing punishment is an amplification of your lack of self-discipline. While you have handed the responsibility of regulating yourself to another knowing that punishment for failure is possible, fear that will occur stimulates your survival mechanism. Within this aspect of your brain, you will find the automatic projection of your perceived low self-esteem onto another. Once the personal detachment is complete, you no longer feel responsible for your actions. "They made me do it," is the typical response.

Offset the fear of punishment with the assumption of your own authority. Upon assuming your role as the only ruler of your personal domain, inner and outer, when confronted by a person or situation challenging that authority, you have no fear. Rather you experience an opportunity to transmit your sense of being within ME alerting the "other" aspect within ME that you know yourself. Fear has no residence within self-respect and authenticity.

Where fear exists, lack of knowing ME is prevalent. Within ME, there is no trepidation, only love without judgment. Since fear of punishment connotes self-judgment, you do not love yourself within this state. In a general sense, fear displaces love within your energy stream. Fearing an action from another expands the energetic transmission from lack of love for yourself to include the one who is exercising authority over you.

Mass consensus in your reality lives in a constant state of authoritative oppression so it is very easy for you to resonate with this feeling and experience. When you step forward as the one true expression of ME as you rather than "running with the herd", you will find yourself living within a much freer state of being.

In answering your question as to how to "let go" of the fear, open your energetic hand. You have a tight-fisted hold on your fear *of the fear* almost as though you are afraid of being afraid. Energetically, this misaligns your energetic signature enabling those who *do* wish authority over you to resonate deeply with your lack of self-response within your life's field.

No one is a punisher. No one holds authority over you. True, there are laws to control the masses within your culture and disobeying those laws results in a variety of disagreeable repercussions. Some of these edicts are for your safety and some are simply in place to keep the "herd" under control. You know the difference and may choose within free will how you are going to exercise your application of those laws. We are not referring to this type of authority within this response to your question.

As with all beliefs, the most productive method to unleash any concept's hold upon you is to spend quiet time following the thread of the fear back to its source. Once at the point of origin you can make a determination whether or not you wish to remain in a state of believing it is true for you. If you accept the ideology as "yours", then you will no longer be afraid of punishment because the belief belongs to you and you hold authority over how you are going to exercise it.

If you decide it no longer serves you, dissolve it into MY Energy Stream to be used in resonance with another, more suitable experience. Nothing is right or wrong within ME. All simply *is* and when that becomes the only knowing you replace all of your beliefs with, fear will have no hold over any situation or circumstance.

## Story Time

Sam was less than happy with having to rehash all of this history and having finished his explanation, left the mess tent for his office. Don lingered behind as though he had more to say and not necessarily to Sam. Nancy watched him thoughtfully as he waited for Sam to depart, remaining silent long enough for him to be out of earshot.

*"Nancy, I don't necessarily feel the same way about Dan and Paul that Sam does though I do believe they have gotten themselves in some hot water. I'm right there with him about their tendencies to make trouble and at the same time, I feel that punishment doesn't always alleviate the underlying problems.*

*"When they first arrived here, they were much more contrite than they've been lately. Both boys were happy to be able to serve their community service time on the reserve while getting*

*a bit of cash held for them rather than picking up trash off of city streets. It's only been recently, and please, realize this is no reflection upon your arrival.*

*"I have a feeling they want more responsibility and less menial labor. So much of the work here is just that, work. There's little glamour to this job. The only place a person feels respect is in being able to take the lead in some of the work crews.*

*"Once Sam has settled down a little, and that's going to take some time, I'm going to see if we can't move Dan and Paul 'to the head of the class', so to speak, and give them a little more authority. When that time comes, I'm going to rely on you to help me, if you will. What do you say to that?"* Don finished his heartfelt little speech.

*"What are you going to ask me to do?"* Nancy asked not sure that she wanted to get too involved with young men she didn't know very well who had anger management problems. Though Nancy knew all about the anger issue due to brother Paul suffering from that same disorder, there was a big difference between dealing with someone you grew up with and people you hardly knew. She wondered how Paul *would* fit in with this motley crew once he got here which should be any day now.

*"I'll want you to be a bit of a cheerleader, if you will, as far as the rest of the crew goes. They might feel some fear and even resentment that the two who cause trouble are being given what could look like privilege. Actually, the fact that they appear to have so much anger tells me they also have the same amount of ambition. I would like to tap into that with them,"* Don replied hopefully.

*"Don, I do have some experience with this type of situation. My brother, Paul, who will be here in the next day or so experiences the same mood swings. Actually, I really think that's one of the reasons he's coming to join us. He didn't really tell me why he got fired from the job at his law firm but I wouldn't be surprised to find out that his anger had something to do with it, so, sure, I'll help. Count me in,"* Nancy replied with only a bit of trepidation.

Once Don had released his concern about the possibilities inherent in this upcoming situation, he called it a night and headed back to his tent, leaving Nancy sitting alone at the end of the "conference table" processing everything that had happened.

She was aware that it was getting late, dark and wet outside the tent and she should most likely head to her own quarters. Yet, a niggling feeling kept creeping up and she didn't know what it was let alone what to do about it. The longer she sat in the chair, the stronger the sensation became.

Making a decision to follow its calling, she stood up and began walking to the tent flap just as she heard an elephant trumpet resound throughout the camp. It sounded very close yet she knew these great grey beasts wouldn't come so close to camp without reason and she had no idea where they were at that moment.

*Well, before you go out in the rain again, you might want to take a moment to congratulate yourself about your promotion and vote of confidence,* Nancy told herself. *It isn't every day that both members of management take you into their confidence. Give yourself a good pat on the back, girl.*

Having soaked in her personal adulation for a minute or two, Nancy began the sloppy path back to her tent looking toward the forest where she believed the elephants would have been calling from earlier. She stopped stock still in amazement.

The majority of the herd was standing only about fifty feet away all facing toward her. In front of the lead matriarch, Talish and Tusk stood in the downpour staring in her direction, as well. There was no sound and no movement. Nancy felt her background processing asking her how she could have forgotten their presence so completely during the last few hours. *Talk about absorbed in the moment!*

Not knowing what to do next, Nancy simply remained standing in the torrent, her feet half-buried in the wet mud. Though she was quite unaware of her physical condition, she was extremely conscious of the feelings within her. She wanted to run, dash right up to the herd, Talish and Tusk. The only mechanism holding her back was pure survival. Running in this slippery, muddy terrain would be risking her neck, at least an arm or leg.

So, she stood still and then she heard Talish in her mind, *"Are you ready? The simple initiation you went through in the tent tonight spoke to your authority. Now we give you our respect."*

# Question Twenty-eight
## What about religion?

When you speak about religion, you most often do so with reference to ME. Since I AM All That Is religion includes itself within ME though not in exactly the same way you may think.

Within the human consciousness exists a desire to know its origin within ME. Since your species developed within the earth from the ground up, it displays a natural derivative - looking "up" to the sky for the source of answers which it construes as ME. And, again, while I AM in the sky, sun and stars, it would be more precise to state they emerge within ME.

Due to the human need to exert influence over those of its kind, as your ancestors began to have what you would now call *mystical experiences* those with the strongest personalities used these occurrences to stand out within the perception of their particular tribe. The more they found this to be of benefit for them, the stronger became the compulsion to create and then deliver edicts and beliefs based upon their own authoritative position.

The earliest religious beliefs included beings that came to earth from other places and included them within their ideology. Some of these "non-earth" beings were seen as "gods" because they were able to fly in the sky harking back in your heritage to the first few humans who looked upward for answers.

While these star creatures are I AM in another form that appears different to you, they are not the agency previously believed. Any creature in form is an emanation of ME within ME as are you. There is no difference with the exception of ideology and evolution of the particular species.

Your present day religions emphasize each of their origin within ME as the one, true, official and only way to know ME. Within that belief lives the lie. There is no *one* way to know ME since I AM you and each of you has an opportunity to know ME as yourself.

Though you typically find yourself "running with the herd" rather than standing out among your compatriots, within your heart is the stronger desire to remove yourself from the constant onset of dictated creed and come to ME within your center. You experience a lack of fulfillment within your chosen religion due to its inability to "fill you full".

Religions live within time, coming, changing and going within the cycles of ages. While you might perceive a specific belief system being of ancient origin, you can only compare its inception based upon your mind's concept of time. I AM timeless so participating with ME *within* time ingrains a certain lack within you.

Stepping outside of time and space within your consciousness, you come to know ME without temple, church, priest and rabbi. Within the no-time no-space of ME, you experience your inception within ME and your arising, emerging as an emanation of ME. Is there more you could possibly wish to experience except ME as purely as your consciousness will allow?

Within you, *as* you, exists awareness of flowing within your original source. Due to the desire you perpetuate to be held in esteem within your "tribe", you bow to the characteristics delegated to you by the "herd master". Remaining distracted within the order, compulsions, habits, patterns and beliefs dictated *to* you, there is little time for silence allowing your experience of ME. While many of your religions offer periods of quiet within their tenets, the axiom stating only the religious leader can know ME prevents your human mind from acknowledging yourself as ME.

The driving force behind all religions is based within your concept of time. There is not enough *of* it so you must do as you are told to make the most of your time *here* in order to get *there* – wherever your belief says *there* may be. Within this concept lives another lie.

You are infinite. Your existence within earth is as a gentle sigh within ME.

When your need to adhere to the ultimatums offered by one set of suppositions or another is no longer within your consciousness, you will experience the freedom of ME. I know no ideology. I support no religion. Each and all of them emerge within ME. So, too, does the person doing dishes for a living, the executive and the woman washing her hair in the river. It is all the same.

Religion separates you from ME while intended to bring you closer. It is not possible to know your mergence within ME when you believe that I AM unreachable. Your structured dogmas instruct that you may only reach ME through their teachings and adherence to their principles. While you may learn and adhere, it does not bring you closer to ME rather it causes you to fear ME because of the apparent distance between US.

Within the teachings you have made a decision to embrace comes the threat of MY wrath, MY anger and MY vengeance. Structured by the threatening, wrathful, angry and vengeful human mind, religion then is an outcropping of the original need to exert authority over a tribe.

Invite yourself to step outside the dark cave of your own making. Release the bonds tying you to the lie of MY inaccessibility. If you desire to remain bound, know that I AM not and within ME, your boundaries are only within your own perception. You are free within ME.

## Story Time

As quickly as the elephants had appeared, so decisively did they disappear. One moment Nancy was standing in the rain being stared at by Talish, Tusk and the elephants and in the next moment the mirage had disappeared within the thick veil of the torrential rainstorm.

Shaking her head to come back to present time, Nancy realized she was soaked through and her feet were covered in mud. Trudging back to her tent, she wondered at the vision. *Was it real? Was the herd truly there together with its apparent guardians? And what did it mean, "give you our respect"?*

*Do I feel lack of respect,* Nancy wondered. *Did I conjure up this apparition to make myself feel better? I can't believe I would do something like that. It's just not like me.*

Nancy continued to muse about her recent journey into the mystical *(or was it?)* as she threw her filthy boots into the corner and peeled off her shirt and pants. *This rain has just got to stop,* she thought with dismay, *or I'll never be able to get these clothes washed and hung out to dry.*

Sitting down in her chair with a sigh, she began thinking about Paul and the discomfort of their youth. His outbursts of anger and rebellion led to many a schoolyard fight. Though he wasn't the bully of the gang, Paul had become viewed as the instigator of most of the trouble during lunchtime. He had spent as much time in the principal's office as he had in class.

*Well, this place will be a good change for him. The hard work combined with the male camaraderie is a chance for him to get his feet under him again. I should probably take some responsibility, own up and tell the crew about him tomorrow. In fact, I will.*

Sleep came easily as the rain continued to drum on the tent's roof and Nancy found herself in a dreamless state. Compared to the visionary dreams she had been having of late, this deeper sleep was exactly what was needed to restore her strength and self-confidence. It was going to be needed.

Silence startled Nancy awake, absolute silence. Darkness still pervaded the tent with no morning birds singing the sun into presence, a strange silence. The rain had stopped. The storm was past.

Nancy lay back down on her cot breathing an enormous sigh of relief. *I didn't know how tightly I was holding myself until I felt that breath,* she smilingly thought to herself.

Rummaging around in her belongings, she found the last pair of dry work pants and a slightly soiled shirt. *Somewhere in today's chores, I'll get some laundry done.* A slight curve of her lips let Nancy know how relieved she felt. Life was settling back down into a more normal pattern.

Striking out toward coffee and breakfast, Nancy saw Sam standing on the office deck motioning her toward him.

"Paul's on the telephone," he announced. "Sounds like he's on his way."

Picking up the receiver, Nancy felt her stomach tighten again. *That's interesting; wonder what that's about,* her background processing nudged its way into her consciousness.

*"Paul, hi, what's up?"*

*"I'm coming to you today, Nanc. There's a train leaving Cape Town at 10 this morning. I'll be there by nightfall. Sam tells me he can send someone to the train station to pick me up."*

*"Great, Paul, I'm so looking forward to seeing you. Was your stay in Cape Town good? Are you doing alright?"*

*"I had a good time, met some great people and really like Sam's Sandy. You'd love her, Nanc. She said she might come visit us at the reserve. Anyway, I'm going to hang up now and get ready for the train. See you soon."*

As Nancy put the receiver down, she checked in with her strident gut's voice. *What am I feeling that makes me so edgy? It all started with hearing that Paul was on the line. What is this?*

Forgoing coffee and breakfast, Nancy went back to her tent to ferret out these untimely, untidy feelings. She really didn't want to see Paul until she understood what her intuition was telling her.

*Okay, to a certain degree I feel free and kind of in charge a bit here. Paul has his own beliefs about life; heck, he's even got his belief in a God outside of him, very conservative in his rebellion. Am I afraid he's going to shake up my supposedly stable existence? Is he going to change the way the crew sees me? Will they think I'm like him? And, what about his anger?*

Nancy sat with these unusual meanderings traveling through her mind, finding every one of them settling repeatedly in her solar plexus.

*Do I think his machismo is going to overtake my authority? There are a lot of guys here who think as he does; even Don mentioned that we should start having church services. But what church? Is it really Paul's religious beliefs that are worrying me?*

Suddenly, in her mind's eye, Nancy saw the elephant herd, Talish and Tusk - and she felt threatened.

# Question Twenty-nine
## How do I differentiate between mind and heart?

The mind is demanding, judgmental and fearful. The heart suggests and waits, does not know judgment and is never fearful.

Your heart contains its own knowledge. It has its own brain and nervous system. Your heart stores the knowledge of what you really desire, what will bring you to a state of the greatest sense of peace and is only awaiting your attention to its information base.

Your mind relies upon knowledge instilled within it from your parents' beliefs, your schooling, religion, peer group pressures and interpretation of what your "past" experiences mean to you. It bases its reality upon survival, never quite sure if the decision it is making will result in a given set of circumstances or not.

Your heart experiences no such fear. It simply *knows* and when you allow it to guide you, you will find that your fears will dissolve within the encouraging arms of your heart's message.

As the voice of your soul, your heart has no specific desire for you. It follows the natural tendencies with which you incarnated into your present life and acts as a translator of what is "in your best interest" whether you know what that may be or not. Since most of the learning you have acquired has nothing to do with what is naturally "best" for you, rather expresses the interest of the person in authority over you, the results you perceive in your world rarely feel as though they are a "correct fit".

Your heart knows the frequency of life always seeking inherent, thriving coherency. The heart can flood your body with harmony when you place your intention on your well-being, when you pay attention to your heart's yearning.

Coherency is the equality within the top and bottom of your frequency wavelength. It is the foundational basis for Creator's manifestation of being.

Your coherent heart instructs your body how to manage its systems. Then you are aligned within all of your bodies. It responds to your sense of well-being. Remember, your body is an environment and every cell within you is reliant on that environment being aligned and balanced.

When you pay attention to your heart and breathe rhythmic, harmonious breaths, you establish a sense of peace within you. You become more aware of I AM from within your inherent yearnings.

Often, your mind says, "But, what about _____?" You can fill in the blank here. Your mind may be afraid that if you are not careful and fearful something "bad" will happen. This refers to the other experiences you have "had" from which you are basing your understanding of what is emerging in this moment.

As your heart and your body experience coherency, doors open to all other dimensions within ME because all life, all creation, responds to vitality. Energy and information respond to your resonant frequency.

You then become the doorway for multi-dimensional information and your coherent brain and mind are able to translate the information that comes through that doorway. And this applies to energy as well, you see, because information and energy work hand in hand.

This is your doorway to experiencing ME. The rhythm of your heart giving life also instills itself into your conscious awareness of ME.

The love emerging from within your heart is a natural vibration that is present when you are not in fear. Fear fuels all of the anger, hesitation, doubt, worry and pain. Love fuels peace of mind, trust, compassion, conscious awareness and communication. Sometimes it may feel like a big leap to agree to be filled with love. It is the experience of ME you are having - no more - no less.

What keeps you from listening to your heart? Lack of practice coupled with a support system in your culture that tells you that you should listen to your mind. It is so much easier to go with the crowd. And yet none of your leaders has ever had that luxury. The surprising fact is that in your present millennium everyone has the capacity to be that leader. All it takes is the willingness to surrender to the voice of the heart and to follow what you know really needs to be done rather than what the mass consciousness has pre-decided for you.

Every one of you is a physical as well as etheric form of ME. Your heart directs your course as you follow its nudges according to the most beneficial outcome for your soul expression. It is not difficult to listen to the urgings of your soul's voice through your heart. It is the most natural and easiest way to experience your expression as ME.

When your mind begins its tussle demanding, fearing, hoping and denying, then you know you are listening to a calculating, scheming voice. The murmuring of your holy heart includes no such plans, fears or schemes. It simply expresses itself as the true demonstration of MY Infinite Beneficence requesting you to formulate your decisions according to its quiet messaging system.

Differentiating between your heart and your mind is much the same as asking how to tell the difference between fear and love. Looked at from that perspective, you can easily answer your own query.

## Story Time

The day sped by due to the amount of work necessary to get the camp back into production mode. Sam assigned two of the newest camp members as laundry stewards much to Nancy's dismay. She hated having other people wash, dry and fold her clothes. It was never done to her satisfaction. Today it was not up for discussion since the storm had left the reserve in shambles and the fewer workers distracted with household duties the better.

Nancy immediately assumed her new responsibilities assisting Don in segmenting crewmembers into groups and assigning tasks. True to her nature, she joined up with a four-man team tackling one of the hardest jobs – reworking the dirt and gravel roadbeds back into traveling shape.

With the intensity of the labor augmented by the fact it felt like it would never get done due to the number of roads to re-work, she hardly noticed the time until the dinner bell rang and the crew came to a much-needed stop. Glancing at her watch, Nancy realized Paul would be arriving in a few hours. She put the thought aside until it was time to address it hurrying to join the men in consuming steaming plates of stew and homemade bread.

Don joined her at a table toward the back of the mess tent where she sat in near solitude with the exception of two others who were just finishing up and on their way out. This gave them a bit of privacy, exactly what Don was looking for since he wanted a short discussion with Nancy before Paul arrived.

"Nancy, I've put Paul in a tent at the end of the row across the road from you, the one that's been empty since that guy left right after you came. I thought being near you, but not too near you, would help him acclimate without being attached to his sister. Does that work for you?"

Nancy's first impression was absolute surprise since she wasn't used to Sam or Don asking how she felt about much of anything. To be concerned about her feelings with regard to Paul was a pleasant shocker.

"Yes, Don, that's fine. I'm not sure how Paul feels about living in a tent but he's about to find out. He's been pretty spoiled most of his life and was never one for camping. I was more the tomboy than he was overtly male.

"I don't mean he's feminine by any means, only that he's more Madison Avenue than African jungle. I was very surprised when he decided to join us. I don't know how long it will last, but we'll see, won't we? Thanks for asking though."

Don's expression told Nancy he was less concerned about her opinion than he was checking the status of Paul's ability to live in the "wild". No one had asked her what Paul's habits or preferences were and since few came to the reserve fully equipped to "go native", she figured Paul would be just like anybody else – unprepared. Though they were well taken care of by the chef and the other government officials who stopped by from time to time assuring that the crew wasn't too sorely oppressed, it was really more of a "make it or break it" situation. You came to the park, settled in and worked your butt off or you left. There were no other options.

Having fulfilled his personal mission, Don excused himself from the table and went over to check on Dan and Paul. They had been doing a pretty good job of keeping their noses clean and Nancy figured that soon they would be given additional responsibility to prove their worth. She was glad that was up to Don and not to her. She had enough on her mind with Paul, Talish, Tusk and the elephants. How she was going to combine all of them within her life was the next quandary.

Heading back toward her tent via the laundry, Nancy picked up her "folded" piles with an eye toward getting into clean clothes to meet Paul. In the distance, she spied one of the mother elephants with her baby as she prodded the youngster into pushing against a young umbrella tree to knock it over. She stopped to watch the natural progression of a mother teaching her young.

*This is how I should treat Paul,* she thought tenderly, *not as a mother but more as a coach when he gets here. I don't know what I'm afraid of about his arrival. My heart tells me I'm safe and my head demands me to be on the lookout, but for what I don't know. He's never done anything to hurt me. Does it have to do with how much I don't understand what's happening with my visions? Could it be that I'm afraid of nothing and am making this all up? Are Talish and Tusk as real as I think they are? What will Paul say if I tell him?*

Nancy's musings were interrupted by the sound of one of the utility trucks coming up the road just beyond the office. From her vantage point, she could see two people in the cab, the driver and Paul.

Hurrying to her tent, she threw her pile of clean clothes on her cot, pulled out clean pants and t-shirt, shrugged off her muddy boots trading them for sturdy, clean tennis shoes.

Once dressed, she sat down in her chair and took a breath composing her mind before walking over to the office to meet her brother. A puff of wind blew the tent flap open. Looking up she saw the baby elephant succeed in toppling the sapling. With great relish, he began to eat the nutritious leaves without as much as a glance at his mother.

# Question Thirty
## How do I find balance
## between enlightenment and 3D constrictions?

Every human being in a physical body within this dimension is there for only one reason: experience. So long as a soul inhabits a physical vehicle, experience is the result. It doesn't make any difference what occurs or does not occur, where you are located or with whom you live or are alone. This is what you are calling 3D or the third dimensional experience as though it were separate from your light within ME.

The teachings you are drawn to are the measure of your own desire for clarity in specific areas. If you find someone with whom you resonate, you can certainly learn from him or her. Simply don't mistake the teachings for an instantaneous life experience that is going to be transmitted to you.

You become aware alone requiring you to drop your mask, take off the backpack of beliefs, let loose the grasp on your spirituality and step forward into awareness of yourself as ME. It requires the decision to be infinite, without need of grounded foundation underfoot and without any claims to perceived past knowledge. Only then will the awareness of your natural enlightened state enter your inner silence without the need for developing new capacities or practices.

This transformative state often ushers in immense fear within the ego personality's concrete structures. The transfiguration being experienced is the most natural state of being yet you know it not in this form, hence fearing that you will lose yourself without boundaries encompassing your perceptions. When you let loose of the river's bank and allow ME to take over your flow, I become all of which you are aware highlighting past belief as an old story. It is a courageous act that you request of yourself. It is within the silence of the heart that you will find your perfect balance.

The arrival of enlightened awareness is inexplicable to the human mind. You cannot predict its advent; cannot foresee how you might bring it about for yourself. The fledging spirituality your mind believes its mainstay employs no arena for this understanding. One moment you believe in searching for enlightenment and the next moment you *know* you are enlightened. You are I AM and all else has disappeared. The observer within no longer exists. There is only I AM. You are simply aware, only aware.

As the part you are playing on the stage of the world increases in visibility, you become aware that you are now conscious of the part you are playing. Yes, you will continue to act out the words, actions and story of your script, yet now you do so consciously aware that it is only a role in an infinite play that I AM creating in form.

The stage upon which you perform your story begins to shift and change. Yet, rather than the setting changing, it is you. The years of desiring, the endless searching, the continual debates and attempted beliefs are now all behind you. The enlivened silence of your heart is all you are aware of in the newly emerging recognition radiating from within ME. The yearning, the longing that constantly shifted and changed within your mind has disappeared.

Balance within ME is without fear, confusion or chaos. While your bodies may tremble at the thought of it right now, when the awareness arrives, all shaking ceases in the firmness of MY Awareness. You are more alive than you have ever been, yet without attachment or need of that aliveness. You know your identity and it is I AM.

I AM eternally vast, infinitely peaceful. If you can name that which you are experiencing, it is not awareness of ME. The naming is yet another means of controlling the experience and calling it yours. The experience leaves you not knowing what you are, who you are, only *that* you are. All questioning has disappeared for answers are no longer needed

Here there is no past or future – only the present, and even that is without conscious name. Attempting to name the moment of your enlightened awareness is a trap of the mind. Do not set foot in that snare that awaits you. Engulf yourself in the vitality of the heart's silent rhythm – that and only that. It is within your heart that you will find the balance of living as enlightened spirit within physical form as ME.

If you fear you have not meditated enough, have not sought long enough, are not spiritual enough, throw away these useless thoughts. There is no prerequisite within ME.

The stillness pervading the silence is all there is within ME. It is inherently *life*. The mind is looking for a goal. It awaits an end to the journey. It wants to know where it is going. The silence has no such intention. The instant awareness of enlightenment ends the knowing unveiling an infinite state of being ME.

I AM already here. I exist within this moment. I am free, accessible and without need of anything. You have no conditions and request the same from your human mind, as well. Without conditions, enlightenment exposes itself within you as ME and you are free – free as the being that you believed you were pursuing yet have found without pursuit. I AM here – right now – right here.

As I AM, you require no balance between this dimension and your enlightenment. It is infinitely present.

## Story Time

*"Nancy,"* whispered Talish as she crawled under the rear tent wall, *"we need to speak before you meet with Paul, again.*

*"You have made many changes since he saw you last and while it isn't important that he understand them right now, it is important that* you *do. While we have been conversing in the dream world and you have had a few short experiences with your herd, we have only cracked open the egg, the door to your heart. When you set full eyes upon Paul this next time, within this space, you will create the same opening within him. I am here to describe to you how to handle his unraveling.*

*"No one in the camp will know what is occurring due to their lack of knowledge of Paul. They barely know you so you have been able to get away with much interaction no one knows as unusual for you. From their perspective, you are simply being who you are. Yet, you, Tusk and I know that you have been taxed to*

maintain normal human interaction as you have played among the spheres. Now you will be welcoming Paul into his own perceptions within those worlds, his extraordinary realities, without much warning and certainly no overt support.

"The last few weeks before Paul left to make his journey here, I visited him within his dreamtime to begin the transmission of information alleviating him of his physical attachment to his bodily reality. I know he has related some of this to you. He will tell you more eventually yet it is not the telling that is important rather your understanding of his lack of acumen in the realms.

"This is why I want to talk with you right now before you actually touch him. Your first embrace will create such an upsurge of awareness within him that he may lose consciousness. This is not because you are harming him only because he is not prepared for it and is very nervous, as are you. Know you are light as is Paul and use that memory, the spirit match.

"This step is a big one for you, Nancy, because you will be embracing this world for the two of you while you are both immersed within the ethers individually and collectively. If you are able to remain balanced, there is a very good chance that Paul will also have conscious experience of the event. He will only succumb to the strength of the wave if you are not able to hold it with him. Within this experience, you will be more than support for him, as you will be merging with him much as the two of you did before birth though you have no conscious memory of that, yet.

"Now let's talk about why this is happening. You and Paul have spent many different lives together. The two of you have played out many distinct roles and within this life, you made a decision to play the role of a woman giving him the chance to be the protective brother. This is not occurring and the script is being re-written.

"Remember that in the realm of the spirit there is no right or wrong occurrence, there is simply life. So the turn in the tide is no reflection upon whether the two of you are fulfilling a mission or whether you have made bad turns upon your trail.

"What has occurred is the two of you accelerating your individual learning through untold experiences you had not *counted on before arrival. You especially, Nancy, have churned up the milk of your soul in a very uplifting way. Of course, this implicates Paul's life structure since you were in previous agreement to have matching interactions together within this life.*

*"Again, remember that the world of spirit does not sit in judgment or expectation. It is in acceptance of what you are deciding moment-to-moment and now there is this. Do you have any questions up to this point?"*

Nancy's world rocked, quaked and then began to settle. Half of what Talish was saying made a bit of sense and the rest she needed a very long conversation to entangle. One moment she was getting ready to meet Paul, and with the next breath, she was thrown into a world beyond her mental comprehension.

*"Talish, I have so many questions that I can't even begin to ask them. We don't have time. I know by now that Paul is waiting for me. Please quickly finish what you absolutely have to tell me and we can agree to meet again to address my concerns. What else do I have to know before seeing Paul?"*

*"There is no way to access this information with speed, Little One. It comes in through me and then throughout you as deemed necessary in the moment of its hearing.*

*"You and Paul, if you decide to agree upon it, have before you an open road within a journey of your own making. Whether conscious of its arrival or not, it is here.*

*"You have seen me, talked with me and interacted with Tusk, your other self, and the elephants. All Paul is aware of is two strange dreams that he cannot forget. Our wise ones would say that you are 'opening the path before him'. Whether you continue to do so is up to him much more than it is your choice. Once the path of spirit is open, each must make the decision to walk the road. The light into the road becomes either a guiding source or an instigator of blindness. He must do the choosing and he must do it soon. There are actions needing to be taken that only you may take part in. If he will join you, the response to the actions will be double-fold. It is time for your meeting with Paul now. Go."*

## Question Thirty-one
## How do I pass up the temptations present on planet earth?

Why would you wish to "pass up the temptations of earth"? Are they not of ME? Why do you feel that you are being "tempted"? Could it be because you believe there is a right or wrong to which you must adhere?

The teachings that inform the belief you maintain about what is to be "given into" and what is to "be avoided" contain their own "temptations", that of attachment. To whose teachings have you committed yourself? Does the person representing your belief system about "being a spiritual being having a human experience" support your truth? If not, why are you committed to them? If so, how are you going to expand out of the perception of your attachment to that person? Are you passing up this "temptation" or giving into it because it appears spiritual to you?

The interpretation your mind uses to evaluate how "tempted" you are is based upon a false assumption. Equalizing head mentality with heart sequencing is undermining your efforts to know ME. What are you doing with the yearning in your heart that craves attention from your spirit? The heart is the voice of the soul asking you to follow the message that is urging you from within your heart. What are you doing to listen and then follow that message?

Guilt, blame, fear and reprisal fuel your belief within ME. Since you experience prohibitive control within aspects of your culture, you assign the same factors to MY Presence. How you fool yourself in that respect. I AM without judgment or blame of you. Creator does not emanate "temptations" in your path, the journey of experiencing within ME as ME.

When are you going to decide, make the commitment, to embrace fully the human body which escorts you through this experience you call life within ME? When are you going to stop wanting to go someplace else, not "stray into temptation" which does not exist? When are you going to come to the realization that there is absolutely nothing to be afraid of within your reality? Yes, you might even say you are *stuck* here because you are. Yet, you can be stuck or enjoying the carnival ride within ME. It is up to you.

Why do you believe you are being subjected to "temptation"? What does it mean to you? Does "temptation" mean you say words or take actions against your personal honor? That is not a "temptation". It is self-indulgence being blamed upon another situation perceived as temptation. All "else" simply *is* and you have assigned it a pejorative connotation and called it real. It is not.

How are you going to understand your enlightenment, comprehend your spiritual self within ME, become a living Master or hear the voice of your spirit unless you become comfortable within the body you are using in this creation of yours right now? Wanting to get away from or pass up what you have created means you don't like your creation. You can change that creation, you know. Actually, you are the only one who *can* because as the emanation of Creator you have full manifestation power. How are you going to change it?

The question you are asking here is your signpost of change. It is saying to you loud and clear, "It is time to shift how you experience your reality enabling you to feel the fulfillment of your own enlightenment." Once you have fulfilled yourself in this way, nothing will appear to be a "temptation" because the desires you now experience will be merged within the sacred light of living fully as you within ME.

There is very little you must presently do to make this shift. It is not a doing at all. You are requiring yourself to transform within your state of being enabling a perception of all experience as existing equally within the expression I AM. Within the transformation is existing freedom from the limitations you experience in a world filled with "temptations".

The beliefs you presently maintain shoring up your involvement in a world of "temptation" no longer serve or support you. Let them go. They no longer exist as an expression of ME within you. They are now outdated and useless.

Rather than feeling you must pass up enticement, decide whether the provocation is actually something you desire or something someone else has convinced you that you would enjoy. Your heart holds the answer to this question for you. Your heart will not ever betray you or lie to you. It is the strongest, surest guidepost within you within ME. Follow its course.

Changing and shifting how you view the reality in which you live right now will give you the chance and the opportunity to fine-tune the view of your personality's reality. Then, in its augmented state, you can bring your creation to the world – whatever the outcome might be. Once you do, when you look back, you will realize you did not ever want to "pass up temptation" at all. What you really wanted was to learn to accept it as *it is*, an emanation within ME in physical form.

## Story Time

Nancy tripped over the edge of the tent flap while attempting to exit gracefully from her instructional period with Talish. Every time she listened to that woman her perception of reality not only shifted, it nearly became extinct. This time in particular, when she was so sensitive about meeting Paul, she had been sorely tempted to try to stop Talish from continuing. Now she was glad she had listened. If anything strange happened upon their hugging each other "hello", she would be minimally ready for it.

*"Nancy, I couldn't wait to get here,"* Paul exclaimed as he continued running toward her. He had seen her clumsy exit out of the tent, remembering how much fun he used to make of her when they were younger. This memory stirred up a whole host of brotherly love symptoms that would best be expressed by a hug and kiss.

As Paul's distance from Nancy became less, it also slowed down in perceived time, the air "thickening" between them as their energy fields converged. Each of them experienced their footsteps barely rising and falling in earth gravity until they were within one yard of each other. At that point, their energy envelopes snapped into place causing Nancy to stop in her tracks with arms outstretched to catch Paul's fall. Without a doubt, she knew it was coming.

One more step forward and Paul transposed position from vertical to horizontal completely missing Nancy's attempt to catch him. She broke his fall just before he hit the ground by sliding her right arm under his chest and lowering him more easily downward. The weight and momentum of his gravitational pull took her with him, slamming her down where she found herself on her back with an arm pinned underneath Paul's neck.

Before she had a chance to open her eyes, which had closed spontaneously upon impact, the world became very dark and she felt herself being drawn into a vortex. The dizziness overcame her and she let go into it even though in the far distance she could hear people calling her name. Down, down, down, she swirled.

Suddenly the world was bright with translucent light. She was standing upright facing Paul who was smiling at her with the biggest grin she had ever witnessed on his face.

*"Well, here we are. Bet you're surprised. I know I am. You know that Talish woman told me this could happen when she came to me in my dreams a while back. To be exact, she told me I 'would fall of my own accord when the time is ripe for picking'. At first, I didn't know what she was talking about but on the plane trip over here, I sat next to an older man from Matabeleland and we got to talking. Eventually, I asked him if that phrase meant anything to him and he told me that it was an ancient phrase meaning 'the fruit is ripe for the picking'."*

Seemed Paul was going to do the talking here and since Nancy had absolutely no idea what was going on, she stood silently listening.

*"Then when I got to Sandy's in Cape Town, I was sitting at dinner one night and a couple approached me. It was a fine looking pair, I'll admit. Turned out they were sister and brother. The woman had been eyeing me from the far side of the restaurant since it was so apparent I was alone. Her brother brought her over to introduce her to me. After the introductions, he sat down next to me and looking deeply into my eyes, he said, 'You may continue on this path with my sister as you are tempted to do or you may fall from the tree like the ripest of fruits.' With that, he stood up, walked over to the entrance and watched for*

my decision. I didn't think for more than a minute and then knew I hadn't come all this way to have a fling so I told his sister goodnight, paid my bill and left the restaurant.

"That night when I fell asleep I had a very strange dream. I was meeting you here and I couldn't walk toward you. It felt like I was stuck to the ground. As I was held in place within the dream world, I began to see myself in a lifetime as a woman named Ann. It felt very unfulfilling and incomplete. The Ann me was waving to the Paul me saying, 'When you fall, go down hard or you won't be able to get up again.' Then I woke up.

"Now we are here and I let myself fall hard when I felt the time and space shift we created together. I have no idea what is going on but I do know that I am following all of the signals that appear as signposts along the way. Everything that I have been up to this point feels like it has led me to this very moment with you. And, like I said, I don't know where this is taking us but I do know I'll go with whatever happens."

This soliloquy stunned Nancy almost as much as being knocked out by Paul's fall. She was beginning to realize that she had read Talish's description of Paul's state of mind incorrectly. When Talish had said Paul had to make some choices perhaps she didn't know that Paul had already made at least one. *Maybe this medicine woman isn't all seeing after all.*

"Paul, I have a lot to tell you. It doesn't have to be said now. I have a few more pieces to put into this puzzle. I must admit you have surprised me. I didn't know you would be able to surrender to what is happening so easily . . . ."

Before Nancy could finish her sentence, ammonia was being wafted under her nose and people were pulling Paul off her. She opened her eyes to see Sam, Don and half a dozen of the crew standing over her looking very concerned. Paul's eyes were still closed and Don had gone over to him with the smelling salts as well. *I don't know what's up next,* Nancy thought, *but I'm definitely not telling anyone about what just happened.*

## Question Thirty-two
## How do I best raise my vibration in my life in general?

Raise your vibration? Now there's an interesting thought. Do you actually know what you mean by it?

Usually you think of "raising your vibration" to mean "become more spiritual" or "more blissful" or "happier". Seldom does a human desire to experience a raise of vibration as a greater awareness of ME.

I will talk about what you mean first and then what you can actually do with what you do not know you are asking. Understanding what you are requesting will immediately move you from "raising your vibration in your life in general" to "how do I best know myself as YOU?"

Those of you who have made a decision, conscious or not, to follow what you believe is a spiritual life vs. a more material, physical life have separated yourself from those who have not made the same choice. They are the "other". They are not of "like mind" and don't usually understand what you are talking about, thus they are of a "lower vibration" within your perception.

When you desire to use a practice or a technique to raise your frequency, it is because you believe that a higher frequency is a better one. Waves of energy are neither higher nor lower. It is possible for them to be faster or slower yet that does not make them more or less spiritual. Energy simply is and in its natural state is neutral within ME.

Your desire to raise your vibration will not serve you in anyway at all until you understand fully what you are asking to experience. Your heart desires to remain firmly anchored within the awareness of MY Presence. You may consider this a "raised" vibration when it really is comprised of ME, that and only that.

The concept you believe in, relating to changing your frequency, requires a bit of fine-tuning. It can point you in the direction you are seeking yet it does not fulfill that which is sought. What is your idea of a raised vibration? Does it feel better than you feel now? Or does it feel more receptive and open to experiencing ME?

The qualities you admire in those you believe have high frequencies are simply resonating mirrors requesting you to open yourself to the same energy wave. Again, it is not a better or worse situation rather a refined alignment within your inner core opening your awareness into an infinite expansion of I AM.

Focusing your attention upon ME will allow you to feel and then physically experience what I mean by aligning with ME. Your constant distraction from within a spiritual practice furthering your belief in achieving a state of vibration will only continue to serve your lack of concentration within and upon ME.

As more human beings come to the Self-realization that the idea of living in an illusion is illusory within itself then the idea of raising or lowering your frequency will no longer apply within your life. In fewer words, you will be free as I AM.

It is important to keep focused upon living your life within ME. Diversion in any direction is simply part of the process of being in existence. Know it as part of the enlightened experience, coming to terms with what you are rather than seeking for ways to become something that you are unable to define. What is a raised vibration?

If you were vibrating a little *faster*, not higher, life would be experienced in a different way. Resonating with this understanding of being ME shifts perception of your life experience. Everything glows, grows and expands within this concept and understanding of that which is possible.

Divining your awareness within ME of you requires you to set aside time in your busy, distracted schedule to do so. If your chattering mind wants to dialogue with you, let it. It is as much a part of ME as the remainder of you. Welcoming your mind's contribution to your silent time will encourage it to be silent, as well. First, it wants to be heard.

While you sit in stillness, you may wish to contemplate what you believe raising your vibration is supposed to do for you. Will it make you more aware of ME? Until you know what the phrase truly means, you cannot answer the question because your response will be based upon your belief about what a raised vibration is supposed to be.

Did you come to this query on your own or did you read somewhere that raising your vibration would be a "good thing" to do? Someone somewhere has informed you that increasing your oscillation will make you feel and appear more spiritual. It doesn't mean it is true. It simply signifies that you made a decision to believe in it, making it true for you. The energy you are attempting to increase doesn't know it as true since energy is neutral. It doesn't care.

Ultimately, the idea of a raised vibration is your own folly leading you nowhere. Dissolve this false concept into the truth of your heart. Move away from attempting to do something that is not possible because it maintains no validity within ME and direct your focus upon the potential within you of knowing ME as I AM.

When the direction of your attention is based upon what you know rather than what someone else told you, you experience the freedom of living within I AM.

## Story Time

*"Nancy, what happened,"* Paul shouted, now on his feet and totally bewildered.

*"Did you fall on me? I started walking toward you and then I felt us falling together. That's all I remember. Wow, this is some welcome!"*

Nancy was more puzzled about Paul's words than what had just happened. He obviously wasn't remembering anything he had told her. *Well, enough of that for now,* she admonished herself, *let's get him to his tent and away from all of these prying eyes.*

*"Paul, you must have stumbled. When you fell, I tried to catch you and we both fell down. I think we bumped our heads together, knocking us out for a few minutes. Let's get you to your tent and after you rest up a bit, I'll show you around. Sam, did you have anything you needed Paul for right away? Can I show him*

*where he's going to be staying?"* Nancy fumbled her way through diffusing an otherwise untenable situation.

*"Sure, Nancy, that sounds like a good idea. We can introduce him around at dinner. Get him settled in,"* Sam replied happily distancing himself from this unexpected turn of events.

*"Great, come on Paul, follow me. I'll take you to your new home."* Nancy proceeded to lead Paul down the row of tents to the last space left of the road. It was one of the coveted spots since its placement had only one other tent on its north side and the south wall was open to the evening breezes.

Entering through the flap, Paul threw the bag he had almost left behind on the road onto the single cot and collapsed in the folding chair.

*"How are you feeling now?"* Nancy said attempting to insert herself into Paul's thoughts.

*"Fine, I think. My head hurts a little. I must have landed hard. How are you?"*

*"I'm good. I caught you with my arm and that's why we both went down. I didn't get hurt, just a little shaken. Do you remember anything else about the fall, Paul?"*

*"No, not really, what else is there to remember?"*

Nancy took a deep breath weighing whether to dive into this conversation now or wait until later. *If I wait until later, when will that be? We'll get involved in work and then I'll have to find another time to talk with him. Now's as good a time as any, I suppose.*

*"Paul, when we landed on the ground together it was more than you tripping. We shifted dimensions. You might say that we changed frequencies and moved into another parallel world. During the short time we were there, you did most of the talking. You told me about a visit from Talish and a meeting with a woman and her brother in Cape Town. You also explained that you keep hearing a phrase about you being fruit that is ready to drop. In fact, you were told to drop hard and you did – when you fell with me. Do you remember any of that?"* Nancy held her breath without any idea about what to expect next.

*"You've got to be kidding!"* Paul exclaimed. *"How did you know about all of that? We've hardly talked at all before I got on*

the plane. This is amazing because that's what's been happening. I wasn't sure whether I was going to tell you about it or not. It's been one mystery after another ever since I made the decision to come join you. Now it's even more mysterious because you know about everything I was going to say and I haven't said a word. What's going on here?"

Before Nancy could answer Paul, Talish appeared in the doorway. Paul nearly fell out of his chair. He had thought she was a dream, a mirage or vision he had conjured up out of stress.

*"Well Paul, seems you made it. And it appears you've told Nancy pretty much all there was for you to tell from within that dream world the two of you jumped into then. That was inventive of you and not unlike what you'll be experiencing from here on out. But you didn't tell her anything about how you learned to float among dimensions or about your focusing capabilities. Saving that for later?"* Talish opened the conversation with a taunt.

*"Oh, my lord, you're real. All this time I thought you were a figment of my imagination and here you are. Do you live here? Has Nancy seen you before? What are you doing here? How do you know so much about me? Why is all of this happening?"*

Talish began laughing with Nancy joining in spite of herself. Paul was so perplexed that he had lost all of his corporate lawyer composure appearing more like a child with a new, unexpected pony.

*"One question and answer at a time and all in proper timing, young man,"* Talish addressed Paul like an old grandmother. *"First, I want to tell you both how pleased I am to have you here together. It has been many moons of waiting I have done, not knowing if you would find your way to me. Now that you have joined up on this land and in this time, we are going to complete a journey begun when the earth was young and new. For right now, why don't the two of you get used to being Nancy and Paul together again before we separate your awareness in many different ways."*

# Question Thirty-three
## How can I experience freedom?

You will not feel free so long as you are burdened by imposed limitations within the physical illusion of earth. And I really mean everything in your life, because every person, place, situation, object or desire you believe is important to you is not important in the way you *believe* it is. You only think each of them might be because of some benefit you believe you will gain from it, him, her or them.

If you don't experience the contributions you consider necessary to a "fulfilled" life, you are very distressed, unhappy and generally frustrated in general. Something is wrong! You deserve to have everything you are told you should want because, after all, isn't that why you are here? To have all of this along with what you prefer to call the "spiritual life" (they're not separate, you know).

Do you realize that everything is window dressing – yes, *everything*. From your beloved relationship to the food you put in your mouth, you have created an attachment to what you believe is due you and when you don't "get it", you feel under-served, left out and generally miserable. What would you say to all the extraneous accoutrements being just that – extraneous? What if these were negotiable points in your life when you are free? What if, they came easily once freedom was put first? What if, as I AM, all you have to do is let go of "knowing" to be free?

Do you have to lose everything you believe is yours to experience this freedom? The answer: You don't need to lose the "thing". You want to lose your attachment, your *need* for the *thing*. You are then free. In that freedom do you recognize your enlightened state within ME.

You have to be willing to walk away from the *need* for the person, place or thing you are tied to thereby losing your attachment to it. This doesn't mean you have to leave your family or your job or anything else. What it *does* mean is you have to be *willing* to walk away from what you believe your family, job, friends *mean* to you so that you can see what they actually *represent* in your life. You can work within this negotiable tenet. It is easily recognized when you begin to dismantle all of the confusion you have allowed to build up regarding your attachments within earth.

Freedom in your heart, mind and soul means letting go of the need to have the same desires as your parents or authority figures and creating an entirely new template of understanding for your life. This means that you take the time to sit down and look at how you are living within ME, what little tendrils of attachment have ultimately connected you to all of the weights in your life and simply take that pair of divine scissors and snip them away – free.

Ask yourself these questions: What do I need to do to experience freedom in my life? What am I willing to give up in order to be emancipated? Do I know that my authentic view of myself is equivalent to being free? This is your enlightenment, liberation.

You are then free. You are unfettered as I AM. Whatever else you desire becomes superfluous and you see it as such. Now life becomes fun because you no longer feel the need to be attached to him, her or it. Everyone and everything are simply in your life floating on the wings of freedom you have created by releasing them into their own liberated enlightenment.

This is exactly how to experience freedom from the burdens, attachments and justifications you have created throughout your long life that seem to be "keeping you bound". These are the obstructions keeping you from sitting joyously on your own mountaintop; stopping you from enjoying the view 360 degrees in all directions, in resonance with all manifestation within the freedom I AM.

What you will discover from this vantage point is how unknowable true freedom is within the constructs of your human mind. As soon as your mental faculties attach onto any person, situation or object, you begin to lose your sense of liberty. It, therefore, can be a very fleeting experience unless you remain focused upon your yearning to be free.

The most beneficial condition to maintain is the release of your past memories and your inhibitions about what the future might produce for you within ME. Relieving yourself of the domination you presently believe is necessary in order to control your expression and experience is the very foundation of freedom.

If you will accept the prospect of being free from your beliefs and attachments, you will find all of your boundaries disappearing. When limitation no longer draws you, your desire to be free will also dissolve since you will only know your own liberation.

Check carefully into every aspect within you within ME for the ideologies you are holding in place enabling you to appear spiritual in your own eyes or within the perception of another. Each attribute binding you limits your flow. It is this feeling within you that has fostered this present question.

As you diffuse the constructs of your personal attachments, you may find other humans drifting away from you. Do not fear this experience. These people only leave your environment because they are afraid of their own freedom. Seeing it upwelling within you suggests the possibility of the same opportunity within their reality. If they are not ready to embrace their own enlightened liberty, they will head for the bounded beliefs they feel will support their limitation. You remain free within ME. They will free themselves in their perfect moment within ME.

## Story Time

No sooner had Talish finished talking than she turned around and disappeared from within Paul's tent. Nancy and he looked at each other with confusion threading its way through their trepidation.

*"This woman turns up at the darnedest times,"* Paul announced shaking his head. *"How can you feel safe or private when someone's always looking over your shoulder, even when you're dreaming? Has she always done this? You seem to know her better than I do."*

*"This is pretty much her style and I've almost gotten used to it,"* Nancy almost reassured him.

She was secretly glad that Talish had shown up right away instead of making an entrance after Paul had asked too many questions. There were so many irreconcilable aspects of this situation and Paul, being a lawyer, could have a habit of inquiring long and hard as though she was on the witness stand.

Nancy decided it was time to change the subject, knowing of course, this also could be subject to change. Making the rounds of the camp would ground Paul and get him up and moving after having hit his head.

*"How about taking a tour of this place with me?"* she suggested enthusiastically. *"You need to get to know the other folks and also get acquainted with the whereabouts of the various multi-purpose tents. With the exception of the office and the laundry, everything here is enclosed in canvas walls, even the shower and bathrooms. It seems there wasn't enough money to go around when this reserve was put in place. You'll get used to it after a while."*

Having forewarned him about what he might run into, Nancy led Paul out of the tent and down the road pointing out her own "home", the mess tent, the laundry building and where everyone else lived down the road from him.

The next logical stop was Sam and the office so Nancy began to head in that direction. Up to this point Paul had made little, if no, comment. Now he chirped up.

*"Are we going to the office and talk to Sam now?"* he asked in a querulous voice.

*"Well, I thought that would be the next step, yes. Why do you ask?"* Nancy replied sensing his anxiety. *What is* this *about?*

*"I want to talk with you before we go in so is there a place we can sit where no one else is likely to hear?"*

*"Sure, let's just go back to my place. It's not far and hardly anyone ever comes to see me. We'll probably be safe."*

Once inside her tent Nancy felt more in control of the situation, whatever that might be, since she was on her own turf. Being surrounded by her belongings gave her a sense of authority and it was feeling like it could be necessary.

"Okay, Paul, shoot. What's up?" She was ready for just about anything.

Paul looked up at her, as he was getting comfortable in her one chair. His discomfort was more than obvious.

"Why don't you sit down on the cot across from me? This is sort of hard to say and I want to be able to look straight at you when I tell you this," Paul requested as several drops of sweat beaded up above his left eye.

"Okay, that's better. Now we're at eye level. What I have to say might make you tell me to leave and if that's what's going to happen, fine. I just have to get this off my chest.

"When I said I would come here I didn't necessarily mean to work. My life had gotten so constricted at the law firm that I was making one mistake after another. All I wanted was freedom and I couldn't see any way to get it. Obviously, I worked myself into a corner and got what I was looking for by being fired.

"As soon as I didn't have a job I began to panic. Where was I going to get money? How was I going to live? It hasn't been easy knowing I was coming here because I didn't have anywhere else to go. If I hadn't left my apartment when I did, I would have ended up being evicted. I couldn't even pay my rent.

"Now here I am and I don't really want to work. I just want to wander around and be free to figure out what's next for me. I'm smart, got a lot of training and skills. There has to be some job I can do that won't get me angry or so mad that I can't function. I just don't know what it is and I don't know how to find out.

"So, now I'm feeling useless, worthless and irresponsible. I just wanted to tell you this before we started talking to Sam because I know I owe him and he's going to want me to work. I'll do it. It's just that I don't want to and eventually it's going to show. So, what do you think now?"

Nancy wasn't surprised. Her sixth sense had told her something was amiss ever since her first conversation with her brother. Now it was out and she was relieved. This was easily resolved. Paul would have to work to pay off the debt he incurred with Sam via the favor with Sandy in Cape Town. Once he got involved in some good, physical labor, nature would take its course. All she had to do was stay out of the way, keep her head down and be quiet.

# Question Thirty-four
## How can I help others on their journey?

I will begin by asking you a few questions in return. How can you help them to do *what*? Help them, why? For what reason do you wish to help someone?

The normal concept most "spiritually driven" human beings believe is the manifestation of being of service or helping. While this is an admirable trait among your peers, it is vaguely useless from the standpoint of being ME in form.

No one can help anyone on his or her journey since no one else knows another person's course. Since every human being only experiences "reality" subjectively, anyone wishing to help or assist another person is applying filters to the event. Once the personal lens is applied to any experience, no assistance is possible since the person performing the "helpful" deed is doing it for him or herself.

Much as those of you who volunteer through various charity organizations to assist animals, the dying or those in any type of crisis do so believing you are being of service, so too those of you who want to help another on their journey do these actions for yourself. You may believe your action is altruistic yet if you sat down and looked deeply into your motivation, you would quickly realize you are doing what makes you feel of benefit and you are - you are of benefit to yourself.

Anytime you desire to help someone, ask yourself first why you wish to do so. Your answer may be that they "obviously" need help or they even might have asked for it. If it is your decision that help is needed in a situation, why do you believe it is true? If someone asks for assistance, what is he or she really asking you to contribute?

Let's look at these two questions separately:

Have you decided someone needs help within the journey? Why have you made this decision? You will most likely say that they look like they are having a hard time or you wouldn't want to "be in their shoes".

Ponder on this: If a person broke a leg, had it set and used crutches to walk while strengthening the leg, would you pick that person up and carry him or her around because it appeared to be difficult to walk with a crutch? If so, the leg would never strengthen and you would be of no service to them. In fact, you would be of disservice.

When you observe a person living their life (their journey) and you decide they need help, you are picking them up to carry them when they need to strengthen themselves. Add that picture to the fact that what you see is only seen through the very hazy lens of your own personal fears and filters and you will arrive at only one conclusion – you need the same type of help you believe the other person needs and you are projecting it upon them. If that were not true, you would let them experience the effects of their journey without interfering.

Has someone asked you for assistance within the journey? They exist within ME. If you have been asked to help, why did they ask you? What do they believe you are able to give them that they cannot give themselves?

Again, another parable helps and it is an old one in your culture: You can go to the river and catch a fish to feed a person. Or you can take that same person to the river, put the fishing rod in his or her hand and teach the art of fishing so food will always be plentiful. The only problem with teaching a person to fish is that you are no longer able to help them. This state of affairs won't allow you to feel better about yourself so you seldom take this route.

If someone asks you for help in any way, ask first what is expected of you. Don't jump in with both feet ready to provide what you believe they need. You do not know their experience within ME and you will not ever know. Unless you ask them to be very specific in the description of their need, you will be unable to assist in any way that bears any meaning for them.

It is always possible to be kind, compassionate and friendly with all physical representations within ME. Comporting yourself in such a manner so as to recognize ME in every human being you meet is the best method you may access to assist another within the journey. Note that not included in this list is figuring out what you believe they need in life. It is not your responsibility to discern what only the other person already knows.

Remember that every feeling, thought, word and action you take within ME is for you. No matter how much you believe it is for another, it never is nor will it be. You only experience for your own soul record. The person you wish to help experiences for his or her soul recording.

I know your cultures believe it is marvelous to assist another person. You believe it is true as well. Since the belief is so firmly rooted within your memory, you will continue to attempt to help others within their journeys despite what I AM telling you here.

Simply remember that when you hand the bowl of soup to the hungry person, you are feeding ME. Since you are nourishing ME, you are feeding yourself. There is no other. There is no other person to assist within a journey. Each of you "travels" within ME, as ME, and can only help yourself to understand your own place within that which you call your journey. Help yourself if you wish to help another.

## Story Time

Heading toward the small 8x10 frame office building (one of the two actual constructed structures in the camp), Nancy remained silent. She wasn't sure if Paul was going to say more, whether she should interject any thoughts or comments and definitely didn't want to open up a can of worms when the lid seemed to have re-sealed itself.

The mud was just beginning to dry up and there were still many ruts in the unpaved road. Though she and the crew had worked most of the day to get it squared away, they had barely scratched the surface. Now with twilight arriving, visual acuity was dimming. Nancy definitely didn't want a reenactment of the day's events so she kept a good grip on Paul's arm as they skirted their way around the lumps and bumps.

Silence finally drove her to speak and she chose general conditions in the camp, which felt much safer than personal issues. There was certainly enough to fill Paul in about when it came to all of the things that happened here. Plus, he would be getting a good chance to start collecting his own "war stories" beginning tomorrow morning.

*"You know, Paul, I'm sure you experienced how dark it gets here at night when you were in Cape Town, but it's different out here in the bush. Once the sun completely sets, it's like someone drew a curtain and all the light just disappears. I keep a small flashlight in my pocket at all times because of that one thing and you're going to want to do the same. You definitely don't want get stuck out here with no light."*

*"Oh, I'm sure I'll be able to take care of myself well enough, Nanc, but thanks for your concern. I brought two flashlights with me and a couple spare batteries so I'll be fine. Don't 'mother hen' me, if you don't mind. I'm a big boy now,"* Paul replied summoning up his usual more forceful demeanor.

*"Okay,"* Nancy acquiesced, *"I'll quit the big sister act but I do want to ask you this one question before we go inside and talk with Sam. Are you going to tell him the truth about how you feel or are you going to let him think you're all gung-ho about working with us? I need to know if I'm going to support you."*

*"I don't want help and I don't need your assistance or support. Just be quiet and let me do the talking. This is going to be man-to-man and if I didn't already know you'd insist on being included in the discussion, I'd tell you to wait outside the office. In any event, you don't need to say anything. This is about me, not you,"* Paul brushed her off while walking in front and opening the door before Nancy could respond or reach the entrance first.

Sam was sitting behind his desk with his feet propped up on a wooden crate sipping on whiskey out of a chipped, smudged glass. He looked up, surprised to be having evening visitors and quickly sat upright.

*"Oh, it's just you two. Wondered when you'd get around to me. Are you feeling all right after your rather comical collision earlier? Thought we might have to take one of you into town with*

*a concussion from the looks of how hard you fell. Good to see you on your feet."*

Paul responded immediately leaving Nancy no room for remarks or assurances. *"We're fine, Sam, thanks for asking. Just a couple of little bumps and they don't mean a thing. Thought I'd come over and talk to you about what's expected of me now that I'm here. Is this a good time?"*

*"Now's as good'a time as any,"* Sam nearly slurred his words. He really hadn't expected to see Paul until the morning.

Continuing, Sam began to explain Paul's role as junior crewmember. *"You'll spend the first day observing each of the crews that go out. I'll have you shadow one group in the morning, another right after lunch and the third from mid-afternoon break until suppertime. We work in three crews every day and rotate the job positions. Once you've had a chance to see what's required, we can insert you into a team on the following day.*

*"The work is pretty hard when we're breaking new ground and tapers off into moderate maintenance once territory has been established. The reserve's about half completed and we still have a lot of acreage to clear and fence. The idea's to make trails through the bush so taking care of everything is easier down the line. The fencing speaks for itself and we have over fifteen square miles still to go. The temporary line that is up does the job to keep the herds in but it doesn't do anything to keep the poachers out, as Nancy can attest."*

She had stood silently listening. The best support she could give Paul was by not saying anything and letting him handle the situation he had created for himself. The last comment Sam made almost untied her tongue but she fought back the urge.

*"Sounds good to me, Sam. I'm a great observer and I'll let you know which team I'd like to work with as soon as I have a chance to meet everyone,"* Paul suggested authoritatively.

*"Well, Paul, as much as I appreciate your honesty, I'm the boss here and I'll be assigning you to the crew I want you to work with, not the other way around. Now if the two of you will excuse me, I've some work to attend to before bed. I'll see you in the morning."* They had been dismissed.

## Question Thirty-five
## How do I help people understand
## they need assistance to be in balance?

People need help to become balanced? Who told you that concept? Where did your belief arise from and why do you believe it?

The summation of all your possible concepts involves a sense of diminution of the human being and his or her personal capacities. It may be more accurate to say that you believe balance cannot be achieved without assistance and, therefore, *you* are out of harmony because you have not received enough help.

The filters you use to demonstrate your beliefs are emerging from within your frequency. You cannot see past them until you make a decision that all is in perfect homeostasis as it is because all dwells within ME. The current understanding among your peers would be the exact opposite because of their attachment to incoherency.

Coherence is the underlying principle of all systems within your dimension. Resonance and harmony are the result. Using two people as an example, the two bodies do not need to be exactly the same frequency of vibration to be in harmony. They each *do* need to be in a *stable phase* relationship within themselves.

While a coherent person can influence an incoherent energy stream to a minute degree, it is the consciousness of the incongruent person that has to change to bring him or her into balance. Another person cannot do this for another and no amount of help will make this so. As each exists within ME, each is perfect in the moment of experience and a belief that assistance is needed for balance is not true.

An authentic state of well-being felt throughout your system creates a state of coherency that floods your field with the coherent light that emits from within you and is absorbed by you within ME. A state of incoherency creates disruption within the phase of frequency. It is disconnected, out of alignment with the status of your natural world and out of resonance with that which is coherent and thriving in your environment.

Yet, you have no way to determine what is coherent and incoherent except by the feeling occurring within you. That perception is colored by your beliefs, expectations, anticipations and present experience. The moment's evidence is based on your past memories and your hope for your future. You can see by these three statements that you have no way to determine whether another person is balanced or not, therefore you have no way to determine what type of assistance they would need.

Contemplating another's requirements is a typical human adjustment to his or her personal imbalance. When you are coherent and in harmony with yourself, you see nothing but the flow of life within all that occurs within ME. Rather than believing that another needs help to be in balance, you perceive him or her as simply *being* as they are within ME and accept them as such.

Whether you are willing to revise your conceptual observations regarding others will be determined by the willingness within you to experience surrender as I AM. No judgment, opinion or point of view assists another to find equilibrium. Rather, it stimulates the incoherency you believe is present because once you place your attention upon what you interpret as existing, you bring it into resonance with consciousness. The transmission of your judgment upon another emphasizes your filtered perception and observation rather than assisting in bringing more balance into the situation.

Your heart, as the voice of your soul, is constantly emitting frequencies that are read by your physiology as it adjusts its balanced status. Speaking for your soul, your heart knows what feeling, thought, word and action (or inaction) is best suited to your soul's expression on a moment-to-moment basis. When you resist the heart's urging, its intrinsic message, relying instead upon the conditioned patterns of your brain waves, you set up a stressful pattern within your body creating incoherency.

This includes the observation of imbalance within another. You cannot view something without increasing your union within it. Since each of you exists within ME, there is no separation between what you are experiencing and what you are observing. You can become conscious of your innate connection by the feelings that emerge within you upon being with someone you consider out of balance. Rather than the belief you are to assist them to become more coherent, check your own energy signature and keep your attention focused upon it.

You know what it feels like to want to express from your heart and yet fight the urge because the fear within your mind is screaming at you out of its mass mind conditioning. It's a habit. And, since the mass conscious support is based upon fear and all that follows in its traumatic wake, it is easier to cave in to the brain's terror than to silence it by turning your attention and focus to the promptings of your sacred heart.

Living a life centered upon your emergence within ME is all that is required to experience your personal state of balance. Once that is your expression, no one else will be observed as needing assistance because you will not be looking for anyone or anything to fix. All is perfect within ME. Know that and only that and you will experience your own personal, perfect balance.

## Story Time

The walk back to their tents was a very silent one. Nancy was determined to keep her mouth shut. It was obvious Paul was struggling with his "anger demons" and she had been on the receiving end more than once in their youth. It was much better to let him sort it out alone than attempt to help him find any peace.

They arrived at her tent long before his and he absent-mindedly nodded his head to her as she turned in its direction. Watching him walk on, Nancy was glad to see Paul reach into his pocket, bring out a flashlight and turn it on to its brightest setting in the enveloping darkness. She remembered all too well how many times she had stumbled home after a hard day's work until she got in the consistent habit of carrying a light with her.

Once inside her tent, Nancy began getting ready for bed although a deep sense of disquiet was prodding her for attention. It was only moments into untying her boots that she heard angry shouting coming from down the road. It was Paul's voice mixed with two others harder to identify. Quickly re-lacing her boot strings, she grabbed her flashlight and headed out through the tent flap just in time to see Paul's light go flying through the air.

Fastening her beam in the general direction of the noise, she saw a fury of fist-o-cuffs going on although the only person she definitely knew was involved was her brother. As her pupils enlarged letting in more of the minimal night light, she recognized Dan and the other Paul as the remainder of the angry trinity. The latter two were going at it, while her brother Paul was on the receiving end of a real pounding though she had no idea why.

Running in their direction, she heard feet pounding behind her and turning to look over her shoulder saw Don coming in her direction. He, too, had heard the commotion and was racing to see what was going on. The two of them reached the point of action together with Don pulling Dan off of Paul and yelling at the other Paul to stop.

The impact and significance of this set of circumstances was not lost on Nancy. Paul hadn't been in camp for even one day and his anger was surging to the surface. At least, that is what she believed was happening.

Don's size and presence calmed the situation down and through the heaving chests, gasping for air Nancy could hear words that she attempted to assemble into some sort of sense.

*"If only you . . ."* followed by *"I didn't mean . . ."* and then from her brother, *"I was only . . ."*

None of it sounded logical and it was apparent that until the three contestants could talk without gulping oxygen no one would understand what had provoked the fight.

Don took charge in his inimitable way by asserting his authority over the camp and demanding, *"I want to know right now why the three of you are causing all this noise. Who's fighting whom and for what? And don't give me some story that you'll be sorry you cooked up later because I'll find out the truth one way or the other."*

Dan was the first one to speak up, obviously worried about their probationary status and seeking to remedy the situation quickly.

*"Paul and I were having words. Nancy's brother was walking down the road just about the time that this Paul here hit me square in the jaw. Paul #2 tried to pull him off and he turned to sock him, too. Then it became more of a free-for-all because I tried to stop Nancy's brother from getting hit again and got the wind knocked out of me. That's the truth. I swear it."*

Don looked at the other two for confirmation and got a general head nod from them. Though rather unconvincing, it seemed they were ready to agree.

*"I'm going to let you two off with a warning,"* Don addressed the offending pair, *"and as for you, Paul, welcome to the camp. Thanks for attempting to stop something that could've gotten a lot worse. Glad to see you didn't get hurt too bad."*

With those rather fruitless words, Don turned and disappeared into the dark knowing the way back to his tent without the need for light. Nancy stood incredulous. Paul had actually prevented an antagonistic situation from getting worse rather than being the instigator which, she had to admit to herself, was her first thought.

Embarrassed by her inner feelings, Nancy offered to walk Paul to his tent while the other two combatants wandered off to lick their wounds.

*"No, thanks, I'm fine. That was interesting. Seeing those two reminded me of myself. That's how I've always been – angry and easily provoked. It's ugly, downright repugnant. And to think that only moments before I was in the middle of a real rage because of the way Sam talked to me. Goes to show that you never know what's around the corner. See you tomorrow."*

With those words, Paul turned and trod off to his tent mimicking Don's lack of need for light. Nancy watched him go sensing a turning point. She didn't know what it was but Paul had definitely shifted something inside himself – and without her help. *Maybe he doesn't need watching over as much as I thought.*

## Question Thirty-six
## Do I always fulfill my soul's purpose?

The answer to your question is "yes" and "no". Yes, because you are always full – filling your soul and no, because there is not a specific purpose you are incarnated to fulfill.

Your soul is similar to a container and the record of all you have experienced since its inception within ME as Creator. Development through every incarnation is recorded within your soul as ME.

Your soul's potential is activated by thought. All endeavors are included within your soul as it is enriched and expanded into the conscious awareness of itself as light within ME. The soul functions within the frequency of your present reality plane, the dimension of duality and contrast. Soul force or substance is infinite, indestructible, vibrating at an ever-evolving rate of vibration within ME.

Your soul united within your human body at conception. When it leaves your body, it does not die. It cannot cease to exist. It simply cannot remain in the earth plane without means of material manifestation so it must return to the realm of "light" within ME. While in form, the soul is always aware of itself as I AM. All earth-manifested souls are in constant union with all "others" and within ME.

When you express as conscious awareness you know your existence as soul. You realize yourself *as* ME, one great cell within MY Being.

This record bears the impression of your every thought or activity written within time and space. The energy expended in the activity leaves an imprint within the etheric waves causing the creation of a memory recording in the time and space continuum. Just as the words on this page convey images, so does the energy of your soul as it goes about its activities leave an image.

Since your soul acts as a record of all experience within form or not in form yet always within ME, it has no specific purpose from one life to another except to gather experience. You may make "soul decisions" before entering this life and then recreate them once you are here. There is no defined purpose for your life, except what attracts you moment to moment.

Your soul is encoded or written upon by thoughts, choices, emotions and actions. Through these impressions, the soul experience expands bringing you into conscious awareness dependent upon your free will choice within each breath.

Your soul is not only a storage device for that which is considered "past experience"; it also holds all of the possibilities for the future-future. It contains the potential for all lives you are living within ME. The experiences already recorded within your soul, the wisdom and knowledge contained therein are the impetus for the potential contained within the learning. Through thoughts, words and actions you delve into personal potential. Through free will choice, the next movement is impressed within the soul.

The qualities within your soul can bring about almost instantaneous illumination, the awareness of what you refer to as your "enlightenment". You experience life through your soul embodied within ME and the realization of this experience "lights you up" as an energetic form.

As your soul continually expands into multiple planes of consciousness, it initiates certain experiences within each earthly incarnation. These experiences in the world of matter create a sense of separation from the world of spirit in order to fulfill certain desires ultimately reflecting the reality and subsequent expansion of each individual within ME.

Each soul animating a physical body forms a part of a group soul. Each soul contributes its essence, its own unique contribution to the group. The collective experience of the group soul ultimately informs the oneness of spirit due to consciousness aligning itself within awareness within ME.

As conscious awareness, you always have the opportunity to refine your alignment within ME. You are able to do so through the attention you place upon ME. Whatever you choose as your present adventure is a delight to your soul and thereby becomes its "purpose". It glories in manifesting every desire of your heart and fulfilling any wish you yearn for within your life, viewing it as the expansion of your consciousness.

Rather than believing that you are here to fulfill some specific purpose, perhaps you would enjoy living the thrill of being ME in form, having an opportunity to share the marvelous opportunities of earth life while contributing your expansion into the whole. There is no choice that is right or wrong except within the interpretation you give it through the concepts you claim as your own. There is no judgment and no judge. Your purpose is the aspiration you deem suitable within the moment of its choosing.

One of the most glorious aspects about being in form in a world of contrast is the constant free will choice moments. If you release the idea that you need to perform in a specific manner, you will begin to realize you are living as the light of human wisdom carrying MY Signature as expression.

What could be more thrilling than to never know from one moment to the next what is going to *be* for you dependent upon your choice? No purpose *is* your purpose. Live it as such within ME.

## Story Time

No sooner had Nancy's head hit the pillow with the blanket pulled up to her chin than she was asleep. It had been a very exciting and busy day. Her body and mind were longing for the release of sleep.

Within the dream world, Talish appeared draped in a lion-skin cloak and little else. Her honey-toned skin shone in the bright light of natural radiance.

*"Nancy, today is a turning point and I am going to use your dream time to set you up for what is about to occur. As you know, I told you that you are a portal for Paul through which he will come to know himself. This applies not only to him, but also to you. As this opening within the void of the spirit, you employ the same effects for yourself as you transmit within Paul's consciousness.*

*"The time has come for the two of you to begin a daily journey with me into areas of consciousness that usually takes years to achieve. I have spent my entire life acquiring the skills I*

now use to project myself into your awareness and to inform Paul as he dreams, as well. He is not sharing this world with us at present, yet he will be doing so in the future-future. There are many aspects you both need to become familiar with to understand the experience and for your personal safety.

"The realm of consciousness, using your terms, in my tribe we would call it the world of atam, is multi-layered in so many directions that it is of no service in this moment to attempt to describe them. Simply know this as I go forward with this learning time.

"You have had an opportunity to visit a select few of these dimensions by allowing me to shift your perception. There was one moment when you were leaving the forest after the flood incident that you nearly crossed over by yourself. I watched to see if you would do it automatically yet you did not which means that you are not quite ready for that leap. Once you stand upon the edge of that cliff, there will be no turning back.

"The choice is made by you moment to moment within the realm of atam which also houses what you call your soul. We would call it the atam-um as an extension of atam-atma that arises with one idea of itself. Consciously you experience yourself as an individual, one human being in a body. This you are not. You are countless human beings within that body of yours yet you know it not. That is what I am going to explain to you tonight.

"I cannot even begin to tell you how many levels of reality you have entered throughout all time. We cannot count that which has no beginning and no end. What we are going to concentrate upon tonight is the direction you want to focus upon for the next few lessons of consciousness travel allowing you and Paul to remember what you are to each other.

"Why this is important is not for your knowing right now. It will become more obvious as time goes on. For the moment, simply know that the two of you have come into bodies together at least one thousand times, by my counting. We are going to concentrate on about four of those experiences creating a new effect within your atam.

"Being here in this land rather than attempting to do this within one of your cities is absolutely essential. The distractions and noise of the many people living so close together in city life set up energy waves that are impossible to overcome when you are not in form. You find yourself merging with others that are curious about your appearing within their life stream whether you want to be there or not. You and Paul created an option before coming into your bodies that if possible, you would find each other in this land and so you have.

"It is made even more significant, as you will learn later, since you have both been here before in several other lives. We will be visiting those within consciousness, the universal atam, and we will be inscribing this experience within your individual records, your atam.

"What is important for you to know tonight and to remember when you awaken is that you are not who you believe yourself to be. You might look like Nancy, act and talk like her yet you are a multi-person who will soon be living as that multiple of personalities. The reason you must remember this before it happens is because you will be practicing choosing which personality you will use day-to-day and moment-to-moment.

"Others in your world are going to find the experience very unusual if you do not learn how to control which of your life streams shows up within any given situation. The same can be said of Paul yet he is going to learn more through observing you than by personal experience at the beginning. Once he begins to understand how the dimensional choices work, then he will become very adept at it since he's done this before, as have you.

"I am going to close now with this information since it is enough for you to begin remembering. I will be close by from now on and you will be seeing me turn up from time to time when you might least expect me. Now as I shift out of your dream reality, I leave you with a set of words to use as a reminder. Remember them. They are:  Atam Atma, which in your language means 'I AM'."

## Question Thirty-seven
## Why does it feel so hard to be here?

Every human being experiences a sense of contention and resistance to being in a plane that feels like separation. The desire to re-member what you are within ME is more than a yearning. It feels much more like an unfulfilled drive that you have no hope of achieving. From the moment the physical body slides out of the birth canal, the very first physiological impression is loss and separation.

Impression number two is survival through alerting everyone in the room that separation and fear are being experienced. It will never feel the same way within form as it feels out of form no matter which dimension you decide to incarnate within as ME. Security will not be as secure, safety as safe. The womb's protective fluid shell is gone . . . never to return.

In its place is the possibility of freedom once you get used to having a body to use within this very short experience of duality. You chose it. You said, *"Give me a human body and I'll go to earth and create magnificent experiences."* And here you are in earth!

Eventually, you begin to understand: I AM an "I"! You are you! So with this new energy bombarding you, you learn that whatever you wish to give power to through your feelings and thoughts will become real, virtually instantaneously and you feel the energetic effect of it as you continue to mature.

All limitations are off and your little feet began the grand exploration. Forgotten is the sense of fear in the delight and glory of discovering this world. You see yourself standing tall in your divinity in complete perfection, living life in absolute delight, embracing, expecting the desires within you to be in your reality.

As you begin going to school, the place of many rules, peer group pressure, right and wrong, proving yourself as capable as the next child, bringing home good grades, life begins to change within ME. The separation between you and the "other" becomes very distinct and, unless you measure up, you feel as though you are an outcast. To a certain degree, you believe it is true. You lose trust in yourself because you have given it away.

So now, here you are – mature, grown up and "living life" or so it seems. The separation is intense because all of the years between being natural and this moment are now filled with a magnification of "not enough", "not good enough" and "unable to live up to expectations". Indeed, you feel separate from everything in your world, most of all yourself. You are seeking conscious union with ME, and not finding it in physicality; you experience life as "hard".

What is missing in your life and why it feels so difficult is because you have lost the ability to trust yourself, the same trust you had when you were so young and letting each new distraction attract you. Now, always, there is an authority. Always, there is someone to become like, something to change, something to control, and always, there is the comparative mind, the mind that says *this* is better than *that*; *this* is preferable to *that*.

Here lives judgment, separation and a constant sense of resistance to what is. It prevents the possibility of being comfortable in your own skin. It stops you from feeling connected to others. It creates adversity, polarity and the world of black and white. Judgment, fear, lack of trust – these are the fibers that weave the veil of illusion together. There is judgment about your presence, judgment about absence, judgment about the seen and unseen and, of course, there is the wish to become something other than what you are - not realizing that you and I ARE always in union.

Beneath it all is this belief that you are alone, without permanent support and that it will always be this way. It feels very hard and it is not true.

"Lifting the veil", realizing your union within ME, is simply replacing judgment, fear and lack of trust with no need to judge, no need to fear and absolute trust in you. Remember, back at the beginning, when you decided to come to earth and enjoy it all? With the removal of the veil of forgetting, you remember why you came. You remember yourself, meaning you remember ME.

When you do this, nothing feels hard at all because it is all effortless.

This is the signal you have moved from forgetting to remembering, the effortlessness of life. When all is in flow, you are rejoicing within each breath because you know you are within existence in union with ME. Nothing is easier, more natural and simple.

Your human mind has made life complex and difficult. Actually, the more sophisticated and intricate your reality is the happier your mind feels because then it has something to play with, to unravel. When you surrender to the simplicity of being alive as ME, within ME and place your attention nowhere else, you will no longer believe that life is hard in any way. It will appear so easy and uncomplicated you will begin to remember why you came to earth to begin with rather than wishing you were not here.

Remember that every feeling you have in this moment creates the next experience and this includes your transition out of this life. If it's hard in earth, it will be hard beyond earth. If it is easy in earth, it will be easy no matter where you find yourself. You are the divine travel director and infinity is the destination.

## Story Time

Nancy awoke with a start as the blazing rays of dawn pierced the crease in the tent's door flap. *Wow! That was some dream! It always feels like I'm* there *rather than in the dream world when Talish comes to talk with me. I wonder if she visited Paul, too. I wonder if I should ask him, probably not.*

Heading to the mess tent for coffee and something to fill her empty stomach, she met up with Paul right from the start. *Well, this is one way to start the day. What's my apprehension about? I don't know what I'm feeling.*

*"Nancy, great night – slept like a log. How about you? Did you get some sleep?"* Paul inquired while falling into step with her on the rugged surface of the rain-washed road. He mentioned nothing about the evening's altercation.

*"Yep, thanks. Slept well and I'm ready to work. We've got so much to do after the storm. You know, I'm so glad you're here no matter what the outcome. We can certainly use another set of hands."*

Grabbing coffee and a donut the two siblings marched over to the office to get Paul's orders from Sam. Nancy didn't really have to accompany him, but she was curious how this was going to work and he didn't seem to mind.

Once inside the office, Sam made short work of the assignment process. Paul would spend the morning with Don's crew working on the fence lines, the post-lunch period on Nancy's crew continuing the clearing of the forest and after mid-break, he would join Sam's group leveling roads. The day was hot, the sun thirsty for their sweat and Sam was ready to get everyone moving.

Heading out to their various assignment areas, Paul turned for just one moment to look deeply into Nancy's eyes. Her gut tightened knowing she couldn't pretend when it came to interactions with Paul. Sometimes this was hard.

Paul was ready to play with her head and she could read the signal loud and clear as he said, half under his breath, *"You know, Nanc, you can't hide from me and lying won't help. Those lives she was talking about last night, they're going to show us a lot. I might just stick around for the show."* With that, he left to join Don on the fence line, leaving her slack-jawed and standing alone.

The morning progressed at its usual routine tempo as Nancy and her crew waded into the demolished forest floor, pulling branches out from under downed trees, chain-sawing trunks into manageable pieces and carving a path for the tractor to pull the wood out into the open clearing. She was so absorbed in the work with sweat swimming before her eyes most of the time that she didn't notice the unusual hush that had fallen over the jungle.

Quietly, the entire crew came to rest. Everyone was sensing an oncoming "something" and no one knew what it was though their natural animal instincts were on alert. Fortunately for the group, they were used to listening and waiting. Africa had made every member of her crew a veteran to knowing that the five senses were their best friends and would bring them into complete union with the natural world.

Nancy was the first to hear and respond. She wasn't sure if the noise she heard was in this dimension or a call from Talish. All she did know was that she could hear a distorted moaning and a subdued crunching of leaves. Following the sound through the trees, she was soon lost to the sight of the others due to the density of the trees.

Nearly one hundred yards from where they were working she found the source of the muffled whimper. A baby elephant, attacked by a lion, was lying in a shallow with its mother standing over it. The damage to the baby was severe. Obviously, the mother had run the lion off evidenced by blood on her tusks and a set of claw marks on her shoulder.

Her child was in much worse condition with a ripped belly, entrails beginning to emerge and a gouged eye socket. He was still alive though barely. *If I can get to him and get some help, we could take him out of here and sew him up. The mother would never let me get that close. I'll probably get killed for even trying.*

Nancy's desire to save the injured infant was quickly overcoming her better sense. She took several steps toward the depression where the mother stood guard waiting for the ear-flapping signals that would tell her a charge was eminent. No sign of disturbance was forthcoming. The mother stood over her baby swaying as her stomach rumbled support.

Just then, Nancy heard several of the crew converging behind her. She turned quickly motioning with her hand for them to stop. They quickly obeyed upon seeing the size of the elephant being challenged. She nudged closer and the rumbling in the mother's stomach deepened. Now she was within touching distance of the baby. *Do I dare reach out to him,* she wondered surprisingly unafraid.

As Nancy got down on her knees to be closer to the baby giving her a better look at his injuries, she watched in amazement as the mother surrendered ground giving her room to work. The gash in his lower abdomen wasn't as bad as it had looked at first glance. *This is fixable,* she thought with relief keeping one eye on the enormous beast only steps away from her. *If I can get a couple of the crew to make a litter, we can pull this little one to safety; that is if we don't all get trampled.*

## Question Thirty-eight
## I want to make big changes in what
## appears to be a perfect life. How do I do this?

When you hold more than one idea about an aspect of life, it creates what humans call *cognitive dissonance*. You state that your life appears perfect yet it is *not* or you would not want to alter your experience. You are living within self-created discord. This means your experience is clashing with your expectations. What you believe is true is not what you see playing out in life – yours or anybody else's – including the world. It creates an *uneasy* feeling because your mind is constantly looking for that which resonates with your beliefs about life. When this doesn't happen, you feel out of sorts, uncomfortable and uneasy.

This is the first change you have to make. You must shift the way you "see" life if you are going to be able to resonate with any change, small or large. So long as you remain in the position of wanting, you will remain in the position of wanting. The frequency of your physiology must match the wave you wish to "be". In other words, you must *be now* what you wish to experience in your future within ME.

One of the first things people do in relieving cognitive dissonance is attempt to justify what they are feeling and that usually results in blaming someone else, hence actually denying having taken part in creating the disruption. Yet this is only a salve to the situation – it is a band- aid over a large sore that wants to be aired out and healed.

Since you desire change within your life, your mind is going to play this game with you. It will tell you that a transformation is necessary because of this person, that situation, or a set of circumstances with which you are no longer happy. Be aware of these inklings cropping up within your mind because they will be the undoing of your choice in frequency by disrupting the coherency of your inherent wavelength.

Allow the natural discomfort you are feeling inside of you to become an opportunity to make changes – in everything, all of your life. So long as you're pretending that everything is fine so that you look a certain way to a specific group of people, you're only adding fuel to an all-consuming fire of deception. You add to the disinformation of the masses when you give yourself away by not saying what is really on your mind, in your heart and, quite literally, in the air.

To bring these changes into your experience, you must first be able to define them within ME. Remain in union with your emergence within I AM as you carve out a new frame of reference for your life. Remove from your mental constructs any ideas you may entertain about what other people or circumstances have to do with where you find yourself in this present moment. Observe every situation as an opportunity to experience yourself anew within ME.

Stop looking for places, people and concepts to secure your freedom from any fear, anxiety, stress and general turmoil. Making changes within you is always an "inside job". No one else can even begin to do this for you or with you. Become fully responsible for every action in your life. The very thought you are having right now is creating the future you are going to experience within ME in what you call the "days ahead". If you can wrap your mind around the idea that only you create everything in your life, then you begin to see there is nothing outside of you whatsoever that will ever be able to give you what you are looking for in any way.

You must first decide how you want to change, what you need to do to make the shift, be it and then do it. As you muse about the transformation of yourself, feel into your body to experience how the change arises first as feeling, then thought. Once you have the coherency of the experience, you can concretize it within your reality.

The key to coming into balance with this concept is to realize that whatever you are seeking is exactly what you want to stop seeking and bring into your conscious awareness the fact that it *exists already within ME*. You enter into contact with your ego personality and your Self, your aspect of ME in form. This means the ego personality blends consciously as one within ME so you see everything you are doing as an aspect of ME bringing balance and understanding to your purpose in life without fear or apprehension. Having removed any fear from the enterprise, you are free to change yourself as you see fit.

This balance I'm talking about is one of recognition. It is recognizing how you are living your life. It's coming to the understanding that if you want to live in a different way, if you are going to bring about the changes in your world you say you want, you have to use your life as the receptacle of information, as the transmitter and receiver of information about you. Remember, that information is impartial, pervasive, all compassing and completely impersonal. *It does not care. You do.*

There are all sorts of things your mind is going to say, "Oh no, no, no, this is essential. You must do this; you must do that." Yet if you will navigate as you would in water, if you will allow yourself to move away from the material particles of life you believe are holding you back, you're going to find the actualization of your future as the emanation of Creator you are within ME. You will realize the future you think is *out there* is only *potential* from the standpoint of your information being the source of the future's outcome.

## Story Time

Despite Nancy's attention being almost fully upon the baby elephant, she was keeping gut-reaction tabs on the mother since she had no way of knowing when she might go too far within the larger elephant's estimation. There was literally no room for error, since there was no room to move away from the situation should it go awry.

Two of the crew members were approaching very slowly yet their presence was causing some concern within mother elephant. Her trunk was curling up over her head as though getting ready to launch a defense. Barely moving her own head, Nancy tucked her right hand behind her motioning them away. Gratefully, she could hear the scraping of their feet against the rocks as they slid carefully backward.

*Well, if I can't get anyone to help me, this isn't going to work,* she thought knowing that voicing anything aloud would signal the end of the present truce. *I absolutely have to be able to move this creature if I'm going to help him. I certainly can't do it by myself.*

As she crouched over the panting baby, the crunch of yet another set of boots came from a completely different direction. Directly behind the adult elephant and slightly to Nancy's left, someone was approaching. She knew this was the end of the tentative comfort zone barely maintained. Reflexively she felt her legs tense, getting ready to run, if possible, to avoid what was surely to come.

Glancing up as the unknown person exited the tree line, Nancy nearly lost her balance recognizing Paul sauntering over as though he owned the forest. She put her hand up to stop his approach and he waved her away easily. Continuing toward the mother, he put out both hands and began making soft shushing sounds deep in his throat. *Where did he learn that?* Nancy thought, still ready to flee.

As Paul reached the rear quarters of the mother elephant, he put his hand on her shriveled, lizard-like skin and began rubbing her as though giving a massage. Meanwhile, he kept up the guttural sounds emerging from within his throat. To Nancy's utter amazement, the elephant responded with definitive stomach rumbles. *They're talking to each other. How does he know to do this?*

When Paul reached her head, the mother turned toward him and wrapped the end of her trunk around his arm. She lowered her head much like a pet dog would for a scratch between the ears and that was exactly what she got except the rubbing was at the top of her trunk where it entered her skull. Nancy watched as the elephant's eyes closed and she released a sigh in relaxation.

*"Nancy, please do as I tell you right now and nothing except that,"* Paul moved from throat sound to English verbiage.

*"Tell the three guys standing behind you in the forest to come over here. Four of you can lift the baby as far as the trees where you can make a litter and cart him out of here. It will be hard but you can do it. I will stay with mom and she will continue to respond to me so long as you are quick about this. Don't dally,*

*girl. Get going,"* Paul finished with some frustration at Nancy's open-mouthed lack of response.

Nancy turned halfway around and signaled the three young men who stood trembling in the shadows to come to her. Reluctantly, they obeyed moving much slower than she would have liked. Once they were within easy speaking distance, she told them that the four of them were going to attempt to carry the baby elephant into the trees outside of the view of the mother. Though it was obvious they didn't like this idea, they continued to move forward in compliance.

Once within easy reach of the baby, they each knelt down next to Nancy, one at the trunk, one at the tail, one opposite Nancy at the back.

*"On the count of three, I want you all to reach down and put your arms underneath the animal. Once we are positioned, I will count to three again and we will lift and carry. You've practiced this in emergency training with humans now just shift it over to this creature. I will be walking backward so I'll have the most difficult time. Therefore, I will set the pace. Keep up with me and, for heaven's sake, don't drop him,"* Nancy gave her orders quickly and succinctly. *No one must know how nervous I am,* she thought as she felt the sweat running down the back of her neck.

*"Okay, 1, 2, 3, position. Take a breath. Breathe again. Now 1, 2, 3 lift."*

They were up and barely moving before Nancy realized that Paul was still standing there stroking the mother who now glued her attention upon her departing baby. The elephant began to take a step toward them and Paul again rumbled in his throat while positioning himself directly in front of her. If she were going to charge, he would get the brunt of it.

Nancy couldn't watch and walk, too, so she decided to leave the mother up to Paul who, for some reason, seemed to know what he was doing. She continued taking small, quick steps backward until she felt the shadow of the trees hitting her dripping back. Her muscles ached for relief. *Well, we're almost into the dense forest again. It feels a bit safer now though I don't know how Paul is going to get out of this one.*

As they reached inside the edge of the trees, Nancy took a quick glance up to see Paul leading the mother patiently beside him. They were coming toward her.

# Question Thirty-nine
## What is in the Akashic Record?

You are surrounded by and immersed within a conscious, living, pulsing, brilliant energy. It is an intelligence of infinite and nonlocal capability within ME. Everything is comprised of vibration, even solid matter. Your physicists call the particles that make up the vibration "wave particles". These wave particles contain information, all contained within ME. Thoughts, actions and feelings continue to exist long after you have forgotten about them. Many of you call the place this energy is stored the Akashic Record or Akashic Field. It is incorporated within the soul and the soul within it.

This impression or record not only contains a history of the soul and all of its events, it also connects with every being. Here is the impetus for your archetypes, the stories contained within myths and the origin of symbolic language within all of your cultures. This field exists everywhere infinitely within ME.

Sometimes you refer to your energy information within ME as light. Light is energy as information so this field is an infinite field of information as well as energy. It contains the history and experience of all matter.

Your science defines a field as a condition in space with the potential of producing a force. Charges within the field create a condition in the space around it so that the other charge feels a force. This creation within ME is filled with fields that create forces that interact with each other. Within these universal force fields reside your notion of space and time totally interdependent within each other.

Your idea of a field is composed of energy that is a force or power manifesting in wavelengths of different frequency. The energy carries information that is a pattern, form or structure. The frequency of the information is created by how many times the energy oscillates in a given time period in your space. The form unfolds itself through a process of emergence within Creator, a non-linear experience for all sharing the field. This is the teamwork of the soul (information) and the spirit (energy) within ME.

Each piece of every field is an entire part of the whole and non-local within ME. Each portion impacts every other piece creating a unified experience for all. Each time an experience is shared, attention is brought to it. This enforces itself within all and attracts more of the same vibration to the awareness of each person.

Within what you identify as the Akashic Field is every experience ever occurring through ME as streaming forth within Creator. One aspect of the emanation within ME is your soul and all that it holds from the moment of its inception through Creator to the present time in which you are able to read these words.

The various attributes of every life you are living (remember there is no time or space within this realm of which I AM speaking) are existent within the Akashic Field as information. You might view it as a network extending infinitely in every direction you can imagine containing every aspect of every feeling, thought, word or action you would say you *have had*, *are having* or *will have*.

Or you might imagine one of your computers that is keeping track of *every* event, *every* thought, *every* feeling that has *ever* occurred, *is* occurring or *will* occur. This computer would not only keep track of words and sounds, it would also provide a picture for the viewer to see relating to each event. Something like this computer does exist, only it is not a computer. It is what you label as the Akashic Record.

Many of you believe this record contains a positive or negative condition relating to what you call karma. This is not true. There is no imbalance within ME in need of correction and there is no feeling, thought, word or deed in need of punishment.

Rather than believing your experiences cause an interchange of good or bad realize that all energetic fields within ME are neutral. The Akashic Field underlies your space and time containing the memory of the universe in what you perceive as a holographic form – union.

Your science would say it is a quantum sea of fluctuating atoms, galaxies, solar systems, living beings foundationed within consciousness. Every thought, word, feeling and action is contained within this living memory, including all that is considered the past, present and/or future. It is the encyclopedia of life for all that exists within ME.

Hence, the universe informs itself through the memory contained within it. What you consider your intuition, sensing without physical senses, knowing without physical knowledge all delve into this living record. It is the dynamic ordering of the universe flowing from within Creator as ME. It is consciously available to all that exists within it. Tapping into the Akashic Field of the soul allows you to re-write that which is not the past, create the future in the present and live a wisdom-filled life in this moment.

If you wonder what is in the Akashic Field pertaining to you, sit in the silence of MY Presence and look into the most natural attributes of your individuation. Within your present form is contained all experiences you are living that comprise your portion of the Akashic Record. Since it exists outside of time, it is present for you right now within ME.

## Story Time

It took very little time for the crew to prepare a litter for the infant elephant since all of the equipment necessary was present due to their brush clearing in the forest. Arnie, Jack and Joe cut up limbs, tied them with twine and made a sturdy, comfortable bed for transport.

Nancy kept the little one quiet though it was not much work since his pain threshold was maintaining a natural state of dazed torpidity so natural in dramatically injured animals. More than having to keep her eye on him, she was mesmerized by Paul and the mother standing watch over them as though it were the most natural thing in the world to be doing.

*I'll talk to Paul about this when it's all over,* she nervously thought to herself. *I can't believe this is happening.* Pinching herself to make sure she was still awake, Nancy realized that, indeed, this was a physical experience. *This is really happening* and *with Paul in the middle of the jungle, no less.*

"*Arnie,*" Nancy called by way of staying in charge of the situation, "*run ahead and find Don. He's supposed to be working on the fence lines somewhere. He was a medic when he served in the army and he's the nearest thing to a doctor that we've got. We're going to need him. And, for heaven's sake, tell everyone to be quiet and stay out of the way. I don't want mama over here to get rambunctious.*"

Arnie ran off to do as he was told while Jack, Joe and Nancy gingerly lifted the baby elephant onto the litter tying him loosely with more twine so he wouldn't inadvertently wiggle off. Meanwhile, Paul and mother elephant stood by rumbling, stroking, and nudging with every intention of walking straight into the middle of the campgrounds.

It took all of their combined strength to pull the litter over the cluttered forest floor. Nancy and Joe held the front much like a pair of mules tied to a wagon with Jack bringing up the rear steering the bottom of the tied limbs over the rugged ground. Plodding along behind, Paul and mother elephant brought up the train's caboose without getting too close for the litter bearers' comfort.

About seventy paces into their journey, Nancy and Joe began to experience a shift in the litter's gravity. It felt as though someone else had appeared to help carry the dead weight of the helpless animal. Nancy didn't turn around right away, because she thought she was just getting used to pulling it. When she finally felt that it was becoming much too easy, she looked over her left shoulder and nearly lost her grip when the sight before her met her eyes.

Right behind her, yet almost ephemeral in presence, Talish was walking with one arm firmly looped through the side branch of the litter. Glancing to the right, Nancy saw Tusk holding the same position parallel to Talish. *No wonder the weight is less! There are more people helping to pull,* she thought as though, for a moment, this was a natural occurrence.

It wasn't until she began to feel herself consciously disassemble that she realized they were stepping out of normal time and space and into that "in between place", the one Talish was always talking about. Within the same moment of her awareness, Paul and the mother elephant plodded past them pushing aside bushes and brush, taking the lead without stopping for even a moment to acknowledge their presence.

Shaking her head to clear her vision, Nancy realized that though it was Paul in front of them, he was no longer wearing his work clothes. In fact, he was wearing very little at all. Clothed in a soft leather loincloth and with black, brown and ivory beads hanging around his neck, he walked barefoot through the thorns, rocks and jagged limbs scattered on the forest floor as if they were not there.

It didn't take long for Nancy to realize that she, too, was no longer in her work pants and shirt, only wearing similar clothing to that of Paul. Looking at Joe and Jack, she couldn't recognize the two crewmembers that had originally been pulling the litter with her and saw, instead, two dark natives who felt familiar yet remained unnamed in her consciousness. Talish and Tusk seemed as they customarily did as they all continued the journey to what she believed would be the park reserve camp.

Not wanting to stop the momentum they had gained, Nancy didn't ask for a halt to the procession. Instead, she decided to attempt to reach Talish telepathically, a first for her since Talish was usually the one making the original communication connection.

"*Talish, what is happening?*" she began tentatively. "*We're not who we were. Are we where we were? Is the camp ahead?*"

"*Good work, Nancy. That was your first attempt at contact with me instead of waiting for me to reach you. Yes, we are where you believe we are while what has changed is your awareness of who you are together with the identities of the surrounding people. It will remain as such until we reach the camp at which time all will reverse itself to the original time and space.*

"*You and Paul have resonated this into place due to being in this jungle forest together, and I might say,* once again. *You are especially fractured in your awareness since you are experiencing yourself as Nancy, Tusk and 'Mao simultaneously. I will explain more later. For the time being, enjoy."*

# Question Forty
## How do I connect with my soul group?

You come from within a soul group to experience life with members of your formation and many others not of your group holding memories within ME. Usually, the beings existing within what you are referring to as a "soul group" incarnate into many different experiences together, gathering a great deal of wisdom from each incarnation. Since they begin to become familiar with each other, it is often times felt that "learning" during an incarnation is easier when the person or persons with whom you are dealing come from your etheric assembly.

All of the lives you are living are present in this now moment. You are a composite of all that you are experiencing. Therefore, all you see around you is filtered through this awareness and composite of understanding. You may also accept and realize you are not alone. You are part of this soul group I AM describing that constantly supports you, communicates with you and sends you energy. This group has been with you for many periods of your time. Your soul group invites you to know, to experience and really apply teachings within experience to daily physical life realizing that every action is an opportunity to experience within ME, as ME.

You tend to reincarnate repeatedly with the same souls with whom you have something to create or balance. Your group is comprised of beings with whom you may have only one contact and some with whom you may be tied eternally. It is your core family and your extended family in the etheric plane. You have been attracted to a certain expression from lives within the parallel realms of your existence. "Negative" events may cause feelings of repulsion and make it harder for you to send love to those people with whom you have incarnated for this purpose within ME. Circumstances often compel you to deal with someone you would rather ignore. Bring the negative emotions to conscious awareness and be willing to "work it through", no matter how long it may appear to take.

Remember that when I say you come with this "purpose" it does not mean that you *have to* fulfill something in particular. What it does indicate is that while you were out of body within ME you decided it would be beneficial to have a specific experience. One or more of your soul group agreed with that decision and offered to play supporting roles within the designated incarnation. Once within the physical realm it is entirely possible that one or more of you will make a free will choice to have another, different experience within ME. No decision is static. All is dynamic flow within ME always and in all ways.

Since you have indicated a desire to connect with your soul group, the connotation here is that you believe you are not already in union with them. Look around you. Who is in your life? What people are playing specific roles with you? Who has come into your life and who has left? What strong feelings do certain people arouse within you as they play out the part they accepted within your earth life?

Every person with whom you have a relationship is playing out a scripted role within ME. Those of your soul group who are not in body in this moment may be supportive from the etheric realm though most often they are going about their own experiences there, as well. The easiest way to make a connection you believe is not there with those whom you cannot visibly see is to sit in silence and open your mind to the group. If they are not absorbed within another experience, they may make contact or they may not. It is not important.

When you are able to understand life at the level of your desire to be here, you remember the vision you had before coming and you merge the power of your relative soul groups in the subtle dimensions helping you to remember more easily. If you are aware that you are more than your physical body, then you can merge with your soul group now through conscious intention. Your focus and attention create and control your reality.

Your intentions and actions here help society on earth and the culture in the other realms as well. As you work together, each of your soul groups comes into closer vibration with you on earth and you with them. On earth, you create through time, space and mass in the physical dimension. Your soul group offers you greater wisdom, prescience and timelessness.

You are presently learning how to transcend your conscious barriers between physical life and multidimensional life. You are learning to make the invisible, visible. Mass consciousness is beginning to feel the effects of this dissolution of separation within ME. When the critical mass number of beings in form on earth accepts the possibility of multidimensionality as their personal reality, the unified field of consciousness in your dimensional reality will shift.

When you connect to your soul group in the more subtle planes of existence and experience, the communities of souls come closer into resonance with each other. The earth dimension is where the physical unification of souls is taking place. A critical mass of people is waking up to its state of existence within ME. You are already in union with all souls. You are connected to the spiritual dimension where existence was first born through Creator within ME.

Etherically connecting within your soul group is effortless. It is only your belief that union with that which you cannot see within ME is either difficult or impossible. That is not true. Your soul group and many others not of your soul group's membership are available to communicate with you.

It simply takes sitting down, being within the silence that mutes your mind's busy thoughts and picking up the soul's telephone line, so to speak. More than likely, someone will answer and the two, three, four or more of you will have a wonderful conversation regarding whatever subject you feel inclined to address. Remember, they are also experiencing in the invisible realms. Make sure you have something worthwhile to contribute. It is not only for your personal information that you communicate. All beings in existence benefit from the wealth of flow that occurs when you are open to it. When you ask how you can assist the world, this is one of the primary ways within ME.

## Story Time

Pulling the litter had been much more difficult than Nancy had expected and when they began nearing the edge of the forest, the spasms in her muscles only wanted to acknowledge the end of the road. Just as this thought passed through her head, Paul and the mother elephant, as leaders of the parade, stopped and turned parallel to the entrance to the camp. Nancy was surprised to see Paul once again in civilian work clothes and her, as well.

*"Nancy, this is as far as we go. This mother is not going to allow you to take her baby into the middle of civilization. When Don arrives, we can work on the little elephant here. If you try to walk past her, I won't be able to control her reaction. Please pay attention to what I'm saying so no one gets hurt,"* said Paul.

*"Paul, can I take a minute to ask you first how you found us and second, how you knew what to do to calm down the mother. I'm astonished to see how you dominated the situation though I'm not sure that's the right word for what I saw you do. It was more as though you merged with her and understood what she was feeling. How do you know to do that?"* Nancy was simultaneously perplexed, pleased and jealous.

*"Okay, answer to your first question is, I heard the sound of the baby since we were working on a fence line that ended at the point in the forest where that shallow he was lying in began. I happened to be mending a fence post hinge right behind that copse of trees and when I heard his horrible moans simply walked in that direction.*

*"I'm afraid the answer to your second question is a little less direct. It wasn't until I actually saw you, the mother and the baby that some natural instinct took over. It was almost as though I could hear another 'me' talking; giving non-verbal instructions that emerged as empathic feelings. I immediately knew what she needed and how to provide the proper amount of soothing for her. Interestingly, the feeling did not extend to the baby, only to the mother. I did what I 'knew' to do. Does that answer your questions well enough?"*

Though Nancy would have liked to continue the conversation, this was definitely not the time or place to do so. She could see Don and Arnie coming their way and wasn't sure how the mother elephant was going to react to the approach of more strangers.

*"Paul, you might want to do some of that empathic merging you were talking about before Don gets here. I don't want our only specimen of a doctor type to be trampled before he can get to work,"* she suggested gingerly.

*"Don't worry, Nanc. We've been communicating and she gets it. She'll just stand guard so long as I'm here and I don't intend to go anywhere. Take it easy."*

Don and Arnie tentatively approached knowing full well the danger of the situation into which they were placing themselves. Paul moved around to a position where they could see him to offer support for their entrance into the forest trail. He could see Arnie talking to Don and as they approached closer, he could overhear him talking about what they had just experienced.

*"And then Paul just calmed that big, old elephant down as though he had been doing it all his life. Look at him standin' there. He's like some kind of whisperer or something. It's downright spooky, it is,"* Arnie said with relish, obviously happy to be the one telling the tale.

Paul kept one hand on the mother while moving a little closer toward the approaching men. He wanted them to know right away that they had nothing to fear. It would make the entire process much easier.

*"Paul, good to see you in charge here,"* Don offered by way of introducing his much-desired presence within the group. *"Arnie was telling me about your new talents; might be able to put them to use in other places here. We'll have to talk about it when this is done. Where's the patient?"*

Paul moved aside voicing his guttural assurances to mom and pointed down the trail about sixty feet away where Nancy, Jack and Joe were kneeling with the baby. Don's arrival had put Nancy at ease since she had faith that he would be able to sew up the infant giving them a chance to save its life.

Don was quick, sure and accurate in his reconnaissance of the scene, immediately going to work. It was tantamount to being on the battlefield, forever sealed in his cellular memory.

*"First things first,"* he said, now in control. *"Nancy, hold his head. Arnie and Joe each take a back foot and Jack I'll need you to play surgical nurse. I've brought what I call my medical bag and I'll ask you for implements, as I need them. Nothing in there is too complex. I know you'll figure it out."*

With instructions given, Don injected the wounded baby with a strong anesthetic to knock it out and keep it still. Once he saw it taking effect, he cleaned the wound, smoothly replaced the entrails inside the puncture and neatly sewed it shut. The other abrasions and cuts responded to cleaning and minor suturing making a quick operation of the whole affair.

Nancy had been crouched over the baby stroking its head and murmuring to it until she looked up to see all of them transformed into dark, ebony, physical bodies she didn't recognize. This group had experienced something like this together in another time and place. Of this, she was sure.

# Question Forty-one
## Do we have past lives?

Before there was time, before there was space, I AM. Some call ME God; some Source; some All That Is and many, many other names in an attempt to name ME. From within ME emanates an attribute I AM calling Creator giving that aspect a label you can use to help you understand how you exist within all dimensions through an emanation of ME.

Imagine ME consciously existing as light for the purposes of presenting a picture to the mind. If I am going to weave a yarn for you, I need threads with which to weave, so let MY first thread be light without purpose or goal. Let's give this light a name – let's call it love – not human love with all of its conditions and expectations – but limitless love, absolute love without judgment or form held within ME as the most perfect manifestation of all of that I AM. The extension of this love is what I AM calling Creator.

The light, Love as Creator is aware, consciously aware of Itself and Its existence within infinity without beginning. It is aware, only that. Love is aware. In a timeless moment, Love begins to express in form. It sends out rays of love-filled light, emanations of ME. This light contains everything that Love is and as it is extending into space, it is creating as it spreads, ever unfolding into the infinite space with each emanation. The waves of light are endless and are composed of all that Love is as I AM.

Each aspect of these waves has an affinity to each other aspect because each is the same. Each emergence contains all that Love is and is drawn to re-unite with all other effusions that are also all that Love is within ME.

Time is created as it begins to pass in this manifestation of Love. Moving through the now created space, time has a place because it has space in which to record its passing. And as time passes, the draw to re-combine, to unite totally in Love's union begins to overtake the waves of light. They join winding tightly together in different forms and shapes. Particles of light begin to take shape as the frequency of the light slows down, ravishingly enjoying this encounter within ME.

The shapes take different forms and within those forms, the consciousness of Love exists. Time is passing. Time is recording in space the happenings within the emanations of Love. A record of conception is being created.

In a given moment in time in space, the various particles of Love enraptured with each other fuse into a form that begins to identify itself as individual. This is a natural outcome of the enchanted delight of Love's forms because it gives Love ever-increasing variations into which to pour its pure Love within ME. Each form takes a name, an identity as Love. Eventually, these forms would be called human beings. They would believe they lived in time rather than knowing they are eternal within ME.

Since Love comprises all - within its properties are also judgment, anger, separation and hate. Love as Creator within ME has been conscious of this yet has not placed emphasis upon any of its attributes because its formless existence found no necessity to do so.

As the human beings, conscious Love in form began to explore all of their individual aspects and properties, their concentration on their physical form, their flesh and all that it feels and contains began to be the center of each human being's attention. Time passed. Each human being began to feel like he or she was the only one experiencing the passing of time, pain within the physical body, longing for union once again; in general a deep sense of loss. As time continued to pass, each human being became so distracted with its physical form that it forgot what it actually was within ME. Meanwhile, Love is holding all of its manifested emanations without judgment in the eternal Love that it is.

Each human being in existence within earth created as its home believes it is the only emanation of Love because it has forgotten through time that every other person, place and thing it sees contains all of the aspects of Love, as well. Yet, because time has passed, each individual has forgotten that it is Love - as well as fear, hate, disappointment, expectation and hope. Each of these attributes is being lived within parallel worlds simultaneous to your present conscious existence. They all exist timelessly within ME.

Each human believes the only way to find peace is by controlling the ground upon which it is standing, the actions of others and focusing its attention on ensuring the form in which it is living feels good, no matter what it takes to do so without realizing in a parallel, present, attainable world all that is desired is available. Meanwhile, Love as Creator within ME is holding all of its manifested emanations without judgment in the eternal Love that it is.

You are made of Love and light. Everything that you feel is part of that Love within ME. It is up to you how you are going to express yourself in each moment of passing time as it records your thoughts, words and actions in created space. Only you know what feels so enrapturing, so enthralling you do not ever want to leave; want to continue experiencing this union with Love in its fullest, infinite, complete form. Only you can create the weaving of the threads for yourself because you are that Love in form. When you accept you are the endless love that you call by any other name, God, Source, Allah, or I AM, then you will realize you do not live in past or future. All streaming emanations of you within Creator within ME are present in this moment everywhere, infinitely.

## Story Time

Once the baby elephant was no longer in danger, Nancy wasn't sure what to do next. So long as she had a goal in mind, she had been able to figure out how to make it happen. Now everyone was standing around directionless.

*"Don,"* she began since the silence was eating away at the group mercilessly, *"what do you think would be the best way to care for this little one now that you have repaired him? Have you ever done anything like this before?"*

Before Don had an opportunity to answer her, Paul stepped in with authority. Even Don made way for his demonstrative voice commanding everyone's focus upon him.

*"This is what needs to happen now. The baby elephant is still on the litter and his mother will not leave his side. While he remains sleeping, I want all of you to pick up the litter and pull it back the way you came until you are just around that first bend in the trail. There you'll find a set of trees to your right that form a natural circle. Take him into those trees and set him down there. I'll follow with his mother. Once we're there, I'll tell you what we need to do next."*

Without a question, Joe, Jack, Arnie, Don and Nancy each took a section of the branches, lifting and dragging it to the exact spot that Paul intuitively knew was waiting for them. None of them had noticed it during the struggle to transport the baby elephant to the camp. Now here it was exactly as Paul had described it, a ready-made home for an ailing child and mother.

*"Okay,"* Paul continued, *"I'm going to make it my commitment to stay here with them including sleeping here. Nancy if you'll go to my tent and get my sleeping bag and water bottle that would help. There's enough food here for the mother to forage during the week it will take the baby to heal. If I stay with them, she'll feel connected to the camp and won't do any inadvertent damage. I'll be fine and I expect someone among you will keep me fed. After all, it's only for a week. You've been working without me so I know you won't miss me that much. This adult elephant will definitely miss me, more than you can possibly expect at the moment."*

Dazed and confused, all the group could do was to nod in agreement since no one had any idea how to care for a baby elephant or how to keep calm a potentially deadly adult. It seemed that all was said and done for now. No one felt like going back to the rather mundane work begun earlier in the day, so the group *sans* Nancy started to head back to the camp. Someone also needed to tell Sam. Paul stopped Don before he had gone too far down the trail.

*"Don, could you leave me some of those antiseptic wipes in case these wounds leak? Keeping them clean the first couple of days will help a lot."*

Don emptied his medical satchel of all the wiping cloths he had shaking Paul's hand before leaving. He was in awe of something he couldn't quite put his finger on and unable to put voice to it at present.

Once they were alone, Nancy felt freer to address her brother though right now she wasn't sure who he was at all. He had shifted from anger-driven lawyer to elephant shaman in skins and beads before her eyes.

*"Paul, what do you make of all that's happening? You must have some feelings about the shifting in and out of worlds that we're doing. I guess what I want to know is if it feels as instantaneous to you as it does to me. Talish has explained some of this to me but listening to a story is a lot different than experiencing what that story means. Would you talk to me about it?"*

*"Okay, Nanc, let's sit down and I'll tell you how I see it. I haven't had much time here to think about what you are asking me though I did give it a good ponder while I was in Cape Town.*

*"Talish has probably told you about parallel planes and lives, yes?"*

Nancy shook her head in agreement. That was one of Talish's favorite topics, it seemed.

Paul continued, *"Before I go on, I want to ask you how many different people you know yourself to be since meeting Talish? How many lives has she opened up your eyes to either in dreams or in other times?"*

Nancy thought for a moment, then answered, *"Well, first I know I'm me. Then I interacted where I was also that kid that was here today with Talish, Tusk. When I was carrying the litter and you shifted I saw myself as someone altogether different, a woman Talish told me was named 'Mao. That's all that I can remember."*

*"Great, good start. And I know myself as Paul, the man you saw today who is Abamti and as Ann who was not here but who I saw when you and I collapsed on the road when I arrived here.*

*"Since we are obviously merging and intermeshing parallel lives within this consciousness together, I would assume that you have a parallel to Ann and I have a match to Tusk, but I*

don't know who those are yet. I have a real strong feeling that we're going to find out.

"As to how I feel when all of this happens, I don't really feel anything at all. One moment I'm Paul and then the next moment I'm someone else. There's no time lapse, no missed time and no moving through space. It simply **is**."

## Question Forty-two
## Is my birth family part of my soul group?

Your birth family may include your soul group or it may not. Often members of your soul family incarnate with you due to familiarity, ease of experience with others who have been in form together before, confidence that someone with whom they are familiar will hold a specific position in life as an experience or perhaps, to have a good time.

Many of you express pain and suffering within your birth family due to your expectations of what *family* means within ME. The human race manifested the idea of "family" at the beginning of its conscious experience to stabilize the species, divvy up duties between male and female and secure the perpetuation of the race through protection and provision.

Now that human beings have covered the globe with the species these roles are less defined within ME yet the belief systems in place documenting how each expresses within the family unit are still in place. This ideology has been exacerbated by movies and television attempting to display a specific type of perfect family unit. If you delved into your cellular memories and your soul record, you would realize you have not ever lived within what you would call a "perfect family" since that does not exist now nor has it ever.

If members of your soul group do not choose to come into form in your particular lifetime, your birth family will be composed of those in similar soul groups or complete foreigners to your soul's expression. I use the term "foreigners" here as a glib way of expressing soul consciousness outside of your usual soul group venue since nothing is a foreigner within ME; all exists within I AM and all "know" each other.

There are very few humans feeling fulfilled and comfortable within their cellular family. This is due to the desire to experience ever-new and expansive vistas while within incarnation. If everything felt or appeared "the same" to you within ME, physical boredom would quickly step in and you would begin looking for additional situations within which to interact.

Since so many of you are not happy with your nuclear family, you tend to blame them for the responses you are presently having within life. If you are unable to support yourself financially, it must be because of the way you were raised, i.e. low self-esteem, no parental support, etc. If you are unhappy within your relationships, it is due to the lack of a model within your family unit portraying how to be within a relationship. All of these projected blaming beliefs serve only to set you up for another set of experiences enabling you to own your own soul experience rather than handing it over to others, whether they are part of your soul family or not.

Nowhere is this more prevalent than within those who consider themselves "spiritual seekers". If you feel that you are more etherically driven than your physical family can understand, then you are beginning to know that you are I AM. You know that you are fully manifesting through Creator within ME. Part of this realization then will be that your family, no matter who they are with reference to your soul, is also ME. Quite a thought, isn't it? Those to whom you cast your blame and criticism are I AM in exactly the same way you are. When you are ridiculing them for their lack of understanding, you are deriding ME in physical form because I AM not living up to your label as father, mother, brother or sister (perhaps aunt, uncle, cousin, grandmother or grandfather, as well).

Given that thought, every experience you have, you are experiencing for and within ME. You are I AM resonating within MYSELF as ME. Every experience, every thought, every word expresses within the Whole, becomes the composite experience and expression of the Whole. There is no exception to this within ME.

These soul experiences become part of your soul and cellular memory trace. There is never anything "wrong" within the journey you experience. There are only different perceptions based upon the indoctrination you received since infancy plus the lives that exist parallel to your earth life in no time within ME. No one has the ability to live in the experience that is relative to your reality in the way that you do. Only you are you, therefore, only you have the ability to answer your questions and to find your own answers. The queries that are unique to your individual frequency of life create a world of choices from which you may choose in each present moment within ME. Others may advise or give a perspective based upon their reality, yet only you have the capability and the aptitude to make the final choice and its corresponding consequences and responses.

Each of your soul aspects is committed to supporting you: The fluid, the matter, the consciousness, the light, the vibration, the circuits is all you. It is totally individual to you, just like your breath. Strengthening your circuitry helps to align within the support you give yourself within ME. You really are the only advocate you have for your own being. Awaken to that which is coded into your circuitry via your soul memory.

No thought or feeling is exempt. There is no thing that you can hide and nowhere to go. You are within ME and I AM within you. So when you are sad, sadness radiates out into the energetic field of ME and now there is more sadness within earth. When you are joyous, there are multiple joys within ME. It does not stop on planet earth. There is nothing in other dimensions holding back your thought, feeling or preventing it from going somewhere. There is no one and no thing that is going to change that feeling or emotion once it has left the immediate field of your energetic influence. You are solely responsible for it within ME.

## Story Time

Having completed as much as she could do for and with Paul while admitting inwardly that the two of them could eternally sit and muse over what was going on, Nancy made sure she had Paul's list of needs memorized and began heading back to camp. The concept of "work" was so far outside her present conscious condition that she didn't even see Sam approaching her at the trailhead that emptied out into the campsite proper.

*"Nancy, I hear that you've had a pretty dramatic morning. I think I'll leave Paul alone in there since Don told me most of what he believes occurred. We can all talk about it tonight. I'm going to call a meeting and let you tell your story so we'll have one version rather than the number of conflicting reports that're rampaging around throughout the crew. I guess that Paul won't be joining us for story time so you can be his spokesperson as well. Meanwhile, do you think we could get down to business again?"*

*"Oh, Sam, I'm so sorry that I've been distracted by all of this. I really did have the intention of coming straight to you so you'd be in the know as well. Glad that Don brought you up to speed. In a nutshell, we just have to leave this part of the forest alone right now and work elsewhere. Paul is staying with both mother and baby elephants and I just need to take him his bedroll, some water and a few other things he thought of then I'll be back on line to work. It'll only take me a few minutes. I'll be right back,"* Nancy offered by way of half-hearted apology. Truth be known, she wasn't feeling apologetic at all, much more amazed and immersed within this multiple-lives drama and really wanting to stay there rather than being grounded in the here and now.

*"Okay, but make it swift. The more time you spend fooling around with Paul's stuff the later it gets. You know how much needs to be done around here and you're now carrying the added responsibility of being a crew leader. Get hoppin',"* Sam added by way of dismissal heading off to the mess tent where he knew he would find everyone else.

It took Nancy mere moments to find Paul's requested items, which she stuffed into a backpack adding a few books he apparently had been reading since he had a good week of solitary confinement within the elephant hospital. Initially, she had thought about how separate it felt having Paul sequestered in the forest without her; now she realized how jealous she was that he didn't have to pretend to work while floating among the dimensional lives they were only beginning to explore.

*"Don't be envious, Nancy,"* Talish began as she appeared next to her while Nancy made her way back to Paul. *"You'll get your chance to immerse yourself within the world of the elephants*

and actually some other jungle life, as well. This is the very beginning of the experience the two of you planned in the world of spirit. Take each step slowly, pay attention to what you see, feel, taste, smell and hear and, above all, don't let it distract you from your physical job. It is daily work that foundations spirit. Let it guide you rather than resisting it."

Nancy was first astonished to have Talish appear out here in the "open" and then nervous that others would either see her or *not* see her and think she was talking to herself. *"Can the crew members see you walking with me or do they think I'm nuts and mumbling to myself?"*

*"Neither actually. I've cloaked us within the veil of atma and no one knows you are here. It is a tool you will come to understand. It allows you the freedom to roam where you will without being seen. This is how I visit you whenever I wish, through pulling a velvet night cloak around me preventing others from being aware of my presence. It is easily spread to include those in close proximity, as you presently are.*

*"I have a specific intention for joining you during your return to Paul and I will wait until we are joined with him to begin telling you the next piece of the story we are unwinding together. Think of it as a lovingly entangled ball of yarn you are playing with much as a child would. You are choosing in each moment which piece of a thread you will follow."* With that, Nancy found herself "magically" seated on a fallen log next to Paul and the sleeping baby elephant with mother still rumbling nearby.

Talish began without preamble, *"I have the two of you alone for a short period of time so I'm going to take advantage of this space to lay a base for what you are experiencing and will continue to see as the days unfold. Defining your aspects will clear up your confusion.*

*"Nancy, you are and will continue to experience you as Nancy, Tusk, 'Mao and John, the last of which you have not yet encountered.*

*"Paul, you will see you as Paul, Ann, Abamti and Great Horn, the last of which you do not yet know.*

*"If you want to look at it from within the stream of atam, John and Ann exist in one wave of the stream, Tusk and Great*

*Horn in another, 'Mao and Abamti yet another and, of course, the two of you in this conscious experience. Yet they all are capable of merging and emerging in different sequences of expression. I have given you this picture to assist you in understanding because as the days continue to rise and fall you will come to know your selves within these different occupations of space. Do you have any questions?"*

"Yes, I do," Nancy stepped in first wanting to make sure she was heard before she had to head back to the worksite. *"Are all of these personalities one soul group? Are we all one big happy family or are we distinct identities with no connection to each other?"*

*"You may think of them as one aspect of the great atam-atma, the I AM, separated into two distinct arrangements. Paul's grouping is one stream and your members are another. Each of the identities shares the attributes of the other three within each assemblage. You would say they are one and the same though appearing different and separate through personality."*

## Question Forty-three
## Do we have strong soul ties to
## the people who are close to us in this life?

All of the lives you have lived are present in this now moment. You are a composite of all you have experienced and so is everyone you know within your life within ME. Therefore, all you see around you is filtered through this awareness and composite of understanding.

The people in your life, close or only acquaintances, may be members of your soul group, groups that are similar to yours, people you have incarnated with in many lives, others whom you have not known before, souls you made commitments to in other lives and are now fulfilling and so it goes. These are only a few of the reasons you may have specific people in your life.

The connotation of your question suggests you would like to believe you do have strong soul ties to the people close to you in this life. You would be surprised to know that most of the people closest to you via the soul realm are those you dislike the most. They have incarnated into this dimension with you in a "best friend" capacity (from a soul aspect) to assist you in experiencing absolution, forgiveness, compassion, empathy and non-judgment.

It is a delight to take on the adventure of being born into earth with those willing to hold the opposite for you within ME. While your ego personality mind wants to believe that those who are close to you are the ones who love you dearly, the unconditional love of those who incarnate to mirror for you all that you despise are the ones who love you more than you can understand. Your human mind has too many beliefs surrounding its concept of love to relish the idea that someone who antagonizes you is telling you how much they love you.

Through your personal will, you are able to draw and repel those who are within your life. It is an energy stream affecting and responding to what is being felt moment to moment. If you presently do not believe you have a strong soul tie with a person in your life and you want to have that connection, create it. If you believe that some of the bonds within your interactive relationships are no longer serving you, sever them. You are in control through your free will as I AM. Use it to free yourself from any perspective that does not serve the coherency of you in this moment of life.

From time to time, you will notice that you'll get a bit of a "hit" as you call it, an expression through your intuition within ME that tells you this enterprise or relating-ship with a person will be of benefit. Your mind begins to explain to you why you should or should not follow that course of action. The tussle between the voice of your soul through your heart and the clarion call of your mental process begins. Which one will win; can both of them? It's up to you.

If you are living within an environment where you feel you are not being served by the connections you are maintaining, realize that you are in control of how those inter-weavings are experienced within ME. If a person is not showing his or herself to you fully and completely, ask yourself if you are letting yourself be seen. If another person is constantly "rubbing you wrong", check in to see if you are not creating the same experience within them.

Of course, this means you have to unveil yourself before their eyes and admit to them and yourself how much this means to you and, perhaps, how hard it is for you to do. If you move into this vulnerable experience with an open heart, the other person is much more likely to open his or her heart to you. You do not know what is going on within their lives, behind their mask of expression. All you *do* know is what you are feeling when you are around them. You will not ever know the answer unless you ask the questions that will provide the answers from within a non-judgmental position within ME.

Know the strong soul ties you have with people may not be what you assume them to be based upon the beliefs or constructs you adhere to so strongly. Oftentimes people who only tap into and out of your life on a semi-regular basis are a prominent part of your soul group who are subliminally sharing this lifetime with you.

Your idea about what a strong soul tie is based upon can only be seen through the veil of your personal filters. When you remove that particular lens and allow yourself to perceive an "other" within the realm in which *they* live rather than from within your personal reality, you will change your expectations of your close relationships.

There are no one-time soul mates or twin flames within ME. There is not a specific soul you are supposed to align with to provoke and promote a specific destiny. Within the over seven billion souls presently incarnated within planet earth, there are at least one billion with whom you may easily live a very fruitful and fulfilling life.

Your intention and the attention you place upon that intention will determine who is drawn into your energy stream. Concentrating upon what you are truly feeling, living your life authentically and maintaining your integrity gives personal permission to commit deeply within the connections you would like to create and maintain as I AM.

The strong soul ties you believe you have may not be of the greatest communion at all. Perhaps those who are waiting in the wings for your attention will prove to be the most bountiful connection within your life within ME.

## Story Time

With those final words, Talish backed out of the tree's cover and disappeared down the path, physically as well as etherically.

*"It's always so hard to tell whether she's here in body or if we're just sort of imagining her, you know,"* Nancy turned to address Paul who was completely involved in soothing the sleeping baby elephant. *"I suppose that's as it's supposed to be since she keeps talking about traveling in dimensions that we're just getting used to. What do you think?"*

Paul raised his head to answer just as mother elephant stepped forward, wrapped her trunk around Nancy pulling her back toward her, stomach emitting a continuous rumble. With one thrust, she lifted Nancy up into the air positioning her within the curve of her trunk as though seated on a chair.

Though she would have believed this would scare her beyond words, Nancy felt at home embraced by the enormous pachyderm. *It's almost as though I belong here,* she thought with a smile.

*"Hey, Nanc, you look real natural up there. Have you done this before?"* Paul asked with a grin.

*"No, not in this lifetime anyway, but I must admit that I feel like I've been here forever. It must have something to do with one of those other lives Talish was talking about earlier. We'll have to ask her next time she shows up. In any event, I'm really glad that 'mom' likes me because it will make it easier to come and go with your goods while you nurse 'baby' back to health."*

*"Okay, Mom, you can put me down now,"* Nancy voiced to the mother elephant hoping she would understand.

Paul intervened as he drew upon cellular memories from another life. *"You have to lightly tap on her trunk twice to let her know that you want down. And don't ask me how I know that; I just do."*

Nancy followed Paul's instructions giving the elephant two subtle touches on the base of her trunk. Immediately, she slowly lowered her to the ground.

Walking over to sit down next to Paul for a moment before heading back to work, Nancy spied Don approaching them on the trail. *"Oh, oh, I'm in trouble now. Bet Don is coming to get me 'cuz Sam is looking for me,"* Nancy voiced nervously as Don drew closer.

Dropping to his knees as he entered the circle of trees, Don made his way to the infant lying snuggled within his leafy bed. Noticeably, the mother elephant made no move to stop his approach or to alert Paul to the fact that she might be apprehensive about this new addition to the slowly developing clan.

Moving quietly, Don stopped just short of actually touching the sleeping baby elephant. *"So glad to see he's doing well under your care, Paul. I must admit I'm really in admiration of your ability to communicate with these animals so well. I tried a couple of times when I first got here but didn't make a dent. Maybe you could teach me a thing or two,"* Don requested by way of asking permission.

*"Why, Don, I didn't know you were interested in the elephants,"* flew out of Nancy's mouth before she had time to censor herself. The last thing she wanted to do was sound judgmental or to stop whatever was unfolding here. The words emerged before she could cap them off.

*"There's a lot you don't know about me, Nancy. Besides being a medic in the service, I was also a chaplain. I have a great respect for spirit in all of its forms. It's not something I speak actively about in camp, but I do let my natural talents for finding common ground and listening come up when needed. I know you've noticed because you've taken advantage of my friendship in your own way. Know that I appreciate your regard."*

*"Don, you are welcome to learn about the elephant world with us if you want,"* Paul unquestionably welcomed him, *"but you might find that there are a few things going on here that you won't understand. I'm not sure that I want to get into it right now, but as time goes by, you might believe that you've bitten off more than you want to chew."*

*"Paul thanks for the 'heads-up'. There's a world I know little about and that I am open to experiencing. There's something about the two of you, Nancy and you, when you're together that intrigues me in a very distinct way. I don't know what it is, but I do know that I want to get to know both of you much better.*

*"Having sort of asked permission to 'join' you two, I have to grab Nancy and get going right now. Sam thinks I've come to haul her back to the 'chain gang' so I'll do just that. Perhaps we could keep this conversation quiet?"*

*"Absolutely, Don,"* it was Nancy's turn to speak up now. *"If you want to become more in tune with the elephants and get to know us better, you're welcome. I just don't know how much we can explain to you and I won't even try right now. Maybe we could come back tonight after work and visit Paul, mom and baby and have another talk. What do you think, Paul?"*

*"Sure, I'm up for company whenever the two of you arrive. Don't forget to bring me some dinner. I'm hungry just thinking about it."*

Neither Nancy nor Paul was sure of why Don had approached them. What they did know was their group was enlarging with or without their mutual consent.

# Question Forty-four
## Why does it seem difficult to
## find a community of like-minded people?

One of the reasons you have a difficult time finding people who resonate with you within a community is because you are experiencing yourself as a leader within a new energetic framework. Leaders within the human species, by nature, stand alone. There is little space for one who points the way to find a group with whom he or she will easily commune on a long-term basis.

While you may find people who seem to listen to you or may even explore subjects similar to those you are interested in within ME, you will inevitably discover that eventually you will lose your interest within the group. You must do so if you are to stimulate your genus into its next phase of expansion.

Think of it this way: Remember when you were in school with one or two people who soared to the "head of the class". They had few friends, knew the right answers and might have been "teacher's pet".

You might have been this person or you may have envied them their position within the classroom structure. Now you find yourself in the self-same position, heading a realm of information in which there are few who understand what you are saying or do not easily resonate with the frequency that you are transmitting.

This position may feel lonely to you since you want to have a "village" of like-minded folks with whom to consort, yet what I AM telling you and would like you to understand is you are creating that which is being considered the *new normal* within ME. Eventually, there will be many more humans expanding and experiencing what you are presently involved within and then you will leap into a totally different space because that is why you incarnated to begin with – to be a leader, not a follower or even a "combiner".

Did you emanate into the earth world to be normal? Did you embrace your new form and say, "make me common like all the others?" Did you say, "I don't want to stand out? I don't want anyone to point a finger and say, 'That one is not like the rest of us.'" Is that what you intended?

Or, did you radiate into the present set of dimensions within ME proclaiming boldly, "Here I come. I AM," announcing your arrival into this world to experience this realm with all of its possibilities, its probabilities as unlimited potential arriving here in this form.

Since I was present at your birthing, not only into this life's matter, also into the experiences out of this form as well, I can tell you with certainty that your statement was the latter: "Here I come". So what happened?

You became dependent, or at least you believed you were, and from the standpoint of this particular plane, yes, you were dependent upon your parents and then your schoolteachers. And then you began to recognize that if you were going to be liked, you would have to fit in, be like the other kids, whatever that meant to you.

And to make it a little bit more complicated, what you didn't realize is that each of those kids was thinking the same thing. So there began to coalesce this uneasy friendship routine wherein each kid was trying to make the other kids like him or her more, better, best and it continued on and on into your teen years and into your more mature life as an adult. It simply takes different forms yet it is all the same within ME.

You want to be seen as *normal* and yet, truly, you don't really know what that means since any definition of what is normal is always relative to the person or group speaking about it. So being normal is really about being safe in a world that appears to be dangerous. At one time, many of your centuries ago, being normal meant that you would be fed by the meat hunters so long as you performed your job in the tribe. Yet, that was a very long time ago in your earth years. Do you want to stay assigned to the tribal mindset or would you welcome becoming a new version of normal through the leadership position you maintain within ME?

Do you know who already knows this? It is the little children you are birthing into your world. All of these beloved beings are attempting to tell you that the creations you are experiencing do not honor your old paradigm; that the normal awareness is asleep. They are awake and the older humans do not know how to understand them and care for them in a way that promotes their abilities. Instead, the mature humans are giving them drugs to keep them quiet, diagnosing them with mental maladies and attempting to make them into the old normal.

None of your society's attempts to quell what cannot be diminished will work. Though the little ones may have to acquiesce to your unknowing proclivities until they come into more mature form, eventually they will do just that and the network of their interlaced consciousness will arise in the glory that only they know is real.

You came into this earth to bring yourself here, not to conform to what you see or experience in this plane or to bemoan not finding a community. The changes you desire so strongly, those that you are constantly talking about, are living within you right now as you read MY Words. You can only experience those changes when you live the life that is normal for you, not for any other human, and when every human heeds MY Words, you will experience the one desire you each have more than any other. You will all be aware of being of like-mind in MY Mind.

## Story Time

Don, Sam, Nancy and the rest of the crew worked into the heat of the day after the unexpected delay earlier in the morning. At mid-day rest, Don took Nancy aside and made her promise again that she wouldn't say anything to anyone about the interaction and conversation in the forest enclosure. And, promising once again to be silent, Nancy pondered why it was so important to him figuring that eventually she might know.

Evening meal came and went and when it appeared as though it wouldn't significantly "stir the pot", Nancy made up a plate for Paul, gave a significant look to Don and headed toward the forest. She figured she had been discreet enough that Don would follow in due course and if he didn't show up really soon, she could at least get a few words in edgewise with Paul.

Heading into the tree clearing, she was met by a very hungry brother who took the offered plate with relish. *"Paul, I think Don's coming right behind me,"* Nancy began quickly before they were interrupted, *"and I want to say this before he gets here. He checked in with me again to make sure I would keep my mouth shut about him with the crew. I don't know why he's so nervous about 'being found out'. What do you think . . ."* was as far as she got before Don appeared behind her.

*"Hey, guys, see you got your plate, Paul. So what's up? How's the baby doing?"* Don was obviously ill at ease.

*"Little one's doing fine,"* Paul offered in quick response. The air was disquieted by Don's fear and Nancy was beginning to feel like it would be much easier to do without him than to include him in whatever was happening here.

Before she could make a decision about whether to say something to clear up any potential confrontation, Talish appeared in the midst of the circle.

*"Greetings and good night's rest to you all,"* she began. *"I see Don has joined you once again and while this is causing a stir in your emotional waters, I am happy to see him take this step. I will clear up the uneasiness you are feeling, Nancy.*

*"During the time that you and Paul are living as Tusk and Great Horn, Don is living as He Who Sees, a medicine man, as I am a medicine woman. This position placed him outside of the tribal boundary just as I am outside of my own local border. We, as those who see what others may not see, are not of one within the culture yet are respected from afar. While we are fed, clothed and housed by the community, we are not allowed to partake of the communal land for we spend our time in worlds that humans usually do not and cannot inhabit.*

*"Don, you have not been consciously aware of this situation within this life though you have had fleeting glimpses of it especially during the times that you were on the battle field with the wounded. I know you often saw those who were dying as their spirits left their bodies. While you had no words with which to address it at the time, you did what your medical and religious*

*instruction gave you to do. Now you are going to begin remembering.*

"*Nancy and Paul, as far as the groupings of lives that we have already discussed are concerned know that Don or He Who Sees will fit in nicely through the Tusk and Great Horn atam-um. My suggestion is that you welcome him as one of you and allow him to find his own footing within the realms most comfortable to him and, therefore, to all of you. Now I invite questions if there be any within your minds.*"

"*I have a couple of questions, Talish,*" Paul began, "*but I'll only ask one. Can Don help me with the baby to increase its healing capacity? I mean, with the memory of being a medicine man, can he apply 'medicine' speeding up the process?*"

"*Don, why don't you answer this question for Paul rather than me,*" Talish requested challenging Don to connect with himself and bring forth any information he may have.

"*I don't know what to say,*" Don replied as he attempted to figure out what he should say to this person appearing in the midst of them represented. "*I can try but I'm not sure I'll succeed. Okay, Paul, here's what I see and please don't laugh at me. If you will move back from the baby and let the mother come closer, she will begin a rumbling in her stomach that sets up a vibration that causes her child to want to live. I don't know how I know this but left to my own devices, that's what I would do.*"

"*If you say that is what you remember, then we will respect it. Paul, pull back. Nancy, step aside. We'll watch and see if Don's words are truth,*" Talish instructed.

As the four of them moved back toward the trail, the mother elephant moved over the sleeping infant, a loud tremble running throughout her body. Rather than the soft murmur of a rumble, the vibration of the sounds emitted from her shivered the leaves upon the ground. Within moments, the baby elephant opened its eyes and began waving its trunk to smell its mother.

"*Well, He Who Sees, welcome. You've come home,*" Talish said with a smile and then disappeared.

## Question Forty-five
## Why do people I consider close to me not like me?

There are most likely many different people in your life all in different relationship with you within ME. It is a sure bet that you want to be with others of like mind, peer group compatriots who feel, believe and experience life as you do.

Have you heard yourself talking internally about how much you wish your friend, family member, husband, wife, girlfriend or boyfriend was more like you, more devoted to spiritual practice as you either are or want to be? Are you disappointed that the people you chose or are choosing to experience this incarnation with don't feel driven to understand him or herself as you're sure you're doing?

The first answer to your question is to reflect upon how much judgment you reflect back to those in relationship with you causing them to choose not to interact with you. The second reference point is your expectations of them.

Let's say you have an intense intention set that you will draw to yourself the perfect friends (since your family is most likely already committed to their view of you) and the ideal mate. You imagine you will live the rest of your life physically and spiritually surrounded by this bliss of perfect union within your friendships and more intimate relationship. The people show up or at least you believe they have and you are very excited making connections within your life as the spirit of divine happiness within ME.

Then something happens; it's been a few years now and all of you have seen a few signs that together you are achieving your, hopefully, mutual spiritual goals. Sometimes it even feels like the strength of your communion is increasing, solidifying in its presence.

Abruptly, life begins to feel like things are changing, especially within you. You begin to see things in a different way as within ME. The little character attributes that exist within your friends, perhaps your family and your intimate partner, that only used to ruffle you slightly become bigger. You might even feel yourself experiencing actual anger.

So you try harder. You attempt to be more spiritual and let everyone know how hard you're trying. After all, you are a "spiritual lightworker", you have come to earth to express all of the heavenly gifts that you know you have and while they're not always appreciated by the masses, at least these people have appreciated all you are; they must see how pure you are becoming in your intent.

It is right here, right in this moment when you are feeling those feelings that you push them away from you through your energetic signature within ME. You are unable to see the opposite side toward that which you are looking; in other words, what you are experiencing is that which you are not looking at within your life.

The first inclination is to bolt, to run away or to fight. It is the typical fight or flight mechanism kicking in so that you may continue to survive within the relationship in the way you construe it to be. That is the human side of your personality telling you your expectations have not been met, you probably made a wrong decision somewhere back there and these people no longer suit you. They experience your feelings and they respond in like kind. This is self-judgment and its reflection upon those in your life you call close to you through the energetic wave you are within ME.

Could it be possible that the people you chose as friends and the perfect mate are being just that? Could it be that they are simply being who and what they are, as authentic as they find it possible to be, and are subtly, by their frequency, asking you to be as well? Could it be that this is an invitation to "step up to the plate", to look in the direction that you have not been looking and express the authenticity of your present feelings within ME?

MY Answer to these questions is yes, yes and yes. You are being given an opportunity to look at your preconceived beliefs about how your spiritual, which is also your physical, life is to present itself, how you are supposed to experience that set of beliefs and how those in your life are supposed to respond to your preconceived idea of your own growth. That takes courage and it takes humility, allowance and acceptance; that the direction in which you are not looking is the direction that is saying, "Look at me, look this way; how about *this*," whatever that may be and it is always your choice within ME.

So long as you hold to any idea about how your life is going to show up, to that degree are you blindsided and you do not have to be. Remove the blinders that cover your authentic feelings. Speak from your heart and let your friend or partner know that you are observing these learnings within yourself. Talk about how you are feeling always remembering that this is about you. Open yourself up to authentic dialogue with your friends and partner remaining humble, observant and loving and as you do so and as they respond, you all have a chance, mutually and individually, to watch your unions grow stronger, truer and emptied of illusionary expectation within ME.

It is not that those who are close to you do not like you. It is much more that you stand as a mirror for them. Now look into the mirror they present to you. Embrace what you see within that reflection. Let it emerge as the new, expansive you, the new normal, able to stand firmly within your presence within ME knowing they are also doing the same.

When you love those "others" as much as you would like to love yourself within ME, they will respond in like kind. Give them what you are wishing to receive from them.

## Story Time

Don was as surprised at the outcome of this experiment as were Nancy and Paul. The baby elephant was healing so fast that it was nearly back on its feet. Paul knew he would not have been able to do that unaided so sat back on his heels in gratitude and a hint of envy.

*"Don, how did that feel when you were talking about what to do? Where did it come up within you? Could you feel it or was it a thought in your head?"* Nancy asked filled with so much curiosity that she simply couldn't wait another minute to find out Don's method of knowing.

*"Can't say that I could tell you that,"* Don replied easily. *"When that woman or whatever she was asked me the question, I simply stated what came into my mind though I cannot say it was a conscious thought the way I usually think. I just opened my mouth and the answer came out. Is that what you mean?"*

*"Yeah, I guess so. I think it's time for me to tell you a little bit about what's been going on here since Talish, that's who she is by the way, appeared while you were here so obviously we're supposed to let you be in the know about what she told us. At least that's what I think we're supposed to do. It feels right anyway.*

*"So here's the bottom line, the short story, rather than dragging you through every event. This woman, as you call her, Talish is a medicine woman who has been appearing to Paul and me in dreams and in the physical world. She has taken us into lives she tells us we are presently living in parallel realms that coincide with our lives here in a variety of ways.*

*"Paul has been told through various experiences that he is like the fruit ready to drop from the tree. It's been explained to me that I am opening the way for him, whatever that means. So we've had these other worldly experiences alone and a little bit together. Now you're here so I guess you're a part of it all and that's about all I know without having to go into a blow-by-blow description of each and every happening."*

Don listened attentively to the summary of events leading up to this moment. He could feel stirrings within him, some aligned with what Nancy was saying and some provoking an entirely different response, almost anger. While he wasn't sure where these emotions were coming from within him, he did recognize them as belonging to the tape recorder of his life, part of the memories from childhood that he had hidden safely away within his inner basement behind a tightly closed and locked door. Now the hinges were busting loose and he had no notion what to expect.

*"Well, I'll tell you how I see this at the moment,"* he began with much less relish than he would have preferred. *"I'm working at an African reserve where no one would even consider talking about any of this. I don't want to lose my job and I don't want to*

*be looked upon as a weirdo so I'm keeping this close to my chest and I caution you both to do the same. If I'm supposed to take part in some sort of mystical undertaking, it'll happen on its own. I'm definitely not going to attempt to bring it to me."*

Nancy was surprised at the vehemence in Don's reply to her summation of events. While she and Paul seemed more inquisitive about what was transpiring, Don seemed to be offended or even afraid of what might come of any junkets into extraordinary reality. Due to her respect and hopefully friendship with Don, she had expected him to jump in with both feet happily accepting whatever might come through Talish's coaching and oftentimes interference within their lives.

*"Well, Don, as strongly as you just voiced your reluctance to accept what just happened, it certainly explains why you were so demonstrative about telling me to keep my mouth shut back at dinner. I think I can speak for Paul here, too when I say not to worry about us blowing your cover. We'll keep our mouths shut about you as well as ourselves,"* Nancy offered with hope of placating Don's eminent explosion.

*"Great and with that I'll head back to the camp and pretend nothing happened here. Nancy, when you decide to return remember to keep your head down. Don't make a big deal out of this. It won't do you any good,"* Don directed as a finale to his now submerged potential volcanic eruption and headed back to the trail.

Once he was out of earshot, Nancy breathed a sigh of relief. *"I thought for a minute there that he was going to hit something, Paul. Did you see how red his face got, almost as though he was going to burst! Wonder what that's about."*

Paul hadn't said a word during the entire interchange between Don and Nancy. A veil of what could only be called peace had descended upon his mind shuttering him off from whatever was happening in the immediate surroundings. Now, with Don gone and Nancy directing her statements only to him, he felt summoned back as though sliding through a slippery stream of viscous fluid.

*"Hmm, don't know what to tell you, Nanc. All I do know is that whatever he did and however this is all happening for each of*

*us I am more at peace right now than I have ever been. While I don't really need to give a great deal of attention to caring for the baby elephant right now, I think I'm going to take advantage of the time I've already set aside from the work crew and stay here in the forest. This is where I want to be, elephants or no elephants. You can join me if you want to but I'm not leaving this space."*

## Question Forty-six
## Why is it so hard to forgive?

I am changing your question to "why is it so hard to absolve?" since forgiveness connotes a wrongdoing while absolution sees nothing as incorrect within the experience.

Forgiveness says, "You have hurt me, betrayed me, disappointed me and since I want to be a good person, be more spiritual, appear loving I will forgive you." Absolution tells you there is no wrongdoing being experienced rather that you and the other person or you within a specific situation are having an experience together as light within ME.

You are constantly in a state of transferring energy throughout your physical system, mind, emotional nature and environment. As such, you are the center point of constant energy interchange among interactions with other people, thought patterns within yourself, the output of physical energy and the decision making capabilities of the conscious and the subconscious playing out through your spiritual and emotional bodies. Within this flow, you are either releasing or holding, doing or undoing and each result determines the outcome of your day-to-day experience.

When you believe it is difficult to absolve another, you must realize that you cannot give to someone else what you do not embody within your belief system. You are as I AM, so the notion that you are unable to absolve is simply a false belief within your present reality. Yet, you must first relinquish the need to hold *yourself* accountable for your imagined transgressions before you can allow *another* to experience the same within you within ME.

The physical body vibrates at a certain frequency that you refer to as solid. Your perception tells you your body exists, and that from time to time it feels separate from ease, filled with stress and lack of harmony. You are at ease when you perceive yourself at peace with the idea of oneness. Re-member, oneness includes separation. There is no thing outside of oneness. It includes everything. It is your belief and action outside of this framework that causes you to withhold absolution from another within ME.

Stress, worry, disappointment and anxiety cause imbalance of the energy within your body. Rather than the capacity of release, there is the experience of holding. Rather than the ability to dismiss, there is a steady perception and concentration upon what is not working through people and situations. Nearly, if not all, of these feelings and emotions precipitate from your perception of life in relation to others. So long as you are holding onto a memory or refusing to come to solution, your energy stream feels stagnant, unacceptable to healthy energy states and confused. It comprises your sense of separation. When you absolve, your mind begins to perceive a change in your body and releases its hold on the illusion of separation within ME as I AM.

Again, this must first occur in relation to yourself since you only see within others what you know lives within you within ME. As you project your awareness of yourself onto another person, you remove from within your reality the ability to absolve or "put back into solution" the experience you have first with yourself and then with them. The occurrence must arise initially within you to enable you to imagine you recognize it within the other. Since there is no "other" within ME, it all cycles back to you within ME in oneness that includes the idea of separation.

Your ability to believe as you do and act on that belief stems from your ability to sense what you have created. If you are manifesting worry, angst, stress and dis-harmony within your body, you believe and act on that belief. If you find a way to change the state you are experiencing, your ability to act on that belief will likewise change. Once you are comfortable with being peaceful, at ease, calm and harmonious and perceive yourself as a person who deserves such states of being, they will remain.

Once again, it is all in how you use your perception within ME. Your ego personality as your individuated self is I AM. Whatever you believe ME to be, from whatever you originally came or emanated, you must be all of ME. I AM, was and always will BE – as are you. All is in solution, dissolved and flowing. When absolution is present within the framework of your life, you are expressing freely as ME. When you make the determination that something or someone has hurt you or caused you to experience anything that is not "in flow", you are attempting to create a separation between you and an aspect of ME. While this is inherently impossible, your mind would like to believe it is real so it changes your perception and maintains an aspect of separateness for you that you believe is outside of ME.

When you begin to believe that no one ever does anything to harm you, that everyone is living life to the best of their capability in the moment, then you can welcome every experience as just that, an experience. There is no one to blame, no fault to assign. You are free. You are healthy and in harmony within ME. Remember, if you hold yourself separate from anyone or anything, your perception causes you to believe you are severed from an aspect within ME. It is not possible to say that I encompass all and then act as if a person or an experience is outside of ME. In absolution, you release the energy of this "blame game" back into the emanation of ME as Creator to be re-used as energy for new creations. Most importantly, you free yourself from any sense of restriction. You are the flow in form as I AM.

## Story Time

Nancy was sorely tempted to take Paul up on his offer even though the pull to continue with the work of the reserve incessantly tugged at her. This definitely did not feel like the appropriate time to desert the crew and, in addition, Paul sitting alone and getting his act squared away would be a much better proposition than having sis right at hand.

"Paul, I'm going to let you enjoy this time alone. I'll still bring you meals if you want. I can even leave them near the trail if you don't want me to disturb you. Just tell me what you'd like me to do."

"Well, Nanc, that's a good offer. Sorry you don't want to hang with me and I understand why. You're much more hunkered in with the crew here than I am. I'll definitely take you up on the *food and we'll see how it goes. Go ahead and bring my food plates on in to me. It'll be good to see you from time to time."*

With Paul's instructions tucked into her mental schedule, Nancy left for what remained of the evening, which wasn't much. It had been an enlightening, challenging, heartening and slightly overwhelming twenty-four hours.

By the time she arrived at the path into camp, it was very dark and most of the crew had ensconced themselves within their tents for the night. She definitely did not feel like going to sleep with all of the day's activities still attempting to find home within her mind. *Maybe Don's around. I wouldn't mind talking to him some more, if he's up to it,* she thought with a hint of anticipation. *Hmmm, am I feeling more for Don than I originally thought? Seems like there's a bit of a stirring going on that I haven't felt for a very long time.*

Expectation gave way to hope as she walked in the direction of Don's tent happily noticing that his oil lamp was still burning. Though Nancy couldn't hear any sounds coming from the tent, she didn't expect to either. In fact, that was a good thing because it meant that Don was alone.

"Don," Nancy said just above a whisper, *"can I come in and talk with you for a minute?"*

Don appeared at the tent flap in his undershorts with no hint of embarrassment almost as though he was used to receiving visitors nearly in the buff. *"Sure, come on in. You can't sleep either, huh? Grab a chair. I've got some soda if you want one or water if you're thirsty."*

*"Soda's fine, thanks. I just left Paul and the thought of going to bed is as far from my mind as possible. There's no one here that I can really talk to about today except you so I'm glad you're still awake provided you don't mind me bringing up what may be a sore subject. Do you?"*

*"If you mean talking about what happened today, I believe I owe both you and Paul an apology. I was really taken by surprise by the whole episode. No, more than that, I was astonished, scared, humbled and agitated because I felt I couldn't control anything that was happening. I'm used to being in control*

and that was definitely not what I experienced with that woman and the elephants.

"So, in any event, I'm sorry that I sounded ungrateful, argumentative and downright stubborn about the whole thing. Not that I want to do it again. No, thanks, but I can appreciate that the two of you are having some type of unusual visitations or whatever you want to call it and seem to like it. Am I right?"

"Yes, Don, we are having fairly frequent visits with Talish and there's much more to tell you about it if you want, but I'm not sure how much to say since you're acting like you don't want to be part of it. Shall I just talk and you can either ask questions or tell me to shut up?" Nancy was feeling a bit brazen after hearing Don actually apologize for his reaction earlier today. Perhaps there's more to this man than I suspect, she thought, surprisingly emotional.

"Okay, I'll just give you a summary. Stop me when you want to," Nancy began with ease. She then continued telling Don what Talish had told Paul and her about their parallel lives, a little about her initial experience with the baby elephant and cycled around to including him in the picture much the same way that Talish had done earlier. She had to acknowledge that she harbored the faintest desire to have him accept her words and want to join in the dimensional game they seemed to be playing.

"Well, that's a pretty fantastic tale you're telling me here and I'm not too sure what to believe or what to discount. I'll admit I want to accept your version of things and yet my mind is so very skeptical. How about if we just let things play out, I'll go along with whatever comes up and hold back on judgment for the time being. In so many words, I'm saying that I'll join up with you and Paul but I don't want you to think I've committed to anything. It's a 'wait and see' proposition I'm making here. Does that work for you?"

Nancy was ecstatic hearing Don acquiesce to her world. Wow, I'm really putting a lot of eggs into this basket; better be careful, don't know how Don feels, and I could really make a fool of myself here.

"Well, now that's said and done how about we get some sleep. Lots of work tomorrow and I have some ideas about *streamlining the crews. There's easier and faster ways to get the same amount of work done. I'm an efficiency expert, have been since my military days and I'm looking forward to trying out some new ideas in dividing the work load,"* Don said in closing as he casually walked her out of his tent for the night.

# Question Forty-seven
## What is compassion?

Humans define compassion as *commiseration, tenderness and mercy*. This definition is quite limiting to your species within ME. I will respond to this question from within your essence as I AM.

Using the word "compassion" divided into two "com" and "passion" changes the connotation of this inherent attribute within you. Since I AM using written language with which to inform you, note that "com" is a prefix meaning "together, with and completely". I will define "passion" as "a compelling feeling". Now the definition of compassion changes to the union of a compelling feeling rather than connoting the existence of a need to commiserate or be mercifully tender.

Each individual walking the earth today has an opportunity and a calling to become consciously awake and aware of his or her compelling feeling within ME. Most of you do not take the time to release and relax from day-to-day activities and suffer from the stress and tension that is consistent with not being aware of the feeling in your body. When you are not taking part in your own passion, it is nearly impossible to extend it to someone else.

Remember that you cannot give someone something you do not already possess within you. This could also be phrased, you cannot give someone something that you are not aware of within you. First, you must recognize your state of awakened light within ME and then you can extend it to another. Since your underlying desire, no matter what you might believe you want, is to know your union within ME, until you recognize yourself as ME, you will have no space for compassion within your life.

There are many different experiences available within which to learn this unique attribute of yours and yet there is no counsel that can be learned from reading books or the teachings of others. Though often accurate, reflections of others' perceptions, books and teachings cannot take the place of life experience and heartfelt compassion, the experience of living within the common union of your compelling feeling and your expression as infinite emergence within ME in harmony and eternal expression.

The current human condition supports, allows and encourages following the mass beliefs as dictated by television, popular opinion and the newspaper headlines. There is not much present encouragement for following "your personal passion", creating individual thought and living life according to the dictates of your own consciousness within ME. This pattern contributes to your state of numbness in the face of increasing complexities and stress.

So, you may ask, "How do I find this compelling feeling within me so as to bring it into conscious union?"

Taking the time to observe, to listen, to breathe and to spend time alone, in nature, talking with friends of like mind and experimenting with any type of creative activity that attracts you will enable you to become more conscious, more aware and awake in this marvelous time and space you are experiencing. No era has held as many options and considerations for you as this present age within ME. Do not let it find you sleeping. Bring conscious awareness into your life through discerning decision.

As you begin to experience the resonance within your energy structures of what your most natural attraction is, you will feel how impelling the compulsion becomes. Eventually you will admit that the invitation has become insistent enough that your compassion within yourself will be heard, followed and lived.

Your original blueprint, that which is you within ME, is love, compassion and harmony. I can redefine those attributes as non-judgment, following the passion of your heart and resonating in balance. The human idea that compassion is commiseration fuels the seemingly endless tide of humanity's dramatic life events. The more intense the trauma, the more compassion is demanded. Unless the compelling feeling is to hold the hand of a person in sorrow, any attempt you make to do so without non-judgment and balance will fall short of your true self within ME. It will emerge as another mask within your personality's closet of disguises.

You are a creator within ME expressed within Creator in this dimension and have direct access to your original blueprint, the initial intention of creation. This originating matrix that is your expression is without perception or concept. It is the impetus within ME, emanating as Creator. It manifests all that is possible within ME. Ideas of trauma, grief, sorrow, anger and frustration are neutral events within ME being experienced through you. Loving the event as the occurrence of I AM is the compulsion of the heart. It is compassion in form manifested as I AM.

There is no fear, no loss, no abandonment nor separation as I AM. Since your perception of lack and aloneness, fear and sorrow are part of the world of illusion perhaps a change in perception will create a new freedom of passion within your life. You might say that by changing perception, you begin to accept your personal, active access to that which is real, the peace and love of creation as well as that not created. What is necessary is the willingness to make the choice for change. As you begin to perceive where you do not embrace the compulsions of your heart, you will see where compassion within yourself is necessary rather than viewing this experience as a need for commiseration or mercy within ME.

## Story Time

Upon arriving at the mess tent in the morning, Nancy found the camp all a-buzz with curiosity. Sam and Don had called a post-breakfast meeting and rumors swirled from someone getting fired to announcement of new additions to staff, from the ever-present fear of Sam's wrath over something yet to be defined to Don's drive to keep everyone happy. Nancy already knew, thanks to Don's hint of the previous evening, and she kept her tongue while applying the self-same device to coffee and bran muffin.

*"Okay, everyone,"* Sam announced in his usual get-down-to-business manner. *"If you'll all quit talking, I'll tell you why we're holding this meeting. All I'm doing is making an introduction and Don will do the rest since it's his idea.*

*"As you all know, the storm damage is far worse than anything we originally imagined not to mention the detour we took yesterday thanks to Nancy's need to be an elephant nurse. Now we've lost Paul for a week while he's babysitting the wounded baby though it's really no great loss since we're used to operating without him. It was a nice thought to have another body, that's all. Don has come up with a way to get more done faster or so he says, so I'll turn it over to him."*

Don was happy to be getting a chance to speak, hoping to undo some of the more pejorative connotations of Sam's "introduction". What he had in mind was going to require teamwork, more than even Sam realized, and smoothing the waters would be necessary before he let the complete litter of cats out of the bag.

*"Thanks, Sam. As you all know, we've been divided into three teams working on three separate, daily projects: fencing, roads and forest. Each day we make some headway, storm or no storm. It's been the protocol since the inception of this reserve. Now I want to suggest a significant change that has the potential for getting more of the torrential destruction taken care of so we can get back to maintenance that is more normal.*

*"What I am suggesting is a technique we used out in the war zone when I was in the military. Much as we have standard methods of working, so too in the service there's a proscribed method of accomplishing every task. From time to time, we found that we needed to change our tactics and that is what I am suggesting today.*

*"Rather than splitting into designated teams that either Sam or I have put into place, I would like to see you divide into three groups dependent upon your personal attraction to the task. The three work zones remain the same. We can't do much about that but I feel if we divide ourselves into three companies based upon what we really feel called to do, we'll get more done because of our personal passion for the task. Each team will appoint a leader from within the group to supervise the work.*

*"This is where the sticky part comes in because for this one exercise it levels the playing field. Sam, Nancy and I will be*

team members only. We will not supervise unless our team elects us as the leader."

Don glanced at Sam to see how he was taking this since he hadn't told him of this additional part of the message. He knew that Sam would have nixed the idea before its birth if he even thought he would shortly lose his management position. Thankfully, Sam had left before Don started speaking since he believed he knew what was going to be said. It would be much easier to tell him privately and face-to-face than in front of what Sam considered the subservient masses.

"Any questions so far?" Don asked gathering steam now that he knew he was flying primarily solo.

"Yes, I have a question," Joe asked voicing what probably many were thinking. "What happens if one group has a lot of workers and another group has hardly any? What happens to the small group's workload?"

"That's always one of the inherent issues within this method," Don began, "and this is how we solved it the last time I tried getting something done this way. As soon as the first group finishes its job, say the road crew has all the roads back to snuff, and then we meet again and re-group into two groups with the same focus. We'll only have to divide twice to get it finished because in the next go-round only one task will remain possibly unfinished. Any more questions? No? Okay, let's divide up.

"The fence crew goes to the doorway, road goes to the back of the room and the forest stays where it is in the middle." It took only two minutes for everyone to make decisions. The road crew was smallest with the fence line next and the largest crew opting for the forest. Oh, oh, thought Nancy, this means that whatever Paul is experiencing might be more easily seen due to the number of bodies. I'd better join the forest crew.

"Okay, now that you've got your groups, choose a leader from among you. Don't take a lot of thinking time. You all probably know who the strongest personality within your group is," was Don's next instruction.

The road crew chose Allen and while he wasn't much of a leader, he did know roadwork. Fencing decided on Joe who was always seen though seldom heard. He had been a ranch hand stateside so was a natural fencer. Since Don and Nancy had both chosen to work in the forest, the choices were a little dicier. No one would speak up so Nancy stepped forward and simply said, *"How about me?"*

# Question Forty-eight
## What is unconditional love?

You are love without condition. What does that mean? How do you *be love*? You usually define love as *affection for or a fond attachment to another person*. Does this make sense if you are I AM? Not unless you realize the being you are attached to is you, then you can be love and be yourself at the same time.

Yet, that love that you are, that love that connects you to you is seldom seen by you. And when it is observed in any way, there are many conditions, expectations and judgments placed upon it.

Anything you feel for yourself or another that is conditional is not love. It is another type of feeling you are calling love that could more adequately be labeled need, attachment, desire, fear or other qualifiers. The experience is not love if there is any condition placed upon it.

Most humans place little importance upon self-love. Your focus is upon getting someone to love you and yet this will not happen without conditions and expectations unless you are first being that love as I AM. You must be what you wish to resonate with and this includes the experience of someone loving you as I do or as close to that as he or she possibly can within ME.

This is why if you want love in your life, you must be love so that the frequency of love will respond to your frequency. If you don't believe you will ever find love in your life, you will not find it. Love does have a frequency, a wavelength. All feelings have frequency. Love and other feelings are all wavelength frequencies within ME, no matter how many greeting cards might attempt to make love into something else.

The love that is you loves you and you are not aware of it. You know that self-talk that your mind contributes to on a daily basis. How often is it saying, "I love you" to you? And if it does, are there any conditions applied to the statement?

Think about the people in your life that you say you love. What happens when one of them lies to you, doesn't do what you want or leaves you feeling betrayed? Where does your love go then? You place that condition upon your love. You love if your "love requirements" are fulfilled.

In desiring relationship, in yearning for intimacy with another fellow human, love is the preface if you want to connect with another in a way that will allow you both to experience the fullness of yourself within the scope of each other as I AM. I AM love.

Fulfilling connections, expanding unions rest only on a foundation of love without condition, judgment, expectation or anticipation. The *fondness of attachment* must be fulfilled within you first. Otherwise, you have two incomplete, unsatisfied beings attempting to find completion and satisfaction in another being that, in turn, is incomplete and unsatisfied.

Love as I love. Love as I AM. Place no qualifiers upon your love. Let it be as you are within ME.

You are a circle of love. It is a wave of love advancing from within you into the omniverse infinitely. There is nowhere you are incapable of emitting this love. You are the center point, the focal point of the love that you give you and then emanate within ME.

You have free will. You can make the decision to withhold the love you are, pinning down the very frequency that is attempting to explode out of you and maintaining that you are doing what is best for you when you deny this love to yourself. True love is without condition. It is MY Blessing. When you send your intention of blessing to another, you are directing the love charge that is your biologic signature to bestow love upon another. How can you do that if you are not love? You cannot.

Oh, I know, you might say that you ask ME to bless someone. Yet, you are I AM, so you are asking yourself to conduct the blessing. It is easier to believe that I AM more worthy to "do the blessing". Nothing could be further from the truth. Not only are you worthy, you are so worthy that in blessing them, you bless yourself as well. You cannot give without receiving that which you give because you live in a world based upon MY Principle of Resonance.

Within this realm exists your anointed awareness of you as I AM. It is the first experience that you had within creation and manifests itself within your soul record consistently and constantly as love with no condition. Since this quality you seek is inherent within ME, it is accordingly innate within you. It is MY Spirit as exercised through Creator. It is the essence of your presence within your human body and expresses through your voluntary desire to be the presence of love.

There is no thing that is keeping you from knowing yourself as love except the separating judgments you use to construct what you call your life. Releasing your personal beliefs about what should or should not be opens the door to divinity. All *you* have to do is walk through the door of love living within you as ME. When you know you are perfect exactly as you are, you will love yourself without placing any condition or judgment upon you or ME. Until that time, the expression of love will be limited by your conditions.

## Story Time

Immediately after the crew groups had formed, everyone went out to their designated areas to begin working under their appointed "leaders". Don and Nancy took their ten-man crew to the forest under Nancy's supervision. She divvied up the work among cutting, hauling and clearing, continually attempting to keep most of the noise directed away from Paul's location.

Don took notice immediately and assisted by directing those he was tree trimming with toward the southern end of the line of trees in which they were working. He and Nancy made a good team and it resonated among their group. Once everyone was underway, Nancy quickly slipped away to check on Paul.

She found him seated where she had left him the night before, food untouched. His eyes were closed and he appeared lost in a faraway world without her.

*"Paul,"* she whispered, hoping not to disturb him yet still wanting to get his attention. *"Are you awake? Are you here?"*

Paul slowly opened his eyes and when Nancy looked into them, she no longer recognized the man who was her brother. In his place were serenity, peace and calm. Though his face still looked like Paul, the aura of tenderness emitted through his eyes left her speechless.

"*Welcome, Nancy. Can you sit? Do you have to work? I have so much to tell you,*" Paul began.

"*I'm working and I have to get back. I wanted to check on you. It looks like something has happened overnight while I've been away. Can I come back after dinner tonight and hear about it?*"

"*Of course, you may come when you choose. Bring me a bit of food and make it light. I'm not eating much right now,*" Paul responded in a tone of voice she hadn't experienced before with him.

Nancy tore through the remainder of the workday without telling Don about her experience with Paul. Though her inclination was to share to draw him closer to her, the loyalty she felt to Paul was stronger. *What could have made such a dramatic change within Paul?*

After dinner, Nancy packed up a few pieces of cheese and some of chef's freshly baked bread, heading back to the forest with Paul. Don hadn't made any overtures during the day or dinner so she figured her feelings belonged to her alone. *They'll most likely fade unreciprocated,* she thought.

She found Paul seated on another log across from where he had been earlier. He awaited her return and greeted her with a great smile.

"*Nancy, so glad you're here. Put the food down over by that rock. I'll eat it later. I want to share with you what I experienced last night. I believe we are close enough, especially through Talish's help, that I can take you where I have been. Would you like that?*"

"*Oh, yes, wherever you've been would be marvelous,*" she responded excitedly. "*Tell me, tell me and show me what to do.*"

"*Last night I slept very little,*" he began. "*As soon as it was very dark, as it gets here, the noises of the forest began to dim into the background. I was sitting over where you found me this morning with my eyes closed, expecting I know not what. All of a sudden, I felt like I was no longer within this physical body though I must have been because I didn't topple over.*"

*"I wasn't sure what to do since I was completely alone. Talish wasn't here nor were you so I took a deep breath and settled into the feeling as she has been instructing us.*

*"Very soon I was nowhere. That's the only way I can explain it. I was nowhere and I was everywhere. It felt like I was a multi-petal flower opening into nothing as me, Ann, Great Horn, Abamti, you, John, 'Mao, Tusk, Talish. I could go on forever. These are simply the awareness labels I can name. None of them was separate from me. The point of contact was all me and not me. I know this doesn't make much sense. I can't verbalize the experience very well. Are you with me so far?"*

*"Yes, Paul, go on. I'm with you,"* Nancy said feeling herself losing contact with her physicality.

*"What I came to realize is that none of our personalities are really distinct. We can say we are each of these people. We can act out their lives. We can have all of these unusual experiences you and I have been having, but none of it is real. What does exist is a love I have never felt before. There was no judgment, nothing expected and everything accepted.*

*"It's the place you would call home. We can get there from here, you know. We've just been taught that it doesn't exist or that we have to die to go there. It's not true.*

*"I was only gone, if that's what you call it, for probably an hour. When I opened my eyes here, it was still late at night, the forest was as loudly noisy as usual and I was sitting here in this spot. Yet, I was very different and the feeling has remained.*

*"Nancy, I believe I can take you there. Do you still want to give it a try with me?"*

## Question Forty-nine
## How do I find my soul mate?

You want someone in your life very much. You wish that the person would have certain attributes, particular tendencies or habits similar to your own. Your mind has a laundry list of what this specific person will be like toward you, others and life in general. You are keeping an eagle eye out for the relationship of your lifetime. You consider this person to be your soul mate.

It will be helpful to define what "soul mate" means to you. Most people believe that their soul mate will have a deep meaning to them in all areas of life, a natural affinity for the aspects of this dimension that they do and will generally coincide with their frequency. In a nutshell, your soul mate will be another "you" within ME.

What is wrong with this picture? Do you see it? Can you feel it? What is missing in the previous equation? What do you need to do, you ask yourself.

You are I AM. This also means that you are Creator since Creator is an emanation of ME. This is an important aspect to consider when you are looking for a mate within your reality. Since you are I AM, there is no mate for you and since you are Creator, you can create a pretend mate for the two of you to believe in together.

Why is this important in relationship building? It is paramount because as Creator, you are creating that which you believe you want. Creation begins in the mind of the creator. So, the creator must be what it wishes to create before it can bring it into existence. You cannot make something that you do not know already exists.

Just as a human mother and father do not produce offspring that is anything except what they are, so too, do you create in your life what you are, as well. This is the flow of creation. It is the creative arousal stimulating coherent flow within what you want to experience in your life. In this case, it is a significant relationship with another person. It is not about wanting it to happen. It is about creating the happening in yourself first and then letting MY Love that you are bring it to you exactly as you are being in your creative capacity.

So, how do you do this? Take the attributes that you wish to see in another person and apply them to yourself. Create within yourself such an energetic, aroused, intimate perspective that you only see in yourself, as well as others, that which you want so much in your life.

So, what is it to be intimate? To actually let another person see into you? What does it mean to let another person see you as you are? Isn't that what you mean by soul mate?

Truly intimate relationships lay bare the person inside of your skin, the person you know you are when you are not pretending to be the person you want people to believe you are. It shows your scars, your scabs, hidden fears, your worst nightmares as well as the loving, caring, compassionate individual you have been prodded to be.

Your ability to show yourself will draw many resonate companions to you. Among them, you can pick and choose through your discerning free will the one who pleases you most. Yet, going back to the question before this one, unless you merge with them in unconditional love, eventually you will find yourself disappointed. That relationship will end and you will go on the search outside of yourself for the next soul mate. Do you see how love with no conditions and your resonance within it is the determining factor to your answer?

There is a totally different aspect of intimacy that it is good to look at within your soul mate search. It is the ability to let yourself be seen not as the person you believe you are, not as the person you want the other person to know deeply. It is the ability to enjoy the experience of letting another person see you as he or she sees you. Therein lays the vulnerability of true intimacy because you cannot change another person's perspective of you. You can either allow it or resist it; you cannot change it.

It is impossible to be intimate with another unless you do let the other person see you exactly as they do see you. The significance of this concept lies in the mirror that you are for every person you meet within ME. Whether the encounter is fleeting or one that will last for years, how another person experiences you is totally dependent upon them. They look through their eyes into the energy space that is called "you" and see exactly what their personal beliefs, filters and truths tell them you are to them.

This is why you cannot "find" your soul mate. You must be the mate of your soul and let the resonance of your frequency attract a person to you who is capable of seeing you as you are. Of course, this is dependent upon you being what you truly are within ME rather than what you want the person to believe you are. If you do not expose yourself to the "other", you will only receive someone who hides from you as well.

When you attempt to change what you are to become something you believe they believe you are, the energy that comprises your frequency, your wavelength, your aura, your vibration becomes confused because you are attempting to align yourself with another person's idea of you, not the being you know yourself to be.

Intimacy is your presence within ME. It is you living as ME allowing all other expressions of ME to see you as I AM. So, unclench your stomach, take a very deep breath and look out of your own eyes at another person remembering they are only what they represent to you as I AM. Love them with no condition as you do yourself. You will mate with your soul.

## Story Time

Nancy felt ready to participate in whatever Paul had experienced. If he had gone to a place that he could not describe, arriving back safe and sound, certainly she could, as well.

*"Yes, Paul, yes,"* she reassured him, *"I'm very ready to delve into the unknown with you. What do I, or should I say 'we', have to do?"*

*"Well, since I haven't facilitated anyone in approaching a new, invisible frontier before, perhaps it would be good for us to make physical contact as we do so. If we hold hands and sit on the ground cross-legged with our knees touching, we will maintain*

*physical connection with the earth and each other. How does that sound to you?"*

"Good idea. There, I've repositioned myself in front of you. So take my hands. I suppose we close our eyes and then you'll direct me. Is that right?" she asked with only a hint of her underlying nervousness.

"I suppose so. Okay, take my hands, close your eyes and focus on your breath. That is what I did originally. As soon as I feel that I'm slipping into the unknown space again, I'll begin guiding you there. Just follow whatever I say and do what I feel called to say to you."

Taking several deep breaths, brother and sister merged physically through hands and touching knees. Sitting with their eyes closed, the noises of the evening began to subside within their consciousness as they matched breath for breath cyclically.

Paul made initial contact as he had the night before easily. Once he had experienced this realm, returning was even more familiar.

"Okay, Nancy, I have made the connection. I want you to look within yourself for a blue glow. Once you see it, follow it further into your core and when that is all that you are seeing, let go. Squeeze my hand when the blueness shows up for you."

It was a mere moment, then Paul felt Nancy grip his hand and then she was fully in front of him within the void. Her focused intention had slipped her consciousness gracefully into the realm of all possibility.

"We're here. This is marvelous. You're right; it feels like home. I want a moment to get accustomed to being present and then I'll see if I experience what you told me about from last night.

"Oh, wait, there is no time. That last thought made no sense within this context. Paul, you're morphing. I see you but I also see you as myself. There is no separation among you, me or any other consciousness here. It's much more than you were describing. And names don't fit either.

"I can experience myself as Nancy plus all awareness at once without time or construct of space. Oh, and I'm not speaking, am I? No, I'm not thinking either. It's more a knowing that I know you also know. This is the reality of union.

*"I notice that where I place my focus, my attention, is what I experience. If I center on Tusk, I experience him. As Tusk, I can release the hold on his consciousness and reemerge as all awareness. I am able to shift from one individual to another with no attachment to form or outcome. Is this what you experienced before and are right now?"*

*"Nancy, you have shown me a fuller view of my earlier participation in this realm. Previously, I had not allowed myself expansion within the fullness of union. Now I see that each is the same though individual. None of the human characteristics or attributes is important. They are much more like costumes worn for a specific role in a chosen life and can be switched at a moment's notice. That is why I feel so at home here because nothing is expected and all is given."*

As Nancy and Paul continued the experience of union, they discovered the dissolution of their desire for personality though their individuality remained. Within the blending, they were able to see themselves as the respective soul expression each contained while enjoying the communion of all. Due to the familiarity of the expression, dividing became less desirable and the common union more the norm.

*"Paul,"* Nancy threaded her knowing awareness through the amalgamation of their essence, *"the truth of this reality is absolute. I now understand that there is no specialness about any incarnation. Each is an emanation from within the whole, completely within unison with all and only experiencing a sense of separation for a very short period of incarnated expression.*

*"No one is more important than another because no individuality bears the significance placed upon it through embodied thought. It reminds me of someone painting a picture and then calling it 'real'. And I no longer question the validity of the teachings of Talish.*

*"Oh, whoops, placed my attention upon her and here I am as Talish. This is amazing. It feels very exciting and almost simultaneously commonplace. Thank you so much for developing the skill to embrace this world through us. My gratitude is now my frequency and I wish it to remain as such throughout my present embodiment."*

*"Talish, oh, you're back to Nancy; okay then, Nancy, it is our mutual pleasure to experience ourselves as one. It is our most natural state of conscious awareness."*

# Question Fifty
## What soul purpose do my partner and I have together?

As you are resting in the waters of life, you exist within a symbiotic relationship as the individual in symbiosis with your soul within ME. And while *symbiosis* means a pairing up, a living together of two dissimilar organisms within your language, I tell you that this is not so. The qualitative difference is that you live in time - past, present and future - and your soul lives outside of time. It is timeless and, hence, you are, as well.

You do not know this consciously. If you did, you would not keep constantly checking in to see if the soul is there and what its purpose could be. You would not need to have so much attention paid to you individually because you would be in such alignment with your soul that no attention would be necessary. You would be aware that you are all that you seek within ME. Since you are not aware of the symbiotic relationship you have with your soul, why would you believe you would be aware of or need to know about your partner's soul or the two souls together? You do not understand your *own* expression and that is where you want to start because it is the *only* focus of any importance to you.

Becoming aware of *you* is a lifelong experience within ME. The person you are presently calling your "partner" is also having the same experience within his or her consciousness. As the two of you have been drawn together, you are mirrors for each other in many different ways. The most expressive of these experiences will be in your dissimilarities leaving more room for you to pay attention to the symbiosis of you with your soul rather than getting lost in the attachment you've made with this individual.

You must align your capacity to love within the identification you hold of yourself as I AM. You are to love yourself, not tolerate yourself. You are to love, meaning no judgment of yourself or the character of the other, for there is no other. The person you see as outside of you is the mirror reflecting your judgments.

While most of you express a desire within ME to be with a partner who is another you, the soul's attraction usually is to a person who will show you how to align the many aspects of yourself. Surrendering to this invitation unites you with you within the relationship you have within your soul and that is all that can be important to you. Why? Because your partner may disappear as the breath of the wind while you will always remain as you as I AM.

You meeting you, recognizing you and accepting you is enlightenment. The greeting is momentous. The welcome magnificent and it is here, right now, in your time frame. What you are looking for within another or between you and the other, bounding about, hoping for and wishing that you could find is already here for you within ME.

If you are looking for purpose among you, your soul, your partner and his or her soul, that is it. Your mate reflects you to you so that you may know your soul and vice versa.
This is you arising from within you within ME as I AM, infinitely. It is you that you seek and submerge at the same time. You are infinite, aware expansion.

Yet, even in the most intimate of relationships, you hide certain aspects of yourself from the other person. When least expected the submerged part of the personality will rear its head surprising both people involved. If you let yourself be seen, the hidden and all, from the get-go, neither of you will be taken by surprise and that means neither of you will wish he or she had not entered into the relationship.

Your love is a "we-ness", not a "you" or "me-ness" within ME. While you might believe your relationship is "special", it is not. Every human being is in some type of relating to every other aspect of creation within ME. As you love your partner, you love the man sitting outside the restaurant begging for food. Love is – plain and simple. Removing the specialness from the idea about your relationship frees you to love without condition instead of attaching yourself to someone else for your own personal, very special, unique, needy support.

Your question is based upon a belief you and your partner have a purpose together. You can make that function be anything you desire it to be since the two of you are in a constant state of transformation and change. While you may be living a loosely scripted role in each other's lives, it is only the expectation of what that is supposed to mean that drives your question.

There is only one truth with which to align regarding your partner's appearance within your soul's expression. It is to mirror to you the transmission of your frequency. Whether he or she plays out this role according to your personal tastes has no bearing with the exception of your personal interest in outcome. You transmit. You receive. He or she transmits. He or she receives. It is continuous, expansive and infinite within ME.

Trust that the person you are resonating with in this moment is perfect for your soul's alignment within your individuated soul expression. If this were not true, the two of you would not be "partnered". Once you have established that trust, constantly look into the mirror held up before your eyes to see what your reflection says to you as I AM. Then say, "Thank you."

## Story Time

Paul and Nancy returned to ordinary reality by common agreement. As they opened their eyes into the dark night of the jungle, they were surprised to see Talish and Tusk sitting knee to knee with them in the circle.

*"Wow, what are you two doing here?"* Nancy gasped as she realigned herself within her physical connection. *"It feels like we just left you and now here you are."*

*"True, in one way you did leave awareness of us in the world of spirit and in another, we are all still there. The material form we are sharing here on the great earth is one extension of atam in which we are aware. The union within atam you were awake within only moments ago includes every expression having meaning for you currently. I know that you felt the hints of other atam-ums that felt very much like you.*

*"It is difficult to put into human words what you have experienced. Even in these forms, I use a special learning with you so that you may understand my native language. It sounds to your*

ears as though I am speaking your English language and yet, I am not. You see, the defined concepts you have been living with are beginning to dissolve. It is one of the reasons I told you to arrange time for yourself, Nancy. Your life within camp is now changed and you will need to deal with that aspect of it in some way.

"As to you, Paul, you have many days before you in which to discover why you came to this part of the world. Nancy will be joining you whether she knows it or not and then we will leave this area for a more secure, private place for your inner investigations. Don may come, as well. There is much afoot of which you do not know and while I have sight into that which may come, I cannot make it occur. It takes the willing compliance of all."

"Talish, can I ask you a question that's been bothering me?" Nancy asked hopefully.

"Yes, of course, and I will answer with truth if I know of it."

"Thanks. It's about you and Tusk. You look an awful lot like his mother. Are you?" Nancy almost feared the response since if Talish was Tusk's mother, then that meant in some way she was also Nancy's mother. This was getting very confusing.

"Yes, Nancy, you are correct. In the world of time as you would see it, in that type of relationship, I am Tusk's mother. And I know that you wonder what that does to my connection with you, as well.

"Okay, go back in your mind to the communion you felt in the world of atam when you felt one with all named expressions. Did it make any difference to you what role was being played by each of the names there? No, I know that it didn't.

"In the same way, you and Paul have played many characters within each other's lives. You have been combinations of mother and father, husband and wife, sisters, brothers and grandparents. None of these expressions bears any importance upon what you are now experiencing with the exception that they are written upon the record, as you would call it.

"So, back to your question about my motherhood: Since I am the physical birthing mother to Tusk in the time and space in which we lived in the physical, you were Tusk during that time and knew me as mother. Though you now perceive us as though we are tangible within your awareness, no one else sees us with the exception of Don. It has to do with your expanded inner sight and our life connections within the realm of atma.

"The human desire to find the design within the soul's life in a particular embodied experience is of no use because no one has the whole picture. The two of you have had the tiniest of glimpses into the world of atam-atma. Have you begun to understand the blinded focus of the human?"

Paul spoke at last having been listening with rapt attention as he resumed union with his materiality. He realized he wasn't use to having guests in his solitary jungle space.

"Yes, Talish, I definitely understand the hubris of humanity since I have been living within the false world of illusion believing it was very real. I am content to stay here within the forest world and open to whatever new learning is to come my way. While I am not eager to pursue this investigation on my own, my gratitude goes to you for any assistance you are willing to offer. I would hope that Nancy would travel this road with me, as well."

Nancy's mixed emotions attempted to usher forth in a great expletive of concern. She felt torn between her brother and the world of the reserve, between the elephants and the human crew and between her desire to learn and her yearning to find out more about Don.

Talish immediately sensed the churning agitation realizing that though Nancy could always retrieve the weaving of this thread within her soul, no set of circumstances would be as appropriate as the ones set before all of them at present. She remained silent for a few moments and then made her decision.

Taking Nancy's hands in hers, Talish looked into her eyes and said, "My child, I have waited for many passings of infinite moons in an eternity of lives to have this opportunity to reflect you to you. If you will honor me with your presence for one month, I will be satisfied in our common union. While fulfilling my soul's commission, we will join as one and bring harmony to all you know."

Nancy shed one tear and then said, *"Yes, I am yours. Take me where you will."*

# Question Fifty-one
## Why do we become immobilized, not progressing to maximum capability?

I will begin by reminding you that all energy is neutral and in a state of infinite movement. Therefore, it is impossible for you to become immobilized. What you experience when you feel "stuck" is a sense of resistance to what is occurring within your life within ME. This persistence in resistance causes you to believe you are unable to move forward toward your personal goals.

Life by its very nature is constantly changing, shifting, morphing, emerging and merging. The natural flow of life is movement. Perception of immobilization is just that, a perception based upon a belief regarding the manner in which you should be living your life.

Allowing your life to live itself is the command of nature to interact within an essential state of flow. The acquiescence of life within itself is far removed from any concept of control, analyzing, goal planning or ambition. It is rhythmic, continuous, inherently coherent and congruent within itself within ME.

Your concept of "progress" may or may not be your soul's expression of it within this moment of your time and space. Since the beliefs you hold about how life is to proceed are contributed to by your intellectual expectations within your culture, you have no way of ascertaining the inherent truth within them. All within your present reality is subjective, relative and constantly contributed to by the complexity of the human's need to appear superior within ME.

Chasing after the next goal or pushing away situations in life that don't please you distances you from allowing your life to unfold within the experience you designed it to be. Yes, that is right – *you*. You created the loosely held blueprint for the unfolding allowances you call your life within ME through Creator. The fear, anger and stress that you experience within the various states of allowance are caused by resistance to allowance with ME as I AM.

As to what your maximum capability may be, you have no hint. Its definition is derived from the belief system you use to define your concept of progress. Within your soul's expression within ME, you have the capacity to "achieve maximum capability" while sitting in a chair in absolute silence. Your mind's drive to become and do sets up its own map of goals and destinations within your world. Since you reside within a completely subjective reality, your contrived ambitions are not real, meaning they have no significance outside that with which you imbue them.

Every aspect of creation, no matter the dimension, form or frequency, exists within a beneficent allowance within ME through Creator. Perception of immobilization along the scale with which you measure your personal goals is the result of resisting the flow of MY Beneficence due to a belief that you know better or something other than allowing life to live.

You are I AM. You are infinite with no minimum or maximum limitation upon your attributes. What you consider the paramount experience in this moment will change dynamically as you immerse yourself within your emergence as ME within your life.

If you desire a goal within your current mindset, reset your ambition to a fuller awareness of your emergence within ME. No momentary, personal achievement can equal the limitless expression within MY Infinitely Emerging Union. When viewed from within this benchmark, your concepts of maximum potential pale in comparison.

Often your idea of allowing pertains to the Principle of Resonance – how you are to allow that which you desire to come to you. Since the natural state of your energy frequency is a reflection of your feelings and your feelings are a reflection of your energy state, allowance paves the way for all you wish to come your way. You cannot fool your energetic output/input within your dimensional awareness within ME. While you may believe you are in a state of allowing and receptivity, if you feel resistance, fear, doubt or lack of trust in the outcome, that becomes your true feeling and that is what is responded to through ME as Creator.

If you will allow yourself to look at your question from a completely different perspective, you could ask why you feel immobilized within your desire to gain something because you are afraid of losing a specific status within your life. The true question you are asking ME is, "Why do I become immobilized as I attempt to gain everything in this reality that will produce a positive connotation of my expression within my eyes and the eyes of the world?"

Within each breath, you have the capacity and the invitation to allow, nothing else. It is not a big step yet your mind says, "How can I allow myself to experience something not contained within my set goals?"

The answer, "Can you simply allow it to be what it is? Can you loosen the attachment you have to the drive to progress and simply allow it to be its own progression within ME?"

Your mind replies, "How can I do that? Can't you see how much this is affecting me? I can't just let it be."

Allowance is the frequency of this dimension *to give you permission to give yourself permission to be*. It is the utmost of your capabilities, consciously being aware of existing as ME. If you truly wish to progress to your maximum, know that you are I AM.

## Story Time

With her acquiescence to Talish's request, Nancy had set her reality ball spinning in a completely new direction with reference to the reserve. *What am I going to tell Sam and Don? How am I going to find out if Don wants to join with us? What would happen if he did? What would occur if he didn't?*

All of these questions and concepts whirled around within her mind while Tusk and Talish become transparent and disappeared. She was left sitting with Paul in the hush of the early morning twilight.

*"Paul, what do you think? Should I just quit? How can I find out if Don wants to come? I'm really at a loss for words now that I've made this commitment."*

"Nancy, I am coming to realize that allowance is the only feeling I want to entertain. In that vein, I allow you to do whatever you feel called to do within your own situation. I know I owe Sam and the same sense of acceptance applies to that debt. I trust that I will have the means to pay him back or reciprocate in some fashion. It is not a concern for this moment. My only focus is on understanding my ability for infinite conscious awareness. Go do what you need to do. I will be here when you return."

Nancy struggled with her sense of abandonment. All of her life she had wanted Paul to be the strong, protective older brother and he had never fulfilled that role. Talish had made mention somewhere along the line that they had rewritten some script. *Maybe that's what I'm feeling, the script rewrite and somehow I don't like it. Boy, I'm so resistant to just letting things be. Do I really want to learn how to do this?*

Slowly rising up from her cross-legged sitting position, Nancy breathed a sigh of nervous anticipation as she considered walking back down the trail. *What am I going to say and do when I get back to camp?* She almost pushed the thought aside rather than entertain it.

"Okay, Paul, then off I go. I'll return as soon as I can, with or without Don in tow and with my head on or not. I'll have to admit that I'm scared and feeling a definite sense of dereliction to duty. Oh, well, I've said I would do it, so let's get it done." With those shaky parting words, Nancy headed out to the trail and back to the camp not knowing whether to find Don or Sam first and what to say when she found either or both.

Halfway down the groomed path, she was surprised to see the water boy who served the crews standing in the middle of the trail. She usually only ran into him when they were deep into their various tasks; otherwise she didn't even know where he lived or came from deep within the surrounding jungle.

"Hi," she said by way of tentative greeting. *"I'm surprised to see you here."*

*What now,* she thought, *as if what's happening isn't enough.*

"I've come to remind you of something that Talish told you once. Your choices make changes within Paul's life. What she

did not add to that, and the true reason I am here since she sent
me to you, is that your decisions shift everything for everyone. You
have no idea what you are capable of bringing about within this
world. I am here to remind you of that one truth as you go
forward to change the direction of many realities."

Nancy was so surprised. *"So, you know Talish? I didn't
know that. Can you see her? I thought you couldn't speak,"* Nancy
asked remembering what Talish had told her about very few
people being able to see her emergence within the physical
world.

*"See her? I live with her, didn't you know? And now I must
return. My message has been delivered and I'm finished here. Oh,
I'm not speaking with verbal words."* With that, the water boy
slipped into the surrounding foliage and disappeared from view
leaving Nancy stunned and even more stymied than she had been
upon setting out toward the camp.

As Nancy entered the campsite, she began to experience
a sense of strangeness that hadn't arisen within her before. It no
longer felt like she belonged in camp. Actually, she didn't feel like
she belonged anywhere at all. The displacement added to her
present sense of confusion causing her to be heady and
unbalanced.

*Oh, great,* she thought as the unsettling feeling deepened
with each step, *not only am I scared, now I feel like I don't even
know where I am. This definitely doesn't help matters.*

Heading toward Sam's office as the first logical step in an
unknown progression, Nancy felt her heart rate speed up and her
palms begin to sweat. Never in her life had she felt such a sense
of fearful anticipation. What the water boy had told her, however
he had done it, only made matters worse. *I don't want to be
responsible for changing people's lives, only my own.*

Shaking her head in disbelief at the locked office door,
she came to the realization that most of the camp was just now
waking up from the night's sleep. Time had lost its meaning for
her, blending day and night into one. *I wonder if chef has the
coffee on,* she mused as she retraced her steps down the office
stairs and over to the mess tent.

Not only was the coffee brewed and ready, chef had just pulled hot muffins and buns from the oven. Nancy realized she had been awake all night with only a light supper the evening before and was starving. *It's interesting how our goals change from moment to moment,* she noticed while pouring the rich, dark brew and waiting for chef to pop the muffins onto serving platters. *One minute I'm dripping with sweat over talking to Sam and the next I'm starving for carbs. Seems nothing can be trusted to remain the same.*

Just as Nancy reached for a warm bran muffin, she heard footsteps behind and recognized Sam's strident step. *Okay, here goes nothing,* she thought in mid-bite.

# Question Fifty-two
## What can we do to "unstick" ourselves?

How long do you take to make a decision? Is it a few years to decide on what college to attend or maybe six months to buy a car? How much time to do you give to allowing someone to enter the sacred realm of your reality? Or even your home for that matter? You came into this world to follow your bliss; do you pay attention to your intention as I AM?

You are looking for ways to go beyond your perceived human barriers and feel "stuck" in doing so. So, I will ask the question again, "How long do you take to make the decision about whom or what is going to enter your inner domain no matter what the situation may be?"

Your experience of life belongs to you within ME. When you see yourself as stuck, mired in the contrast or too immersed within discontent, you are looking through your personal filtering system – a frame of reference for how you see the world. This veiled perception of life gives you goals, measuring sticks and a tallying method to let you know whether you are keeping up with yourself or not. Most likely, this way of taking stock of where you "are" has to do with what others tell you about yourself.

One of the pitfalls of looking outside of yourself for confirmation of that which you already know (and you *do* know) is that anyone you seek out has an opportunity to play out their own story within your drama. Since each of you is a standing wave, transmitting and receiving simultaneously within ME, you only experience that which you are transmitting and so does everyone else. Acceptance of yourself exactly as you are is the point of departure for an acceptable, meaningful effort at self-transformation wherein you do not ever experience the feeling of being "stuck".

Your soul knows no time, judgment or condition. It simply is and within that realm is only beneficence and love while being in a constant state of change. The emotional realm is within the noosphere in which exist all of the feelings and thoughts of humanity. It is constantly changing and moving contributing new information to the whole in every way.

Your physical life is a mirror of your soul's world since your incarnated experience is your desire for just that, experience within ME. If your soul is always transforming and the emotional envelope of your earth is in infinite shift, how can you, as an expression within those dimensions, be stuck in any way? You cannot, any more than I can be stuck.

You, as a human being, are beginning to understand and realize that you are I AM. This means that your human heart is taking the driver's seat, driving not only the physical body, also the personal desires of daily life. This opens the door to unlimited possibility because as I AM, you are unlimited possibility. Now you are beginning to know it. Embrace this unlimited knowing. Be vivacious within it!

Act in that knowing by using your sacred discernment in determining who and what you are going to allow into your life. If someone says you "should" do something or "shouldn't" be a certain way, you immediately know he or she is attempting to project a belief system upon you and it is all a loop within a mirror.

From within the concept that you are unable to move from one aspect of experience to another, you arrive at a boundary line that does not exist within ME. If you believe you are "stuck", you are telling yourself or someone else is telling you that you do not measure up to what you believe you should be doing. Perhaps the issue lies within your belief about yourself and its confirmation by the people with whom you have chosen to associate.

The judgment that maintains a stranglehold on your heart reflects you believe you are not worthy of love. You are guilty of something, deserving of blame and separate. The world of illusion is actually a world of delusion. Within this world, you reference yourself as a victim within ME. This self-referencing is your acceptance of your idea of being unable to move within your concept of personal transformation.

Your ego personality's concept of your inner war demands everything and gives nothing. Love, self-respect and inner honoring give all and ask for nothing. Yet, you always have free will and if you make the choice to live in fear, anxiety and "stuck-ness" or "immobility", a sense of separation becomes your norm. Your awareness of the connection to your origin within ME appears severed, the basis for the feeling you describe as being "stuck". The connection is still there, only you do not know that it always remains. Separation, by its nature, defies ME. Separation is included in union within ME.

The emanation you are intends to collect and record ever-moving, changing, transforming experience. All of your perceptions are built upon the events of your life. Each experience contributes to your beliefs and your perceptions. Your personal truth will only be revealed and the fear of being stuck relinquished when you stabilize your awareness within ME, releasing your programmed belief systems.

The original intention for experience is the expansion of conscious awareness. It is natural to expand and grow. It is only the distortions of your belief system that cause the confusion, worry, pain and fear of being unable to "move" that you experience as real. When you realize your harmony within ME, the idea of being "stuck" will not enter your mind because it is not in MINE. Your resonance with MY Cosmic Mind will fill your heart and you will be at peace.

## Story Time

Turning to address Sam and get it over with, Nancy was doubly surprised to find Don behind her also, standing next to Sam. She definitely wasn't ready to take on two such disparate conversations and quickly made the decision to shut up.

*"Hi, guys, and good morning. Rolls and buns are fresh and hot. Let me move out of your way so you can get at the coffee."*

*"Well, Nancy, nice to see you up and about so early,"* Sam said with a note of sarcasm. He was not unaware that she had been hiding out in the forest with Paul. Her behavior was unacceptable according to his personal camp rules and he knew she knew it.

"Yep, sun got me up," Nancy lied and feeling stuck in the middle of this non-conversation decided to make a fast exit. "I have to go back to my tent for something. I'll catch up with you two later."

"That's good," Don piped up, "because we've got a full day ahead. As soon as the rest of the crew is up, we're going to get an early start. I'll see you back here."

Oh, God, what can I do now? Nancy thought with dread as she hurried to hide inside her tent and figure this out. I can't go to work as if nothing has happened. Paul's waiting for me and who knows what Talish is doing. I'm stuck; I'm stuck, oh, I am so stuck.

Collapsing on the bed, exhausted more from stress than from the long night, Nancy quickly dozed off. Within moments, she was in the dream world standing before 'Mao, an aspect of herself she had had little contact with as yet.

"I, too, make a similar decision as you in a world seemingly distant from yours. My choice is whether to live or die. I know your deciding point right now feels as extreme. Within the time to which I am referring I, that is also you, either leap into a raging river or die through the shot of an arrow I can see will be coming in my direction. Stuck within the decision point due to the depth and strength of the turbulent waters and presence of crocodiles, I hesitate just long enough for the arrow to find its mark. In a matter of speaking, the decision is made for me because I cannot act quickly enough.

"The reason I am telling you this story is because we are one. You stand on this precipice as me, the edge of the river, with no space within time and no time within space. Your decision in this moment shifts the tide as to whether you live in the reality of your physical world or step into the waters of the dimensions with a foot in both worlds.

"Though you have given your commitment to Talish, all experience within atam is open to being reconstructed with no judgment. The blame you are creating within your mind I, too, share. The arrow hitting me causes my death leaving my two children alone to face life without direction. Again, each breath creates the outcome of the next connecting all within all.

*"Whatever you decide to do you will live with within all of the aspects of yourself you are meeting. There are many attributes of yourself you know not of and will not meet within this physical life if you choose to walk that path. If you choose yet another fork within the trail, there are experiences within the physical realm you will not have, as well. Yet, you must choose because you are at the choosing point within the journey."*

Nancy bolted upright gasping for breath as though she had been suspended under water far too long. *What am I thinking? How could I believe I was stuck in this self-created paradox? There is only one decision and I know now what it is. I've got to talk with Sam first and then Don.*

Jumping up from her cot, Nancy peeled off her dirt-ridden work clothes and hopped into another clean set for the duration. *Clothing will be the least of my concerns, I'm sure,* she thought with a dazed smile on her face. Once dressed, she headed to the office figuring Sam would be breakfasted and back at his desk before he headed out with his team.

She arrived at the office door just as it opened to Sam leaving for the day. *"Sam, I need to talk to you before you take off,"* she began with élan. *"This is important and will only take a moment."*

*"Do we need to go back inside or can you tell me here?"* Sam queried as he attempted to skirt past her at the top of the stairs.

*"Here will do. I only need to tell you that I'm either quitting or requesting a one-month leave of absence. I'm going into the jungle with Paul and I need the time. Whether you let me go and then come back or I have to quit is up to you."* Nancy found herself surprised at her own newfound courage and integrity without mincing of words.

*"What the hell! You can't just walk out on us after I made you part of the admin team. What do you think you're doing, anyway? Paul shows up and you go all woo-woo on me. So, you think you can just come and go as you please. No, I don't think so. Either you stay now or pack up your things and get out."* Sam was nearly stammering with frustration, anger and disappointment.

"*Well, I guess that does it then,*" Nancy responded with relief. "*I'll get my bedroll and pack up my clothes though I don't really have any place to put them.*"

She hadn't seen Don approaching behind her as Sam announced his verdict. She only heard his voice as he quietly said, "*I'll store them for you, Nancy. Give them to me.*"

# Question Fifty-three
## I have an innate understanding
## of the bigger things, so where is my direction?

Wanting direction is part of experiencing a realm of contrast and free will within ME. Without those two components, you would not be asking the question because direction would not enter your mind.

A world of contrast is naturally conflicted. Duality and polarity create a constant state of decision. This is where free will comes into play and, hence, the conflict or the belief you need direction within the "bigger picture".

If you were left to follow your own devices, you would much more easily "go with the flow". As I AM, you are preconceived to navigate this realm of duality and choose that which pleases you, serves you and helps you thrive. That is your natural state. Your ego personality has constructed a reality in which you believe you know an overall "plan" within ME and it wants to know how it fits into that Plan.

The beliefs you are programmed to live by are filled with *should, should not, can, cannot, do* and *don't* directives. The reason behind these control mechanisms *is* control. Behind every single belief exists someone's desire to maintain power and control over one aspect of the human population pursuant to those edicts and convictions.

If you truly want direction within the experience of conflict, follow that which serves you first and foremost. Make your happiness the focus of all that you feel, think, say and do within ME. Follow your natural instincts.

I "source" ME within expansion through infinite experience in every dimension. A dimension is a frequency. There are infinite frequencies. The idea of direction within contrast is part of your differentiation within your dimension.

In other frequencies, the idea of direction may be very different or not exist at all. It is through preference that you decide what you wish to experience within your reality and this can lead to attachment.

If you trust your intuition, the feeling of the 'rightness' of things, you cannot go wrong though your actions may appear foolish to others, or to yourself, if you try to analyze them from within the rational mind. Trust is the key, not skepticism and past experience.

Inasmuch as you have stated you have an innate understanding of what you call "bigger things", you may ask this question of yourself: Where within the "bigger things" do I feel I want to fit? What direction do I desire to follow?

Posing the question *outside* of your personal, current understanding hands your innate power within ME to someone or something else. It exhibits a dichotomy within what you believe is true.

If you truly believe you understand the "bigger picture", why would you ask for direction outside of your current understanding? In other words, if you *know that you know*, why are you stating you do not know your direction?

Now, if you are willing to admit that you do not understand the bigger things, then you will open yourself to a state of surrender in which you can actually come to terms with the direction most desirable to you. Your belief that you possess a comprehension that does not include your direction does nothing to support your authentic experience within ME. It is a mask you wear to project the appearance of knowing. You know you do not know, yet you would have others believe you do.

Are you ready to release the hold you have on your world and your attachment to everything in it? First, this is not something you can seek after - you can only let go of everything that is holding you back from following your natural directive within ME. Otherwise, all you do is attempt to grasp hold of something that is one more attachment. You must dismantle your mental constructs. You must see through the image you have of yourself in your mind.

Examining all of the beliefs you believe are real and finding out where they come from is the first step. After that, you can begin to experience what is real for you, true for you rather than what someone tells you is supposed to be valid. If you live a heart-focused life and only allow that which you know to be personally authentic into your life, you will find there is no need for direction because your experience is ever changing. You will find out that there is nothing to hold onto, no place to go and that you effortlessly move from within one aspect of ME to another.

Then you stop struggling and attempting to figure out. You simply are being within ME. Stay with what is happening right now – as you are experiencing your life – not the past or future of your projected personal management.

You will *know that you know* when the fear of lack of direction no longer visits your doorstep. Life will be simple harmony and you will not get lost in the day-to-day even when watching the evening news (though you will most likely do less of that since you will see it for what it is – human drama.) This knowing is only found in moment-to-moment awareness within ME. Once you are no longer attached to the idea of this body's need for direction, you will not be so concerned about where you are going since you will see it all without attachment to the contrast – the right/wrong, the bigger or the smaller of anything.

## Story Time

Don's words slapped Sam in the face. His "right hand" was siding with a deserter. At least that was the way Sam was seeing it in the early morning light. Shrugging his shoulders and throwing his hands up in the air, Sam turned and walked away to the waiting crewmembers he would be working with for the day.

*"Nancy, I know this is hard for you and I'm not sure I completely agree with the direction you have decided to take, but I do know I'm willing to help you out by storing some of your stuff in my tent. Do you want to go get it now or what?"* Don asked and in so doing took the first step to lighten the density of the cloud hanging over them.

*"Thanks, Don, that's really kind of you. Yes, let's go get my things right now so I can get back to Paul. I don't have that much but what I do have has to go somewhere. I'll be gone a month. Is that too long to use your free storage?"*

*"Nope, not at all. I'm not going anywhere that I know of so you can leave it as long as you need. I doubt anyone's going to take ladies clothes around here."* Don's cavalier attitude was relaxing Nancy after her tongue lashing from Sam. She never had done too well with criticism and Sam had really let her know how he felt. It stung.

*"Don, I'm going to ask you one more time, just to make sure. Don't you want to come with us? Talish is offering us one month's training with her somewhere in the jungle. We've had some pretty exciting experiences thanks to her and we definitely want more. I would love to have you join us and I know Paul would, also."* This was Nancy's final plea to not only let Don know how much she wanted to see more of him, also to give him the opportunity to learn more about himself.

*"Nancy, with you gone, I can't just run off and leave Sam. When I came here, he was running the place all on his own and it was a bit of a mess. It's shaped up a lot due to our mutual efforts, not to diminish your own contribution. I can't walk out on him right now."*

*Is that a hint of wistfulness in Don's voice,* Nancy thought to herself. *Is it because of me or because of what Talish is going to teach us? Do I dare ask? Maybe, not.*

Once at her tent, Nancy piled her belongings into the two rucksacks she had brought with her and handed them over to Don. Looking around her erstwhile home, all she needed were the clean clothes on her back and her bedroll. Innately she knew through her inner direction that nothing else was needed from her old life.

*"Okay, Don, thanks. I'm going to go now. I want you to know that I'm sure Paul and I will be at the same place you found us before through today if you change your mind. Don't be shy about joining us. After tomorrow morning, I don't know if we'll still be there since Talish didn't tell us when she would be coming to get us for the journey. I hope you change your mind."*

With a quick squeeze of his arm, Nancy turned around and headed toward the forest to join Paul leaving Don standing next to her tent, rucksacks in hand. For just one moment, she turned to wave goodbye and was astonished to see Talish standing behind him.

*Does he know she's there? Can he see her? He saw her before but she is standing out of view so maybe he doesn't know she's there. And why is she there? Is she going to talk to him? Oh, maybe he'll come after all. I'd better stop putting too many eggs in that basket. He's given me no sign that he is interested in me personally. This is all me, not him.*

Nancy walked toward Paul's hidden enclave much more slowly than she had anticipated she would. Her earlier excitement about going with Talish and Paul and finding out what direction this would take her was now being overshadowed by her reluctance to leave Don.

Still, she maintained her stride until she hit the trailhead toward Paul's hideout. Once out of sight of camp and into the forest, she began to feel better about her decision. *It's not that I regret doing what I'm doing or having said what I said,* she told herself. *It's just that I feel like I'm missing a chance to get to spend time with Don and see if there are any feelings growing between us. After all, he did offer to help me even knowing how mad Sam would get.*

As she approached Paul's seated figure, a movement caught her peripheral vision just to the right. Turning quickly so as not to lose the presence, she sensed 'Mao even more than she saw her. Within her inner awareness, she heard the voice she was now coming to know as her own as 'Mao.

*"Do not forget what I told you about my choice at the river. You will spend a great deal of time going over your decision, second-guessing what you might have done differently. Every time you lose trust in yourself, you diminish your journey just a little bit.*

*"Since I know you as me and you are coming to know me as you, take these words as coming from yourself. You have set your foot upon an unknowable path. You will not understand any of it one breath to the next. The only comprehension you will find real for you is surrendering to what is happening as it occurs. Once you begin to flow within that wave, you will cease making choices. Rather you will allow the choices to inform you."*

## Question Fifty-four
## What are effective strategies to
## recognize we are not reaching our capabilities?

First, you must recognize what you believe your capabilities might be. Since all perception regarding what you are capable of comes from beliefs you have learned and maintained, it is most certain that what you believe your aptitude for any endeavor may be is false.

When you come to the realization that it is impossible to know anything about yourself until you understand your emergence within ME, then you are truly free. Freedom is the absence of necessity within your choices or actions. Therefore, the belief that you have a necessary potential you are not reaching imprisons you within your own thinking. When you sit firmly rooted in the sense that you do not know, you are then free of the necessity to choose or act.

What does that say to you on a daily basis? How does that free you from the conditioned responses that seem to drive your life? To begin with, it allows you to live in the moment in which you are breathing. It allows you to observe, witness and quietly see that which you are a part of around you. You no longer have to deliver a certain aspect of yourself; rather, you are able to be free within that which is your greatest aspect as ME, no matter how that shows up.

This practice allows you to go beyond the teachings of your parents, your schools, your religion and social structure. It invites you to feel what is being called forth from you within your heart and soul and to follow that road no matter where it leads. It means that no matter what the fragments look like, they are all I AM and you are invited to pay attention to them. It frees you from personal obsession and creates the space to see the second-to-second play of creation.

When you learn to interpret the messages of your heart as the voice of your soul, your perceived capabilities change. One day they are in one form, the next day in another. Static living within non-flowing potentials is the human being's undoing. The mental body believes it knows what is to be "reached" and thus sets benchmarks within ME attempting to define what, where, how, with whom and sometimes why. None of these questions are asked by your conscious awareness within I AM. They are only curiosities of the ego personality.

When you awaken in the morning, open your eyes wiping clean the slate of your mind and be in the present moment only. Allow yourself to become awake to where you are and what you are. Do not attempt to program the day. It will take care of itself. As you get up, dress, eat breakfast and all of the usual early morning happenings, be present within the moment of each occurrence. Know that you do not know what the day will bring. Allow yourself to feel what it would be like to stretch yourself during that day as far as you could possibly expand. Yet, you do not know how far that stretch will take you or even if you will be aware of it. Simply allow.

As you go about your day, there is an awareness that is available to you. You will begin to live with more compassion for yourself and for those with whom you interact. You will start feeling that all is available to you because you have not circumscribed your circle to include only the few. Diversity becomes harmony in your vision. The whole begins to become that which it is, ME rather than an abstract concept.

When this occurs, you will begin to perceive your potential and your various attributes within a different light. Right now, as you ask the question, you have a set of projected abilities you wish to believe you can fulfill. Yet, since you are asking for strategies to recognize lack of fulfillment, you do not know what your capabilities are or you would understand how to bring them about for yourself. Your question admits to that fact.

What your ego personality's mind is asking within this question is "tell me how to go further than I am going since I don't recognize how far I can go". You want to know how much you are capable of and are hoping someone will tell you that so you will have something to compare yourself to in this present moment.

There is no strategy because there is no limit to the potential existing within you within ME. Recognizing this one fact will free you infinitely better than attempting to give you a list of *do's* and *don'ts* to follow fulfilling your mind's desire for a to-do list based upon personal judgments.

If you ask your heart what strategy it would like to apply to recognition of your capabilities, it would simply tell you to be. Once you are aware of your beingness within ME, then whatever else you do can only increase whatever potential you may observe within yourself.

You are a natural observer, a witness to all that occurs within you and around you. As you sit silently as the beholder of ME, you will quiet your busy mind, leaving room to hear the subtle whispers of your soul through your heart. You will recognize how infinite your ability to be is within ME and that you have barely noticed the capabilities within you.

This recognition is beyond any recognizing you have done to present date. Your question is your prison and it lives within your mind. The mental body loves strategy. The heart loves only the being within ME. Invite your mind to relinquish its need for control and surrender itself to the openness held within your sacred heart within ME. That is the only strategy you need.

## Story Time

'Mao's words rang in Nancy's heart as much as in her ears. This was the confirmation, the support she needed to take the next step. On a broad level of understanding, she knew what she was capable of doing, and had proved to herself time and time again her ability to rise to the occasion.

Yet, this was no ordinary occasion and she had to focus hard to move her mind's turmoil from questions about Don and back to the task-at-hand. While she knew Paul was waiting for her, she was also aware that he was having his own mystical experiences and had very little need of her. There was a deep, dark part of her mind needing to be needed. She was not finding that need present here.

It wasn't long before Nancy arrived at Paul's circle of trees to find him sitting steadfast with eyes closed and breathing slowed. Quietly, she put down her bedroll and lowered herself to the ground facing him. He did not open his eyes, only continued breathing within the same slow, methodical rhythm.

Nancy closed her own eyes and picked up Paul's waves of breathing, flowing into and out of the quiet inbreath and outbreath in sequence after sequence. Slowly, she felt her shoulders relax and her back begin to relinquish its strain as she merged her mental processes into the world of meditation.

It was some moments before she was quiet enough to connect with Paul. She found him within the realm they had started to recognize as their own. Emerging slowly into the light of their souls' expression there, relief swept over her as she noticed how natural it felt to move among these frequencies. She felt more at home here than anywhere else because her mind could not strategize in a plane where that type of action was not recognized.

*"Nancy,"* Paul began easily, *"I see you have been having a difficult time in the earth space realm where you had to sever connections with the camp. Do you realize that nothing is ever separated only released for the moment to be picked up again at a time of your choosing?"*

*"Yes, Paul, I do,"* Nancy telepathically responded to the image she received of her brother in earth space, *"yet, I forget because of attachments I create to the people and happenings I consider important. I know that this experience we are having and will continue to expand into with Talish will assist me in dissolving those connections into a more generous stream of flow. I am looking forward to bringing the feeling of this plane into the denser earth world.*

*"The hardest part of the experience was leaving Don. I know that you have observed my desire for a greater union with him and I don't know if he feels the same way. It mystifies me that he is so nice to me, overly helpful even, and yet that is as far as it goes. My mind is afraid that I will make a fool of myself and so it draws back when it wants to move forward."*

*"Okay,"* Paul offered, *"let's take a look at how Don plays out in the realm of spirit so that you can have a better understanding of what is possible for you and also for him. Here*

there is no judgment so we can simply watch and learn and I will assist you in remembering when we are aware within our physical forms.

"Do you see how we are able to merge and emerge within any and all souls that are within our focus? Okay, now put your attention upon the frequency you read as Don and feel into that aspect of this moment. What do you feel? What do you see? How is he experiencing rather than how are you experiencing? That will give you the answers to your questions and you can commit them to your soul record for easier retrieval later. I have learned this while sitting waiting for you since I had the same type of questions regarding your return. No so much about a greater union, rather my questions were about whether you would return at all. I saw the potential of you coming back from this vantage point and that assured me of our mutual time together."

Nancy spread her consciousness into that which she regarded as the Don expression. Now she could experience what Don was living within in earth and what potential existed for him from the realm of spirit and soul. She invited Paul to join in her observation.

"Paul, do you see how Don has always been a member of our soul group? He has offered to play the role of outsider if it suits the greater expansion of the entire group. He has had many similar experiences in a number of different incarnations in this role. I'm not sure he is enjoying it as much as he thought he would. Though the offer was made in all sincerity, I feel strongly that my desire to unite with him will break that pattern and bring him into greater awareness of his own soul expression. I'm going to look into the realm of possibility and then probability to see what I can fathom there.

"Okay, what I see is that Don can possibly make any changes within his future that he desires. He does not know that of which he is capable in human form. The number of earth incarnations is small within his record in comparison to yours or mine. So he is used to playing this part and does it by nature.

"Within probabilities, he is also capable of changing the outcome if given another set of variables with which to work. Hmmm, it seems that Dan and Paul have commissioned *themselves to offer those chances to him. Maybe that's why he felt like he wanted to give them more of an opportunity to assert their independence and be leaders rather than to see themselves as probationers and looked down upon."*

## Question Fifty-five
## Where do we turn for internal
## and external support and direction?

Your question presupposes that you require internal or external support and direction as ME. I talked about direction in the last question, so in this answer I will respond regarding support. Humans are constantly looking for support, usually external much more than internal. If you only looked for internal confirmation, you would find it much more readily than any exterior guidance. You are always your best advocate.

To begin, I will ask you a question in return. What is on your mind? Stop here for a moment and survey your internal environment. See what you are truly playing on the image screen of your mind. There are many, many mixed messages going on right now, all at the same time, rather than concentrating on one object; simply one action or thought that you grace with your full attention.

Distraction within your surroundings, whether internal or external, is the proponent for your belief in the need for support. When you focus your attention on your internal environment, bring it into harmony and then use that frequency to resonate within your reality, no additional foundation is needed.

For the truth of the matter is that you truly have nothing to support. You might believe you do. You might even believe that your thoughts and your actions are in constant need of confirmation from without you since you are not receiving it from within. You live in your own universe, one created by thoughts, feelings and observations so how can an "other" support you.

There is a misleading belief within your mind that objectivity is the key to understanding your world. There is no objective reality within your dimension. Everyone and everything is the result of a subjective perception belonging to the perceiver. No one can understand what you see or experience in the same way you do so no one can offer quality guidance for your experience. You are your one true guide.

As light in form within ME, you are enlightened, fully aware within MY Cosmic Mind and capable of receiving and transmitting information within your light. The belief that this is not true is the sole reason you may not experience the flow of informing light within you. Therefore, you believe you must seek guidance and support from either outside of yourself or have some "other" tell you how to listen within. A simple change from "non-believing" to "believing" transforms the possibilities always open to you. You are in charge of the shift. Your trusted intention becomes the portal of emergence within the informing light you *are* - accessing ever-expanding information in form. The light you are is information slowed to a frequency that appears physical within ME.

Since you are light within ME, you are a constant source of information within yourself. That informing energy is subjective to the experience you are having as spirit incarnate. When you believe you need or desire support you are saying within your frequency vibration that you are not enough and someone or something else must shore you up within ME. I AM all. You are all. What support could possibly be needed within that truth?

How can anything be sacred within ME and not completely of ME, simultaneously? Your body is in a constant state of informing you as to what is happening in this breath, then the next and then the next. It is when you slow down enough to live that breath that you receive the message contained within it, the support within yourself.

I know that you are thinking it is hard because you are a human being and believe you need help. It is your perception of what a human being is that requires redefining. When you realize that the human species is a slowed down frequency of ME within ME, you will stop declaring how much help, support, confirmation and direction you believe you need.

You have the one exponent you require within your body. It is your heart. It speaks the words of your soul, directing every feeling, thought, word and action when you allow it to do so. It is the beliefs held within your mind limiting the awareness of your heart's voice that you are invited to release. No one can do this for you. It is a personal, subjective decision within your own mind.

In fact, many people will protest that you are not acting rationally when you make the decision to step away from external authority figures and strike out as your own guidance system. The only reason people will ridicule you is out of jealousy and longing. Pay them no mind. Listen to the urgings of your heart as it speaks your inner truth requesting that you align with ME within ME.

The complexity of your mental processes will attempt to defer this decision to a later space and time. You may do so if you wish. I will not judge you if you ignore MY Voice within you. You do a very good job as your own judgment source. Eventually, you will become uncomfortable enough that you will realize you have only one choice left. In that moment, your heart will be waiting for your listening inner ear.

Will you change your view of yourself to an enlightened being within ME resonating within the experiences of your life? Will you be as unconcerned about the mind's intent control as the leaf is unconcerned about the blowing of the wind? Will you remain neutral to the comings and goings of daily life to be informed by the light in form that is constantly informing you? You make the choice. You experience the result and you can change your present choice in *this* moment. Your heart awaits your decision within ME.

## Story Time

Not too long after Paul and Nancy's meditative journey into the realm of spirit, they returned to ordinary consciousness seated on the jungle floor. Taking a few deep breaths to bring themselves back into awareness of themselves and each other, they breathed a sigh of satisfaction at their interaction.

*"Paul,"* Nancy began breaking the silence, *"I am beginning to understand a feeling I have been having that I've mistaken for intimate love. I want to support Don in his ability to expand as we are learning. In that desire, I project onto him my*

own ambition for him and attempt to make it his. It's not. If he wanted to be with us, he would be. In fact, he may still come. I told him we would be waiting for him through today in case he changed his mind. Now I have to find a way to let it be whatever it's going to be."

"Nancy, you cannot be supportive of Don's decision to know himself. He is the only one who can guide himself to that termination point. I know that he is feeling very pulled between his duty to the camp and his curiosity about what we learn with Talish. You must allow him to decide. Now, come and share this food I saved from the plates you left here for me while we wait for Talish to come for us."

While Nancy and Paul finished up the remains of the meals Paul had sequestered away, back at the camp Don was performing his usual duties of crew supervisor. He had long wanted to give more responsibility to Dan and Paul; with Nancy's departure, the door had opened wider for this possibility. The only block to firming up the positions for them was Sam. How to get around his predilection to keeping crews subjugated was a constant dilemma Don faced.

The teams were still working within the protocol that Don had set in place allowing members to join up in groups that had common work interests. Nancy leaving the forest crew only put them down one person in that crew yet she had been the self-proclaimed supervisor largely due to no one having the courage to override her self-appointment.

As Don thought about who else could take her place outside of him, he realized that Dan and Paul were also working in the same jungle crew. Here was the opportunity he was waiting for and he was going to take it.

"Okay, crew, listen up," Don said as he jumped into this new situation with both feet. "Since Nancy is taking some time off and, yes, I see the surprise on your faces which we will address later, we need a new team leader. I am going to appoint Dan and Paul to work together as co-captains of this crew. They will make joint decisions and you will consider their direction as coming from one person. Any questions, except ones about Nancy?"

The only raised hand was Dan's and it was a comment rather than a question. *"Don, though you didn't ask us if we wanted to take this on, we both want to you to know we'll give it a go. I suppose you didn't have to ask us, being our boss and such. So, thanks for the thought, anyway."*

*"Okay, if there's no other questions or comments,"* Don concluded, *"head out to the forest with Dan and Paul. Stay to the south of the path and work down toward the bend in the river."*

As Don followed them toward the forest, he veered off to the right, heading quickly down the trail so as not to waste too much time before catching up with the crew. *I've got to let Paul and Nancy know there is a chance I can join them. I don't know why I'm thinking about this, but my gut feeling absolutely won't leave me alone. I'll end up with an ulcer if I don't follow my own lead. Hell, Sam is going to be so mad!*

Nancy felt Don approaching before either she or Paul physically saw him. Her heart jumped within her chest as she leaped up to meet him.

*"Nancy,"* Paul admonished, *"whatever you are doing is disturbing the calm here. Sit and let it happen."*

Nancy meekly retook her place on the dirt realizing she had let those old beliefs about relationship propel her action rather than her newly developing sense of allowance. *I don't even know why Don's coming anyway. He might be bringing us a message from a disgruntled Sam.*

As Don approached the cloister of the circle, he slowed down, took a breath and composed himself to enter. *Dare I allow this side of me to rule the show,* he thought with anticipation. *If I do, there'll be no turning back.*

*"Paul, Nancy, may I speak with you for a moment?"* he began tentatively.

*"Sure, Don. Come sit,"* Paul offered hospitably since he felt this area of the jungle had become his personal domain.

*"I'm attempting to make a decision about joining you. It's a real tug of war. The scales have shifted since I realized that Dan and Paul could step up to the plate as potential crew leaders. That still leaves Sam running the camp by himself for what, Nancy,*

*didn't you say a month. I know what I want to do and then there's the other side. Can you support me in my decision?"*

Paul and Nancy looked at each other meaningfully. The question in their eyes was *who was going to respond to Don.*

Nancy made their decision for them by calmly announcing, *"No, Don, we cannot support you. This is for you alone to decide."*

## Question Fifty-six
## Is it possible for negative energies to attach to me?

It is not possible for energy to attach to you because no "attaching" energy exists within ME. What you label "negative" energy is any frequency that does not resonate with you to such a degree that you feel it is harmful. While I am telling you that it is not possible because energy does not attach within ME, it will not stop you from attempting to manufacture it within your personal reality.

All energy is neutral. The only evaluation you apply to a wavelength of activity is what you believe is possible. I stress the word "believe" here because your belief does not create it. Through your assertion that a concept is true for you, you resonate with the frequencies of that construed belief within ME. It does not mean that it exists for anyone else. By the question you posit, you are connoting that "negative" energies are "bad" or "evil" meaning that you are converting neutral energy to a personal significance.

Planet earth is vibrating at an increasing frequency right now. It is moving within a plane where the thoughts and emotions of humanity are more readily discernible by you within ME. The envelope that holds these thoughts and emotions you call the *noosphere*. It is an etheric container of the mental and emotional bodies of humanity surrounding and infiltrating the earth.

This envelope holds the fear many people are feeling, the very emotional extremes of human experience. Many people are easily upset as they experience the changes and transformation, individually and collectively. On a larger scale, it is mass consensus within ME.

Due to the amount of fear present for you if you wish to resonate with it, it is easy for you to create within your mind a "negative" energy or form and call it real. It is given life by you resonating in your world. You say it is "attached" to you. You have it backwards. You are attached to it.

Another reason many of you decide that there may be an unwelcome presence around you is to draw attention to yourself. You feel you are not fulfilled within ME so you look for additional attention from outside yourself. If this does not come fast enough, in a great enough quantity or quality, the manifestation of something that can possibly harm you is a fast-track method to attracting attention.

There is no "other" force aside from ME, no devil, no embodied force of evil with the power to harm you in life or after death. The "evil" or "negative" energy existing in the world is fed by your fear. You endow evil with power when you believe in humanity's "inherent evilness" or when you scorn your spirituality as meaningless within ME.

Everyone creates his or her own negativity within through being trapped in rage, horror, guilt, envy, jealousy or terror. What you term "positive" acts on earth carry much weight and can outweigh numerous "negative" actions you have created out of fear. It is all emerging within your consciousness if you will surrender to the understanding.

When you own what is going on inside of you as ME, you can move past the belief that negativity resonates within your reality. Many of the difficulties you create for yourself can be traced to disembodied thinking. You have cut yourself off from what you feel in your bodies. You have separated your emotions from your experiences, your heads from your hearts and your souls from your being within ME.

When you fully acknowledge and live within the knowing, not believing, that you are ME in physical form, the idea of anything harmful existing within your sacred reality will no longer be a probability for you.

Yet, since I AM all and you are I AM, if you make a decision that you wish to resonate with, and therefore create, a sense of negativity within your life no matter how frightening, scary or harmful, I will not stop you from doing so. It is your reality. Make it what you will. Since you are within ME as Creator, you will resonate with that which pleases you no matter what it feels like in the moment.

If you are determined to live within a reality that includes "negative" energies that can attach to you, you might want to ask yourself why you made that decision. Of what benefit is it to you within ME? What are you gaining within your soul life experience by bringing into existence within you something you proffer that you don't want? What does it take to detach from your attachment to it?

The answers to these questions will cycle you back around to your need for attention at all costs. No matter the stakes, your ego personality will create and resonate with anything that will feed it. When you don't have enough outside confirmation of your worth and you are unable to produce it from within yourself, you will resort to any tactic available to acquire focus upon you.

Will others pay as much attention to you if you say, "Oh, gosh, I have all of this positive energy attached to me?" No, they will not. Yet, if you use your victim voice to tell another that you have negative energy attached to you, doesn't that make you feel special? Yes, it does even if your uniqueness is based upon relentless fear.

Since focusing upon an energetic source increases its availability to you, the more you pay attention to your negative manifestation, the stronger it will appear to you. Eventually, your belief will be potent enough that you will truly believe you cannot detach from the negative energy you believe is real. Remember, it is not attached to you. You are attached to it.

## Story Time

As Nancy voiced their common knowing as brother and sister, events began to unfold very fast. The calm, quiet circle morphed from serenity to activity as Don twitched with nervous anticipation of his own answer, Talish appeared unannounced and Sam's voice was heard in the distance calling Don's name.

The tremendous shift from peace to disarray challenged the meditative states within which Paul and Nancy still existed.

Tantamount to an energetic tsunami, decisions were demanding to be made by every member present.

Don knew he should answer Sam's call. Nancy understood it was time for them to leave with Talish and Don hadn't had time to give his answer whether he would accompany them or not. Paul was anxious to get going on their journey into the jungle and wanted to start right away. The only person who did not join in the furor was Talish who stood patiently to the side awaiting the perfect timing and moment.

"*Don,*" Nancy, throwing caution to the wind, broke the silence, "*are you going to answer Sam? He sounds like he's in distress. Maybe something's wrong and he needs you. Oh, this comes at a terrible time for you. What are you going to do?*"

Before Don could respond, Sam appeared running down the trail toward them. The look on his face was one of anger and fear fueled by frustration at not being able to find Don. Rounding the bend in the path, he stopped short at the edge of the circle.

"*What are the three of you doing?*" he roared. *Obviously, he can't see Talish,* Nancy thought with relief. "*Don, I need you right now. One of the crew has had an accident. Joe drove the auger through his foot and he'll probably lose it. I need you to drive him to the hospital in town. What are you doing here anyway?*"

"*Sam, I've come to talk with Paul and Nancy and to make a decision about whether I want to join them in their one month journey together. That is what I am doing here right now. You've caught us in the middle of making that decision.*

"*I want to thank you for being the catalyst to my process. While I felt some wavering at first, not knowing how to resolve my allegiance to you and the camp with my desire to find out more about myself, your request has given me my answer.*

"*I put Dan and Paul in charge of the forest crew. I left them for a very short time to come here to talk with Paul and Nancy. If they cannot handle this situation then I made the wrong decision and shouldn't be supervising at all. If they do handle the decision, they don't need me. So, in any case, you see the decision has been made. I will stay here and we will eventually find out whether Dan and Paul are worth what we pay them. I won't be coming back with you."*

Sam stood open-mouthed, nostrils flared. Then, closing his mouth, he raised his fist intending to strike Don in the face. As he did so, Nancy saw Talish wave her hand and suddenly Sam put his arm down and shook his head.

*"I don't know what you three think you're doin' and I don't want to know. I'll tell you this though. You're off the payroll and off the crew. As far as I'm concerned, I don't even know you. Don't bet on your stuff being there when you come back. I'll be hiring some replacements and they can throw it away for all I care. Good riddance is all I can say."*

With those closing words, Sam turned and stormed down the path back to the dwindling camp, alone. His carriage belied his parting remark.

Paul, Nancy and Don stood in silence. Feelings were shouting. Words were useless. Talish watched quietly, head bowed and hands at her side.

After several minutes, Nancy voiced their common question, *"Are we leaving now, Talish? Is there anything else we need to do before we depart?"*

Talish raised her head slowly. *"I would like to take this time to begin teaching what you have learned through action. Each of you, Don especially, has become attached to a certain way of being. You believe it is a positive method of creating a reality suitable to you until something comes along to unsettle that perception.*

*"You have each experienced and observed what has happened in the last few moments. None of these experiences exists outside of your mutual creation. Even Joe's supposed accident is an intentional response to an agreement among all of you made through the realm of atam-atma.*

*"Don, you may wish to remember in the future that Joe's actions were in response to your indecision. His spirit shouldered the process with you and since you faltered in your heart-driven reaction to your soul's calling, another member of your soul group made a move. It is neither negative nor positive. It simply is his acknowledgement of and with you. In another space within atam,*

*you will balance that response with him through mutual deciding points within both of you.*

*"Now, I would like you all to sit down and breathe with me for a while so that we may enter a state of pure serenity for our very long voyage. We will be traveling by foot for several days. We will be journeying within infinite atam as we walk. It is imperative that each of you is fully anchored within your physical bodies before we request that you place your feet in many simultaneous worlds."*

## Question Fifty-seven
## Why don't I feel safe here, especially at night?

Belief that you are not safe stems from fearing your perceived lack of control. Intrinsically, the realm of contrast is filled with insecurity due to the need for choice. Since human culture removes the full free will ability from the young very soon after birth, the need to know what you can do or can't do is removed as well. It is then simply a need to do what you are told or face some consequence.

Safety is based upon knowing that you are held, nurtured and nourished within a container of security. It relies upon a capacity to relax within life the same way you would relax within the womb.

Since your concepts of safety and security are built around conformity, you live in a constant state of attempting to conform whether the confines of your culture are in agreement with your inherent understanding or not. Most children, if left on their own, would come to understand how to function within your reality within ME. They are usually not given that chance because parents are conformists also desiring to raise a child or children who mirror them.

Your society does not have many words to describe or converse about divergent thinkers. You are taught convergent thinking. Your schools are foundationed and stylized with this type of student in mind. Children often struggle to learn, especially when it comes to detailed directions, rules of grammar, spelling and math. The underlying potential of the consciously aware child often goes unnoticed.

Children display creative and energetic natures that are subjugated into conformity. This is an important concept for all adults to grasp. Children's sense of security and nurturing comes from having parents and teachers who believe in them, accepting and supporting them. This is critical to the secure child and probably the hardest asset to acquire since the adults did not experience it, either.

Since nearly all children within duality are raised in this sense of insecurity, life begins to express as a lack of safety. Additionally, the present human mindset professing the need to look outside the individual for the missing security rather than within, wherein it lies, fuels uncertainty because it cannot be found outside of oneself.

If children were raised to know they were respected, seen and heard, they would automatically rely on themselves to supply the security and safety so necessary for thriving. The parents' model would instill this foundation within the child or children within ME.

As you mature, you have the opportunity to realize you are the authority within your physical body and reality. You no longer have to resort to asking others what to do, how to act or what to say. Yet, within the culture you are raised, the norms take precedent if you want to feel accepted. Within this concept is the fact that acceptance does not make you feel safe. In fact, it is just the opposite. The more you attempt to conform, the less secure you feel.

The basis for this lack of safety in conformity is the desire to measure up to a median imposed upon you by others. If you allow yourself to be your standard, you will begin to understand what security feels like because you will be living as your true expression within ME. As this occurs, no thought is given as to whether you are meeting a certain illusory criteria. Rather, you are setting your own precedent and living as that personal truth.

I know you will question how lack of attention to mass consensus can assist your feeling of insecurity. The doubt is based upon your conditioned beliefs about how you are to appear within your role as human. Since you are programmed to believe that there is safety in numbers, the concept of standing out or "being alone" is terrifying to your physical brain and mind.

As an emanation within ME, your inherent awareness is foundationed in safety. Your physical ego personality wishes to control what your emanation means to you. Your mind can only give it meaning through your programmed beliefs. Releasing the hold these concepts have upon you will result in absolute security in form as I AM.

When the dark night comes and you have less control of your visual sense, you feel an increased insecurity. Though you may wish to believe it stems from your days without electricity, the original human being quickly found ways to assist the darkness through fire. The primal fear of being attacked and eaten was the mother of this necessity. Yet, that initial fear resides within your cellular memory and you resonate with it when you remain a member of the mass consensus.

A quality of conscious awareness is possible within your emanation if you will accept it. Dissolve and release your preconceived notions about what it means to be human. Listen to MY Voice within you through the stirrings of your heart. If fear raises its head, welcome it the way you would a very old friend. Your angst has been present from the moment you were conceived so rather than pushing it away, offer it a home. As you do so, you move from a sense of separation within your body to incorporating all areas of experience as the "home" you seek.

There is safety and security in only one human condition. It is found within your awareness of existing as ME in a very temporary form playing in a field of experience. Once you allow it, safety is your natural state within ME.

## Story Time

Once Nancy, Paul and Don had begun to breathe in unison signaling their mutual alignment, Talish continued her instructions.

*"We are going to begin this journey by bringing you face to face with your inner most fears. Physically, we will sit here until dark descends. Within the realm of atam, I will direct you individually though it will originally appear that it is a collective instruction.*

*"My intention surmounts any resistance you may have to following the path that will emerge within your inner vision. Your acquiescence to this journey is the stimulus providing your passage. At no time will you be rendered assistance within this*

venture. Failure is not an option now that you have set foot upon this path.

"If you have any question, now is the time to ask. Once we begin, you will be forbidden to question or comment upon any directive unless I request you to do so. Though it may appear that you are submitting to my authority, it is just the opposite. You will be surrendering to the realm of atma within which you exist. I am merely the holder of the torch through which you will see.

"Now, does anyone want to ask me a question or are we ready to begin?"

The three sojourners looked at each other as though hopeful that another would ask what was in each one's mind. *If I ask a question, will I be seen as weak,* Nancy was thinking as Don posited what was in everyone's thoughts.

"Talish, please don't think I'm backing out here. I only wonder if we will be able to say 'stop' or declare we don't want to go any further once we begin whatever you have in store for us? Is there a way to opt out of continuing somewhere along the way?"

"Don, as well as each of you, you may stop the journey anywhere along its pathway that you wish though you will find yourself feeling a little lost if you do so. Since I will be fully merged within each of you as atam, I will be unable to assist you in finding your way back to purely physical. If you make a decision to stop your unfolding within atam-atma in this way, only you will be responsible for finding the point of attention you will require to resume living solely 'here'. It is a dangerous choice and one I do not suggest though it is always possible for you."

Don thought for a moment about the connotation of Talish's words, then summed it up for the three of them by saying, "So, if we're too scared or believe we are unable to continue, what you are telling us is that making the choice to leave will only make it worse. At least, that's the possibility. Am I correct?"

"Yes, Don, you are correct. I would strongly suggest that if you have any reservations, you make the decision to abandon this quest right now or surrender fully to it no matter the outcome. Once you have stepped into the realms in-between, you always have a chance of being lost among them. I have seen it happen and there is nothing I can do to change your course once you are experiencing within them.

"So, having listened to my response, does anyone want to change their mind about this experience?"

Nancy and Paul had lowered their heads and closed their eyes in contemplation. Don stared at Talish as he quested within himself for any signs of desertion. No one raised a voice.

"Okay, then, it seems you are in agreement to continue. I will take your silence as acquiescence to the entire experience and proceed according to the ancient ways.

"Now, I would like each of you to remove your shoes and fill your water bottles. You will be bringing only water with you on this journey. If food is necessary, it will be provided. You will remain shoe-less for the entire experience. You will take nothing with you except the clothes you are wearing which you will set aside toward the end of the journey."

The three travelers did as instructed and then sat in the circle waiting for their next directive. Aware of the strange silence that was descending upon them, no one was about to do anything except what they were told, at least not yet. Talish had succeeded in frightening them into submission.

"Now, please sit in a circle with me, knees touching and place your hands palm down upon your knees. As soon as this rearrangement is complete, I would like you to close your eyes and breathe with me."

Since everyone was almost in the requested position already, the change in positions was easily accomplished. The only one who really had to find a seat within the circle was Talish. She gracefully slid in between Nancy and Paul.

With their eyes closed and hands positioned, each began breathing in rhythm with Talish's undulating breathing pattern; inbreath, followed by a lengthy pause then outbreath. During the outbreath, Talish would whisper a soft "ahhh" and then return to the inbreath continuing for what seemed like hours.

After a good length of time, Talish asked them to open their eyes and look around. Darkness had descended yet now the obscurity was total. There were no trees outlined in the night.

Looking toward each other, they individually realized they could see nothing and no one, only Talish.

## Question Fifty-eight
## What should I focus on to protect myself?

Why would you protect yourself from ME? What would you believe is harmful within ME?

When you ask what to focus on to protect yourself, the connotation is that you are afraid something "etheric" is going to hurt you in some way. Usually, this question is in regard to your view of "negative energy" or "evil", as you call that aspect of ME.

Your ego personality is the conscious accumulator of your experiences in the body you are using and it believes it is separate and distinct from the "others" in its reality. In this separation exist apparent independence, safety and imagined security. As your ego compiles its idea of life through these events, the experiences are added to your soul, your etheric record, and the composite of you is enhanced.

Within this record are all incarnations you are living. If you believe that something negative has the ability to do you harm and you are experiencing that feeling in this dimension, it is most likely that you have done so before. The existence of a parallel life or lives resonating with the same belief enhances the fear you experience in this world.

Conversely, if you make the decision that there is nothing to protect yourself from in this realm, it will affect any, and all, parallel experiences, as well. You have complete control over the type, quality and quantity of your experience or experiences within ME. The world you live in is so sensitive, so responsive to your every thought, feeling and action, that you imprint yourself within it because you are not outside of it; you are within its electromagnetic frequency.

Take the earth's water, for example. You might be familiar with the human theory that you can impress the molecular structure of water with your biological signature. In other words, if you are feeling, thinking, experiencing gratitude, you can intention this feeling into water and, if that water is then frozen, it will create a crystalline structure that was not present before your intention of gratitude. What you might not know is that the water also remembers. It holds the frequency of gratitude within itself. It does not dissolve within the water stream. The memory remains within ME.

Now, think about your vehicle, your body. A major portion of your body is water. What intention are you sending into the water that is you? Consider how the embedding of thought, feeling and emotional frequency creates the belief that you can be harmed or that you are safe in life. Once your intention is firmly in place, the transmission of your frequency becomes a receiver for that which your vibration resonates with within ME.

When a situation appears that sends you into a feeling that is one of belief you may be harmed, your mind starts to think a thought that will bring resolution to the experience. The instant you begin to look for a solution, you stop to remember what happened the last time something like this occurred. Then come up the feelings of fear, stress, insecurity and terror. Your mind doesn't even get up a good head of steam in its problem-solving mode before you have de-railed yourself.

Therefore, when you ask what you can focus upon to protect yourself, the only thought to pay attention to is the one that tells you there is no need for protection. Any other focus will create the perceived need *for* that protection and then you are caught in the never-ending spiral that prompted you to ask the question in the first place.

Consider what might happen if you decided that every time you began to feel this fear, this need to be protected, this "I'm going to be attacked", or what it is that makes your ego personality feel like it is separate from what is "out there", that you dismiss it as not true or possible. You are the creator of the experiences within your life. No one or nothing is "out there" with the intention of hurting you in anyway.

As you transmit your frequency within ME, you believe you attract to yourself harmful manifestations. You also believe that by focusing on something else, you may protect yourself. It is not focus assuring you of the most beneficial experience. It is your feeling creating the energy wave as your consciousness contructs an illusion for you to live within and calls it real.

Mass consciousness revels in believing that it is separate from ME within ME. Since I AM all and in absolute union within you, even the idea of separation is in union within ME. There is no place to go and no belief to be held enabling you to separate yourself from what I AM and you are within the union of ME.

When you hold the belief that you need protection, you are stating that you believe I can harm you because all is I AM. This is the ultimate in separation anxiety because if you feel that you must protect yourself from an aspect of ME, what are you going to use to do so? Focus is of little use when you are attempting to separate yourself from the source of your life within your life within ME.

Rather than focusing on something to protect yourself, perhaps you would be willing to entertain the thought that you can open yourself so fully to the awareness of ME that protection will be the last thought in your mind. Once you surrender to yourself as ME, you will realize that the only protection you could possibly desire is from your own restless mind. It thrills to the concept of separation and fears union. Ultimately, it will surrender within ME.

## Story Time

"Yes," Talish now continued, "you are each without personal physical sight or so you believe. This reality will remain during the onset of our journey enabling you to fine-tune other extraordinary senses.

"In a few moments, we will be standing up and walking on the path. We will remain upon the trail for the first two miles. At that time, I will lead you deep into jungle after you have become accustomed to the depth of darkness in which you are now experiencing.

"If you desire to connect with each other, you may only do so by accessing your atam connection. You will have no physical access to each other during our walking journey, only that of your atam sense. I suggest you spend less time wondering about each *other and more time paying attention to what is occurring as you walk.*

*"The path is clear for these first two miles so there is no need to consider any type of protection for your physical selves. Once we leave the trail and begin our trek through jungle, you will be using your energy field to sense the presence of objects around you or lying upon the ground in which you are walking.*

*"This is the beginning of knowing yourself as more than form which has been your perception up until this present time. Now it is time to stand. Rise up slowly as you have been sitting for quite some time and your body must get used to this new awareness."*

Nancy, Paul and Don slowly stood up which did nothing to shift the opaqueness of their surroundings. Everywhere they attempted to look, pitch black was the outcome. Unnerving as it first appeared, once each of them was standing up, a feeling of belonging to the dark began to emerge. Personal perception melded with the aphotic surroundings allowing for no separation between the individual and the eclipse of light.

*"Step on the path and follow me. You are each able to visually see me. I will slowly advance faster than you are able to match so pay attention to where your foot falls. The sole of your foot is your constant contact with the living earth. Through your feet, you tell her what you are and she responds in like kind. If you step upon a pebble or stumble, it is her signal to you that your vibration is uncomfortable to her outer skin. Pay attention as you begin this infinite journey."*

With these final words, the three travelers stepped onto the dirt path behind Talish who was the only being they could presently see. As the walk began, realization dawned that they had no physical idea where the other two were short of sensing their presence through the energy field. Taking Talish's words to heart, each began concentrating upon his or her personal journey rather than wondering where the other two companions might be.

The typical African night is filled with a density of animal and insect sound. Many of the nocturnal creatures are readying to hunt, hungrily roaming while the insect world shouts its joy at the cool night air. Not so in the world that Nancy, Paul and Don traveled. There was as dense a silence as there was darkness. The silence was *so* present that each one began to become aware of the sound of a beating heart.

Up ahead, Talish became increasingly more translucent as she left their physical sight, what there was of it. The threesome was now walking in pitch black, soundless and sightless wonder at the experience. Fear oscillated with thrill at the prospect of what this was to mean individually and collectively.

Each step upon the path was increasingly deliberate, the farther they traveled. Minds slowed down because there was nothing to stimulate the brain. Individual breathing slowed. After what seemed only moments, Talish's voice appeared within each of their consciousness. She was no longer visible. Only through the tenderness of their feet could they discern the path ahead.

*"You have acclimated well. I am happy to see that none of you has lost yourself fully to fear. Nor have you attempted to speak or search each other out. This is a welcome sign of your ability to participate in the unseen way.*

*"Now, as you walk, I would like each of you to attempt to reach into the atam world of one of your companions. Don't worry about clashing with each other if two of you choose the same person. There is room for all.*

*"It is vitally important that you succeed within this step because it is the only sense you will be using for communication during our month together. Verbal language is of no use where we will be traveling soon. This skill must be perfected this night before we can go further into the many faceted world of atma."*

The identical message having been heard by each of them, Nancy spontaneously reached out to Don sensing what felt like a wall she could not surmount. Don attempted to connect with Paul yet the self-same barrier prevented the experience. Paul united with Nancy turning her attention from the frustration of reaching Don to delight in being able to perceive her brother within her consciousness.

*"Paul, you did it. Great,"* she silently announced with joy. *"I'm trying for Don and can't get in. Don't know what that means. Maybe Talish will help. Hold on a minute and I'll try to ask her*

*what to do in this situation."* Nancy reached out for Talish only to find her nowhere.

# Question Fifty-nine
## Can mechanical objects negatively affect me?

What do you consider a negative effect? Are you impressed negatively when you have to use the vacuum cleaner? Or perhaps you feel harmed by lifting a piece of cloth to dust your home? What is the meaning of "negative" to you within this context? Since you asked the question, it will be answered in a variety of ways so that you will understand that everything you experience is a matter of your free will.

As you bring mechanical objects into your home, workplace or play space, you begin with an intention about their use. From a dishwasher to help in the kitchen, to a computer on your desk, from an automatic tennis ball-throwing machine to air conditioning, each article is selected by you for a purpose. How you feel from the moment you make the decision to purchase the object to the times when you make use of it, the commodity takes on different meanings for you within ME.

Most of the objects you purchase are bought to assist with the ease in your life. Some of them are purely for entertainment while others do work that would normally take you much longer to complete thereby giving you more free time. The sports equipment you use has been designed specifically to assist you in re-creating yourself.

Many factors go into the purchase of an item no matter what its use may be or where it is to be used. Usually, you look for the best quality for the least amount of money. Sometimes you spend extra cash because it makes you feel good to treat yourself to something you consider expensive. Often, you regret this later changing the significance the object has for you in your life within ME.

The initial belief you have regarding the object's purpose is going to be the basis for how you experience its use. If it performs up to your standards, you will be pleased that it does so. If it fails you, the once-desired article becomes fuel for your antagonism.

It is right here that your question leads because if you entertain a notion that an item can affect you negatively, you maintain an interpretation regarding what it is capable of within your energy field. Take a vacuum for example; since it makes noise, follows you around or you push it, swallows what is in its path and generally portrays a devouring monster, it is easy for you to project negative attachments upon it. It is you attaching to it, not the other way around.

Once you have determined that the vacuum "possesses" negative energy, everything in your life that is not going according to your desires becomes its fault. You blame the vacuum when you are tired, upset, not feeling well or having a bad day. If the vacuum were not in your home, these things wouldn't be happening to you.

So, you give the vacuum away to a charity in your town and purchase another one that has the potential to provide you with a better experience. Now you are pleased to be using the new appliance because you are proud you tuned into the "negative" one and saw it for what it was rather than being duped by it. The days go by and you begin to realize you are still tired, upset, not feeling well or having a bad day. Perhaps it is the coffee pot causing your experience. If you throw the old one away and buy a new, more modern coffee pot, all will be well. And so it goes.

The material objects you purchase have no will of their own. They do not "throw off negative energy" affecting you or your environment. Any of them may be noisy, smelly, loud or of poor quality, yet that is not their "fault". They did not build themselves. A human being constructed each one of them.

If you find you have a habit of blaming your mechanical devices for your experiences, take a moment to ask yourself what your feeling or emotion is when you use the object. Are you upset because you have to rinse the dishes and put them in the dishwasher? Does it use so much water that you pale when you look at your water bill? Do you believe your computer is affecting you negatively because you still haven't quite figured out how to use it? Get down to the root of your feeling regarding the object and you will understand why you blame it for your life's upsets within ME.

Human beings have an inherent creativity within their minds. This streaming focus emanates from within Creator within ME. It is the reason many of you call yourselves co-creators with ME. Though you cannot be a "co" anything since you are I AM, it does display that you understand the idea that your reality is your creation.

While your living creations are those that issue from your body as other human beings, your life's work is an act of creativity no matter what you do. You are constantly invited from within your soul to focus upon everything that gives you joy within ME. This includes what you call your "work". Choosing an occupation that gives you joy is consciously making use of your awareness of I AM.

Many of these occupations are the creating of mechanical objects. From the nuts and bolts holding items together to the finishing touches of the labels and decorations, each point of assembly is a cause for creative expression. There is no "negative" or "positive" energy involved. There is only neutral energy doing its work as ME within ME through MY Emanation as Creator.

## Story Time

Paul and Nancy are connected consciously through no physical mechanism except their awareness of each other. Nancy is aware that Don appears to be unreachable.

"*Paul,*" Nancy conveyed her message within their united consciousness, "*since we can't locate Talish, most likely on purpose knowing her, we have to find a way to reach Don. The three of us cannot continue without communing and Talish said it was imperative we learn this skill tonight.*

"*I reached out for Don to unite with his awareness and was stopped. Why don't you give it a try and see what happens.*"

Paul acquiesced to Nancy's request. He focused upon Don in the same way he had linked up within Nancy's awareness.

Reaching for Don felt like attempting to scale a turbulent wall of rushing water to no avail.

*"I'm getting the same response, Nancy,"* Paul reported within their union. *"I know he was sort of afraid of all of this. I wonder if it is fear that is holding him back. He felt so agitated to me, much like jagged edges but slippery like water."*

*"Okay, Paul, I'm going to try something different. Since we're just doing what we usually do, especially you and I, kind of thinking about the other person and reaching out to meet them, I'm going to change my pattern. I'm going to open to Don without attempting to make a connection and see what I receive that way. In other words, receive him into me rather than attempting to unite into him."*

Nancy's consciousness expanded with her awareness focused upon her experience of Don. As she opened more to the idea of him, she became filled with guilt, remorse and fear. These feelings were unlike her and did not resonate within her consciousness. Aware of them as she was there was no place to unite within them.

*"Paul, I'm learning something new here. When I open to Don, I feel sorrow, guilt and fear. They are foreign experiences to me. It's not that I've never felt them within my physical life. It's just that the way I feel those emotions from him do not fit into my energy pattern.*

*"I wonder what we can do to shift his feelings so that he is able to be reached. There's something here Talish wants us to learn on our own and if we place our attention upon it, we're bound to understand how to change the outcome.*

*"I have an idea. Let's attempt to connect with Don together. Not as though we are going into him rather we'll do what I just did, open to him. You know what I mean. I know you can feel what I'm describing. When we both experience what he feels like it might give us enough information to merge with him."*

Within their union, Nancy and Paul opened their awareness to Don's consciousness. The confusion within his feelings crashed incoherently into their awareness yet they maintained their connection as strongly as possible. Seeing there was no change, they pulled back to discuss the situation, again.

*"Nancy, I'm getting an idea about what Don's experiencing. If we were in physical right now, we'd call it a 'man thing'. His guilt for what happened to Joe based upon his own indecision is causing him to feel blame, guilt and fear. Since he hasn't spent much of his life connected with others, short of his military stay, he doesn't have the same access points we do.*

*"If we are going to be able to connect within him, we're going to have to shift our energy from our normal state of awareness to one of absolute compassion and absolution. In other words, when we approach him, we are to have our focus upon what it feels like to be absolved. That frequency within this realm will then have an opportunity of resonating with his perceived need for it. It's almost as though he's asking someone to forgive him and he can't say it. Do you understand what I'm communicating to you?"*

*"Oh, yes, Paul, I understand completely. How wise of you to come into this realization. Okay, let's try it and see what happens."*

United within their mutual awareness, Paul and Nancy focused all of their attention upon absolving Don of any wrongdoing. Expanding the confluence of their consciousness to include Don within that union, ignoring the turbulence emerging from within his field of awareness, they held him firmly within their loving compassion.

Slowly, the incoherent wave of Don's consciousness began to harmonize within their union. Oscillating, accepting, opening, then surrendering, Don joined within their awareness. Now the three experienced themselves as one.

*"Thank you, thank you. I am filled with the utmost gratitude. You felt what I was experiencing and opened a space for my self-absolution. I would have arrived at it eventually yet I do not know how long it would take. Since there is no time where we are, that is hard to estimate.*

*"I understand now that I perceived the auger as an extension of my indecision, first placing blame upon it and then accepting the blame within myself. There is no wrongdoing here at all, only Joe's acquiescence to his own self-appointed commission. I am so grateful to you."*

Within the union of that message, Talish appeared within the merged realm of atam.

## Question Sixty
## Why am I sick?

I will refer to *dis-ease* as *unease* since it is caused by the illusion of separateness - separateness from your core essence, each other and ultimately from yourself. In keeping with this illusion, you begin to fill yourself with self-hatred and fear that eventually causes unease, stress and dis-ease of the body and the mind. You have forgotten you are I AM and, therefore, have forgotten you are master of your life.

You must step out of the normal bounds of your ordinary idea of knowledge to align within your awareness of ME. If you are to connect with your physical body as the vehicle of your manifestation and the accompanying mental and emotional selves, you must allow yourself to use extraordinary sight. If you remember the core essence of your being and become quiet enough within, you will hear the soft, quiet voice of your soul speaking through your heart calling you in the direction that responds to your inner yearning.

Any discomfort anywhere in your body is a direct message of misalignment of your experience within ME. Rather than allowing your life to be lived as it unfolds, you are in resistance to the current of energy creating your reality. The energy in your body does not flow; feels lifeless and tired, lusterless.

Too often, the prescription for such a malady is one or another chemical meant to mask the symptoms so you are not totally aware of the risk to your life that is occurring. You attempt to change your diet, take copious amounts of supplements and vitamins, abuse alcohol and tobacco, all smothering the pain and discomfort you are feeling. Rather than working on the cause through profound and vibrant use of energy, you usually give your body one more substance with which to deal to pretend that all is well. This condition cannot last for long. Your body becomes accustomed to the substance, demands more or a different one and, eventually, the ingested solution's efficacy is depleted and the cause has not been addressed.

Human medical professions do the very best they possibly can to assist you in your needs. They diagnose, prescribe and administer using their scientific techniques. When you follow the guidance of your personal doctor, it assists any decision you make regarding your health. Remember that all learning and experiencing arises within ME. As aspects of ME in form, you have mutually consented to create a variety of ways to bring yourself back into balance. Choosing a modality that serves you without judgment moves you within greater conscious harmonic union within ME.

Balance is attained by listening to the body's needs, addressing them as they arise and promoting health and well-being through direct communication with its compelling voice. When you override your needs, as is so often the case within your world, your body begins to suffer until finally, the dis-ease physically appears and it becomes only one more issue with which you feel you must contend.

Your ego personality's solution to the matter will be to push you further, harder and with additional expectations of all you are supposed to be for those in your life. It takes little consideration of MY Voice that is guiding you to stop, breathe, rest, relax and let go. Since your ego personality does not want to release control, it will compel you to continue on, as though nothing is happening within you even though your body is shouting at you to stop and care for it.

If you find yourself in a state of dis-ease, a state of not being in ease within life, or even simply general stress and anxiety, you may be hard put to find a method of controlling or regulating the flow and flux of the energetic states of your body. Your mind is preoccupied with the activity or situation that is causing the condition, and, therefore, not at hand to alleviate its cause.

Since it is energy within your body that actually causes the illness or discomfort to appear, the rearrangement of that energy will not only result in the disappearance of the symptoms, potentially also of the dis-ease itself. Your intention, and your attention upon that intention, allows for rearrangement of energetic flow in your physical body, impacting your mental, emotional and spiritual bodies causing change in your total being within ME.

Stress, worry, disappointment and anxiety cause imbalance of the flow within your body. The equilibrium of energy and the acceptance of its movement through your body begin the improvements you seek. Your mind begins to perceive a change in your physiology and initiates the release of its hold on the illusion of separation. It is when you begin to comprehend that your bodies are becoming balanced that an awareness of the changes occurring begins.

Illness in all of its forms is the result of imbalance in the physical body that will incorporate the other bodies as well. Asymmetry within your body is the result of forgetting what you are within ME and allowing that forgetting to become a vast portion of your life. Forgetting what you are creates unhealthy life practices. Tracing the steps back to the divergence is the method that leads to remembering which converts to health, well-being, peace and calm. You are then living from within a state of union including the incorporation of your individuated ego personality.

Since you are self-defined by what you believe is real, as that reality broadens and expands, so do you. Change within the physical, through the movement of energy forever alters and expands your ability to perceive the world in which you live. The clarity creates an ability to be clear of distress in the future. It is a life-altering event within ME.

## Story Time

Talish's presence within their conscious union was a two-edged sword. Happy to have her back among them, a wave of excitement was followed by anticipation. A shared desire to be commended for their recent achievement pervaded the triad's awareness.

*"I see you have connected,"* Talish began drily. *"Good. Now we can begin to proceed further into the jungle. I would like each of you to focus upon your physical body once again by*

*feeling your feet on the ground. Most likely the soles will be highly sensitive to the earth's magnetic field right now since you have been slightly disconnected from your vehicles. Once you are each balanced within your forms, we will begin the walk into the jungle."*

Nancy, Paul and Don were quite nonplused by Talish's lack of recognition of their masterful performance in absolving Don and recognizing the need to do so. A murmur of current flowed among them unacknowledged by Talish, as well. Within moments, a sense of separation pervaded their atmosphere as their perceived union disassembled.

Sensing the disturbance, Talish consciously surrounded their diverging awareness as though corralling a herd of horses. Not only was she aware of what each of the three was experiencing, it was only the beginning of her much more expansive plan.

*"So, I sense discordance among you. Have I missed something here? Are you not in accord with me in the initial stages of our journey together?"*

None of the threesome wanted to bring the conscious thought into awareness for Talish's discernment. Yet there was no place to hide within this invisible world. What they were experiencing was as easily read as a book on a table under the bright sunlight.

*"So what I pick up within your merged awareness is a disappointment in my lack of recognition of your recent efforts. Paul and Nancy, you two opened a space for Don to absolve himself of his apparent guilt for Joe's destruction of his foot. Don experienced self-appreciation after having experienced the release of blame within himself. Now the three of you would like me to honor this achievement among you.*

*"Yet, what you are not aware of is my part within your experience. It is relatively easy for you, Nancy and Paul, to merge within atam since you have been practicing doing so since you were children. Don is a different matter. He knows little about the two of you and you are not very acquainted with him. Your positioning gave me the perfect opportunity to model influence for you.*

"Don, your guilt was my stage. Even the barest reference to Joe's choice set up an enormous wave of failure within you. The misalignment of your belief regarding your part in Joe's free will decision resonated with my intention to enhance your sense of disgrace. I merely amplified the frequency within atam and you merged into the offending position. Once there, you were out of sync with Paul and Nancy so they were unable to commune within you.

"Nancy and Paul, you deliberated for some time about how to approach Don's perceived disappearance. Once you agreed upon a method of approach, you found that it worked. Your mutual absolution invited Don into the same vibration and he accepted it. So, now here we are.

"The point I would like to make is that the momentum behind the experience was my coercion within Don's atam-um due to his innate state of guilt. If he had accepted Joe's offering for what it is, I would have had no influence over him at all. He would not have been susceptible to my frequency. It would be inharmonic within him. The two of you had a preconceived idea about how Don supposedly feels which made him inaccessible to your present awareness. If you simply opened to connection without your mind's idea of how Don might be feeling or how you personally would experience him, he would not have appeared to be unreachable.

"It is this same frequency signature that re-shapes humans into illness. When they set up a frequency that is discordant with their natural state, no matter how it comes about, there is a resistance asserted within the cells. The basis for all ill of ease within human life is the repelling of that which is natural to that particular life. Due to beliefs and perceptions, many different manifestations of disharmony result.

"Now that you have had a taste of what your beliefs construct for you within the realm of atam, we are going to remain within the physical, stay merged within the dark and complete the first leg of our journey. You will find that this initial experience of union is setting the stage for expansion of all of your selves – the physical, feeling, thinking and atam-um. Come now, we have a long way to go."

With those closing words, Talish accepted what appeared to be a physical form at the head of their small troop of adventurers abruptly turning off the path and into the middle of the jungle trees. There was no clear footing or actual physical space within which to walk. The barefoot trio simply had to follow her figure as it slipped through bushes, brush and twisted branches blocking the path.

*It feels as though when I concentrate on Talish, I walk easily within our group,* Nancy thought. *When I lose my awareness of the moment in which we are walking, the brush appears to be blocking my way making it harder to walk through. I wonder if I'm the only one feeling this.*

# Question Sixty-one
## How can we clarify the vision of our possibilities?

Humanity's viewpoint of linear time has caused much of the chaos experienced by all of you. There is very little understanding of the realm of possibility that exists within ME. Within that sphere, no system is independent. Every system in operation is affecting every other aspect in some way. Your future is in the making in each instant and based upon interactions that are being created in each moment. Therefore, it is impossible to know your future-future though it is possible to present possibilities and probabilities based upon what is happening at present.

When you desire to bring clarity to the vision of what is probable within you, it is important to remember that when you label a perspective, you limit the endless possibilities that exist within ME. The desire to bring clarity to the limitless, limits it. I would ask you what your intention is within the infinite potentials within which you exist?

Your question comes full circle to humanity's consciousness creating that which it wishes to experience and thus actually bringing it into existence within each moment. The catch to this active manifesting is that most of you create from remembered experience and some of those experiences were not necessarily comfortable or joyous. What can you do about that? How can you change the memory of what you have experienced and, thus, create a totally new future more to your liking? That is what you are asking within this present query.

If you open yourself to the world of all possibility, you will find it shifting, changing and morphing moment to moment within your consciousness. The clarity you desire to perceive within that reality will always be subjective. The infinite expanse of possibility is neutral to your cares and concerns. You are not. When you ask for definition of what is possible for you, you already have a preconceived picture based upon experience relating to what you want to see. You provide your own clarity and do not believe it is real.

Are you open to understanding that you can change the notion you have about your potential? It is important to consider this possibility because you truly can and you must if you desire the future to be the joyous, loving perfection that you really wish to live within ME. It is imperative that any negative memory you have be transformed into the ideal situation or experience if you are to change the wavelength of your frequency and by doing so usher forth a new set of vibrations that is you within ME. The future you desire requires coherency in your frequency.

This does not mean you actually need to "enter" the past. It simply means you are to create a new way of remembering that which you call the experiences you have already lived. Since you anticipate what is coming based upon what has been experienced, the changing of the memory then changes the future events within the realm of possibilities. There is absolutely no limit to what you can manifest should you choose to do so. First, you must disabuse yourself of the belief in your limitation. That creates the clarity you seek.

Since you are actually unlimited potential holding conscious awareness within ME in this dimension, you have the opportunity to decide what you remember, what you experience and how you perceive each of those happenings. The trick is to let go of the negative expectations that have become a habit believing that by thinking about them you can, in some way, allay what is to come – whether it appears or not. In the place of this mental abuse, you are invited to create what you wish to experience, hold it in your consciousness and your heart and know that, since you are creators as emanations of Creator within ME, you have set in motion exactly that which you wish to add to your list of earthly experiences. This is the way to gain clarity of perceived possibilities.

Since the present moment contains the energy of the future, it is the perfect space and time to begin the creation. See it. Envision it. Feel it. Smell it. Know it.

If it is necessary to change a past event to know that the future will be different, reassign new memories to the past. Look at what happened and ask yourself why it happened the way it did. Ask what you could have done differently and see yourself doing exactly what would have contributed to a different result. Do this sufficiently so that you can actually feel the change in the memory. The chemical reactions in your body are now shifting and assisting you in recreating a feeling that will align with your desires for the future.

You may feel that I AM dwelling overly much upon what you have already experienced rather than focusing on the realm of your possibilities. This is intentional, I assure you. Without redefining what you believe you *are* based upon the occurrences that have shaped you, it is impossible to be clear about what you wish to bring forward in what you label your "vision". All human reality is subject to significance assigned to it by beliefs and the playing out of those concepts. Until your understanding of this is firmly in place, you will simply recreate that which you believe you have already lived within as ME. As I AM, I know no time as you do.

Bringing clarity to what is possible within your present existence can be an invitation to the limitlessness existing within you. Asking how open you are to surrendering to the unknown will bring your greatest clarity. *Know* that you are limitless and you *will be* within ME.

## Story Time

Nancy's musing was cut short by interference within her consciousness from Don. He appeared to want clarification about her feelings. Now that the three travelers had merged their awareness, all was exposed to the inner light of clarity.

Nancy had no way to "turn off" Don's intrusion into her private space because she had created a frequency in resonance with him out of desire for him. Now she had him, so to speak, and wasn't sure what to do with him in the manner in which he appeared.

*"Nancy,"* Don transmitted within her, *"I'm experiencing you wanting to know me on a much more intimate level. This is a great honor though I am not clear why you didn't speak up about it when we were back in camp. Though we seem to be mind*

readers in this atmosphere, we certainly are not when in the physical only. Once we are complete with this journey, perhaps we can look into this aspect of ourselves a little more. What do you say about that?"

"Don, this is most disconcerting. I feel as though I stand before you completely naked and I don't know if I'm ready for that or not. So all I can tell you is that you're right. Can we put this on hold until we're finished with Talish? Talking about it in this environment feels strange, almost inappropriate. Basically, I just don't want to go there right now. Okay?"

"Of course, Nancy, we'll put your feelings on hold until we're done here. Sorry for the intrusion. I just couldn't help noticing." With these words of apparent regret, Don withdrew his presence from Nancy's consciousness leaving her abruptly alone.

"You're never alone," Talish expressed into the triad. "Merge your inner perception because I want to explain something to you as we walk. It will be most easy if you focus your visual eyesight upon your perception of my back and simply follow my ongoing path. Then you can concentrate upon what I am expressing.

"Paul, for your benefit since you weren't actively taking part in Don and Nancy's recent interaction, Don accessed Nancy's desire to be in a more intimate relationship with him. Nancy expressed her reluctance to discuss her feelings right now. I would like to use this experience as a pointer toward other areas of living within our earth.

"If we begin back in the moment that Nancy realized she had a yearning for Don, it will emphasize for you how energy begins to create your life. And, Nancy, while I know you don't want to address this right now, we are going to do so anyway. This is a time and space of learning. You are the student. I am the teacher. I will choose what and how you need to learn.

"Once the frequency of Nancy's feelings was put into motion, the realm of all possibility began to clarify itself within her experience. This does not mean that she received a clearer vision of how it was going to turn out. It simply means the potential for either Don wanting her in the same way or not wanting her in the same way became the two options. Within that personal framework, there is little optional room for any other outcome.

"This manifestation then begins to take on a life of its own. Based upon Nancy's experience with intimate relationships in the past, the environment in which the energetic achievements may be expressed shape shifts dependent upon her memories. If she has been successful in other physical unions, she will expect Don to acquiesce to her. If other relationships have left her feeling abandoned and alone, she will be on the alert for this within Don, as well.

"Because the vacuum of all possibility within atam-atma includes everything that could possibly happen in your concept of past, present or future, the potential for any outcome outside of Nancy's awareness is always available. While she does not include this in her survey of the present territory, it does still exist.

"Now here is the learning aspect of the moment's interaction: As we continue in our exploration of the visible and invisible, you are going to be invited to stretch yourselves to edges of awareness you have no existent knowledge of right now. To the degree you believe you know where you are going, to that degree will you limit your progress at the edge of that boundary which is actually a portal to the unknowable.

"When I express this space as 'unknowable' I do so intentionally to allow you to realize that what you believe you know and what is actually capable of being acknowledged can become divergent paths for you. While your present awareness encompasses a very small portion of the possibilities of your existence, your vision is obscured due to your beliefs. My intention is to take you to the edge of those ideals and kick you off into the unknown. Once that is accomplished, my job is done and you are all on your own.

"If this frightens you, well it should. You three have displayed an aptitude for loosening the holds on your concepts. If this were not so, you would not have traveled from the western worlds into the jungles of Africa. At the same time, you each have attached yourself to an enormous amount of fear thereby deriving some comfort from attempts to control what happens next. When you can no longer exercise that control, you will understand it *does not exist. It never has and, eventually, you will no longer look for it."*

## Question Sixty-two
## Why do I feel I have been
## intuitively working toward something all of my life?

The first reason is that the etheric realm, the subtle realm, that which is unseen, is where you originally emerged. This plane houses your intuition that is reliant upon your body to communicate its contents within you as I AM. Actually, you unfolded into the subtler realms when I intentioned manifestation through MYSELF as Creator. What you call creation exists in endless dimensions, frequencies of expression, in every possible manner infinitely. That is an enormous sentence, an almost incomprehensible idea for you.

When you feel you have been intuitively working toward something you are listening to yourself in another frequency of vibration. It is your soul speaking through your heart, which in turn, uses your body to convey the message.

You need a physical body to use intuition. It is different from receiving information directly from within MY Mind though it does flow from within ME. Each of you intuits differently. Some of you feel the message, others hear, smell or taste it. Your intuition is reliant upon your physiology, therefore it is inherently within your nature to "intuitively know" what desires to be expressed as you.

Every possibility that exists within ME is connected with the physical realm, as well. In the sense of Oneness, nothing is separate; nothing is disconnected. Again, even if you believe you don't want to interact with other dimensions of information within your intuitive capabilities those vibratory frequencies are interacting with you as I AM.

The oneness of union simply *is* whether you believe it or not. Everything that exists in every dimension is connected by a web-like force within ME through Creator. It is the basis for telepathy, energetic remission of lack of health in the physical body and the reason you can feel what you call "vibes" from people, plants and animals. It is even the reason why you like to look at some pictures, movies or scenes and not others. It all depends upon the resonance you have with that at which you are looking during that moment in linear time. Look at the same picture a year later and you will see it differently even if you do nothing consciously to change your perception of it.

The field within union is literally embedded within your DNA acting as a template for oneness to be expressed in and through you in harmony and coherence. So when you feel you have been working toward something all of your life, you have been "headed" toward being aware of your emergence within oneness within ME. No matter what your mind may tell you might come up within the future with which you resonate, the result of all is awareness of ME within ME and as ME.

Communication with the etheric through your intuition while in your physical body is one of the most natural experiences. It has been conditioned out of your culture to keep you under the dominion of the government of your country, the leaders of your religions, the teachers in your schools and, inevitably, the peer group you decide to associate with at any given time.

If you step back from the industrial and technological world you presently live in and look at your ancestors in the natural world, you will see that unequivocally all of the earlier peoples had constant communication with the unseen. Those countries, tribes and national groups living outside the world as you know it still do communicate with the etheric and use their knowing, their nightly dreams and their voyages of seeing into the unseen to create, organize and administer their daily lives. They live present and aware within ME.

Making this much more personal, you intuitively feel and experience the loosely held idea you constructed within your soul before you incarnated into your body. Now your physiology is reminding you through its intuitive sensing mechanisms of some of the reasons you decided to become human within ME.

Your busy, distracted mind often doesn't want to pay attention to what your extra-sensing ability is telling you. Sometimes you ignore it completely rather than make a decision to move toward another way of living. This is the "working" you are talking about and you will only understand it, honor it and follow through upon it when you loosen the attachment you have to material control. It is impelling you through its energy rather than it being an actual action you are undertaking or *needing* to undertake within ME. It is a shift in your being.

The world you live in, the world you came from and the world to which you are going is not physical. It exists and is available to you when you make the decision you want to live your life more consciously aware of, and consciously linked to, that which already exists. It is not outside of you and it is not inside of you. It simply is and in that, so are you. You simply *are* within ME. In truth, you cannot keep from having communication with the subtle, etheric realms. All you can do is keep yourself from knowing it.

Ask yourself what it feels like to accept your intuitive knowing at this point in your life. Question whether you are listening to the voice that incessantly reminds you what you are within ME. Your body has the answer if you will respect its bio-transmission to you. Then it is no longer "work", rather it is the harmony of resonance with your own truth.

## Story Time

Talish continued, *"While we are traveling to our place of rest, I would like you each to be very quiet and let your physical body tell you what is happening around you. Disconnect your awareness from each other. When I am through talking, disconnect from me. Then place all of your focus upon what you smell, feel, hear and taste with your physical senses and your body's intuitive sense.*

*"Tell yourself to keep a memory of each of these sensations. You will need them later when we are again not focusing on being in the body. Are you ready? Disconnect now."*

Nancy, Paul and Don slipped away from within their common union. Now they were experiencing themselves much more as they were used to day-to-day. The only difference was the intense dark that remained. They couldn't see much at all though their other senses had grown more acute due to the lack of eyesight.

As Paul walked directly behind Talish, he recognized her smell as that of the natural world around them. It was hard to separate her from the odor of the ground, leaves and tree bark. He placed his hands palms out so as to touch whatever leaves or bushes they might be passing and felt the sharp spines of thorn bushes surrounding them.

Nancy first focused upon what she could hear. The birds were singing though they usually didn't announce their presence so loudly at night. In the distance, she heard the deep, overwhelming roar of a male lion staking out his nocturnal territory while the wings of night hunting birds could be heard flapping overhead.

Don was lost in taste. He always had a propensity for different flavors so he stuck his tongue out as he walked to let the night air drift upon it. From tangy to bitter, the essence from vegetation filled the moist surroundings alerting him to potentially edible fruits. There was the random taste of old flesh announcing that they were sightlessly passing old hunting grounds.

Talish let them play in the grounding world of the senses for some time as they logged the miles toward her home. She made a decision to deepen their experience. Turning around to face the line of travelers behind her, she provided a wall into which Paul abruptly walked.

*"Oof!"* he announced as he hit her chest on. *"Excuse me. I can barely see anything and I was lost in feeling. I didn't see you stop. I'm sorry for hitting you so hard."*

*"It's fine. I'm going to change your experience right now to heighten your body's awareness of the use of your senses through your intuitive powers. Paul will be my partner and Nancy and Don will team up.*

*"We are going much further into jungle, arm in arm. Each of us will assist the other to navigate through without walking into trees or spiny bushes. Since you can see very little, you will have to use your intuition to know where to step and what objects to avoid.*

*"Having a partner will assist you for a while. After we have traveled a few miles, we will let go of our partner and walk alone using the same technique. I will keep track of you and you will not get lost so don't let that occupy your mind. Simply pay attention to what you need to focus upon to walk safely."*

With that being said, Talish slipped her arm through Paul's and turned directly into a wall of trees slipping among them gracefully. Nancy and Don shyly linked up and took a few steps into a barrier of brush. Don gave her a gentle pull around a set of protruding branches that his body's feelers told him was looming in front of them.

As the group walked, it almost felt as though the forest was opening up for them. The longer they proceeded intuitively, the easier the going became.

At one point, Talish announced, *"Okay, let go of your partner and walk alone. We do not need to travel in single file. Step where your body tells you to place your feet. Relax, breathe and feel for each other as you progress. We will continue in this pattern until first light at which time we will stop for refreshment."*

Though they might have been walking in this fashion for hours, it did not seem overly long to the three. Nancy decided to close her eyes completely allowing only her senses and her intuition to guide her. There was no difference whether her eyes were open or closed. She still knew the way. Don and Paul advanced in much the same fashion though they remained with eyes opened. No one ran into anything harmful nor did anyone lose track of each other.

The dawn light first began to announce itself with the morning star emerging over the horizon. Talish stopped the group and pointed out the reference point she was using now to guide them to her home.

*"I always travel by the stars at night. When the morning star presents itself, it is my only signal and I then turn toward it. As soon as we can no longer see its brilliance, we will be at a place to stop and refresh ourselves. Once rejuvenated, we will walk quickly throughout the morning stopping only to sleep through*

*the hotter afternoon. After one more night's travel, we will arrive at my home."*

They continued for a short period and then the sun proclaimed another day with its fiery presence. As the rays lit up the jungle ceiling, a clearing appeared directly ahead perfect for a space of rest, food and water.

## Question Sixty-three
### How can I know that what I do is for the highest good?

I will begin by asking you, "How can you believe that anything you do as ME is not of benefit?" Humanity is taught that its consciousness is flawed, that a human being cannot know itself. Hence, there is always another person or authority figure to whom to look for information or assistance. Autonomy appears futile. This is why the mass consciousness, humanity at large, constantly looks for a happy ending.

Personal plans, goals and far-reaching achievements are humanity's attempts to control the world of natural order. This does not mean that your actions are not good, simply that they stem from your desire to perceive yourself as "doing" good, whatever that may mean to you.

You live in a reality that responds to each moment sometimes referred to as a "just in time universe". Everything happens just in time without prior planning or preparation. Creation lives in a realm of the eternal present within ME. Every experience occurs now and is perfect through Creator as I AM.

In each moment, you experience a heart storm of desire. It is your passion. If you are not experiencing it, it is because you have suppressed your feelings and cannot feel what your deepest desires are or could be. What do you want to be and do? What gets you juiced up – like riding a tidal wave of feeling? What gets you excited? Why do you want to get out of bed in the morning? What is your message to the world within your reality?

The answers to these questions release you from focusing upon whether you are "doing something for the highest good" and redirect your attention upon your heart's desire. Once you realize the passion of your heart can only be of benefit, you will no longer be questioning your motivation. Until that time, all comes under scrutiny within you within ME.

Your subjective response to your reality is based upon an ego personality that believes everything happening within the earth is because of it. This translates into "I have to be good so bad things won't happen." The ego personality wants to believe that its actions determine the outcome of its reality. While observing with an open mind rather than always believing you know can expose a completely different state of reality, remember that your experience is particular to you only.

At the same time, you encompass an energetic frequency so large that you are affecting the entire globe by simply paying attention to this information within ME. It is your intention that determines whether you are resonating with beneficial frequencies, though what is "good" in your viewpoint may be different from someone else's concept of it.

While you may argue there are "givens" within creation outlining what is "good" or "bad", reflect upon differences within cultures. What is deemed perfect in the society of the United States is opposite to what is considered appropriate in the Mideast countries. Your mind immediately pops up in response, "But we're right," as a United States citizen. Pay attention to that message. It is your personal response to consideration of all being perfect within ME. A human being in a European country believes he or she is just as "right" in believing what that culture dictates.

You are what your science calls a "standing wave" of information transmitting and receiving simultaneously. Both actions are happening at the same time. If you place this picture in your mind and use it in your relating to the world, it will change your view of reality. The wave that you are comes from your heart as an expression of ME. It stimulates and responds to every interaction you experience in every moment based upon your attention. When you talk about being sure that what you do is for the "highest good", all that it comprises is an increase in your personal coherency through attention based upon your present belief system.

All beliefs are based upon the need of a person to control an interaction. This includes your desire to assure yourself of "doing good". Trace every belief you have back and you will find this to be true. Believing is seeing and what you see is what you get. What you believe is going to be present for you creates what is there.

All energy is neutral. It has absolutely no significance. Energy doesn't care until you decide it means something. Your belief creates a perception that what you believe means something. Its significance is only yours. You do not ever know how another person is interpreting a situation. Your idea of what is "good" in a specific environment is subjectively charged with "what is good for you".

Your feelings are personal so own that which you have created and see where you want to make changes for your own benefit since those are the only shifts you are capable of making. As you do so, you will influence the whole within ME without having to exercise a judgment about whether it or not it is for the "highest good". Not only can you not know that, your opinion is not important since it stems from a limited belief of what is possible.

Focus your attention on your present intention to live fully as you are within ME. Shift your focal point from a desire to operate for the "highest good" to *being,* aligned within the limitless love, compassion and absolution of ME. Translate your need to know the outcome of your feelings, thoughts, words and actions into a state of benevolence within your awareness of ME. That will clear up the confusion inherent within this question.

## Story Time

While the quartet sat in the semi-shade downing water and nibbling on what the bushes had provided as snack, Don made a decision to clear up the confusion he was experiencing. His decision stemmed from wanting the remainder of the journey to be as clear as possible. Since he still held a residue of doubt about his interaction with Joe's "accident", now felt like as good a time as any to bring it up.

*"Talish,"* he began tentatively, *"is this a proper time to ask you a personal question?"*

*"Don, yes, now is a good time for me to relieve your mind. You are remaining confused regarding how much you contributed to the pain Joe caused himself due to your indecision. I will explain it to you for the benefit of everyone.*

"Much of what humans contrive to do is based upon a concept about what is for the good of all. Even when you are making decisions about what you want to happen or you are running away from that which you don't like, your mind reconfigures the experience into something that resembles a beneficial outcome. This is what is bothering you right now. You can't find a place to fit Joe into that scheme since it leaves you feeling as though you were in control and then lost it.

"This limited viewpoint is due to your tiny frame of reference for life. You are not alone in this opinion. Nearly every human being believes that he or she must act and speak in a way that will be seen as conducive to good for everyone in their personal reality. The problem with that need is that you have no way of knowing how the other person or people will experience your offering. You can only see it through your own eyes. That point of focus is very narrow.

"In this moment, you believe that if you had made a faster decision, one way or the other, Joe would not have 'needed' to 'harm' himself. It is a personal feeling you have about the experience. Please remember you have not even asked Joe about what he felt during the entire episode so the construction of the event is completely limited to your mind.

"I am going to take the three of you into the inner worlds to show you what I am talking about. Close your eyes, breathe with me as you have learned to do and let's align with your parallel selves that you have recently been introduced to in the realm of atam.

"Breathe, relax, breathe and perceive. Slowly you are becoming aware of Ann, John, Tusk, 'Mao, Great Horn, Abamti and He Who Sees. Don you are only experiencing one alter life rather than the number Paul and Nancy have awareness of due to the influence this one life has within your experience as Don. While it is important for Nancy and Paul to merge within each of the other experiences with which they have been presented, it is not the same for you.

"Now, Nancy, I want you to focus upon your life as Tusk and witness first how much natural wisdom is included and then how little connection with humanity is allowed. Whenever you contribute to your own social network as Nancy, Tusk experiences greater fulfillment of an interaction he did not have in the Tusk body. It doesn't make any difference whether these communications appear to be positive or negative to you. Within the awareness of Tusk, they embellish a networking he did not know until you incarnated as Nancy. My emphasis here is on the idea of 'bad' or 'good' from your standpoint. It is only your opinion and it is relative only to you.

"Paul, I would like you to focus upon your experience as Ann. Relate to how little you felt fulfilled as a woman and realize it was that desire that fueled your decision to come into form as a male in this lifetime with Nancy as your younger sister so you could protect and guide. These were the self-same feelings you felt lack of in your life as Ann. Now you find yourself here without the capacity to enact that which you believed would be the purpose for this life. It is neither 'bad' nor 'good', important nor unimportant. It simply is and since you were not aware of it until this moment, you have a choice, right now, whether to shoulder blame for your perceived lack or to simply let it be.

"Now to your question, Don. I have left it for last. I want you to focus upon your life as He Who Sees. As you recognize yourself in that way, look behind the medicine man, He Who Sees, and notice the young woman standing there. See how she looks at you longingly. This is Joe in that life as R'em, a beautiful virgin who wished to be your bride. Your devotion to your shamanic way of life left no room for communion in this way and R'em remained celibate her entire life in her dedication to you.

"In this life, Joe subtly remembers his alliance with you in that parallel life. I stress subtly here since he has no awareness of it as Joe. The energetic fabric that contains the memories intermixes within his expression as Joe without him having to acknowledge them.

"Since all is in union, when you were hanging at a pivot point of decision regarding whether to come with us or stay in the reserve, Joe's atam-based memory was triggered. It just so happened he was using the auger. It could have happened in a number of ways. He didn't make a personal choice. He simply responded to your energy signature within atam yet not from his Joe mind of knowing.

"As I mentioned before, in some realm, the two of you will play out more of this particular set of vibrations. Now the only experience you can have that will contribute to an ongoing unfoldment easily is to be grateful he responded as he did. Whether you believe in the benefit of it is of no importance. In the realm of atam-atma, it has no meaning. It simply is."

## Question Sixty-four
## Is my soul purpose in alignment
## with this mission, or is it time to move on?

The key to alignment with what you consider your "mission" is what you are feeling in this moment within ME. Since you are asking the question, you already know the answer.

Step away from what you consider your "mission" to be and ask yourself if you feel complete within it. Your soul does not have a purpose, as you would imagine. The soul's desire within ME is only to experience. How you decide to create within each moment of your life is not the "purpose" of your soul. It is the desire of your ego-personality.

As an individuated aspect of ME, you incarnated within your present body to experience a realm of contrast through free will. Here ends your "purpose" or your "mission". You may *commission* yourself to have a particular experience through committing to it. Yet, there is no judgment included if you later make the decision to change the course of your ship and head in a different direction. The only person who cares is you through your ego personality's attachment to its persona.

Your soul is always in alignment. It is not ever out of balance or harmony. When you project the idea of chaos or lack of harmony upon your soul's purpose, you manufacture a condition of being out of resonance with your soul's eternal state. It is much more appropriate to admit you are either tired *of* or bored *with* the present set of circumstances. Rather than attempting to foist your frustration upon your soul, own it as a construct of the personality's mind within ME.

Your present incarnated life is one of countless experiences you are having in a limitless number of dimensional realities. Within each one, the personality you have acquired manifests as a specific "you". While this is occurring, the soul remains inviolate as it records the various feelings, thoughts, words and actions you create within it.

From moment to moment, you know if you are in a state of harmony and congruence within yourself or not. You feel it within your body, think it through your mental state and express it emotionally through actions. The difficulty emerges when you feel the desire to "move on" and then spend hours, days, weeks, months, even years attempting to figure out what it means to you.

You know the answer to the question in the moment of its asking. Now you are asking for confirmation from ME so you won't feel alone or completely responsible for your decision. Rather than allowing yourself to say, "I feel it is time to make a change. I am no longer happy within the present situation," you dress it up in fancy language thereby removing yourself from the experience of it and relegating it to the soul as a task within ME.

Stepping away from the practical, day-to-day decisions and free will choices doesn't leave you feeling any better. It simply adds to your present confusion because now you have given away your authority. Since your authentic self makes decisions within ME, giving that self away serves no purpose. Instead, it creates chaos within your physical, mental and emotional bodies.

Within that created state of incoherency, the urge to "move on" becomes increasingly insistent without definition as to where, what or how. You begin with a question that is based in confusion, run from its answer and end up in an even greater sense of conflict.

Since attraction is your natural state, you have a free will choice whether you are going to make shifts in your life's structure or not. It is your decision-making ability to decide what you are attracting rather than letting it all happen by default. Your reality will continue to do what it does no matter what you are attracting. That's what creation does – align different attractions together through Creator.

I bring this up right here because your desire to know the answer to your question is attracting what your true feeling is directly into your life. That is the foundation of your present dimension experience. You have placed your attention upon the decision to "move on" or "not move on" so your true feelings will bring the choice point into your awareness.

If you advise yourself to live your life of attraction by constantly turning your attention to those ideas, thoughts, words, sounds, sights, experiences that make you feel good, you will always know when you are in harmony within yourself within ME. Then you are following the direction that your true nature flows easily. You are no longer attempting to obey a law outside of yourself. You are in alignment with the attraction that makes your world revolve around all of the wonders you so truly wish to know.

When you ask if your "mission" is in alignment with your soul, I would request you release the idea of a *mission*. Release the concept your soul cares about what you are doing. Your ego personality will voice its disgruntled opinion because it wants to feel important no matter what's at stake. Once your mind lets go of its attachment to the outcome of your life, you have a chance to use your true motivations to attract and create the fulfillment of your life's incarnation as soul recording experience.

Despite what you may believe about why you are alive, know this – your experience in a physical, human body is one of infinite choices you are making. None of them is more or less important. Each one is equal within ME as I AM. The realization of this truth is the greatest freedom you can possibly experience no matter where you focus your incarnated attention.

## Story Time

Snack consumed, bodies hydrated, lesson given and received, the foursome began their trek toward Talish's home village. The heat of the day would certainly slow them down in mid-afternoon yet for now they could walk in the morning's evaporating mist.

Nancy, Paul and Don were lost in their personal inner realities relying on Talish to head the march and direct them along the correct pathway. They were so immersed within themselves that they did not see the elephant herd grazing among the trees until they were almost upon it.

Talish stopped moving and motioned them to do the same. Surveying the herd's proximity to the group, she signaled Nancy to come forward toward her stealthily.

*"Nancy, here is one of the many opportunities you will have during this month to investigate your connection with the untamed world. You will do so as Tusk. This herd has given us the perfect chance to begin practicing the shapeshifting all three of you will be learning during your time with me.*

*"I would like you to shift into your Tusk embodiment and demonstrate for all of us his union with the elephants. So long as you remain in the Nancy body, they will fear you, even to the point of attacking. As Tusk, they view you as one of them. Don't rely on your recent experience with the wounded infant. That was an exception to the rule. Now, focus on Tusk and then shift."*

Nancy focused her attention on the young native she knew as Tusk feeling the familiarity it created within her body and mind. She felt a slight twitch within her nervous system spreading into physiological musculature and then out into her extremities. Looking down at her body, she witnessed herself as Tusk. The body of Nancy was no longer her experience. Her reality had transformed itself.

Tusk's natural propensities took over nearly stumbling over his eagerness to be with his best friends. Leaping on top of the log at his feet, he raised his hand in salute running toward the foraging animals with delight.

The herd's matriarch raised her head from the local branch and looked in his direction. Recognizing their two-legged companion, she signaled safety by trumpeting a welcome from them all. When Tusk reached her trunk, he leapt into its curl and she lifted him onto her back with ease. This was Tusk's natural position as an elephant rider.

Paul and Don had been observing the interaction between Nancy and Talish in silence. One aspect of each man's ego personality was jealous of Talish's special attention to Nancy. Another part was glad they each had not been singled out for another lesson in loss of personal control. Their security was quickly threatened when Talish then pointed to Paul and summoned him to her.

*"Okay, Paul, you have witnessed Nancy shifting into another reality within this plane. Now it's your turn. As Great Horn, you administered to your tribe and the natural world, plants in addition to animals. You still carry the inherent instinct as you demonstrated when you instructed Nancy how to care for the wounded infant several days in your past.*

*"This is your opportunity to transform yourself into Great Horn and join Tusk among the herd. Your natural inclination will be to look for any of the elephants that might need remedial attention. We are not going to be remaining here very long so don't use your allotted time focusing on one animal. Simply let yourself feel what it is to be Great Horn so you can understand yourself from that aspect.*

*"Paul, since you haven't had as much experience shapeshifting as Nancy has had, breathe with me to set your mind at ease. Then focus on the idea of Great Horn as your fondness for nature emerges within you. Okay, close your eyes, breathe, sense the forest, breathe, shift."*

Paul dropped into his center core where he had been focusing during his days sitting in the tree circle. Imagining Great Horn came easily as the image of him welled up in his mind. His physical body felt as though it was expanding to embrace a much larger "him". When the developing amplification ceased, Paul opened his eyes as Great Horn.

Taller, broader, more expansive now, he surveyed his surroundings and slowly walked to the herd to join Tusk. The elephants barely noticed his arrival due to his resonance among them. Placing his hand on the matriarch's trunk in mutual recognition, he meandered among the animals keeping an eye out for any that may need his assistance in any way.

*"Well, Don, you're next. Come breathe with me and watch this scene as He Who Sees,"* Talish called him to her.

*"As you walk to me, feel your breath becoming my breath, my heart, your heart. That's right. Keep walking. Together we will shift you into your other self."*

As Don took one step after the other, he felt the rhythm of his breathing slowing down to match that of Talish. His body felt as though it was slipping into a much more graceful way of being, naturally. By the time he reached Talish's side, he looked down to see himself in lion-skin loincloth only.

Talish reached out her hand for his saying, *"Welcome, mate of my belly. Let's watch the children play among the elephants. We have taught them very well."*

## Question Sixty-five
## What is my highest contact
## of light when I need help or information?

Many of you talk about other points of contact within your belief about "higher" light beings. Though there are many expressions in existence within all dimensional realms, very few are there to give you information or assistance in experiencing your own existence. I will ask you a question in return. Can you, outside of this linear time structure, recognize yourself as ME? Remember you are I AM. There is nothing to do. It is all realization; there is no doing. It is only being. That realization is the foundation of being. It is I AM in which you access all help and information . . . and it is you.

The only distraction to becoming aware of your own unlimited wealth of available advice is within your mind, you see. There is only this awareness that you need to step into which is your honesty. It is your integrity. It is what makes you what you are, without believing that you are supposed to be anything other. The only reason you believe you need to be something else, or seek a "contact of light" to give you instruction, is because you do not own your divinity within ME.

You are honest when you are being what you are in every single moment of your day. Do you feel like that is a *given*? In the life that you are living right now, you know you are not being what you are within ME consciously. You are being what you think you need to be to appear enlightened, to "ascend" or whatever idea you have of what you think spirituality is all about in your reality.

To know yourself as light, to take that concept and to make it concrete, you must think about what it means to increase your frequency so fast that you are literally vibrating at a speed that no one can see with physical eyes. That is what light is, you know. It is vibrating at a frequency that cannot be seen by your earthly eyes. You can call it your light body or anything else you want to label it within yourself. Simply realize you *experience* it as light, you do not "see" it.

When you ask for a highest contact of light to assist you or inform you, what you are really asking for is something you cannot see that is supposed to know more than you do within ME. What or who do you believe that would be, since you have absolute access to all that I AM?

Your desire for "exterior" assistance is keeping you from believing it is possible to know the answers yourself. It is not that you have to be good or better. That is a judgment based upon what you think good and bad is and that is different for each of you. If you desire an increase in your understanding, be what you are without attempting to please anyone, to be good enough, whether that is being a vegetarian or practicing yoga or burning incense or lighting candles or meditating or any of the other myriad practices that you believe will assist you or enlighten you. What all of those routines do is to slow you down enough and make you comfortable enough in your bodies that you are able to look at yourself and see what you are expressing as within ME.

Yet no one can give you the strength, no one can give you the courage and the capacity to be your true self as ME. There is no amount of "higher light contact" that can show you the way to you. Only you can do that because you are the one and only interpreter of your energy frequency.

You don't need to do anything that is different; you don't have to change yourself into some magical spiritual being so that you can be enlightened and a "lightworker". What you realize is that by stepping out of experiencing yourself with the small "s", you step firmly into your Self with the big "S" and then nothing else truly matters. You are enlightened and you know it and you do not care. You are your own assistance.

You are utterly filled with knowing within ME in this very moment yet you stop yourself from the awareness that is already present within your being. Loving you is all that is required; simply that and when you do that, simply love yourself, you can do nothing except be what you are because you then realize that you are as I AM.

If you want to ask a "highest contact of light" for help or information, ask yourself. You are the brightest, most informed and glorious being in your environment. No one knows you as you do. No one and no thing can give you advice about how to live the existence of your soul the way you do because no one understands what you are experiencing except you.

Though you might want to believe that there are "higher beings" who are sitting around just waiting for an opportunity to give you advice, this is not so. Some invisible entities may have "words of wisdom" to give the human race from their perspective yet they are very few indeed.

Most of the intelligences from which humans claim to receive information are aspects of themselves they have re-labeled with a convenient, lustrous name in order to garner attention. Sometimes the advice they offer in the name of these beings is wisdom-filled and sometimes it is only a projection of their personal wishes. Despite the wording, it comes from within their own conscious awareness even though they would have you believe otherwise in light of their desire for notoriety among you. You have instant and absolute access to ME, MY Mind, of which you are an integral part. Do not doubt it. Do not look for information elsewhere. Trust your own wisdom within ME.

## Story Time

While Talish and He Who Sees stood watching the children of their union, it was time for a new experience within the realm of consciousness. Talish intended to exhibit to them how easily they could switch among their soul's aspects garnering wisdom from each experience within atam.

Addressing Tusk, she told Nancy, *"Okay, now I want you to focus on being 'Mao and walk toward me away from the elephants. They will tolerate you in that guise yet not as easily as they do as Tusk. Slide down from the elephant, walk toward me and focus on the other aspect of you."*

Nancy did as she was told and found herself morphing into the image of a woman dressed in a soft, short leather skirt with a string of beads hanging around her neck. The fact that she was topless didn't seem to bother her at all.

As 'Mao continued walking toward Talish and He Who Sees, she experienced a sense of slipping away that left her alone in the jungle. Everyone who had been there previously had disappeared within her awareness. At first, she felt a sense of shock and then familiarity began to set in as she found herself walking in a direction that she knew would be her village.

Back at the scene of the elephants, Talish was instructing Paul, directing him to shift his attention to awareness of himself as Abamti. As he did so, he too, experienced Talish, He Who Sees and the elephants disappearing and found himself walking slightly ahead of 'Mao. Sensing her presence, he stopped and turned around.

"*'Mao, it is so good to see you here. I did not know you had ventured into the forest so far from our living village. Are you alone? It is not safe to wander such distance without a weapon or a companion. May I join you?*" Paul as Abamti offered Nancy as 'Mao.

"*I have no fear of this living world, Abamti,*" 'Mao retorted with pride. "*I have lived past my most fertile birthing years and no one will do me harm. The lives in the forest are always within me and we become as one very often. Why do you attempt to hinder that which I would do?*"

"*It is not that I would stop anything you desire to live out here. It is only that I know the living village requires you as the seeing vision and I would have it be no other way. I would not wish to lose you to the worlds you behold rather have you continue to guard us with your wisdom.*"

With a downward motion of his head and both hands, Abamti requested forgiveness for his apparent transgression.

"*I open myself to your forgiveness or judgment as we are commanded to do in all things. Transgressing upon the spirit walking of another is a great offense and I would not be seen by you in that light. Please accept me back into the heart of your vision.*"

"*Abamti, you do me no grievance by your concern. There is understanding living within me of the weight the living village places upon my head. With that, one would believe our tribe* would know I would see my own passing if it were to happen in these places in which I wander."

Complete in that statement, 'Mao continued quietly strolling toward the village stepping through the underbrush as though upon a newly-mown lawn. Abamti followed her silently. His feelings for her bewildered him yet he found no appropriate way of expressing his love. It was much easier and an honor simply to be in her presence and be silent.

It was not many footsteps later that 'Mao stopped and looked about as though she heard someone calling to her. Indeed, within her visionary capacity, she could sense her name being summoned from planes unseen.

Opening her inner vision, 'Mao immediately saw Talish beckoning her with guttural tones plus hand and arm motions. She read her message as, *"It is time to leave. Bring Abamti with you. You know the way."*

Turning to Abamti who was watching silently, 'Mao asked, *"Do you trust me completely, enough to follow wherever I lead you?"*

Abamti bowed his head in submission responding, *"'Mao, you may lead me to any place of your choosing and I will follow willingly in my living flesh and spirit. You have only to summon me and I will come."*

*"Good, then take my hand,"* 'Mao instructed. *"We are leaving this place and may not return. I do not know where we are going yet I do know the way. Close your eyes, hold tightly to my hand so we do not lose each other and let your living flesh and spirit follow with mine."*

With those words, 'Mao slipped both she and Abamti back into the awareness of life as Nancy and Tusk, Paul and Great Horn where Talish and He Who Sees, who now had returned to Don, awaited them. No one seemed surprised to see them appear as though out of thin air.

"Well, that was excellent," Talish commended them. *"And to make it all a little more educational, I showed Don as He Who Sees how to see among the atam planes so he was able to follow the two of you as I did, also.*

"Nancy, you did a fine job of finding the way back for both of you. It was of assistance that you did not know it was possible for you not to find your way back for some time, since coming back 'here' was not part of your desire at that moment.

"This learning experience is the cliff of leaping now for the three of you. We will continue our journey."

## Question Sixty-six
## How do we gain support from
## others when they don't believe we will change?

Why do you wish support from others? Are you not sufficient unto yourself? Yes, I understand that you believe you cannot stand alone and yet I AM. Within the context of ME, no support is necessary rather the establishment of a firm foundation within yourself sustaining you as ME.

The connotation of your question suggests you are creating a change to please another person and you want that person to believe it is possible. It is not possible to alter yourself to please another. It will not last and you will inevitably, begin to revert to that which you naturally express within ME.

If you re-frame your transformational idea to discount your desire to make another person happy with you and consider only what you are satisfied being, do you still want to change? Perhaps the shift is something that is hard for you and the constant urging of another has stimulated you to consider it. Or it may be that you wish to make this alteration yet haven't felt courageous enough to take it upon yourself and now you want to base it upon another's request.

The reason I make a point of *why* you wish to alter your present configuration is because the impetus to do so will become the strength with which it occurs within you. If you have a strong desire to change a habit, a lifestyle, a belief or any of the many attributes you consider part of your life, you will do so with or without the support of another. If you are asking the question because another has asked you to make changes you don't necessarily want to make, then no amount of support will assist you in doing so. It is always and in all ways up to you and you will only transform yourself into a pattern of your own desire not that of another person, no matter who they may be within ME.

If you are being asked to shift a habit pattern in your life because a family member, friend, co-worker or associate finds you to be abrasive, controlling, abusive or detrimental to the relationship, it is their viewpoint they are speaking from about you. It does not mean they are incorrect. It is simply their way of experiencing you and because they do not like the behavior, they are asking you to change.

Now that the request has been made, you are considering the value of the relationship, noting that if you don't make the changes your mutual communion may dissolve. Since you don't want to lose this person in your life, your mind decides to attempt some shift of your habits. Note I said "your mind" rather than "you". This has very little to do with your true expression and all to do with what you "think" you "should" be doing under the circumstances.

Since your decision to release your attachment to some of the conditions within your life stems from the request of another who feels impacted by your life's expression, it does not belong to "you". It belongs to your mind through your ego-personality's desire to conform to another's wishes. While it may secretly be an underlying desire of your own, it has not been strong enough to create the shift without the impetus of the other person. Therefore, it is not foundationed with enough energetic input to maintain itself. This is the reason why you are looking for the support identified within your question.

Your comment that they don't believe you will change stems from having watched you live as you say you desire to live. The person's request that you make changes for their benefit, even if they say it is for you, carries with it an energy signature stating that you are not capable of doing so. A frequency within them resonates with your own inner knowing that this is not entirely your desire.

Now if you have made a decision to make changes in your life that has nothing to do with anyone else, you will find all of the support you desire within you. This resonate frequency will call to you those who will be responsive to you desiring to offer their assistance in many ways.

The difference between making a free will choice to transform and doing it at the insistence of someone else is due to it being *your* life that is changing. You make alterations in your personality as you see fit rather than to please or conform to another. Not only does it make a difference why you decide to change, it also shapes the ultimate result.

If it is not your sole choice to re-create the patterns of your life, you will not remain in the transformative position you initially manifest. It may remain for a while, yet eventually you will return to what is most natural for you within ME.

Perhaps that is what you are experiencing in the lack of support from others whom you say do not believe you will change. If you are surrendering to their persuasion, they already know why you are doing so. Even in their attempt to convert you to their way of thinking, they inherently know it is for them and not for you. That is always true.

If you have made a conscious decision to live life differently, why do you believe you need the support of those you are presuming to impress? Is not the change sufficient reason to resonate with it? If your answer to that question is "no", then you are attempting to make shifts that will not last. They will come; they will go because they are not imbued with the energetic power to maintain their structure.

Look at why you want to become a different person. See if it is a choice of re-modeling yourself in your eyes or within the eyes of another. Only one may exist within ME.

## Story Time

The remainder of that day and through most of the night, Talish led the trio through the jungles of her home. They slept little, ate even less and subsisted on water and air. Surprisingly to all three, they felt no real need of food and were tired only a little from this very long voyage.

During a rest period just before dawn, Talish began giving Nancy, Paul and Don their final instructions before entering her village home. It was important that they were able to stand on their own. Whatever changes had occurred within them during the journey so far, the people they would meet would only know them as they presently were. This was important because there were many protocols needing attention within this new version of reality.

Talish began by instructing, *"When we enter into the center of my home community, you will be surrounded by those who live within its safety. They will form a circle around you and expect me to join them quickly within that formation. I will do so leaving the three of you to act as I am now revealing to you.*

*"As soon as this gathering feels complete, our chieftain will come out of his stone hut to address you and those gathered around you. As he approaches you, please put your heads down and keep your eyes averted until he asks me your names. One by one, Chief 'Rhumti-eben will call you by name. What he will be doing is giving you your name at that time. Only those named by the Chief may be housed within our village.*

*"Now here is the part I really want you to pay attention to because it will determine the next week of your reality. We will be staying with my people for that amount of time and then moving on to another secreted location for the remainder of your training. The portion of this that carries so much import is which name you tell me to choose when I present it to Chief 'Rhumti-eben. The name you choose will be the identity you will use during our stay in my home village."*

Don was the first one to voice a question asking what was undoubtedly on everyone's mind, *"Talish when we choose the name which makes the choice of the change in reality we will experience does it mean we will be enacting that life for the week of our stay? I remember that 'Mao and Abamti left our reality during that last shift. What would happen to them? And if I choose He Who Sees am I your husband for a week?"*

*"These are good questions to help define what you may expect to experience. It is important that you make your choice based upon what you really want to know as you.*

*"As to 'Mao and Abamti, since it is of import that you three experience and learn together for purposes you will understand later, if those personalities are the choices of Nancy and Paul then they would appear here as visitors from another country. Though my people understand spirit walking they do not see it in the context in which we have been working so reality will*

*shapeshift itself to match what is necessary for all concerned. As to being my husband, yes, Don, if you choose He Who Sees not only will you be my husband, you will be a guest seer among my tribe.*

*"Also, Nancy and Paul, you don't have to choose the same mutual soul expression if you do not desire to do so. All reality will reshape itself to conform to our needs at present.*

*"Now, as the morning star loses her brilliance and the mighty sun arises to form the new day, close your eyes and open your hearts and align with the decision that is perfect for each of you."*

As Talish closed her eyes as well, holding the space of personality formation for the three shamans in training, she was aware of how far she had taken them and herself in a short time. Few humans were able to morph themselves within the world of atam as easily as these three. *Unique indeed, they are,* she smiled to herself.

Moments passed silently as bird song began erupting within the air in welcome to the awakening day. Nancy was the first to open her eyes sending a ripple effect among the others. Very soon, each looked around their small circle expectantly.

Don spoke up. *"Talish, if you will allow it, I am happy to serve as husband and seer as He Who Sees during our stay in your home village. I am honored not only to be at your side but also to learn about myself in this humbling way. Thank you for this enormous opportunity."*

*"You are very welcome to stand beside me in this capacity, He Who Sees. I will address you as such from this moment forward. Paul and Nancy what will your decisions be?"*

Though they had not consulted each other verbally, both Paul and Nancy knew how they wished this experience to unfold. Almost as one voice, they offered their decisions.

*"Tusk."*

*"Great Horn."*

Then Paul continued, *"We would like to ask that we have opportunity to later investigate Abamti and 'Mao in more detail."*

*"So be it,"* Talish acknowledged. *"Now, shapeshift."*

# Question Sixty-seven
## How much of the "transformation process" is guided internally and how much externally?

Internally? Externally? Is there a difference between the two in your mind? If so, why? There is no internal or external, no inward or outward that is separate within ME. All emerges, emanates from within ME including what you consider inside and outside of your body.

True transformation is experienced alone. As you unwind the persona that you believe is you, your attachment to your spirituality, your preferred belief systems and all that you consider important to you drops away. Within the inner silence, you find that all of these bonds have bound you tightly within a web of your own making. Only you can untangle that which you have woven.

Being alone can initiate your ego personality's fears regarding what it believes is its perpetuated structures. Though your transformation is a natural state, your ego personality does not want to recognize that because of its security within its delineated boundary lines. As you make the decision to deliver yourself from the grasp of your mind's tight hold, the changes you witness may usher in a totally new set of apprehensions.

As this occurs, you find yourself standing at a great crossroads. It is here that you may choose whether you will emerge from this transformative embryo with your wings unfurled or submit to the anxiety attempting to assert its hold over you. The sense of separation is always paramount within the mind's eye and during this pivotal moment, it will rear its head summoning your attention.

While thought processes struggle to draw a line in the sand for you, your heart sits silently by awaiting the outcome. Will it be a fear and separation selection or a shift within your reality as the union you are within ME?

If you make the choice to alter your perception, to transform, you will release the need to consider yourself as separate, the "I" of you. The belief you are alone as the "I" limits your awareness of the possibilities open to you. Once you accept your infinite emergence within union as ME, all potentials are present before you.

There exists an inexplicable understanding that occurs when communion becomes your focus within ME. In *this* moment, you have no comprehension of its meaning because you believe yourself to be in an "untransformed" state. So long as that concept is held within your mind, these words will only flutter around your ears. They will not penetrate.

You ask your question as though transformation is a process you experience much the same as you take a shower to cleanse your physical body. This is not true. Since you are eternally emanating from within ME, there is no process. You limit yourself with this human thought. What you believe to be a course of action is a shift in conscious observation so slight as to be almost imperceptible. Yet, as the witness, you realize you are I AM and you forget that you did not perceive in that way previously. You are aware, only aware.

When you accept your conscious awareness of your true "form" as ME, all of the lives you have sought ME dissolve into this realization. The desires, searching, debates and controlling arguments merge into the common union that is your actuality. Your waiting heart ceases its encouraging yearning, enfolding your mind within its welcoming embrace.

Does this occur externally or internally? This is the question you are asking of ME and, if so, how much of each? Can you begin to see how the question in itself simply exists within union without linear process?

You within ME exist within this moment and only in this moment from your time perspective. Then, you within ME exist in this moment. Within ME, there is no past, no future. There is only the present so the concept of your transformation being a process has no home within ME since I AM without time. You are I AM. You are timeless. No process is necessary for your metamorphosis, nor is one possible. Your instant awareness of you as I AM unveils your state of beingness within ME – that and only that.

Your transmutation is without price and asks no price from you. Nothing is required of you except the release of the many beliefs you maintain about how separate you are from other humans, your earth and ME within which it all exists. When you no longer include personal opinions or judgments about what you consider "to be another" within your perception, you will experience only ME. Your origin within ME includes all that you would separate from so it is impossible for you to live without being in union with all.

The glory of realizing your own transformation, which you also call your enlightenment, is that you no longer have need for personal truth. All that you now label "truth" is but a moment's fleeing glimpse of a belief that pleases you. Until the moment of your transformation, all of these truths are very important to you. They dissolve within ME, as you are aware of being I AM.

This is freedom. It is the embracing of liberation in every aspect of your present life and will continue to be your awareness infinitely. Once you know yourself as ME, you do not lose that remembrance. Be not afraid that the transformative moment is a transient perception. It is not. As you recognize yourself as I AM, you will remain anchored within that awareness. Let it be now, if you will. Your will and MY Will are one. Accept that as your truth and observe your reality become as MINE. Then you will no longer believe in process because you will BE.

## Story Time

As Talish drew the triad into the village's center, she pulled He Who Sees aside for additional instruction. If Don were to act as her mate, he would have to do so immediately.

*"He Who Sees, as my mate, there are certain aspects you need to be aware of before we proceed. I will be walking ahead of you only during the time in which I bring all of you into the circle. Once there, you and I will remove our presence to the outer rim of the gathering and I will stand behind you. So long as we are mated in the eyes of my tribe, I will always be behind you. While this may appear subservient to you, it is exactly the opposite.*

"All women of our tribe carry my people's power. We stand behind the males to show that we support their actions and that we are their mainstay always. When decisions are made, the women speak first. Although we have a male chief, it is only to free his female counterpart to observe the actions of the tribe in order to be apprised before a decision is to be made. Our chief is what you would consider a figurehead.

"Within our tribe, those who are mated do not live together as you do in your world as Don. The men live within one quadrant of the village and the women in another while children over the age of seven live in still another area. Only young ones under seven years of age live with their mothers.

"This will give you enough information for the moment. If you access the memories of He Who Sees, you will easily fit in with the village. You will be given a separate hut in which to live as I also maintain since we are seers and do not live among the general population. It is believed that our gifts may be tainted by the daily activity. We are allowed much time alone and in silence in order to perfect our abilities to see and give forth the knowledge we gain from doing so."

Coming back to Nancy and Paul, she had a few last words for them as well. Reality was going to shift dramatically for all of them and they needed a bit of forewarning before stepping into these new perceptions.

"Now, Tusk and Great Horn, I want you to realize that the village will see you as our children come back from a trip into the jungle to share wisdom with the animals. While you have been living in many different spaces, my village only knows that I have gone off into the forest and died. Since my family, which is comprised of the four of us, has also passed from this earth rather than appearing in spirit bodies, I have created a shift in the time/space rift to allow my people to believe as they did when we walked among them.

"You may have concern about damaging the flow of time and need not be concerned. You, too, will come to know how to manipulate the forces in order to transform instantly all into that which is most relevant and appropriate. Come now, it is time for us to proceed."

Having given her final tutelage, Talish gathered the three who had now fully physically shifted into Tusk, Great Horn and He Who Sees and began the entrance into the village. Just as she had predicted, the people came to meet the four travelers in the middle of open ground. The men circled around them followed by the women behind them. As soon as the circumference had been completed, Talish and He Who Sees moved to the outskirts leaving Tusk and Great Horn in the center.

Chief 'Rhumti-eben emerged from his hut and entered the village's common ground. His aging female mate walked behind him. He approached the circle, speaking briefly to Talish, and waving a long staff to part the crowd focused upon Tusk and Great Horn. As he did so, the two lowered their eyes as previously instructed and awaited the name calling ritual.

*"Tusk, I see you,"* the Chief began. *"I know you have been in the world of the elephant and that you have painted your scent upon their great trunks and ever-growing tusks. Welcome back from your journey, you who are Tusk."*

Turning toward Great Horn, the Chief stumbled for just a moment. A tear began to well up and slide down his cheek as he observed him closely.

*"Great Horn, I see you,"* he continued. *"You have walked into the worlds of the rhinoceros without fear and given them of your wisdom through the essential authority you carry in your loins. You cause to emerge within me the day I was given to take the spirit of the great rhinoceros in my first hunt. Though it was not my intention to bring down that most magnificent of beasts, I was called to choose between its life and that of my son. I chose to continue the life of my child and thereby took the spirit of the rhinoceros that I have carried as my burden all these years. Welcome back from your journey, you who are the Great Horn."*

Having completed the welcoming naming ceremony, Chief 'Rumti-eben took his long staff and raised the chins of Tusk and Great Horn to meet his gaze. Nodding his head, he met each pair of eyes for a long moment and then retreated quietly backward from them melting into the circle.

This was Talish's signal to gather her little flock and show them to their quarters. Tusk and Great Horn went to the huts prepared for the men while she took He Who Sees to the single hut set aside for special guests.

*"You will stay here and food will be brought to you,"* she explained to him. *"Do not leave the hut until I come for you. Later tonight, the four of us will meet for a ceremony of transformation in my hut. Be silent until that moment."*

# Question Sixty-eight
## How do we ensure we remain
## on the path to achieve our dreams?

How do you know what the path of your dreams encompasses within ME? How do you know you are on a path? I ask these questions because you are not walking or traveling on a path though you often use that word to connote your journey as a soul within ME.

Since you believe you are navigating some*where,* it must mean your mind concludes it "has come from somewhere else". Herein lays the dilemma your mental faculties confront because the journey is infinite, beginning-less, endless and limitless. Can you understand that idea for a moment?

The concept that you have a "path" to travel that will allow you to "achieve your dreams" is not truth. It is a concept you have created that is constantly confirmed by your mass consensus. The consciousness of the human masses use this idea to create marketing tools in news media, television and any other place where advertising may be appropriate.

"Do *this* and you will find your dream." "Buy *that* and your dream will come true."

The underlying cause of your attachment to a path to a dream is derived within your sense of separation from ME. Though it is not true, and can never be true, you persist in believing that something, somewhere, somehow will flip a switch and you will feel fulfilled and content. Though your heart knows it will not be discovered within the contrast of your physical world, your mind keeps dreaming that it might happen anyway.

Laying down your attachment to the pursuit of a dream opens your journey to recognizing you as ME. Once you distinguish what you truly desire from what you believe you want, life becomes much clearer.

The path that you perceive stretching before you is filled with daily challenges, obstacles, fear and anxiety as well as intermittent delight, joy and contentment. This is the reason you are asking the question because you are afraid it will always be so. You worry that the stressors of life will continue and hope that the arrival of insurance regarding your chosen path will change the result.

Now I tell you there is no path and your mind is in a quandary with no place to go in its constant search. That is a very helpful occurrence because now you may open yourself to experiencing ME as I AM as you. If you have no path and if dreams are attachments, then what is left? I AM left expressing as you.

The question then becomes, "Is that enough?" AM I enough for you? If so, why do you look for anything else?

You see how you have created this endless spiral for yourself. Your ego personality is very good at using your mind to do so. An expert at making you believe you need physical experiences and material objects that will not serve to resolve your emptiness, your assiduous mind is unwavering in its belief structure.

You emerging within ME, share MY eternal love and peace. Though you think and believe you are separate from ME, you are not. You do have access to MY Cosmic Mind. You can change your perception and gain that access. All that is necessary is a willingness to perceive nothing else. If you perceive both dream and lack of dream, both good and evil, you are accepting both the false and the true and making no distinction between them. You have no need of a dream.

What is a dream and why do you want one, or two or three? A dream is a vision and it is an illusion. It is an image and a chimera. It is what you use to keep yourself excited when things aren't going your way within ME. A dream can be entertainment so long as it doesn't become a replacement for that which you really desire which is to know ME.

Your desire for your fantasy comes from the belief that you are powerless to remember what you are within ME. You create a visualization you call real while envying that which you perceive as power and knowing. This is the fear of straying from the path to that magical dream of your own making. It makes you silent and troubled, turning your helplessness against yourself.

The question remains: Do you wish to live in a world where you believe you are on a linear path to an imaginary dream? Or are you willing to experience the truth of existing consciously aware of your existence as I AM?

Given the chance to recognize your union within ME, you will be able to answer these questions to the fullest. You need only go inside, feel your heart's answers and come full circle within your love of yourself as ME.

What is the single prerequisite for your shift of perception? It is only the recognition that your ego personality's fear of losing the path is a construct of your mind and has nothing to do with reality. What does this cost you? It will cost you your attachment to your dream.

I do not mean that you cannot envision some marvelous castle in the air to which you would like to go. I do not constrain you ever in anyway. It is only that there is nothing to imagine, no place will your image screen take you that compares with knowing yourself as ME. When you realize your thirst can only be quenched by remembering ME, I become your only "dream".

## Story Time

The dark night descended as it only does in the African continent and Talish summoned Tusk, Great Horn and He Who Sees to her hut. This evening was to be the initiation into that which this journey promised to encompass, walking fully among the worlds.

*"Now that we have all secured our positions within the tribe for this short period of time, I am going to use our moments together at night to expand your awareness far beyond that which you have presently encompassed. Though you may believe each of you has experienced a great deal of learning within atam, I tell you now you have only placed your toes into the stream of its flowing depths. Tonight we will wade much further in together.*

*"Since this new territory can be potentially disruptive to your awareness, letting you merge with it without detailed instructions would be negligent of me and I would dishonor you. I*

am going to give you specific directions as to what is desired and I want you to follow them as I set them forth. This will assure you of a safe exploration from within your own perspective.

"The initial journey will take you into atam as you presently are as Tusk, Great Horn and He Who Sees. I will accompany you and continue to do so throughout our travels together. Once we have linked consciousness within this accelerated realm, I will give you your first guidance. Are there any questions before we begin?"

Silence pursued Talish's announcement and then Tusk took a deep breath saying, "This might sound a little ahead of what you are doing with us, Talish, but I'm curious if each night is going to be the same. Are we going to be doing the same set of exercises every night or are they going to be different?"

"No matter that you are curious, Tusk. You always are and I am happy to fulfill that natural curiosity.

"Each night will build upon the previous for the first three evenings. Then we will see how desirous you are of experiencing alternative expansions. There comes a time when you become your own teacher and we are very close to the arrival of that occurrence.

"Are we now ready to begin?"

Three heads nodded in affirmation as Talish reached to bring them closer into the center of her hut by motioning with her arms. As their small circle narrowed its circumference, she began toning a deep, sonorous sound that led to a semi-hypnotic state for each of the three.

"Close your eyes. Breathe with me, as you are accustomed to doing. Let your grasp on this reality loosen. You are going to travel with me into the realm of atam, purely and without form, shape or creation. Do not attempt to confine your experience in anyway. Simply let yourself forget your physical vessel and slide into the stream of atam with me."

Many moments passed, as the four-some sat in absolute silence releasing their physical awareness. The silence became the carpet upon which they magically rode until suddenly each was aware of arrival with the others.

"Good. We are here with no disruption. I do not expect that there will be disturbance within our field yet it is always possible," Talish began transmitting information wordlessly.

"Now, what you are going to do is dissolve any concept of whom or what you might be in any form and take on the form of another. We will tread easily tonight to acquaint you with the wholeness of atam. Each of you will now take on another awareness with which you are faintly familiar yet have perceived as belonging to another.

"Tusk, I would like you to enter into the consciousness of Abamti. Great Horn, please experience yourself as John. He Who Sees and I will exchange awareness for the sake of this first practice. On another evening, He Who Sees will experience much more.

"Now, as I begin to exist within atam as He Who Sees, you each will make these transitions into the realm of one that has always, up to this present time, been outside of your design. Tusk, connect with the spirit world of Abamti. Great Horn, align with John.

"To present, you have believed that Tusk is at one time in your reference, John and Great Horn is Abamti. Now you are one in atam."

With these words, the four experiencers within spirit traded places in consciousness with the existence of the designated realities. Abamti was the first to transmit information into the group through merging awareness. He couldn't help exclaiming, "This is delightful, to be able to know another on such a level. I earnestly wish to take this knowledge back to the physical realm and express as this common union."

John followed with, "I had no idea how much the one Nancy wished me to be her big brother as Paul. Now that I am John who became Nancy, I can reflect on my awareness as Paul and see where I did not fulfill that commission. Though I feel no judgment within this realm, I re-commit to our experience when we return to the physical world as Paul and Nancy."

He Who Knows and Talish, within their switched awareness, energetically held their children in this discovery. Enormous strides of awareness were taking place for all.

## Question Sixty-nine
## How do we maintain balance
## and momentum as we move to the next level?

The earth has gone through many, many different shifts, many, many different configurations since it began its existence within ME. Shifts or changes do not mean imbalance. There are billions of sacred, divine humans living within the earth at this moment and none of them are out of balance either, though many of your perceptions believe that is not so.

As to the "next level", there is no "next level" to "move" to within ME. You are as I AM. What you consider a stage is no achievement at all since there is nothing to achieve. You exist in a constantly fluctuating, infinite realm of possibilities. Every potential you can imagine is present for the asking without the need to create motion in which you gain momentum to reach an invisible nothingness.

The magnificence of you, the power of you is what is being shown to you in what you are calling the "earth changes". The earth will always shift and change just as you do. Since you are an integral part of the earth's frequency, as it transforms so do you. It is graceful, balanced and always in harmony within ME.

The concept that you need to maintain balance and momentum is the subject of much debate among your religions. Many believe it is nearly impossible to realize ME within the human body. Others conceive many different practices and techniques promising to bring you closer to that which you already are within ME. Attachment to these principles can easily unbalance you, yet within your devotion, you will not find a re-balancing. You will be using the same discordant perspective to attempt equilibrium. It will not work for you as you might project.

You know within your sacred heart, you are a benevolent being. You generally wish those within your life to be well and thriving. Often you get confused by the various teachings that emerge from within communities telling you one or more ways of being more benevolent than you consider yourself to be. Often there is great competition among you to be more enlightened, appear more divinely guided and to create as much momentum as possible to reach a peak of understanding that does not exist within ME.

It is not necessary for you to do anything at all to recognize your divinity as I AM. You can make the choice to experience yourself as such and when you place your attention upon that aspect of you, remain within that focus. I know you will say that distractions come to "tempt" you away from your version of your sacred self, yet there are no temptations within ME. All is expressed as ME and you are always able to discern whether you wish to take part in a particular activity within your reality or not. Nothing tells you that you must or must not.

The beliefs most of you hold are so threatening as to remove from your mind the slightest ability to know yourself in your authentic form as ME. When you express the words, "I AM God," among your friends and family, they are astonished at your arrogance. It is not audacity at all; rather it is the truth of you as ME. Were they to embrace the self-same truth, they would no longer be surprised.

Within the infinity of ME, you constantly make a decision how balanced you consider yourself to be as the human you express. Incongruence within your energy signature for any reason feels very uncomfortable yet it has nothing to do with what "level" you are experiencing since a standard does not exist within ME, so it is not in you.

Your focus and the feeling it creates within you is the creator of your present set of circumstances. Do you feel you need more harmony? Are you experiencing a lack of symmetry and alignment within your life? Again, this has no connection to momentum within stages of upliftment because you already are as divine as you can possibly be within ME. What it does concern is your belief about what you are expressing *as* within your present incarnation.

So much of your conversations and writings detail great concern about the changes within humanity now. Many of you believe there is going to be a sudden shift within consciousness that is going to make your lives appear "better" to you. Rather than depending upon an external event within your life, create such benevolence within you that you are alert in each moment to whether you are *being aware of* all that you can possibly be in the glory you are within ME.

You are all creating this, you see. You are co-creating it with all of the humans who are living in planet earth. Will you look through MY Eyes at all that you perceive? Will you assign yourself the privilege of only seeing ME in all that occurs within your life?

Reach inside yourself for the feeling that benevolence connotes, that it brings up for you and allow that to be the revelation of what you really are no matter what anyone says, no matter what anyone gives back to you. You are the aspect of Creator capable of eternal balance. You are that attribute within ME that knows itself as eternally present and consciously aware.

There is no balance to maintain. There is no momentum to be had because you are going nowhere. You are as I AM. Know that and only that and you will be free to experience the joy of your infinite harmony within ME. To do so, you will first release yourself from the belief that it is not possible.

## Story Time

The following evening, Talish summoned the threesome to her hut once again. They had spent the day living among the tribe members in the new roles that felt unusually natural to them. And, each of the trio was quite excited to see what Talish had in store for them this night.

*"Now that you each have traveled with me into atam and witnessed your ability to shift into the frequency of what you would determine to be another aspect of you, tonight we are going to go further within the releasement of your identities. He Who Sees will also be given an opportunity to shift into areas he has not yet experienced without me.*

*"Your focused attention is paramount within this transaction. Distraction is not an option until I tell you that you may relinquish that focus. The reason this is important is because you may feel a strong drive to remain in the realm of atam*

without physical form if you find an apparition occurring for you that is extremely inviting. Up to a certain point, I can retrieve you and pull you back within me. After that point, I cannot.

"We are going to experience two separate realms of travel this night. First, I will assist you in choosing a being with whom you will merge in order to experience a set of memories having nothing to do with you as individuality within the aspects you have been recently visiting.

"After you have assimilated that information, I will assist you in expanding into the infinity that comprises the world of atam. I say 'comprises' as though it is made up of a substance yet that is far from true. Often language fails when we are discussing that which no words may describe. It is during this time that you may relinquish focus. Up until that moment, there is always the chance you may divert into a consciousness you experience yourself being partial to and I cannot control that moment for you.

"Do you have questions before we begin? Do not let any thought or comment remain unspoken because you will need absolute clarity for this journey," Talish said in momentary completion of the description of what the night's potential held.

"Well, Talish, I can probably speak for all of us," Great Horn said, "first I say 'thank you' and second, we trust you implicitly. I know I will do my best and I feel strongly that the others will, as well."

Two other heads nodded in agreement with no additional questions or comments to voice. The time with Talish was so enriching and she comprised such a field of safety that there didn't appear any reason to feel fear or trepidation of the next learning.

"Then, breathe with me, eyes closed, as you naturally do. Our circle is unified. Our oneness is felt by all as we release into the realm of atam as Great Horn, Tusk and He Who Sees. I go as Talish and remain as such during the entirety of this journey. If you feel any doubt within atam, connect with me remembering my initial warning."

The dimensional journeyers left the dense realm of physicality finding their etheric footing in what had come to be almost familiar territory. Once stability was accessed among all four, Talish began transmitting her next instruction.

*"I am not going to tell you exactly what to do now. I only want you to transmit your desire to merge with another within atam and see what comes up for you. Your resonance within your own experiences in atam will determine what awareness appears to merge with you. For these moments, I remain silent."*

Great Horn immediately sensed a benevolent comprehension merging within his consciousness. It appeared within him as an ancient being of different incarnations in many different realms. Tusk joined with an apparently talented being that demonstrated a variety of learning within other planetary structures while He Who Sees melded with one who had birthed him in many lives throughout a variety of frequency dimensions.

Talish watched approvingly as her three budding shamans maintained focus, embraced the information transmitted within their individual unions and shared their own wisdom easily. They were embracing the learning of the star traveler's functions as quickly as she had hoped. Now they would be ready for the greater tests.

As soon as the three were actively returned within her consciousness, she first inquired how this experience had been for each of them. Each felt delighted to report how fluidly they could combine with what humans would call 'another' yet was really simply an aspect of atam.

*"Now you will completely release yourselves from any experience. This may take days in earth time for your full understanding. You are going to intend yourself free of any constraint or memory. As you do, you each and atam will become as one within your reality. You may imagine moving from being a drop within the ocean to awareness of being the ocean itself.*

*"I will remain steadfastly here for the duration. Do not rush. Take your time. You have seen yourselves as other selves. You have experienced another as yourself. Now you will unfold into no self and as awareness only. You will not get lost and when you feel the impetus to take up atam-um again, you will do so.*

*"I bid you now to turn your attention to no thing and be it. Completely let go of any desire and be no thing."*

# Question Seventy
## The transition is unsettling;
## how do we maintain spiritually and physically?

Your physical body is in a constant state of flux and change. There is a continual transference of energy throughout all of your systems: the body, mind and emotional nature within ME. Here is the center point of perpetual energetic interchange among interactions with other people, inner thought patterns and the output of your physical energy.

The aspect you refer to as "unsettling" is your inexperience with thinking of yourself as an energy wave. You believe you are static, unmoving and usually without much change. So when an idea, physical experience, emotional interchange or a sudden shift in your familiar outlook takes place, you think something unusual has happened.

That is why you experience the changes you call the "transition" as unsettling. Your mental picture of your life is fixed and headed toward an unmovable goal. At least you hope it is non-moving since it is something you desire within your future. Human beings are routinely revising themselves, exteriorly as well as interiorly within ME. Each variation either requires realignment of thought patterns or strengthens the ones already present. Every time energy is applied in a different manner to any situation, the ability to grow and sustain an evolving pattern increases. Your spiritual development follows the structure of the energy system in its constant fluidity.

The agitation you are expressing within the question is the result of your resistance to this natural changing flow. When you release your control of how you are expanding and transforming, simply letting it occur, it will be less unsettling.

There exists within ME a conscious awareness that all are invited to experience. It lives within the inner core inside each of you allowing you to know the freedom of being. Within this space is the acceptance of not knowing anything at all. Within this awareness, you realize that what you do believe you know is only based upon conditioning you have accepted within your lives and called it real.

When you come to the realization that it is impossible for you to "know" anything, then you are truly free. Freedom is the absence of necessity in choice or action. When you sit firmly rooted in the sense that you do not know, you are then free of the necessity to choose or act in a certain way. Within this liberation lies your transformation, the transition to which you refer.

As you transfigure within yourself, you go beyond the teachings of your parents, your schools, your religions and social structure. You invite yourself to feel what is being called forth from within your hearts and souls and to follow that road no matter where it leads. It means that no matter what the fragments look like, they are all part of ME and you are invited to pay attention to them. It frees you from daily obsession and creates the space to see the second-to-second play of creation emanating from Creator within ME.

All of this magnificence requests of you only one attribute, that of allowance. You make an offering of it to you. You will either accept the invitation or reject it. If you decide to spurn your own request, no one will judge you except yourself. The energy of this judgment is experienced as the unsettling feelings you are describing within your question. Only you have the capacity to change that feeling.

As the natural wave of energy curves its way from Creator within the creation itself, its original impulse is well-being, peace, cohesiveness and the perpetuation of its expanding impulse through the points it creates in time and space. This is the fulfillment of the transition in your life. It is the serenity of peace, love and the sense of community acknowledging that you are not alone. It cannot be recognized so long as you believe it is hard, you must control the outcome or that you know what it is to be within ME.

Your choice in the moment is a decision between loving and controlling out of fear. Your personal selection is made with each breath whether you are aware of it or not. It directly impacts each molecule of your physical body within ME. It is the choice between being undefended or defended, of being connected and individual or disconnected and separate. Your decision to flow allows your core essence to shine forth. If you find it too difficult to be fluid, your next option is to accept that your present state of being is inviting you to work through another cycle, becoming more aware of your desire for transformation.

If you feel severely disconnected from your core essence, you lose awareness within ME. You do not experience yourself as being divinity as I AM. You don't know yourself as a unique center of light in the universe. If so, you have forgotten what you are and have trouble connecting to your union within ME. Once you experience the essence of your core being, you will be able to find it everywhere. Nothing will unsettle you. Your focus of intention, of your life energy field, in your physical body and in your present existence is where your essence is most fully expressed. Imbalance is a signal that in some specific way you have become disconnected from your core essence, from your inner Divinity. It is not necessary because it is not so within ME.

## Story Time

Silent comments from within atam-atma:

Nancy, Tusk, 'Mao, John: *There is nowhere to go. There is nothing. I am and I am not. These thoughts of mine are nothing but waves lapping upon an endless shoreline with no meaning. I contemplate nothing and I am everything. There is no experience only being yet to be within this awareness is not. It is a sense of expansion that is limitless and I am all of it. Nothing can contain me because I am not, yet I am.*

*Immersed within myself I am beyond experience or knowing. There is nothing to know for there is no import in any or all. It is not union because that means there is separation, which is not. There is no way to divide the indivisible and it is I. There is no one and nothing to see because I have no sight. There is no need for I am all.*

There is no movement for I expand into infinity with nowhere to expand into as me. All lives within me and nothing exists for all creation is embraced within my being.

Reality is not for there is nothing that is real or unreal. There is nothing, no one, no division or segregation. I sense no one for all is I. I only know myself that is not a "me" rather the entirety.

There is only peace, contentment, harmony without any thought of other than those conditions of being. Each and all of those aspects I am.

Paul, Great Horn, Abamti, Ann: Now I know what it is to be free. I have no desire to go or be in any other realm. Only this suffices. I am and I am all.

I loose myself from any boundaries and release any thought, feeling or impression as I dissolve into myself. There is only dissolution of all within me as me.

There is no experience and no experiencer, only being. There is no desire, yearning or sense of want for I am all fulfillments. I simply am and that is all; there is no wish for more or different. How could there be? I am everything, everywhere in every way.

I am all and I am nothing. No words are necessary; no thought but this reflection of an eternal state. It holds nothing apart from itself as me and looks for no evidence of its beingness. I am the root of all and rootless because there is no need to express. Beyond expression, I am.

Don, He Who Sees: It is only from here that I remember my beingness, my inclusion as I AM within all. I release any need to be other than this utterly devoid state of union, holy and unholy, sacred and vile; it is all and it is I.

Refraining from reflection, I pause enough to give credence to that which I am, have always been and always will be. This is a familiar state of being as I loosen any awareness diffusing into the nothingness.

With no need to control or let go, no desire or despair, nothing is expected or accepted for all is as I am. Thoughts are as shimmering shadows within me and leave me with no desire for them.

As she released her wayfarers of spirit to their own freedom in the realm of spirit, Talish was very satisfied with herself that she had given due consideration to having several of her previous shamanic students monitor the bodies of the three travelers. They were journeying for quite some time and it was now appropriate to move them to her secret, sacred cave location and out of the village. She knew she could rely on her students, now shamanic masters, to make the applicable accommodations. All she was responsible for in this moment was the well-being of her developing triad.

The shamans who had been under Talish's tutelage during another life in the tribe moved the physical bodies of the travelers to her teaching cave outside of the village's vicinity. This was the place where she had lived and worked when training potential medicine workers in her knowledge when she was in form. Since this group had experienced what the trio was now experiencing, each knew exactly what was needed.

As Tusk, Great Horn and He Who Sees began to become aware of their physical bodies, they were astonished to find themselves in different surroundings. They had left physicality from the village hut and now found themselves embraced within the walls of an enormous rock cave complete with ancient writing and pictographs on the walls. Light came only from candles made of rushes held in wax set within the cave's walls.

Quietly, each one opened their eyes to survey first where they were lying on the ground supported by pads of twined leaves and then whether they were alone or still together as a group. Everyone was present including Talish who quickly assuaged any undue anxiety.

*"Welcome back to the realm of the physical. You have been immersed within the void of atam-atma for a little over two weeks. I know it is timeless within that formless form so you have no awareness of this.*

*"You have been moved from the village since we had exhausted our allotted time there and placed safely in the location of your next learning. For the remainder of today, you will sleep, eat and be silent until you have acclimated to your new surroundings."*

# Question Seventy-one
## How can I be free to be who I am on my own terms?

Every day you have conversations and communion with family, friends, co-workers and your various social connections. Within these associations, you are hoping that you will be seen as you are and sometimes you are open to experiencing the other person as *they* are. Usually these interactions are with two or more people responding from the perception of what each believes are expected of him or her.

Life by its very nature is constantly communicating within ME, yet if you do not know who you are to *you*, there is no way that you can take part in anything meaningful to you. This is what you mean by "freedom on your own terms". You desire to feel the liberation of being who you are, as you experience yourself and, most importantly, being accepted as that person.

If you allow your life to live itself rather than attempting to be what another person or institution expects of you, then you will find yourself easily connecting within a natural flow. The acquiescence of life within itself is far removed from any concept of control, analyzing, goal planning or ambition. It is rhythmic, flowing, inherently coherent and congruent within itself.

You may perceive the "acquiescence of life" to be "your own terms" yet life exists within itself naturally. That which you call your "terms" is more correctly labeled your boundaries or limitations. The essence of existence knows no limits so yours do not confer freedom, rather imprisonment.

You have become your own prisoner. You have placed yourself in a cell of your own making, locked the door and thrown away the key – at least you believe it's been thrown away. Yet that is not true because you can easily use the voice of your heart to open the cage door, step forth as you know you are and begin to allow yourself to live your life within ME as ME.

You created the loosely held blueprint for the experience you call your life through Creator within ME. The fear, anger and stress that you experience within its expression are caused by not allowing yourself to unfold, as you naturally know yourself to be.

No one knows you as you do and no one knows you as ME as you do. You are the only one who can decide if you are going to be yourself or continue to succumb to your ego-personality's fear that if it doesn't perform by a set of dictated standards it has failed. The sense of failure you experience is not conducive to your thriving rather feels much more like a threat to your survival.

I AM within a constant state of formless being. Any form you perceive as ME is an expression through ME as Creator. Every aspect of creation, no matter the dimension or frequency, exists within a beneficent allowance within ME. Your perception of suffering or unhappiness is the result of resisting the flow of this beneficence due to a belief that you know better, more or something other than allowing life to live as it naturally desires. When I say "life", I am referring to your energetic expression within your physical form within ME. It wishes to embrace every breath, every moment with the richness possible within it. I allow life to be; do you as ME?

As you live, you search for means to relieve the uncomfortable feelings through attachments to people, situations and things. Yet the resistance to being you comes right along with you and the discomfort continues. Pleasure and enjoyment is a natural gift of life itself, yet it is a constant, dynamic flow – not a need, requirement or demand. When you live as a requirement in your life based upon the perception of another, you betray yourself and therefore betray all of life within your sacred union. It is a very uncomfortable feeling within you and one you need not resort to if you will release your "terms" and live infinitely within ME.

Since the natural state of your energy frequency is a reflection of your feelings, being in a constant state of integrity wherein you know *you* within your true reality paves the way for all you wish to come your way. That is the interesting aspect because you cannot fool the energetic output or input of this dimension within ME. While you may believe that you are in a state of authenticity, if you feel resistance, fear, doubt or lack of trust within yourself that becomes your true feeling and that is what is responded to within your life.

Within each breath, you have the capacity and the invitation to live fully as you are without compromise or regret. Allowing yourself to do so is the nature of this dimension giving you permission to give yourself permission to be yourself within ME as I AM. When you are authentic in your offering of yourself, you give everyone and everything else permission to be themselves. Knowing who you are implies that all that is experienced within your life is perfect exactly as you are. When you no longer feel a struggle or resistance to that which is your choice through vibration, you are free within your free will contrast to enjoy every aspect of your life.

There is absolutely no reason within your existence why you should choose to be anything less than the completeness you are within ME. Any thought you have to the contrary is a lie, a deep betrayal of your inner most knowing. You know exactly why you may decide to live as less than that which you know yourself to be. You are the only one who knows you as you do and you are the only one who can truly live your life as you, as I AM.

## Story Time

Talish used this time of rest to re-set her energetic template for the tasks ahead. Once the three initiates were awake and ready to travel again, she would be holding an entirely different etheric space with and for them. Every initiation process ended within this final set of experiences. Each set of students posed a new learning cycle for her and for this Talish was always very grateful.

*"Talish, we've been sleeping for quite some time haven't we,"* Tusk asked upon opening his eyes and recognizing the cave once again. *"Am I the only one awake now?"*

*"Yes, Tusk, the rest will awaken soon. I suggest you go to the water pots over in the corner and refresh yourself. Splash water on your face and drink a goodly amount since your body is calling for hydration. I will have Great Horn and He Who Sees do the same upon their awakening which I see has begun."*

As the two remaining members of Talish's sacred trio opened their eyes and began to stir, she instructed them to also wash their faces and drink a quantity of fluid. They would need it for the next period of interchange among the worlds.

*"Now that you are rested and refreshed, I want you all to join me around the fire circle in the center of the cave. Remove all of your clothing for you will take the next set of journeys naked in spirit, mind and body. This set of tests will determine your ability to withstand the daunting task of attentive focus called for in mastering the calling as medicine man or woman."*

The threesome did as requested and sat upon the earthen floor of the cave stripped of all pretenses. Though they wore no clothing, the cave was strangely warm and almost comforting in its semi-lighted, shadowed embrace.

Talish continued, *"One of the most important aspects of shamanism is being able to take on the body of those whom you are working with or to assume a disguise as an animal. Today we will practice becoming an animal of your choice. Then, once you have felt through that experience, I will assign you a different animal to become; one that is not necessarily easy for you to resonate with to advance your abilities another step within the ancient medicine way. Does anyone have any questions?"*

*"Yes, Talish,"* Great Horn voiced, *"as we become these animals are we likely to harm each other if we choose adversarial predators? What happens if I choose a lion and Tusk chooses a gazelle?"*

*"Good question and one that would naturally come to mind, Great Horn. That is my role here. I will observe, protect and manage the energy field of each animal you become. There is enough room within the cave for any creature to have space to roam. I will let each of you know when you are to change form.*

*"The most important aspect of what you are now going to experience is remaining true to yourself. The existence of the animal will be colored by your inherent traits, as you will be influenced by the animal's aspects. Betraying those attributes may cause much discomfort for you. Stay true to yourself, as you innately know yourself to be. Now close your eyes, breathe with*

*me, travel to atma and choose an animal's nature and body to embrace."*

Within the space of He Who Sees' seated figure suddenly appeared a python snake. Talish knew this was daunting magic and was not surprised that He Who Sees would choose the native symbol for transmutation.

Tusk quickly transformed into an elephant, a natural shift for one so attuned to these enormous, benevolent creatures. The strength, honor and stability of the elephant were fitting traits for Tusk. Talish led him quietly to a corner away from the python for his privacy and comfort.

Great Horn began flying around the cave as a goshawk, the messenger. His choice reminded Talish of several other students who felt that bringing a message was their calling and had chosen one among many different hawk forms over the years. She watched her three trainees enjoy their bodies and feral natures for about an hour as each of them moved with grace within the cave that had withstood the magical properties of shamanism for centuries.

Approaching the python, Talish picked it up and held its head firmly in her hand. *"Transfigure into a desert fox,"* she instructed, dropping the python to the floor to shapeshift into the next shape. The fox carried the message of camouflage and concealment combined with the cunning of instant knowing. He Who Sees would need these attributes in the years ahead.

Stroking the elephant's trunk, Talish grasped one large ear and directed, *"Become the jaguar filled with integrity, resolve and fixed attention."* She watched the elephant's trunk subside and the magnificent face of the African jaguar take its place. This animal's aspects would dissolve Tusk's easily over-stimulated sensitivities. From a lumber to a stalking pose, the cat circled Talish curling its tail around her legs. She gave it a calming stroke down its back and headed toward the goshawk that had landed on a ledge near the cave's entrance.

*"Mighty hawk, become a wild boar,"* Talish commanded and observed the goshawk float to the ground as his ferocious tusks emerged. Great Horn's need to confront himself would feed from within this animal's daring nature.

# Question Seventy-two
## Does awareness separate
## some people from others at this time?

Awareness of yourself as I AM does not separate you from other incarnations of ME. If you perceive yourself as any other occurrence of spirit in form besides ME, you may then experience it as separation. Even believing you are a co-creator with ME is a dividing belief within you because it connotes "two". I AM all that is and within that statement is contained all that I AM.

One of the perceptions occurring within the human mind that causes your question to arise is your level of unease; what you often refer to as "stress". This degree of anxiety often arises within you when you begin to discern your spiritual life "separate" from your physical actions. You term this "awareness" and use whatever techniques you find available to separate you from the daily earth experience. Within this concept, you forget there is only one, that which I AM, that is also you.

Few people do not know what stress feels like. The personal realization is that you believe only you are stressed. Everyone else usually looks calm, cool and collected to you separating you within your mind. Once again, the mind through your perception separates you from the "other" in an effort to keep you in control of your reality. When you are in stress, you are in extreme separation, which in turn, accentuates the stress.

This is where you begin to really become aware of how divisive your view of your spiritually is within you. As you feel the loss of control of your reality, you tighten your hold upon the practices you believe will emphasize for you that you are spirit in form. Therein lays the next division. Spirit and form are one within ME.

Time is one of the stress factors you experience. Because you believe you are "ruled" by time, you often feel you do not have enough of it or that it will "run out" on you. You talk about how fast the years pass and that you don't know where time has gone. When you are grieving or waiting, time weighs heavily and appears to move almost in slow motion. Nearly every stressful situation has a common factor involved in its energetic dynamic. That element is time and how you perceive its use.

When you remember that you are I AM as conscious life without need of time, infinite, your experiences begin to lose their overwhelming significance. Your awareness within consciousness no longer sees any aspect of creation as separate from you no matter whom or what it is within your reality. Your contribution to the whole is the whole's bestowal within you as ME. There is only one.

It would be of assistance for you to experience living in silence, without your concept of separation. Actuating a state of inner stillness carries with it a tremendous amount of peace, calm, relaxation and becomes a very centering experience for you within ME. This state of being allows you to feel more in union with ME dissolving your awareness of any separation. It brings you into awareness of the present moment. You stop thinking about what just happened. You are no longer worrying about what might happen in the future. You are not experiencing another disassociated from you. You are simply being within ME as ME with no sense of separateness or other. Within this moment, those concepts are inconceivable within you. This experience is infinity.

Be mindful of what your belief may be about your spiritual awareness. Modifying your life in even little ways can make a big difference. The very act of focusing on union causes you to stop and consider what you might believe is true that foundations your idea of awareness causing separation. In the silence, your ego personality is invited to make friends with ME. If you persist in the practice, it will begin to lose its fear and common union has an opportunity to blossom within your mind.

The calm, relaxation and peace that come from letting go of your separation perception alter your experience of your life when you step back within your inner observation. It becomes possible to flow along with MY Infinite Stream rather than feeling driven by it. The more you practice allowing this space within ME, the more it infiltrates your day and your thoughts. No matter what is experienced, you can be centered in perceiving and accepting it for what it is in infinite union. Your future can be viewed without losing perspective or feeling anxious. In that space, the ego personality's grip on your mind succumbs to your inner peace within ME. You live *as* union.

Know that you are an individual within ME that cannot be divided from ME or from any aspects of ME which is all. Awareness of this actuality dissolves your perception of space in which you are *here* and another is *there*. Reference is made within this statement physically, emotionally and mentally. There is no separation. There is only union.

If you will begin to become aware of absolute inclusion rather than harbor any concept of division, you will be expanding into a new frame of reference for your soul's experience as you within ME.

The depravation caused within your approach to awareness is your ego personality's attempt to divide itself within ME. I cannot be divided. If you believe awareness can cause separation, you are not experiencing awareness. Your mind is stressing its desire to appear separate, spiritual and superior from what it believes is another. I AM indivisible. Your mind's attempt to divide ME is included within ME.

## Story Time

Talish quietly corralled her animal companions directing them toward the opening that led out of the cave. She mused that a jaguar, a wild boar and a fox were three of the easiest combinations she had worked with recently. Sometimes the blend chosen either by the student shamans or by her for them were less easily maneuvered together.

She had been teaching medicine men and women the tools, techniques and ability to travel among the dimensions for centuries. Beginning with the first physical class that she had decided to take to this sacred cave, Talish had been using its womblike container even longer in her less than material body. It would be the final learning for each of them in due time, as well, and could not be accessed so long as physical life was present within the corporeal vessel. This alchemical avenue was reached only in spirit.

Once outside in the jungle, Talish commanded each of the transfigured forms to return to that of Tusk, Great Horn and He Who Sees. There was a transformational adjustment period always experienced when the DNA shifted from that of the animal form back into the human embodiment. Sometimes it took hours, often only moments. Today it was the latter.

*"Now that each of you has encompassed two different animal forms, one of your choosing and another of mine, you are going to stretch yourself even further. Now you will become part of the natural world of the flora forest. This particular morphogenesis will be of your own choosing only. I would like to suggest that you make it a random choice among three or four different species.*

*"The most paramount thought to hold within your minds is that there is no separation. All is one. Atam-atma is. Everyone, everything is one within atam-atma. Since this is true, you will travel within atam-atma to distinguish which categories of plants you would like to become. There is no rule you must follow. You may choose to be a particular tree and then segue into a flower followed by a thorn. It is the concept of following the stream, the flow of the atam-atma within all things that is the point of this learning. Do you have questions?"*

*"Yes, Talish I have a couple of questions,"* Great Horn began. *"My first question is regarding the animal forms we just became and used. There was a great difference between the first form and the second. I don't mean a distinction between the type of animal, or in my case, raptor. I mean the residual feeling after we shifted back into these forms. Can you explain that for us?"*

*"Great Horn, you are observant. I believe the remainder of you may have the same question in your mind and heart. Yes, there was a distinctive difference between your first embodiment and the second.*

*"The first animal, bird or reptile you each chose was one that was the easiest for you to resonate with at the outset. Once you got the feeling of slipping among the emanating frequencies that resolve into form in this aspect of atam-atma, I then*

*commanded you to take on a form that would have characteristics more in line with what you each need to experience to complete your training.*

*"Great Horn, you became the wild boar because you will need to confront yourself in a much deeper and intense way as you proceed upon this medicine path. Sometimes it will be obvious to you. Often it will sneak up upon you when you least expect it. It will do you much service to practice being the wild boar and to align yourself fully with its frequency.*

*"Tusk, you were directed to become the jaguar to strengthen your integrity and attention. Very often, you allow yourself to feel the victim or put upon and the jaguar's energy aligned you with the potency of your self-authority. Merge with its vibration and practice walking in pointed attention focused within your own power.*

*"He Who Sees, I suggested you into the desert fox for its stealth, cunning and ability to camouflage itself at any and all times. Your forthright nature is very respected yet you must learn how to remain unseen when necessary and to watch with observant eyes before making a decision. The soul of fox will help you become more decisive which you already know is something you desire to learn."*

*"Now, Great Horn, your second question?"*

*"You've already answered it, Talish, as usual. I wondered what the others had experienced and now I know. Thank you."*

*"With that said, each of you will now morph into tree, leaf, flower, thorn, branch, bush or log, to name a few of your selections. I will remain here for your return. You are completely on your own.*

*"You have completed the two hardest aspects of your training. One was the formless atam and the second was flowing among animal forms. Those were the crest of the wave. This next experience will be a bit easier though I will warn you that I have met with many interesting characters within the forest world's species. Be on the lookout for two students who chose not to return. Now be off with you."*

The trio lay down on the ground releasing their minds into the atam-atma within the jungle while Talish watched their transparent shapes change from green to brown, yellow to mustard, all the while following the course of each. That would be their final lesson on the morrow – to be consciously aware within atam-atma, separated within union.

# Question Seventy-three
## How do I know I have arrived at Self-Realization?

When you believe you have arrived at realizing yourself, you are present as ME. You are realizing you are present and it allows you to be visible to others without your mind scripting a part you play in life with them. You are able to see yourself. When you are in that act of communication with yourself within ME, you hear the words and those words are going to tell you about yourself. You are witness to your motivations and intentions. Within ME, you experience only union and there is no "other".

Some of you call ME your Higher Self or the Essential Self. I AM the One Self for I AM All That Is. I AM timeless, space-less, eternal and, hence, so are you. And yet you do not know this consciously. If you did, you would not keep constantly checking in to see if I AM there. You would not need to have so much attention paid to you individually because you would be in such alignment with ME that no attention would be necessary. You would be aware that you are all that you seek.

The ego personality says *pay attention to me* then comes the moment when you become consciously aware of yourself as ME, that which you label Self-Realized. While much acclaim and credence is given to this positioning within your spiritual belief system, it is the most natural state in which to experience your life as a human being.

You love yourself as the ego personality though your mind does not realize the depth of the love that is present. If you truly wish to realize yourself as ME, you must align your capacity to love as ME within the identification you hold of yourself. You are to love without judgment, opinion, attachment or expectation. This means no self-judging or the characterization of any other for there is no other. The person you see as outside of yourself is the mirror reflecting your opinions. When you do not like or appreciate the reflection you see, you blame the person reflecting yourself to you until you are able to stand as the witness to your self-imposed limitations about what should or should not be. In that reflection, you see your own boundaries. You *are* the limitation that you see. *You are your own limitation.* There is no thing outside of you that is limiting your Self-Realization *at all*.

You can only have command of your life, the power of your own presence, when you are the witness, the observer, of your own awareness. This "Self" is the realization of being ME that you are discussing here. The power of your presence is in direct proportion to your awareness of life in the present moment. Eventually, you realize you are searching, bounding here and there, looking, hoping for *something* – often you call it "enlightenment" as though there is something called "being enlightened" that allows you to know more than "not being enlightened". You are already enlightened because you are I AM. You are simply not conscious of your own enlightenment. If you *were* conscious of it, you would be aware of it as you within ME.

While you talk of Self-Realization, enlightenment and all of the other various experiences you believe connote spirituality, there are no special spiritual experiences because everything *is* I AM. Since you want to know how you will realize that you know your Self, it is when you only know ME, when everything you feel, think, say and do is I AM acting through you and you see it all as such.

Know that you are I AM and then you will experience everything in your life as a spiritual happening. Let go of the search and step into the power of that realization now. You realizing you as ME is enlightenment, realization and all of the other labels you place upon the experience. Do not be concerned about where, when or how you are arriving at awareness within ME. You are I AM. That is all you need experience.

Then you awaken to the truth of your awareness as I AM. You have no care what spiritual name you are giving to your experience as ME because the very beingness of it is wordless. When there are sounds, your words come from your heart. There is so little to say within the full awareness of ME. And you realize that, as well.

You are awake in your consciousness as ME in this moment. You experience yourself as light within ME. You have no doubt about the strength of your presence within ME because it is your only experience as with each breath, you breathe light. Be aware of this breath within ME. Use it to convey your inspired frequency into your reality. Experience every breath as your only breath in this moment of awareness. Accept your life as the presence of your essence within ME.

As you do so, you are aware of the connection of all things within ME. You are this connection as fully as I AM. You are the connection of all things and you express as such. All is valued as ME including all experiences within your life.

Be awake to your commitment to awareness as ME. Open to the eternal wisdom of being aware of your emergence within ME. Awaken to all flowing through you as eternal conscious awareness without form and within form.

Knowing your Self is knowing ME. Realizing yourself as ME leaves you not doubt and no question. When you no longer wonder, you will know you are the answer.

## Story Time

Once the three trainees had finished merging with the jungle environment Talish called them back to her. It was time for review and the final lesson, then a surprise.

*"Please shift into your Tusk, Great Horn and He Who Sees forms and follow me back to the cave. You've done well and we still have quite a bit to cover. Your time with me is shortening and I have more to impart. Come this way."*

Talish led the trio back to the cave in their more familiar forms as she formulated the assumption of the connections she was now going to request of them. Though she had facilitated this portion of the shamanic teachings hundreds of times, each group had their particular needs and strengths. Playing to those aspects was very important in relation to the outcome.

*"First, I want you to shift into your physical forms as Don, Nancy and Paul. For a moment, you may be embarrassed in your*

nakedness unlike the ease with which you accepted yourselves as Tusk, Great Horn and He Who Sees. Your clothing is where you left it and you may put it on now. I want you to begin to become familiar once again with the identities in which you will do your final traveling since these are the personalities you will be taking back into your world."

Each of the three changed physical configuration and hastily walked to their folded clothing, donning it as quickly as possible. Talish was correct in understanding their reluctance to be naked within this identification. Once clothed, they followed her instructions to take a seat around the fire.

"I would like to review with you where we have traveled and answer any questions you may have. There will be one more opportunity tomorrow morning to request additional knowledge of me if you haven't formulated all of your questions right now.

"We have come from learning how to be silent within, to trusting your ability to navigate the world without sight. From there we practiced shapeshifting into different forms both non-physical and physical. You had an opportunity to acknowledge a few of the expressions you have taken in various forms and to merge within aspects of atam. You also let yourself experience the realm of atam without assuming a specific individuation except that of witness. Then you all moved from your present forms into one of your choosing to live among my people. They cared for your bodies while you experienced more shifting. You have been animal and plant, some of your choosing and some of mine. That is a brief summary of your work as students of the ancient medicine way. Do you have questions?"

The group sat wide-eyed and appreciative acknowledging how far they had come in less than one month. Indeed, Talish was a teacher of strength and accomplishment.

As usual, Paul voiced the question in everyone's mind, "Talish, you sound as if we are going to be parting soon. Can you talk more about that?"

"Yes, of course. This is the last night you will be within my teaching cave. Tomorrow we will have a closing ceremony and the three of you will begin your journey back the way you came with me. I will escort you part of the way and then leave you to finish *the walk on your own. I believe that answers your question, Paul. Anyone else?"*

No one raised another question as their minds absorbed the reality of this being their last night in the cave with Talish. Each had to admit personal attachment to her.

*"For your last learning, I am going to take you back outside in your present forms. You are to each decide what shape you would like to take. You may choose among your identities as human beings or you may choose an animal or plant. The object of this exercise is to be what you wish to become and then shift within atam to be a witness within the two others in whatever form they have chosen. The emphasis is on remaining aware of yourself while you are fully following the awareness of the other two.*

*"It is what I have been doing with you as you learned. I remain as I am and I merge with each of you within atam to follow your progression. Now it is your turn to do so. Do you understand?"*

Three heads shook in agreement with some perplexity being silently registered. This was sounding like a very expansive, demanding task.

Talish took them back to the front of the cave to begin this practice. *"Now I will watch from here. I will not intervene though I will monitor. Choose your forms, become your choice and then unite with the other two in their physical assumptions. Begin now."*

Nancy quietly slipped into the form of a springbok believing it would give her range of movement. Don preferred the python once again and Paul slipped back into the goshawk form. As they did so, each reached out for the other two and found to their amazement that they realized their union fully. As a springbok, Nancy flew on the wings of the goshawk. Don slithered through the brush and leapt as the springbok. Paul flew overhead while the leaves swept along his back as a python. They interchanged in union completely, knowing no separation no matter the form.

# Question Seventy-four
## How can I do more good
## when I feel limited in my outreach?

You came to earth to experience as soul within ME. Within these occurrences, there are times when you believe you know you are doing good, being good, expressing good, when you are feeling full of light and times when you are having what you would call a spiritual experience.

What happens during the times when you are not feeling full of light? Are you still "doing good"? When your world is going round and round? When everything seems upside down? What do you believe about those times? Where is your "goodness" then? Here is where you want to pay attention to how you understand your value.

When you are feeling angry, impatient, resentful, judgmental, vengeful, jealous or any of the unfulfilling feelings that you have every day, you are face to face with the promise you made to yourself to incarnate into a world of contrast within ME and to be the superb expression I AM in all ways, always.

You are anger or you are joy; churning for revenge or brimming with compassion; judgmental or accepting. You are resentful or appreciative. You *are* the experience I AM. You are the facilitators of the experience through your choice. Free will choice is your presence within you no matter what you choose. Do you choose to be the beneficence you perceive as ME always? Do you believe that being human is a flaw rather than the most divine of experiences within ME? How can you be anything but "good" if you are as I AM expressing the wholeness I AM?

Within ME is no limitation as to time or space. As I AM, you are. When you express that your outreach is limited, it is a belief you have had impressed upon you through various concepts giving rise to your thoughts of limitation. No such inhibition exists within ME.

Your question suggests the necessity for having a person or situation physically present within your "reach" to flow your goodness "into" it. This belief is based upon your view of a separate existence within the realm in which you presently exist. If you dissolve that assumption within your realization that you are I AM including everyone, everywhere, your outreach is no longer limited.

Do you realize there are dimensions upon dimensions of frequency available to you? There are timescales of experience you have no conscious knowledge of and yet, if you would look into your whole, you would see that everything you're attempting to do as "good", everything you are attempting to stop from happening is what you are creating everywhere, infinitely. Your attention and emotional input inform all with the subject matter of your focus.

While there is a majority of human beings believing that doing good warrants additional attention within ME, it is not true. All of creation receives an equal distribution of MY Presence. There is no less or more within ME. Therefore, every deed is comprised of ME, fulfilled within ME as it emerges from within I AM.

The key to coming into balance with this concept is to realize that whatever you are seeking to do as "good" is exactly what you want to stop *seeking* to do and bring into your conscious awareness the fact that it exists already. You enter into contact with you as ME and acknowledge that your desire is based upon the idea of separation. This means the ego personality and your concept of ME blend consciously as one so you see everything you are doing as an aspect of ME bringing balance and understanding to your purpose in life without fear that you are not enough.

How can you tell what you are creating? Do you know if it is "good" or "good enough"? You will easily notice whether you are actually in balance with what you desire to express, or not, by feeling inside for evidence of struggle or effort. Or is it a flow within ME? If it is not a flow within you, if you don't feel like you're fluidly moving from one moment to another, then you are literally creating struggle and effort in the desire to make sure you are exhibiting goodness into the limited reality that knows no limits.

This balance of performing commendably is one of recognition. It is recognizing how you are living your life rather than how others perceive your actions. It is coming to the understanding that if you want to live in a different reality, if you are going to bring about the changes in this world you say you want, you have to use your life as the receptacle of information, as the transmitter and receiver of information about you. Remember, the information is impartial, pervasive, all compassing and impersonal. As an expression within ME, it does not care. *You* do.

Take on your commitment to this world with ease within ME. Turn away from, walk away from that which you fear. If you are afraid you are not doing enough of value, remove the energetic input you have been giving to it. Every time you feel fear, anxiety, stress or discomfort, literally walk away from whatever it is that is causing it. You are the only one who can do this for yourself.

If you truly want to fill the world with "good", then it must begin with how you perceive yourself within ME. Fully loving yourself as ME, devoting time and attention to what pleases you and makes you feel good transmits itself into the whole without boundary. Release your idea of limited outreach. This misconception does not deserve your attention within ME. Align your focus on relishing every breath within the life you live within ME and know that you are giving yourself wholly to the world as I AM.

## Story Time

The following morning, Talish awakened the trio with an ancient song from her native tribe. Her melodic voice filled the cave with a tremulous blend of vocal sounds calling forth the wisdom of the ancients. The frequency of these currents soared up through the cavern and out the opening sixty feet overhead, where normally only smoke was emitted feeding into the surrounding jungle.

As her song completed, Talish approached the sleeping area where Nancy, Paul and Don were beginning to open their eyes. They had come into the cave from their various states of intertwining in the jungle in the early hours of the morning so sleep had been brief. Talish knew that this, too, was to be for they were now fully fledged as shamans and lengthy hours of sleep were no longer a prerequisite of the body.

*"Come with me before you fully fill your conscious awakening. I wish to share my deepest secret with the three of you. Only those who have studied with me in the last one hundred years have had privy to what I am going to show you. It took me many moons to retrieve and then preserve what I will share. Walk over this way behind the curve in the cave's wall."*

As Talish talked, she led them to the space she was describing in a dark portion of the cavern they had not investigated during their stay with her. There hadn't seemed a reason to enter this area of its environs. Now it felt more like it would have been inappropriate to do so.

Squatting down, Talish took up a long branch that had been carved into the shape of a trowel to begin digging into the dirt. Obviously, she had done so before because it looked as though this place had been previously disturbed. She dug inside a circle of stones all pointing toward the center where something was buried.

After some minutes passed, Talish stood up and moved aside from what now was obviously a gravesite. The figure within the deep hole was curled in a fetal position with beads, rattles, gourds and various animal skeleton pieces distributed around it. The bones were very dry, brittle. It appeared to have been buried for some time.

*"You look at my bones, as I was when I left the body. It was many centuries ago as you count time that I used this form. Originally, it was buried in ceremony high on a hill overlooking the village. I waited a hundred turnings of the earth before contemplating that I might be able to retrieve it as a whole and bring its potent medicine to this cave. I was successful in doing so with the assistance of one class of shamanic students who were willing to forego portions of their training to assist me. As*

repayment for their devotion, I set aside spaces for their burial here as well. You will see their graves just over there."

Talish pointed to another section of the cave further back from where they presently stood. As Nancy, Paul and Don followed her outstretched arm with their gaze, they realized that this cavity extended far back into the mountain, much further than they had previously experienced.

"May we go back to their graves and honor them, as well?" Nancy requested graciously.

"Yes, we will walk there together. In distinguishing them, you give deference to me since they are extensions of what I am. Come, we will do ceremony at their burial sites."

Once they had walked about forty feet further into the darkness, Talish turned to the trio and bowed. This was the completing moment of their training. She was pleased they had decided to experience their finale here at the graves of her willing students who had given so much.

The threesome looked at four graves that were decorated with stones, gems and a variety of growing plants. It was strange to see green, flourishing flora in the dark interior of the cave. Yet, there was so much magic here that nothing was truly unusual.

"If you each would stand at the head, the left and right of this burial mound, I will stand at the foot. Now is the moment of your final achievement before you take that which you are out into your world.

"I summon the spirits of Manash, Cohal, Tomminga and 'Brungia to come forward now and be acknowledged within your presence."

As Talish said these words of summoning, four shapes appeared over the burial sites. They were human in form yet transparent and glowing. Each of the spirits placed two etheric hands on the shoulders of the four physical beings as Talish completed the ritual.

"In this moment and in the presence of the invisible and the visible, I commend each of you: Nancy, Tusk, 'Mao, John; Don, He Who Sees; Paul, Great Horn, Abamti, Ann to the realm of the spirit. No longer will you walk the earth in only physical form. Where you are will the realm of atma be graced by the bridging of the worlds. No longer are you human beings, rather beings that walk among the humans. From dawn to dusk you will find that you work most readily within the physical world. As darkness descends upon the realm of the living, will you live among the world of atam-atma most naturally. Though this will be your most instinctive progression of form, it will not limit you in any way. From this day forward, you are the Keepers of the Medicine, Walkers Among the Worlds."

After the pronouncement of this blessing and commendation, Talish joined her four etheric spirit students in an ancient chant of belonging. Then, with these final words, the four spirits disappeared and Talish stood alone with the three initiated shamanic shapeshifters, formless and in form.

## Question Seventy-five
## How can we experience heaven on earth?

You are heaven. You are earth. You are also the fires of hell that dwell in your own imagination.

There is no way you can possibly *do* anything that will bring you to the peace, happiness and stillness in the core of your humanity that you wish within ME. There is only your state of being, an ever-changing, expanding beingness occurring within you. That is the change that you call heaven on earth. It is what so many of you are talking about with great expectation.

You have been told that heaven is within you. I will tell you that it is not "within" you; it *is* you.

When you ask this question, you posit it as though the concept of what is called "the coming of the kingdom" is an occurrence without relationship to you. There is no "kingdom" to come. You are the sovereignty you believe I AM. All that I encompass, you also embrace. Your belief that this is not true creates what you term to be "hell" and some of you take this to an extreme within your assumptions.

As you ask "how" you may experience what you consider nirvana in earth, the use of the word construes an action as though there is something you are to do to bring heaven about for yourself. Within ME, there is only paradise even though you may believe otherwise due to the space and time in which you live. If you are experiencing a pain, it feels like it will last "forever" even though the lapse of time is less than a breath when viewed within infinity. You have forgotten that you are eternal and believe that your life within this incarnation is comprised of a type of longevity. When you live as ME within ME, you are thrust into a completely different point of view liberating you from the boundary of time.

When you place your attention on the moment within which you are living, you activate your will to be alive, to create; you feel your union with all life. That is why you often call it "being in the flow". You lose the sense of having to strive and are actually alive in the actual continuity of being conscious, *being* life. This is what you construe as heavenly because you are not paying attention to the concept of issues occurring within your existence within ME.

If you would take a moment to review what you describe as problems within your life, you will begin to understand that in the midst of each one you have a choice. You choose to experience the moment as an issue, challenge or problem within ME based upon what your ego personality's mind construes should be happening rather than what you are experiencing.

You have the ability right now, as you are reading these words, to experience your life as "heaven". You are the only one who can make the determination to do so as ME. You exemplify a concretized participation within a dimension of contrast in which you have the full ability to choose delight, every time. Once you fully understand this, you will call yourself a master of this dimension and you will live as such content within ME.

What you feel and think about is what creates your reality. If you are feeling that there should be no more war, feel in your body what you feel when you think that thought. Does "no more war" create peace in your body? No, it creates the feeling of fear of war. Does holding peace in your thoughts create feelings of peace? Perhaps, yet with that thought appears its companion thought of "no war". Once something is resonated within, its dual nature is also present. There is only one feeling and thought that can actually shift your vibration enough to hold you in a sense of heaven. That feeling and thought is love, as I love, with no condition or judgment attached to what you say you impart as love within ME.

Your mind acknowledges ME as love. I AM neutral, encompassing all that is not neutral. That which is identified as good and bad, I AM. That which is neither right nor wrong, I AM. And I AM love.

Love is a facet of Creator using the property you label *love* to extend into Its creation within ME. Through the essence of this expression, Creator within ME balances the concept of duality accessing infinite counterpoints of presence. Looking for the source of love, you will find it in Creator. I AM that Creator which operates within ME. The eternal bliss available within you is your awareness of yourself as ME emerging within Creator. The heaven you say you seek is an aspect within MY Creation.

So long as you consider yourself part of your present duality and construe your life from within that context, you will seek for something other than that within ME. You are as I AM and your mind suggests that there is something else to find somewhere. There is naught but ME, which means there is nothing except you, as well. Accepting that reality as yours will shift you from believing there is a heaven to create into being the harmony that is sought.

When you stop seeking, you will have found ME. I AM eternal, without beginning or end. MY Infinity is your eternal beingness. There is no other except ME. Simply stay in MY Love and see how different it feels to you. Love promotes bliss; love brings peace; love resonates as contentment within you infinitely. It is all that you need be and know to create "heaven" within yourself daily. When you resonate with your own glory, you are all that you actually can be to create "heaven in earth". Holding love in your heart within ME brings a resonate frequency within you and, therefore, within what you consider the whole. All are affected by your feeling in every moment. Make that feeling love within ME, and you will experience the heaven you believe you need to seek.

## Story Time

Talish accompanied the trio throughout the first portion of their return journey. Passing through her village, they had a bit of time to stop and express gratitude to the elders for allowing them to stay as guests within their lodging. No mention was made of where they had adjourned to when they left and none was needed. Nor were they questioned about their present appearance.

Once the foursome entered into the jungle proper, Talish began singing her songs of nature, conjuring up visions of devas and sprites that emerged from within the trees and plant life. None of the three had ever seen the energetic life forms of the floral world in this way so they were very excited to experience the flow of divine essence as it flowed around and within them.

About noontime, they stopped in the heat under the outcropping of a great boulder to sit in the shade and share water and food. Talish found this the perfect moment for a parting and final instruction to the group.

*"I will be leaving you after this meal and you will go on alone. If you follow the sun toward its place of setting, you will arrive at your destination. There is yet another experience lying in wait for you and it must be accomplished without my presence.*

*"I am honored beyond my heart's deepest desire to have brought you this far in your learning. The three of you are the first westerners to have been able to maintain and sustain that which you have experienced with me. Only one other group attempted your path. Then, we mutually chose to disrupt the teaching before we reached the village due to their overriding fear. To a certain degree, you may give yourselves this inner approval though it was something you had all called to you, individually and collectively."*

As Talish was completing her thought, a presence was felt joining them as it emerged from behind the boulder. It was the water boy from the reserve. Nancy mused over how she had nearly completely forgotten about the park and its staff during the last month or so.

*"Here is my son, Tocami, come to join me for our journey to the next place of stopping. He served you all as water boy before you made your decisions to follow the medicine way. Now he may reassume his role as my assistant while teaching. I did not summon him for your learning because he already had a place within your reality that would have been distracting for you.*

*"It is now time to say farewell. We will meet again upon the way. Know that you may call upon me by summoning me through these words, "Talish, shecuma promuda. It means 'Talish, she walks with me'. I will appear with you if you have need. Do not take this offer lightly. Use it only upon due reflection. Now we leave you all."*

With those words, Talish and Tocami disappeared from the sight of the three newly initiated shamans and they sat under the boulder alone. As Nancy looked at Paul and Don, she realized she was seeing them through unfamiliar eyes. Not only were they male in form, she now viewed their energy bodies and the emission of their feelings as though they were streams of light flowing and emerging from within them.

*"Are you seeing me the way I am seeing you?"* she asked both of the men at once.

Paul was the first to respond. *"Yes, I see you, Nancy, yet I also see your atma body as well. It is a rainbow of light constantly changing shape and color."*

*"I am having the same experience,"* Don agreed. *"We have clearer sight to use in the world now."*

The triad began walking with the sun as Talish had directed. Though their minds told them it should take them many days to return to the reserve, they realized quite quickly that much of the surroundings looked very familiar. Eventually, Nancy pointed toward the east as she saw the herd of elephants that she had first come to know in the reserve, keeping pace with them.

*"Paul, look. It's the elephants from the park. Could we be that close already?"* she asked incredulously.

*"It must be, Nancy. Don and I were just noticing that everywhere we look seems to be an area that tells us that we are very close to the camp. I thought it took us days to get to Talish's village and now we're almost back in less than twenty-four hours. This is wonderful."*

*"I wonder if this is what Talish meant when she said we had something yet to experience,"* Don began to say and then the three of them stopped still in their tracks.

The elephant herd had come right up to where they were standing in the midst of the trees and there was a man with them. He left the assemblage and walked right up to Don.

*"Don, I am so glad you went with Paul and Nancy. Talish and I had put the plans in place yet we couldn't know if you would follow through with them. Welcome back. You will find the camp was only to draw the three of you together. Now you will learn the ways of the animals with me,"* Joe said as Don looked at what should have been his damaged foot, which was whole and perfect as he stood upon the ground.